Capitalism Russian-Style

D0198268

For a decade Russia has been dismantling communism and building capitalism. Describing a deeply flawed fledgling market economy, *Capitalism Russian-Style* provides a progress report on one of the most important economic experiments going on in the world today. It describes Russian achievements in building private banks and companies, stock exchanges, new laws and law courts. It analyzes the role of the mafia, the rise of new financial empires, entrepreneurs and business tycoons, and the shrinking Russian state. Thane Gustafson tells how the Soviet system collapsed and the new market society was born. Evaluating the impact of the crash of August 1998, Gustafson shows how the crisis revealed the flaws of a Russia still halfway to a new order, but also the resilience and energy of the Russian people. Identifying investment as vital to preserving Russia's status as a major industrial power, in his final chapter he examines the prospects for an economic recovery in Russia in the twenty-first century.

THANE GUSTAFSON is a Professor in the Government Department at Georgetown University and Director of the Eurasia/Former Soviet Union Service of Cambridge Energy Research Associates. He is the author of *Crisis amid Plenty: the Politics of Soviet Energy under Brezhnev and Gorbachev* (1989), (winner of the 1990 Marshall Shulman prize for the best book on Russian affairs), and *Reform in Soviet Politics: Lessons of Recent Policies on Land and Water* (1981), and co-author of *Russia 2010, and What it Means for the World* (1993).

Capitalism Russian-Style

Thane Gustafson

CAMBRIDGE
UNIVERSITY PRESS

PUBLISHED BY THE PRESS SYNDICATE OF THE UNIVERSITY OF CAMBRIDGE
The Pitt Building, Trumpington Street, Cambridge CB2 1RP, United Kingdom

CAMBRIDGE UNIVERSITY PRESS
The Edinburgh Building, Cambridge CB2 2RU, UK http://www.cup.cam.ac.uk
40 West 20th Street, New York, NY 10011–4211, USA http://www.cup.org
10 Stamford Road, Oakleigh, Melbourne 3166, Australia

© Thane Gustafson 1999

This book is in copyright. Subject to statutory exception and to the provisions
of relevant collective licensing agreements, no reproduction of any part may
take place without the written permission of Cambridge University Press.

First published 1999

Printed in the United Kingdom at the University Press, Cambridge

Typeset in Plantin 10/12 pt   [SE]

A catalogue record for this book is available from the British Library

Library of Congress Cataloguing in Publication data

Gustafson, Thane.
    Capitalism Russian–style / Thane Gustafson.
        p.   cm.
    Includes index.
    ISBN 0521 64175 6 (hardback) ISBN 0 521 64595 6 (paperback)
    1. Russia (Federation) – Economic conditions – 1991–   2. Capitalism
Russia (Federation)   3. Post-communism – Russia (Federation)
    4. Russia (Federation) – Social conditions – 1991–   I. Title.
    HC340.12.G87   1999
    330.12′2′0947 dc21   99-40307
                                                                  CIP
ISBN 0 521 64175 6 hardback
ISBN 0 521 64595 6 paperback

To Dan and Angela,
in friendship

Contents

Foreword
Russia in the New Century

Daniel Yergin

As the new millennium begins, one of the biggest questions for the emerging global economy is the role that Russia will play in it. Russia's power and wealth are at their lowest ebb since the 1920s. Yet for how long can it be counted out? Its enormous natural resources and talented people, spanning eleven time zones, and its vast strategic position, argue that Russia could be a major player in tomorrow's world. But in what role? Will Russia be an important and constructive player in building tomorrow's global economy and a world order based on peaceful technology? Or will it be left behind, nursing bitter resentment over a lost empire and a dead ideology, concentrating its meager resources on rebuilding militarily? The answers depend on the outcome of the new Russian revolution. At the beginning of the twenty-first century – almost eighty-five years after the Bolshevik Revolution that sent such shock waves through the twentieth century – Russia is again caught up in a revolution. It is partly political – the effort to establish secure foundations for democracy. And it is partly economic – the struggle to transform the very archetype of the centrally planned economy into a market system that is anchored in the new global economy.

What will be the outcome? That depends on whether Russia can make good on its historic bet to build an open market economy, founded on private property, contract, law, and enterprise, and on the free movement of people, capital, and ideas. Only a market economy can generate the wealth and the dynamism that will renew Russia. Only a market economy will enable it to be a major force in contributing to the global society that is transcending the old boundaries of nation-states and empires.

All that is the story that Thane Gustafson tells in *Capitalism Russian-Style*. This book is an absolutely essential companion for anyone in the West seeking to do business in Russia and the rest of the former Soviet Union. It provides the framework and insight they need to understand the business environment in which – and with which – they are seeking to work. Simple prudence requires that they read it to understand the risks and challenges. The book is essential for those concerned with Russia's turbulent transition from communism and its place in the world of the twenty-first century. This narrative will also prove fascinating and illuminating reading for anyone interested in markets and the shape of the global economy. And, I am convinced, Russians themselves will profit from the clarity and structure – and agenda — that it brings to the great drama through which they have been living.

Thane Gustafson is uniquely qualified to tell this story. He is Professor of Government at Georgetown University and Director of the Eurasia Service at Cambridge Energy Research Associates (CERA). We have worked together as colleagues for many years, and as co-authors, including on *Russia 2010, and What It Means for the World*. There are few westerners who can match his deep knowledge of Russia and his balanced judgment of Russian reality, and his commitment to exploring and understanding in an informed and open-minded way the great transition through which Russia is going. His standing as one of the leading scholars of both the Soviet Union and Russia was underlined by his selection for the Shulman Prize, one of the most prestigious awards in the field. He also has the practical and hard-headed knowledge that comes from working with western companies as they struggle to find and develop businesses and investments in the former Soviet Union. He brings this rich perspective from the new scenario project he is leading, *Rekindling the Future: Russia Scenarios toward 2020*. He understands both conceptually and in a very down-to-earth way what a market system requires, and what is missing in Russia. And he is deeply schooled and engaged with Russian culture. To the many other talents he brings to the present task must be added the unique one of having had the Russian newspaper *Izvestia* describe his command of the Russian language as "impeccable."

All this enables him to capture the positive side of the drama of Russia's forced march towards capitalism – the excitement, the energy, the entrepeneurial creativity. At the same time, he brings the negative sharply into focus – the corruption, the crime, the instability, the human costs, the inadequacy of the institutions. He does something else very unusual: he tells his story in terms of people – whether it be the new tycoons to emerge out of communism's rubble or the scientists who gave up their careers to operate a tour boat on Lake Baikal. But he puts the people and the human story into a rigorous analytic framework of the making of a market society.

The "Wild Nineties"

It has been nearly a decade now since the Soviet Union collapsed and Russia was thrown, almost without warning, out of the familiar world of state planning and one-party control in which it had spent seven decades. The new leaders had no recipe for the future. All the rules were gone. Many Russians felt as though they had abruptly been transported to the other side of the moon.

There followed a decade like no other: Russia's "Wild Nineties". It began with the attempted coup of August 1991, which broke the back of the government of Mikhail Gorbachev and ushered out the Soviet era. And it almost seemed to end in August 1998, with the disastrous default and devaluation by the Russian government. And yet by the autumn of 1999, the Russian economy was once again demonstrating vitality, and some confidence was returning. The Wild Nineties have been rollicking years of fortunes made and lost, a spectacular boom for some, set against the backdrop of one of the deepest industrial depressions in world history, years of a frantic scramble of Russian against Russian for power, property, position, and rents. These are years of great hopes raised and dashed, of commitments made and broken and, yet, years in which Russia has moved towards the market economy.

For, obituaries notwithstanding, the Russian market economy is not dead, the reforms have not been reversed, and the post-communist generation continues to expand its influence. Russia's journey continues toward the next crossroads, now looming immediately ahead, with an impending change of president and the advent of a new generation of Russian leaders. Whoever follows Boris Yeltsin into power in the Kremlin, it is certain that there will be no going back to the Soviet era. Today in Russia, the market is not a theory as it was a decade ago. Whatever its many and grave imperfections – it is a reality.

Just what is this new Russia? The first decade of market reforms produced a badly flawed quasi-market, what Thane Gustafson calls "a no-man's-land" between socialism and capitalism. Building a new economic system is turning out to be far harder than the hopes of the early 1990s. "What the Russian Nineties have also taught," he writes, "is how enormous an undertaking it is to change from one world view to another, from one political system to another, and from an old economy to a new one." Reversing seventy years of history would be an enormously daunting job under any circumstances. Russia did not have the advantages of China's slow opening to the market, nor access to a dynamo like the overseas Chinese, with their entrepeneurship and capital. Nor did Russia have the advantages of a Poland – with its border with Germany and a tradition of private property that been preserved in its agricultural system. Except for the black market, Russia had no market institutions, no market culture, no market memory on which to draw: all that had been wiped out. The job was made even harder by the false starts. The new institutions of the private sector are badly built, in all too many cases geared more to extracting (and exporting) quick profit than to promoting efficient growth. The political leadership of Boris Yeltsin has, at least since 1996, been destabilizing and demoralizing and has cost the Russian people heavily. Crime and corruption have spread far more deeply into the fabric of society than market behavior or money. A good part of the country's new private property has become part of an elaborate "virtual economy" based on barter and subsidies. Counterpoised against the virtual economy is a "shadow economy," which is "strictly cash" and "lives by its wits." The state itself has barely begun adapting; indeed, in many respects Russia resembles a country that has been abandoned by its government.

Yet, as Thane Gustafson asks, "how could it have been otherwise?" Better and more consistent leadership would surely have helped. As it is, the Nineties have been ruinous to Russia's prospects as a great power. For a decade there has been essentially no investment in Russia's resources and its people. Russia has been saved by its exports of commodities, but those will run down inexorably if they are not renewed. There is a growing health crisis, the result of bad care, polluted air and water, and the self-destructive lifestyle of a population adrift. The wrangling of the political system has bred cynicism. Little wonder, then, that Russians remain deeply ambivalent about this quasi-market system that has brought most of them wrenching change, hardships, and demands for which they had no preparation.

Where will Russia go from here, under the new leadership that will soon take the helm? The nation, once again, is at a vital crossroads. Russians face a crucial choice, either toward a renewed commitment to the market and to closer integration with the global economy, or toward a return to some form of state interventionism, likely to be aimed at restoring the Soviet-era heavy industry and military technology. Many Russians, however, fear that citizens and elite alike will duck the hard choices, and opt instead for muddling along, milking the inheritance of the Soviet era as long as possible. More and more, young Russians express their fear of a second *zastoi*, or "era of stagnation," the name they gave to the corrupt and lazy Brezhnev period of the 1970s.

The New Economy

The central message of Thane Gustafson's book is twofold. First, as flawed as the new Russia may be, the feverish building of the new private institutions that took place in the nineties succeeded in laying the basis for a new economy, which obeys, however imperfectly, the laws of the market. Second, the changes that have taken place are so deep and fundamental that they will continue to drive Russia forward in the first decade of the twenty-first century. Russia's transition to the market may be flawed, but it is real, and it is irreversible.

Yet, while Russia struggles through its change, the rest of the world has not been standing still. Russia today faces intensified competition from a fast-moving global economy, based on services and information, in which heavy industry and commodities, on which the Soviet economy were built, are no longer at the forefront. That is the deeper challenge for Russia, and it is one for which its experience in the twentieth century leaves it poorly prepared. The best resource it can bring to bear for this new competition is, of course, its people. The challenge is to harness their talents, education, and skills, to a competitive economy.

Russia's experience in the twentieth century is that although its first revolution ultimately led it down the wrong path, 1917 did create the conditions under which Russia became, for a time, the second most powerful global power and a model, if a severely defective one, to many throughout the world. It is ironic that Russia's second revolution, despite bringing Russia back to the mainsteam of western nations, is so far having as its first result – at least in the eyes of many Russians themselves – a vast and humiliating loss of status and power.

Will Russia continue its odyssey to join the global market, and will it gain the wealth and pride and standard of living that its energetic and talented people have suffered for so long to attain? Thane Gustafson's book explains, with balance and without illusion, why such hope has real basis. The results will be something unique. Call it "Capitalism Russian-Style."

Daniel Yergin, chairman of Cambridge Energy Research Associates, is co-author with Joseph Stanislaw of *The Commanding Heights: The Battle Between Government and Marketplace that is Remaking the Modern World.* With Thane Gustafson, he co-authored *Russia 2010, and What It Means for the World.* He received the Pulitzer Prize for his book, *The Prize: The Epic Quest for Oil, Money, and Power.*

Acknowledgments

Westerners of all backgrounds, once exposed to Russia at some point in their lives, are often hooked permanently, fascinated by a country that seems forever at a crossroads. It happened to me when I was twenty. The literature and then the language of Russia entranced me first. In the mid-1960s, as a Peace Corps volunteer in West Africa, I spent the tropical nights reading Tolstoy and Gogol, and in my imagination I was transported from palm trees to the wintry nights of St. Petersburg and the snowy mountains of the Caucasus. Russia was in my blood, and I've never looked back.

I've been a Russia-watcher ever since, living and traveling in Russia for the last twenty-five years, trying to understand how the political and economic systems of the Soviet Union, and now of the new Russia and the other successor nations work. Since 1990 I have combined university teaching with advising businesses, crisscrossing Russia in every direction for clients, mostly Western energy companies and financial institutions. This has given me the opportunity to observe the new Russia in many settings. I have had the good fortune to witness some of the key symbolic events of post-Soviet Russia, from the raising of the new Russian flag over the House of Soviets in Tiumen', the capital of West Siberia, to the barricades in front of the White House and the first shareholders' meeting of a privatized defense industry. I have spoken to thousands of Russians in every setting, from jobless geologists above the Arctic Circle to ministers and bankers, and at least one of Moscow's powerful godfathers.

This book is a reflection on the new Russia that emerged in the 1990s from the ruins of the Soviet collapse. It follows an earlier book, *Russia 2010*, which I wrote jointly with Daniel Yergin and Angela Stent a few years ago. We asked then, "What paths will Russia follow?" Our answer was, "By 2010 Russia will have its own unique form of capitalism." But back in the summer of 1993, when we were writing *Russia 2010*, describing capitalism Russian-style was no less a work of imagination than the nineteenth century Russia that had captured me originally; indeed, it was practically science-fiction. Now it is becoming a fact. Whether it will survive and prosper is the subject of this book.

Any book about Russia in the 1990s begins with a miracle – the miracle that it has become possible to travel freely in Russia, to speak without hindrance to nearly any Russian, and to share views without masks or euphemisms. This book owes everything to the many Russian friends and colleagues who have given their time and thought to answering questions and debating ideas, sometimes over hundreds of hours, with the sincerity and wholeheartedness that are the special hallmarks of the Russian character.

I would like to give special thanks to four close friends, Vadim and Marina Eskin, Aleksey Reteyum, and Vladimir Bokser, who more than anyone else made this book possible. For their many suggestions, criticism of key points, and valuable reflections, over many hours of pleasant conversation, I am deeply indebted.

Many other Russian friends and colleagues, scholars, businessmen, and public figures, gave freely of their time to speak to me over the years, and I am grateful to them all. Particular mention goes to Vitalii Ermakov, Sergei Eskin, Egor Gaidar, Rafael and Tamara Goldberg, Valerii Graifer, Leonid Grinfel'd, Mikhail Khodorkovsky, Olga Kryshtanovskaia, Igor Malashenko, Arkadii Maiofis, Alevtina Nikitina, Vladimir Pechatnov, Marina Pereverzeva, Leonid Roketskii, Iurii Shafranik, Sergei Shatalov, Igor Sher, Lilia Shevtsova, Petr Shikhirev, Grigorii Tomchin, Grigorii Yavlinskii, and Ilya Zaslavskii.

Special recognition goes to Viktor Krotov, the Moscow painter who created the icon of Capitalism Russian Style for the cover of the book.

This book also takes its inspiration from the support and guidance of many western friends, but none more than Dan Yergin and Angela Stent, my close colleagues at Cambridge Energy Research Associates and at Georgetown University. Both of them read through several drafts of this book and offered innumerable and valuable points of advice and criticism. To Dan and Angela, warm and staunch friends for over twenty-five years, this book is affectionately dedicated.

I owe a special debt to my home university, Georgetown, and my colleagues in the Government Department there. This book would not have been possible without the support of my chairmen, Robert Lieber and Eusebio Mujal-Leon. But even more important has been the laboratory provided by my students over the years, especially my graduate students in two research seminars, Government 612 and 684.

Warm thanks are also due to the team at Cambridge Energy Research Associates, especially Joseph Stanislaw, James Rosenfield, Stephen

Haggett, Richard Hildahl, Kelly Knight, Laurent Ruseckas, Helen Sisley, Izabella Tabarovsky, Sue Lena Thompson, and John Webb. I am particularly grateful to Kelly Knight, Tatiana Ustiantseva, and Irina Zamarina of CERA's Moscow office, Celeste Plante and Anastasia Rozhkova in Cambridge, and Marianne Frederick and Ellen Perkins in Washington, D.C., who came to the rescue time after time with key sources, statistics, and many useful suggestions.

Many Western fellow scholars, business colleagues, and personal friends provided valuable ideas, insights, and sources. I am particularly grateful to Michael Alekseev, Martin Andersson, Harley Balzer, Smith Bobbitt, Peter Boone, Howard Chase, Timothy Colton, Peter Davies, Paul Drager, Todd Fogelsong, Timothy Frye, Clifford Gaddy, Joel Hellman, Simon Johnson, Craig Kennedy, Georg Kjollgren, Maurice and Lelie Kurtz, Eugene Lawson, Trevor Link, Joel McDonald, William McHenry, Douglas McKay, Robert Sharlet, Ben Slay, John Paul Smith, Peter and Susan Solomon, Christopher Speckhard, Murat Talayhan, and David Woodruff.

And last but definitely not least, I thank wholeheartedly my wonderful family, Nil, Peri, Farah, and Carolyn, for their patience, affection, and support.

Can Russia ever achieve a functioning market economy?
Why not? It already has a malfunctioning market economy.
Boris Fedorov, former Russian finance minister[1], 1992

In September 1991 it seemed to us that it would take only
a year or two at the most to build a new economic system
in Russia. But as you know miracles occur only in fairy
tales.   Sergei Stepashin, former Russian prime minister, 1999[2]

Prologue

Arkhangel'sk, January 1992:
The man was so drunk he could hardly stand. After three tries he hauled
himself slowly into the bus, dragging a huge dried fish behind him. An
overpowering smell of fish, vodka, bad tobacco, and sweat filled the air.
"Those *bliadi* (whores) haven't paid us in six months," he railed. "What
the hell do they expect us to do? Starve to death?" He kicked the dirty
snow from his boots.

"He's one of the oil geologists from Narian-Mar, up on the Arctic Sea
coast," my host whispered to me. The drunk went on, his voice mounting, every third word unprintable. "I've got a wife and children down in
Zhitomir. My savings are all gone. And there are sixty thousand of us up
there, all like me. What do we do now?" The other passengers stared out
the window, hardly paying attention. They had obviously heard the same
story from many others. The drunk exhaled and closed his eyes.

Moscow, December 1996:
The young bank president had agreed to meet me for dinner on the
corner of Kamergerskaia ulitsa. I was suddenly surrounded by bodyguards as the bank president emerged from a parked car across the
street. Without a word he led me into an unmarked doorway and down a
dark shabby hallway. There were more guards everywhere, and nobody
was leaving us out of sight. Down a flight of stairs, we emerged into a
palatial dining room. Waiters bustled about, wearing smart uniforms
with gold filigree monograms on their jacket pockets. The maitre d'hotel
ushered us to our seats with practiced deference. "This is Klub Sergei,"
the bank president explained as he unfolded a linen napkin. "It's where
politicians and bankers go when they want a quiet place to discuss a
deal." He smiled smoothly. "I've bought many a deputy here."

[1] Quoted in Daniel Yergin and Thane Gustafson, *Russia 2010 and What it Means for the
World* (New York: Random House, 1993), p. 6.
[2] Sergei Stepashin, speech at the US–Russia Business Council, Washington, D.C., July 26
1999.

Capitalism Russian-style: introducing the book

On August 17, 1998, a pale-faced Sergei Kiriyenko, Russia's thirty-five-year-old prime minister, stepped up to the microphones of a crowded press conference. It was almost exactly six years since the failed coup against Mikhail Gorbachev had led to the disappearance of the Soviet Union. The Russian Federation was its main successor state, and during all the years since, Boris Yeltsin had been its president. Kiriyenko, however, was Yeltsin's third prime minister, having just taken the position just five months earlier. His appointment had been hailed as a sign that further reforms were to come.

But that was not Kiriyenko's message on August 17. His announcement was terse: the Russian government had declared a moratorium on its debts and would no longer defend the ruble.[3] The prime minister assured his listeners that the government would stand by its obligations, but no one could mistake the announcement's real meaning. The Russian government had effectively declared bankruptcy.

The announcement ripped like a bomb through the Russian economy. Especially hard-hit was the new private sector that in the space of one decade had grown to supply over half of Russian economic output. The top twenty commercial banks were gutted overnight; bank transfers and settlements froze; transfers of taxes and pension funds halted. In the weeks that followed, credit disappeared and imports plummeted. Russia's GDP, which after a decade of decline had finally shown signs of bottoming out, began falling again. By the end of the year, the ruble had lost over two-thirds of its value against the dollar, and inflation, which had been subdued in the previous three years, had returned in force. A blizzard of dismissal notices blanketed Moscow, as banks, brokerages, and private businesses of all kinds laid off tens of thousands of young employees, who only days before had been the stars of the new Russian market economy.

As dazed Russians set about picking up the pieces, the prospects were grimmer than at any time since the Soviet collapse in 1991. They faced years of work simply to regain the lost ground, and in a much less favorable environment. World commodities prices, which had sustained the Russian economy throughout much of the 1990s, had dropped to record low levels. Foreign investors, badly burned by the Russian default, had withdrawn from Russia, and the country's international credit was at rock bottom. But the most discouraging knowledge was that the decade-long

---

[3] "Zaiavlenie pravitel'stva RF i Tsentral'nogo Banka RF." The text of the official announcement can be found on the Internet at the web site of the National News Service, http://www.nns.ru) Excerpts from the prime minister's press conference will be found on the NNS's web site under the rubric "Biznes-novosti."

effort to build the institutions of a new market-based economy – banks, insurance and pension funds, brokerages, private companies, commercial courts, regulatory agencies – had gone disastrously wrong.

Yet as the months went by after the crash, a kind of normalcy settled back over Russia. Beneath the devastated top tier of the largest banks, a second layer of several hundred smaller ones had survived in good shape. The export sector, which had carried the Russian economy through much of the 1990s, continued to ship oil and gas and other commodities and to bring in essential hard-currency revenue. Imported goods re-appeared in Moscow shops, alongside new items from Russian producers, for whom a devalued ruble spelled an opportunity to regain markets lost to foreign competitors. As a result, industrial production recovered quickly. Outside Moscow, where the market had penetrated less deeply to begin with, most people were less affected by the crash than the capital. Their lives were depressed before, and so they remained. Despite a blow that would have crushed a normal market economy, Russia somehow resumed muddling along, under a succession of caretaker governments whose main virtue was that they did little to rock the boat, while the country waited for new elections and whatever a new leadership would bring. As former prime minister Sergei Stepashin declared on a visit to Washington, D.C., in July 1999, "Russia's exit from the August crisis was much faster than any of the experts had predicted."[4]

But the real change was psychological, and that will be slower to fade. The shock of the crash caused a change in the attitudes of the Russian elite. Prior to the crash *transition Western-style* was the official script, and *markets* and *capitalism* were its slogans. Market reformers either led the government or played key roles in it. But after the crash the elite mind-set shifted. The slogans of market reform were abruptly discredited, and the notion that Russia was on a fast track to success was abruptly dispelled. The chief casualty of August 1998 was a state of mind.

Thus the crash of August 1998 provides a dramatic symbolic close to the period that began with the launch of market reforms in January 1992. Between those two conveniently placed bookmarks lies the extraordinary first chapter of Russia's uncertain emergence into the post-Soviet era. ✓ Russia ends the decade as it began it – in crisis, divided over its past, uncertain of its future.

To most observers, it is a story of failure, or at best a false start. Russia today has sunk to a level of weakness not seen since the early 1920s, when the country lay prostrate after a decade of war, revolution, and civil war. The gap between the Russian economy and that of the United States has

---

[4] Speech by former prime minister Sergei Stepashin at the US–Russia Business Council, July 26 1999.

grown immense. One telling statistic is the difference between the two national governments' resources: the revenues of the Russian federal government in 1999 are expected to be in the range of $16–17 billion; those of the US government will be about $1.7 trillion, or 100 times larger. There is an even greater gap in private-sector investment. As the twenty-first century begins, Russia is on the verge of falling out of the ranks of the industrial powers.

Yet Russia is never as strong as she seems; and Russia is never as weak as she seems. Dollar measures exaggerate Russia's weakness and understate its potential wealth and strength. It has a highly educated population with a strong scientific and engineering culture. Its natural resources are the world's largest. And it still has thousands of nuclear warheads and missiles, backed by strong martial traditions and a 500-year record of military success. Russia will rise again. Indeed, it will be the worse for the world if it does not.

But in what guise? As a democratic, free-market economy? To many, the crash of August 1998 signaled the failure of Russia's transition to the market. Yet the Nineties were a crucial decade of creation, in which a new post-Soviet order, for better and for worse, began to take shape. To understand where Russia is going now, it is essential to understand what happened during the crucial years after the Soviet collapse. Why did the nascent market economy crash? What, if anything, was achieved of lasting value? Is the present quasi-stabilization viable? What lies ahead, as Russia moves toward the end of the Yeltsin era and a critical leadership succession?

These are the key questions of this book.

A decade like no other

Only a surrealist painter could do justice to the Russian Nineties. The Russia that has emerged from the ruins of the Soviet Union is a crazy-quilt of contrasts and contradictions in which the implausible and the impossible coexist daily. The country is mired in the worst depression any industrial country has ever known. Yet alongside the idle factories there has sprung up a new market-based sector, driven by commodities exports, imported consumer goods, and financial speculation, which bubbled and frothed so long as high world commodities prices and plentiful short-term capital sustained it. Even as Russia's manufacturing and military industries lay paralyzed, Moscow became, for a time, the world's hottest emerging market and a city of golden opportunity.

The combination of collapse, boom, and depression has turned Russian society upside down. In the mid-1980s, the two men described above – the bitter, drunken geologist and the self-confident, cynical young banker – might have been equal in status and income. Ten years later they were at the top and the bottom of a ladder that did not even exist before, and though today the banker may have been humbled a bit, the geologist's plight has only grown worse. Russian society has been torn in two by a revolution in property ownership, distribution of wealth, status, and moral values.

For a fortunate few – perhaps 20 percent of the population, concentrated mainly in Moscow and in regions with something to export – signs of new wealth began to appear within two or three years of the Soviet collapse. By the second half of the decade the streets of the capital were choked with foreign cars, old buildings were being refurbished and new high-rises were going up. Russian passers-by downtown were not merely well-dressed but often flamboyantly so. Anyone flying into Moscow could gaze in wonder at the thousands of new luxury houses (quaintly called *kottedzhi*, or *cottages*), many of them marvels of bad taste in red brick, dotting the suburban countryside. The excesses of the Russian *nouveaux riches* became legend, but the rich were not alone. An emerging Russian middle class bought expensive imported electronics and cars, traveled to foreign countries, and grew accustomed to the good life.

For the rest the price has been horrendous. Most Russians have told pollsters all through the decade that they are worse off than when the market reforms began, and since the August crash the polls have sunk to new lows. Russian cities are plagued by organized crime. There are beggars in the streets and prostitutes in the hotels, and in the railway stations, where refugees arrive from the periphery, the misery is beyond description. Unemployment exceeds 13% of the workforce and could grow much larger, while the remaining safety nets of the Soviet era continue to unravel. Infant mortality has risen, average lifespans have dropped sharply, the Russian population is growing smaller and older, and infectious diseases like tuberculosis have reappeared in force. In the statistical manuals, in the hospitals and the morgues, in the courts and the orphanages, Russian society reveals the shock it has undergone and the tribute paid by its weakest citizens for the sudden move from one system to another.

The extremes of the Russian Nineties also polarized the views of observers. Two views came to dominate. For some it was the sordid story of the collapse of an old regime. A rent-seeking elite, sprung from the Soviet nomenklatura, had grabbed the country's property and made off with it. What they built was not free enterprise or a market economy, but a corrupt imitation – "crony capitalism," some called it – based on financial-industrial cartels, mafia gangs, and wholesale plunder. On this view, the very idea of a transition to a normal market economy was naïve, since the "cronies" could hardly be expected to undermine their own power and profits. It was a structure built on "chicken legs," as one chastened banker put it after the August crash, and it was doomed to fail.

Yet for others, the building of a new order made Russia in the Nineties the most exciting and hopeful place in the world. It was a time of feverish building, not only of offices and kottedzhi for the rich, but of new businesses and institutions based on new skills and products. An entire new tertiary sector of trade and services-the area most neglected by the Soviet era–roared to life, as a generation of young Russians leapt to the task of creating private companies in fields as diverse as advertising, consumer credit, television, franchising, and computer software. In government, reform-minded politicians, though never more than a handful at the top, dismantled the Soviet-era controls and set about building new state institutions to regulate a private economy. For those who took their inspiration from the powerful trends in the global economy in the 1990s, the transition to a market economy in Russia seemed unstoppable.

The strange thing is that both views were true. The question no one could agree on was, What did they add up to?

August 1988: the music stops

The crisis of August 1998 suddenly provided a brutal answer. It was as though the music abruptly stopped and the lights went on, revealing appalling corruption and weakness. The August crash brought out in sharp relief, as no other event could have done, how deformed and fragile the emerging political order and economy had proved to be when tested. It showed that Russia's transition to a money-based economy and a national market were still only partial, and that large parts of the country still stood outside it. Much of the "new" economy hid underground, out of sight of the tax collector, while much of the "old" economy had retreated into a virtual world of barter and quasi-monies.

But August 1998 also showed something else: there was no longer any bridge back to the past, and those who initially talked of turning back found that they could not. What the crisis revealed above all was how dramatically Russia had changed over the course of the decade. For better or for worse, a revolution has begun in Russia.

The word revolution is much abused, and in the next chapter I will spell out what I mean by it. But the key point is this: to call events in Russia by their right name reconciles the "collapse" story and the "transition" story, and provides a sounder basis for understanding what is happening now and what may come next.

First, the "collapse and takeover" story. It is right but it does not go far enough. The Soviet system collapsed and was taken over by its survivors, but it is much more than that. An entire order – the entire political, economic, and ideological system of Soviet Marxism–Leninism – has been overthrown. The basis for the command economy and the one-party dictatorship no longer exists. It has been replaced by a new set of economic and political institutions, founded on different constitutional and ideological premises, which though still fragile and uncertain are a world apart from the past. A new class has come to the fore, and has seized property and power. The individuals within it, to be sure, are descended from the Soviet administrative class, the nomenklatura. But they no longer owe their rank and privileges to the communist state and the command economy. They are in business for themselves, and that central fact is changing their roles and behavior.

Secondly, the "transition" story. Those who describe the Russian Nineties as a transition to the market have likewise only captured half of the picture. The revival of liberal economic doctrines in the last generation, and the tidal wave of globalization, privatization, and liberalization that has swept the globe, are the story of our age. Market transition has been the single most powerful revolutionary force in post-Soviet Russia – and the forces driving it – technological change and global competition – will continue to act powerfully on Russia.

Yet transition was not the only game going on in Russia in the Nineties. The reformers' agenda overlapped with those of other players who were busy extracting rents, gaining power, salvaging a collapsed state, or simply trying to do their jobs and get by-and for whom "market transition" was an unfamiliar or threatening foreign ideology, or simply a convenient opportunity for stripping assets or advancing political causes. Transition as a driving force is real. But so are the complex reactions to it in the Russian setting, which is undergoing massive political and social upheaval at the same time.

It is the combination of these two forces – the collapse of the Soviet order and the worldwide tide of economic and technological change – that makes the Russian Nineties a revolution. But thinking of the situation in this way has one important implication: revolutions are not a matter of a decade, but of a generation or more. This one began well before the Nineties; it will go on well into the next century. The tide of change in Russia is not spent; indeed it is still building.

Yet the Russian Nineties have also taught how enormous an undertaking it is to change from one world view to another, from one political system to another, and from an old economy to a new one. It was naïve, in retrospect, to believe that capitalism in Russia could be built in a decade.

The world constructed by the Soviets was in its way as unique a system as has ever existed. It had its own ideology, its own culture and institutions, and its own language, formed over more than thirty years of revolutionary upheaval and reinforced over another three decades. It was as internally consistent and highly evolved, in its way, as its market-based Western counterpart. Today's Russians (at least, those over thirty) grew up in it, spoke its language, learned its customs, and knew no other. For those who were adults when Gorbachev's reforms began, an inner core of Soviet habits, beliefs, values, and expectations remains. The revolution will not be complete until those who were children when the Gorbachev reforms began are running the country.

Overcoming the Soviet legacy is more than a matter of culture. Russia remains "hard-wired" to its Soviet past, by the layout of its pipelines and its power-lines, the location and technologies of its industries, and the geographic distribution of its workforce. There is also an institutional legacy, which shows up in the way accountants measure costs or the financial system treats value, in the managers' habit of relying on their friends rather than their lawyers, in the restrictions on setting prices, changing jobs, selling land or real estate – all these and a myriad more are inherited from Soviet practice.

If undoing the old is difficult, building the new is even more so. Of all the countries in the world today that are trying to build market economies or liberalize them, none is coming to the task from as great a remove as the Russians, or in the midst of such political and social upheaval – not the East Europeans and not the Chinese, and certainly no Western country. For the second time in this century, Russia is performing on itself a vast experiment in social engineering, reshaping its state and its society and its economy all at once.

Seen in this broader perspective, the Russian Nineties were only the first chapter of a story that will take another generation, if not two or three, to finish telling. Russia, especially in the major cities, looks on the surface like a "normal" country. There is peace, the buses run, the streets are lighted, people go about their business. But Russia cannot yet be considered normal. Society has been badly damaged. The political system is still in flux. Above all, as the August crash showed dramatically, the economy is still a no-man's-land, neither socialist nor capitalist. In its first decade, the attempted transition to the market created far more losers than winners, and the consequent build-up of popular disillusionment and anger is dangerous political tinder. Until a post-Soviet order emerges that can produce growth, pride, and a reasonably shared wealth it cannot be considered more than temporarily stable.

Why did this happen? Why did the Russian Nineties prove in so many respects a false start? What was achieved that might yet provide a sounder base? What changes will prove viable and lasting? This book looks for the answers in the origins and evolution of the market-based institutions and players that grew up in the first post-Soviet decade. There are chapters on the banks and capital markets, entrepreneurship and privatization. Crime and corruption have a chapter of their own, but so does the law. Other chapters describe what is happening to Russians' health, families, occupations and values. Lastly, and most important, we look at the Russian state – at once partner, accomplice, and antagonist of the new private sector.

The book's central finding is that Russia is still in motion. The twin forces that acted on it so powerfully in its first post-Soviet decade – revolutionary collapse at home and the tides of change in the global economy – are far from spent. The quasi-stabilization we see in Russia today, founded on what remains of the Soviet inheritance, is not viable over the longer run, because it cannot generate growth and prosperity. A new post-Soviet order is still evolving, even though its final shape cannot yet be known. Only one thing is sure: if it stays on the road to capitalism, Russia will no more resemble the models of liberal theorists than do, say, the capitalist systems of Brazil, Mexico, or for that matter Italy or Japan. Capitalism Russian-style, if it survives long enough to evolve to a stable final form, will be a uniquely Russian amalgam.[5]

"Old Soviet hands" like me bring their own perspective to the new Russia, because they know how different the old system was and how far the country has come in a remarkably short time. The distance is truly from one civilization to another. Whether at the end of the road Russian capitalism will be prosperous, efficient, democratic, or just, are questions that are not yet foreclosed. They are the Russian agenda for the twentieth century.

---

[5] This is a central argument of Rose Brady's excellent book, *Kapitalizm: Russia's Struggle to Free its Economy* (New Haven, CN: Yale University Press, 1999).

For a whole century Russia has been turned into a gigantic
laboratory. Only the experimenters have changed.

Nikolai Petrakov, Russian economist[1]

Est' u revoliutsii nachalo, net u revoliutsii kontsa. (The
revolution has a beginning, but it has no end.)

Popular Soviet radio song of the 1970s

1   The new Russian Revolution: false start or dead end?

Tiumen, December 1992:

The sleepy central square of a typical Russian provincial capital. The
new Russian tricolor floats over the former Communist Party headquarters, now renamed *administratsiia*. Above its Grecian columns the
Russian two-headed eagle has replaced the hammer and sickle. But
inside, the same policeman in grey uniform checks the documents of all
who enter, and the same endless oriental carpets lead down the corridors of official doors, thickly padded with maroon leatherette.

In the closed executive lunchroom, located behind the public *stolovaia*
of the administratsiia building, the local influentials, many now recast as
private businessmen and traders, still meet for lunch every day. All are
na ty – on a first-name basis – from their years together in the Soviet
apparatus. Outside, in the central square, a marble statue of Lenin still
points the way to the future.

Kaluga, June 1996:

We are sitting under the apple tree of Vadim and Marina's country
dacha. It is a warm, lazy day in June. In the distance rise the tall stacks of
the first Soviet nuclear reactor at Obninsk, now idle. As the bees buzz
about the apple blossoms, Vadim is interpreting the Russian revolution.

"The real revolution came in 1992, when they decontrolled prices.
Overnight, Russia became a money economy. You Americans have no
idea what this means. Our whole life used to be built around the struggle
to find things that were in short supply, *defitsit* – things everyone had to
stand in line for. The search for things dominated your whole life; you

---

[1] Nikolai Iakovlevich Petrakov, *Russkaia ruletka: ekonomicheskii eksperiment tsenoiu 150 mil-
lionov zhiznei* (Moscow: «Ekonomika,» 1998), p. I. Petrakov, a senior Russian economist
and academician, was briefly Gorbachev's economic adviser in the late 1980s.

organized every waking hour around it; you built your friendships around who could get you what; people took jobs just to have access to a flow of goods 'on the inside.'"

Vadim sat back and smiled. "Now that's all gone. There is no more *defitsit* – except of money itself."

How to interpret what is happening in Russia? As always, it is the most basic questions about Russia that are the most controversial. The decade of the Nineties can be summed up as a debate between two points of view: market transition versus collapse and takeover.

Market transition has been the most powerful slogan of our time. Worldwide, if the first two-thirds of the twentieth century was the era of faith in the state and suspicion of the market, the last third has been its opposite. From a modest ripple at the backwaters of intellectual fashion at mid-century, the resurgence of pro-market ideas built to a tidal wave in the 1970s and 80s, overwhelming the previously dominant belief in the welfare state with an equal faith in the power of the market and of neoliberal economics. The doctrines of free markets, competition, privatization, and deregulation captured the commanding heights of world economic thought and policy,[2] and by the 1990s, they had become the new orthodoxy.

At both ends of the century these opposing tides washed over Russia. But there was a significant difference. Whereas marxist ideas began penetrating into Russia a generation before 1917, at the end of the century it happened that the Soviet system collapsed before the swing in economic thinking in the west had had much popular impact inside Russia. To be sure, Russian thinking and attitudes from the 1960s on (especially those of young urban Russians) were powerfully shaped by Western consumerism, pop music, fashions in clothing, and even some intellectual movements such as environmentalism and cybernetics. But ideas about markets, free enterprise, and private property had hardly any impact at all (except on a minute handful of intellectuals). In this respect, the 70s and 80s of this century were quite unlike the 80s and 90s of the nineteenth century, when notions drawn from Marxism penetrated deeply into the Russian working class and contributed to undermining the *ancien régime*.[3]

Thus it was almost a coincidence that as the Iron Curtain crumbled, Russia encountered a revolutionary doctrine at the height of its power and self-confidence. At the end of the 1980s only a small number of

---

[2] The phrase comes from Danel Yergin and Joseph Stanislaw, *The Commanding Heights* (New York: Simon and Schuster, 1998), p. 365.
[3] From a vast literature, see Orlando Figes, *A People's Tragedy: the Russian Revolution, 1891–1924* (New York: Viking Penguin 1997), Chapters 3 and 4.

Russians had been exposed to market thinking. From 1990 on the new market doctrines spread powerfully among the better-educated young urban Russians. But it was a last-minute and superficial conversion.

Transition dominates the Russian Nineties

Little wonder that market transition was embraced enthusiastically by those who suddenly found themselves in power in the fall of 1991. Market ideas provided a ready-made substitute for the vacuum left by the collapsing Marxist–Leninist world view. They appeared to explain the West's phenomenal success and the defeat of the Soviet Union, but they also offered a blueprint for Russia's reform and recovery. And last but not least, the new ideas provided a nationale for the wholesale transfer of state property into private hands, which was already happening spontaneously as Soviet power collapsed.

Western governments, international financial institutions, and a host of economic advisors were confident they knew what the Russians had to do. It was a deceptively short list: decontrol prices, stabilize the money, create a new tax system, privatize and restructure companies, and protect property rights and contracts. At the core of the transition idea was the conviction that if this list were implemented quickly and vigorously (the approach that came to be known as "shock therapy"), the essentials of a market economy would begin to function almost immediately, and recovery and growth would soon follow. This blueprint was not theory only, but had been tried out with success in many places around the world. Especially relevant was the experience of Eastern Europe after 1989, which appeared to prove that Soviet-style economies would respond well to rapid marketization.

Anyone who experienced the Russian Nineties at first hand will remember the conviction and enthusiasm of the first years of the market reforms. Step by step, the Russian government went down the list of transition policies, implementing first price decontrols, then privatization, and finally macroeconomic stabilization. The reformers soon went beyond the naïve initial agenda of "shock therapy." By the mid-1990s they had broadened the reforms to include regulation of natural monopolies, elimination of housing subsidies, policies to improve corporate governance, fiscal reform, and many others. If the first half of the 1990s amounted to dismantling what remained of the command economy, in the second half the reformers' agenda shifted to rebuilding the state around market principles.

Yet the economy did not turn around, it did not invest, it did not grow. Worse, marketization brought with it such crime and corruption, inequality, and suffering, that by the mid-1990s it had begun to lose the support – which had been thin to begin with – of most of the population. Considered superficially, the government and the private sector had gone an impressive distance toward setting up the institutions and policies required for a market economy. Yet the collapse of August 1998 showed that much of it had been built on sand.

As marketization bogged down, criticism mounted. Initially, most of it was of the "if only" variety. For some, market reforms were implemented too slowly,[4] or in the wrong order. Prices were freed too soon, or restructuring or legal reforms should have preceded privatization.[5] Those who had been on the inside returned fire, justifying the reformers' actions and their own.[6] Most of this debate – which involved primarily Western economists or Russian reformers – accepted the premises of transition doctrine, but sought only to make it work better. By the mid-1990s, once inflation appeared to have been conquered but still economic growth did not occur, the debate shifted to the need for liberalizing the economy, overcoming the obstacles to entrepreneurship, or improving tax collections – but all under the heading of getting transition back on track.[7]

Not transition but nomenklatura takeover

Yet from the beginning there was another view – that what was happening in Russia was not really "transition" at all. The Soviet system had

[4] Jeffrey D. Sachs, "Russia's Struggle with Stabilization: Conceptual Issues and Evidence" (Washington D.C.: World Bank Annual Conference on Development Economics, April 28–29 1994).

[5] Alice H. Amsden, Jacek Kochanowicz, Lance Taylor, *The Market Meets its Match: Restructuring the Economies of Eastern Europe* (Cambridge, Mass.: Harvard University Press, 1994). The same debate went on among economists inside Russia. For an example of the "shock therapist" view, known in Russia as the "monetarist" position, see V. Popov, "O perspektivakh makroekonomicheskoi stabilizatsii," in Tat'iana I. Zaslavskaia, ed., *Kuda idet Rossiia? Al'ternativy obshchestvennogo razvitiia*. Proceedings of an international symposium held under the auspices of the Interdisciplinary Academic Center for the Social Sciences, December 15–18 1994 (Moscow: "Aspekt Press," 1995), pp. 99–103. For the industrial-policy view, which in Russia goes under the name of "structuralist," see the articles by A. Klepach, N. Karagodin, and S. Aukutsionek in the same collection, pp. 62–88.

[6] See for example Aleksandr Livshits, *Ekonomicheskaia reforma v Rossii i ego tsena* (Moscow: "Kul'tura," 1994), p. 42; Joseph Blasi et al., *Kremlin Capitalism: Privatizing the Russian Economy* (Ithaca, New York: Cornell University Press, 1997); Anders Aslund, *How Russia Became a Market Economy* (Washington, D.C.: Brookings, 1995); Maxim Boycko, Andrei Shleifer, Robert Vishny, *Privatizing Russia* (Cambridge, Mass.: MIT Press, 1995); P. Richard G. Layard and John Parker, *The Coming Russian Boom: A Guide to New Markets and Politics* (New York: Free Press, 1996).

[7] Barry W. Ickes, Peter Murrell, and Randi Ryterman, "End of the Tunnel? The Effects of Financial Stabilization in Russia," *Post-Soviet Affairs*, vol. 13 (No. 2), pp. 105–133; Daniel S. Treisman, "Fighting Inflation in a Transitional Regime: Russia's Anomalous Stabilization," *World Politics*, vol. 50 (January 1999) pp. 235–65.

never really vanished; it was taken over and adapted. The old nomenklatura became the new owners, and behind the façade of privatization they stripped the best assets of the former Soviet economy and settled in to extract rents from the remainder. Russian politics became the story of powerful business "clans" doing battle for control of state favors and subsidies, united only in opposing any changes that might weaken their power, while society sought refuge from taxmen and mafiosi by withdrawing into the shadow economy. By the mid-1990s, on this reading, the transfer of property into the hands of the "crony capitalists" was essentially complete, and a new economic system, based largely on barter and political protection, had taken shape. "Transition" was largely illusory from the beginning; but such as it was, by the mid-1990s it had stopped.[8]

The contrast between these two narratives-transition vs. takeover – was at times so stark that they hardly seemed to describe the same country. For those who held the transition view (perhaps typically a Western economist or investor, or a middle-class Muscovite), by 1997 or early 1998 marketization was already a success. They pointed to the dismantling of the command economy and the rapid building of key market institutions. They hailed the development of new skills among a whole generation of young Russians, and the emergence of a market-oriented middle class. Russian society appeared to have stabilized and the economy was beginning to turn around.

The very things that were positive in the transition narrative were negatives for those who rejected it. The new institutions were little more than fronts; the new skills mainly serviced Western speculation and the laundering of mafia profits; the middle class was a pseudo-class, enjoying a one-time bounty from exports of non-renewable commodities. The apparent stabilization of society and the turnaround of the economy were largely statistical artifacts, while the suppression of inflation and the strengthening of the ruble by 1997 were achieved only by massive withholding of pensions and wages by the government. Transition was not simply wrong; it was a hoax.[9]

August 1998: a reality test

The collapse of August 1998 was a critical test, because it revealed the deep flaws in both narratives. It was a crisis on four levels.[10] The stage had

---

[8] The most extreme statements of this view come primarily from journalists. Long-term observers of Russian affairs have been more measured, blending elements of both the transition and takeover stories. For the most sophisticated statements of this view, see Joel S. Hellman, "Winners Take All: The Politics of Partial Reform in Postcommunist Transition," *World Politics*, vol. 50 (January 1998), pp. 203–234; and Clifford G. Gaddy and Barry W. Ickes, "Russia's Virtual Economy," *Foreign Affairs*, September-October 1998, pp. 53–67.   [9] See Petrakov, *Russkaia ruletka*, p. I.

[10] Two Western accounts of the August 1998 crash are "The Russian Crisis," in European

been set in southeast Asia the previous summer. Over the following months falling oil prices and the worldwide exit of capital from emerging markets weakened both the private and the public sector in Russia. The immediate cause of the debacle was the federal government's simultaneous devaluation and default, caused by the government's short-term borrowing to offset its chronic deficits and the mounting burden of debt service, which at the time of the crash absorbed nearly one-third of its revenues.

Underlying the deficit was the government's failure to curb spending and to raise revenue, caused by political divisions and the lack of a coherent budgetary policy. Beneath these, in turn, was the weakness of the state in dealing with tax evasion and payment in barter, and the failure of the state to provide basic protections and services. At the root of it all-the fourth level-lay the failure of state and society to develop a stable and productive partnership. August 1998 was like an explosion that blew open the sides of a building, exposing flawed architecture and rickety construction on every floor, but above all at the foundations.

The impact of the August crash was highly uneven. It hit hardest the new service economy of Moscow and St. Petersburg, which depended on the trickle-down income from commodities exports and financial operations. But the rest of the economy was much less affected. Commodities exporters hunkered down, cut their costs, and stepped up their exports. After the initial financial shock, the subsequent decay of the ruble actually made their exports more competitive. The Soviet-era manufacturing economy, the heart of the so-called "virtual economy," was protected by its isolation from the money economy. Life in the drab secondary cities of Russia went on at the same depressed level as before. As a woman in one of these "rust belt" towns told a Western correspondent, "How can you have a bust if you've never had a boom?"[11] The irony of the reform government's default and devaluation was that it was most damaging to the new Russian market economy – precisely that part of the economy that the reformers had worked so hard to create.

Yet the greater significance of the August collapse is that it also revealed how far Russia as a whole had moved away from the command economy.

Bank for Reconstruction and Development, *Transition Report 1998* (London: EBRD, 1998), pp. 12–19; and Ben Slay, "Overview," in *PlanEcon Review and Outlook for the Former Soviet Republics* (Washington, D.C.: PlanEcon, Inc., October 1998), pp. i–iv. For three perceptive Russian reviews, see Aleksandr Ivanter, Nikita Kirichenko, and Iurii Beletskii, "Schast'e v dolg ne voz'mesh'," *Ekspert*, No. 1 (1999), pp. 7–13; Vladimir Mau, "Politicheskaia priroda i uroki finansovogo krizisa," and Andrei Illarionov, "Kak byl organizovan rossiiskii finansovyi krizis," both in *Voprosy ekonomiki*, No. 11 (1998), pp. 4–19 and 20–35 respectively.

[11] Quoted in Serge Schmemann, "How Can You Have a Bust if You've Never Had a Boom?" *The New York Times Magazine*, December 27 1998, p. 28.

Russia's very vulnerability to world commodities prices and movements of capital showed how open the economy had become. The fact that the collapse of the top twenty commercial banks could paralyze the country's system of payments and credit underscored how deeply private banking had taken over the country's key financial functions, including some that in other countries (such as processing tax payments) are performed by the state. Many enterprises in the "virtual economy" had bet heavily on government debt and were among the losers when the bubble burst. On the positive side, Russian industry responded to devaluation by increasing exports or filling the gap left by imports. This testified to the growing profit-mindedness of many Russian companies and their capacity to react to market signals. In short, even in its worst moment of crisis the Russian economy showed clearly that it was no longer Soviet, and indeed that the market had penetrated deeply into Russian thinking and behavior.

Moreover, the August crash did not lead to a dismantling of the post-Soviet structures, a major push for renationalization, or a significant retreat from free prices or ruble convertibility – even though such a backlash had been widely predicted in the months following the crisis. Most of the remaining reformers left the central government and were replaced by a new set of players with long Soviet-era résumés. Yet at this writing the new government has made no move to undo the marketization achieved to date. Indeed, it is too weak and too divided to do so.

By the end of the Nineties, in sum, the changes in Russia have reached a depth and a complexity well beyond the simple narratives of transition versus takeover. Both narratives are true, as far as they go, but they do not capture the full sweep of what is happening.

If we are to capture what is going on in Russia we must take a more long-term historical perspective. An entire order, the whole political, economic, and ideological system of Soviet Marxism–Leninism, has been overthrown. It has been replaced by a new set of economic and political institutions, founded on different constitutional and ideological premises. If that is not revolution, then what is?

Thinking of the recent events in Russia as a revolution has three useful implications:

First, it is not yet over. Revolutions take decades until a new political, economic, and social order is built. The present quasi-stability is illusory. There are still strong forces pushing for change. Thinking in terms of revolution makes us look for them.

Second, the end point of revolutions is a synthesis of old and new. The new Russia is being built with pieces taken from the old, and thus both transition and takeover are part of the same story. Many of the people now on top in Russia already had status and connections in the old system, even if most did not belong to the front ranks of the nomenklatura. The question is not where they came from, but what roles they play in the new system, and what the basis of the final synthesis will be.

Third, the final political result of revolutions is a rebuilding of the state on the basis of the new economic and social structures and the new distribution of power and wealth. This is not a one-way street: the new economy, society, and polity evolve simultaneously and influence one another. But revolutions typically result in stronger states, not weaker ones. So long as the Russian state remains as weak as it is today, and Russian politics remains as fluid, we can be sure that the revolution is not yet complete.

Revolutions, like volcanoes, come in all shapes and sizes and degrees of violence. How does this one differ from the classic eruptions of the century, and especially from the first Russian revolution? What clues do we have to where it might go from here? Those are the questions discussed in the rest of this chapter.

A revolution by accident?

As late as 1988, no Russian would have imagined that his familiar world would shatter as it did. The break-up of the Soviet system came for most people, as the Russians say, *kak grom sredi iasnogo neba*, "like thunder in a clear sky." The shock of the first few years had barely worn off when the second shock of 1998 occurred, and Russians are still coming to terms with the enormous and unforeseen disappearance of the system they grew up in. Very few would claim that they were mentally prepared for anything remotely like what happened.

When a familiar world abruptly collapses, it is only in retrospect that one can see how it was silently undermined – "we recognize," as Marx once wrote, "our friend the old mole, the revolution." But in the case of the Soviet system, the undermining had long been apparent, and both Westerners and Soviets (and not just dissidents) had been writing about it for years. Still, in the mid-1980s the end seemed far away. There was little reason to suspect, when Mikhail Gorbachev became leader in 1985, that the collapse of the Soviet Union was just around the corner.

The fatal catalyst was the well-meaning but inept tampering of Mikhail Gorbachev and his fellow reformers, as they attempted to breathe legitimacy into the old system. In retrospect, Gorbachev played the role of the sorcerer's apprentice: he took apart, one after another, all of the Soviet state's principal mechanisms of control, without seeming to realize that in doing so he was undermining the supports of his own power and of his government, setting the regime adrift.[12]

From 1986 to 1991, the Soviet state successively lost control over its revenues and spending, the state enterprises, the banking system, foreign trade, credit, money, and wages, the apparatus of censorship and repression, not to mention political and police control over the outlying republics and regions. How and why Gorbachev did this is not the subject of this book.[13] But one thing is clear: the collapse of the Soviet Union in 1986–91 was touched off by blundering reform at the top, followed only afterward by popular response.

If Gorbachev was the catalyst, what about deeper causes? At first glance, most of the usual precursors of revolution – the kind that announce a new order decades ahead of the event – were lacking in Russia in the mid-1980s. There had been no generation of Russian liberal *philosophes*, preparing people's minds for capitalism and free enterprise with their writings. There was no underground "Free-Market Party," no Lenins or Trotskys plotting in exile, armed this time with Russian translations of Adam Smith or Friedrich Hayek; no wealthy middle class chafing over its exclusion from status and power; no expanding peasantry desperate for land or uprooted industrial working class, no civil society noisily asserting its rights against the state. The USSR as late as the mid-1980s was remarkably quiet.

And yet the old mole was at work, beneath the surface. Russians themselves became aware of the changes in their society from the 1970s on. Most people did not consciously reject socialism – that was like an old pair of shoes, shabby perhaps but comfortably familiar. But they were fed up with the *nachal'stvo* – the bosses – and the wooden language of the official ideology, and the grayness of life in a system that could not even produce a decent pair of blue jeans or elegant shoes. The political system had become soft, corrupt, and contemptible. The economic system could no longer deliver growth, and living standards had ceased to improve.

A common sign of the decay of an old regime is a silent appropriation of wealth and power by second-tier members of the elite, loosening the leadership's grip. In the Soviet Union under Leonid Brezhnev this was clearly happening. By the 1980s the local managers of the state economy were well on their way to becoming de-facto owners – "stakeholders," the academic literature delicately calls them. Meanwhile, society as a whole

---

[12] On the Gorbachev reforms, see Archie Brown, *The Gorbachev Factor* (Oxford: Oxford University Press, 1996) and Jerry F. Hough, *Democratization and Revolution in the USSR, 1985–1991* (Washington D.C.: The Brookings Institution, 1997).

[13] For Gorbachev's own reflections in retirement, see Mikhail Gorbachev, *Memoirs* (New York: Doubleday, 1996).

was becoming less closely controlled. A shadow economy was growing strongly, outside state controls. Virtually all Russians bought private goods and services "on the left," that is, through a black market of friends and connections. There were already underground millionaires, and mafia gangsters to prey on them.

Soviet culture was being undermined as well. State controls from the Sixties on failed to keep out influences from the West. But even more important than the West in shaping the minds of the last Soviet generation were the Russian songwriters, poets, filmmakers, and comedians who worked just inside the edges of the system, long before *glasnost'*. Hundreds of thousands of students joined informal organizations such as the KSP – *kluby studencheskikh pesnei* (Student Song Clubs) and gathered in mass songfests in the woods. The values of a private, more individualistic and materialistic consumer-oriented society were seeping into Soviet life for a generation before the final collapse.

As the economy slowed and the gap between the regime's slogans and everyday reality grew wider, young people reacted with mounting cynicism. The Komsomol – the junior version of the Communist Party – became a cover for careerists and entrepreneurs.[14] Anti-regime jokes – the famous *anekdoty* that Russians traded when they thought "Sofia Vasilevna" (the Soviet equivalent of "Uncle Sam") wasn't listening – were now told openly. One of my own favorites is about the man who is arrested on Red Square for handing out leaflets. The astonished policemen discover that all the leaflets are blank. "What's the big idea?" they demand. The man shrugs, "Why write anything on them?" he asks. "Everything is already clear." On the economic front, the message was indeed clear. Only the massive Soviet oil exports of the 1970s and early 80s, at the high prices of the day, gave the command economy a reprieve – while enabling the Soviet leadership to avoid change.[15]

For many intellectuals, the break with the Soviet order was already more complete. Some – but as yet only a handful – were already thinking actively about alternatives to the command economy. The future reformers of the Yeltsin era could be found in ones and twos in the late 1970s in the academic institutes of Moscow and Leningrad, in the media, or even in the apparatus of the Communist Party. Egor Gaidar, who as acting prime minister and then finance minister led the first radical reforms in 1991–93, was economics editor on the staff of the official monthly of the

[14] Steven L. Solnick, *Stealing the State: Control and Collapse in Soviet Institutions* (Cambridge, MA: Harvard University Press, 1998).
[15] On the failure of Soviet-style reforms in key economic sectors, and the rise and fall of the oil bonanza, see Thane Gustafson, *Reform in Soviet Politics* (Cambridge: Cambridge University Press, 1981) and same, *Crisis amid Plenty* (Princeton, NJ: Princeton University Press, 1989).

CPSU Central Committee, *Kommunist*. He came from one of the most prominent families in the communist upper crust. His grandfather, Arkadii Gaidar, was the author of a hugely popular novel for boys, *Timur and his Team*, which was published in 1940 and became a classic, eagerly read by two generations of Young Pioneers, the Soviet boy scouts. (Later on, old-line communists would accuse Yegor Gardar of betraying his grandfather's memory.)

"I started out as a convinced communist," Gaidar recalled, as we sat in his large pine-paneled library in the summer of 1996. "I was six at the time of the Cuban Missile Crisis, and my family was living in Cuba. My father was a journalist. Che Guevara was a frequent visitor to my father's house. My doubts began when I was twelve, at the time of the Soviet intervention in Czechoslovakia in 1968. I had many Czech friends, I started asking them questions, and I could see that the official version had nothing to do with what actually happened."

"In the late 1970s I began post-graduate studies, and realized that halfway measures or hybrid compromises – 'market socialism' – simply wouldn't work. I was gradually moving toward acceptance of the private market. There were plenty of like-minded people to talk to, and it wasn't so difficult to find things to read. Sometimes they were kept in the *spetskhran*, the classified area of the library. But for the most part, if you read foreign languages and were willing to take the trouble, you could find a lot to read on market economies."

"The major influence on me," Gaidar continued, "was the Hungarian economist Janos Kornai. His analysis of the economy of shortage, in the early 1980s, had a great impact on all of us. He was addressing *our* problems. Among Western writers, the most importance influence on me was Friedrich Hayek. He gave a very clear and consistent picture of the world, as impressive as Marx in his way."

But most of this ferment still went on out of sight. The repressive apparatus of the state was still strong enough to make most people cautious. Sedition was confined to the kitchen. Young people and intellectuals had gotten as far as talking quietly about what they did not want, but few had begun to think actively about alternatives. In that respect, Gorbachev was representative of his generation. In time – perhaps in another generation – this mixture would have started to bubble, and then to boil over, first at the non-Russian periphery of the Soviet Union then in Russia itself. But before it did, Gorbachev broke the kettle, while trying to repair it.

When that happened, very few Russians were consciously ready to throw off the old system – but fewer still were prepared to go to great lengths to defend it. What violence there was occurred in the outlying republics – in Alma-Ata, Vilnius, Tbilisi, and especially Baku. But in Russia itself there was hardly a break in the daily flow of life. In most revolutions the population becomes radicalized and pours into the political arena.[16] But the Russian population did not. Only a few thousand people, mostly in Moscow, were directly involved in political activity, while the rest of the country, and indeed most Muscovites, went about their daily business.[17] The Soviet state fell victim to indifference and opportunism, not least among its own elite.

And most certainly the Soviet order did not collapse because of the pro-market ideas that had gathered momentum in the West over the previous three decades. This key point helps to understand two things about what followed. First, when the Soviet system collapsed there were only a handful of people who understood even so much as the basics of how markets worked. The team led by Egor Gaidar, who found themselves at the top of the government in 1991–92, promoted ideas that they themselves had never experienced in real life, and which were totally unfamiliar to the population at large. The common slogan, "We want a normal, civilized country," was revealing in its vagueness. When the end came, many Russians who had never heard of neoclassical economics proved remarkably well prepared to step into the vacuum, but the market as they understood it was essentially the freedom to do whatever one pleased, without restraint or limit.

Second, the political support for radical market reforms, thin to begin with, weakened further as soon as the first reforms began to bite, in the spring and summer of 1992. The reformers knew they had to move fast if they were to achieve anything at all, and they became obsessed by the need for speed. But because the revolutionary wave that carried them was comparatively weak, they soon faced determined opposition. After the first few months, market reforms turned into trench warfare, and from that time on progress was achieved only through constant compromise. The patchwork quality of the Russian market economy, the pattern of stop-and-start of economic reform, reflect the deep popular ambivalence and the lack of broad elite conviction that have been characteristic of Russian marketization from the beginning. The most striking symbol of

[16] For the classic statement on the explosion of popular demands for participation in revolutions, see Samuel P. Huntington, *Political Order in Changing Societies* (New Haven, Conn.: Yale University Press, 1968). For a Russian analysis that also argues that the present situation is a revolution, see Valdimir Mau, "Ekonomicheskie reformy i revoliutsiia," in Egor Gaidar, ed., *Ekonomika perekhodnogo perioda: ocherki ekonomicheskoi politiki postkommunisticheskoi Rossii, 1991–97* (Moscow: Institut ekonomicheskikh problem perekhodnogo perioda, 1998), pp. 9–36.

[17] M. Steven Fish, *Democracy from Scratch: Opposition and Regime in the New Russian Revolution* (Princeton NJ: Princeton University Press, 1995).

this lack of consensus is the inability of the Russian government, to achieve a lasting victory over inflation.[18]

Nevertheless, the combination of reform and collapse launched three revolutionary waves that have penetrated deeply – though as yet not completely – into Russian society: the renaissance of money, the transfer of wealth into private hands, and the weakening of the central state

Three waves that launched a revolution

Well before the final collapse of the Soviet Union at the end of 1991 three revolutionary changes were under way.

First, wealth flooded from the state into private hands, on as large a scale as the Russian Revolution of 1917, but in the opposite direction. Second, the basis of the economy was transformed, as money displaced political power and connections as the chief purchasing medium. Third, as Russia began to shift from a state-owned to a privately owned economy, reforms began to refashion the mission of the state. However, all three waves have penetrated only part-way, leaving Russia in an awkward middle ground. The grip of the national state over politics and society was lastingly weakened, which initially catalyzed the rise of the private sector but subsequently weakened and distorted it.

Behind these changes is an upheaval of values, social status, and roles. Russian Marxism–Leninism had abolished the market as the prime mechanism for allocating scarcity, and relegated money to the role of a secondary, passive unit of account. It reverted to a medieval Russian concept of state service as the basis for all rewards. It subordinated society to the state, and systematically fed the state's needs while ignoring those of society. The planner and the bureaucrat, not the consumer, were sovereign. The prestige occupations – down through the end of the 1960s, at any rate – were those of military officer, rocket scientist and cosmonaut, engineer, and Party official. Lawyers, bankers, economists, accountants, and traders were despised.[19] Most Russians in their everyday lives, until

---

[18] Daniel S. Treisman, "Fighting Inflation in a Transitional Regime: Russia's Anomalous Stabilization," *World Politics*, vol. 50 (January 1998), pp. 235–265.

[19] At least, this was true to down to the 1970s. In the last two decades of the Soviet era, engineers, scientists, and military officers began losing social prestige, partly because their earnings slipped. People in the trade system earned far more – mostly by selling their goods into the unofficial economy – and gained steadily in informal status from the 1970s on. Respectable Moscow matrons affected to despise mere *torgovtsy* – but strove to make sure their daughters married one.

The surest informal measure of this trend is applications rates to specialized institutes of higher education. Beginning in the 1970s the most prestigious scientific and military academies began to lose applicants, while students besieged the doors of institutes leading to occupations in the trade sector.

well into the 1970s, lived practically free of market forces, something Westerners can barely conceive of. A world of beliefs and expectations – particularly the expectation that the state would provide – which encased every Soviet citizen from birth to death, has been smashed like an eggshell.

The incomplete penetration of money

For most Russians, the real revolution in Russia was the return of money to center stage in economic life. In the Soviet system of central planning, goods were produced and distributed through a combination of planners' orders from above and vigorous bargaining from below. "Money," said Peter Karpov, deputy director of Russia's federal bankruptcy agency, "was like an amusing but insignificant little musical accompaniment."[20] In actual fact, the interesting thing about money in the Soviet system was that its value varied depending on who spent it and where. One hundred rubles, in the hands of a well-placed nomenklatura family shopping in one of the closed stores for the Party elite, bought a fortune. In effect, three currencies circulated in the Soviet economy – money, power, and connections. The price of any given object was a blend of the three.[21]

The effect of decontrolling prices in January 1992, despite many local restrictions at first, was dramatic and immediate. The Russian State Statistical Committee (Goskomstat) has run regular surveys of 132 cities all across Russia to monitor shortages of consumer goods (in Russian, "defitsit"). These found that by April 1994 there were practically no lines. Only 12% of Russians surveyed still complained of shortages.[22]

Decontrolling prices wiped out instantly the huge monetary overhang that had built up over the previous three years, and brought goods back into the stores-just as economic theory predicted.

Much of the Russian economy – perhaps as much as three-quarters-now functions on money, whether rubles or dollars. Consumer purchases take place in cash, as do imports and exports. The new private sector of trade and services-or at any rate what is left of it after the shock of August 1998–also runs largely on cash. The money prices of consumer goods and most services reflect supply and demand, and are driven by consumer decisions. The money supply and the price of money are as closely watched in Moscow and Vladivostok as anywhere else in the world. The

---

[20] Quoted in *Financial Times*, August 12 1994.
[21] For this point and many others throughout this book, I am grateful to Dr. Vladimir Bokser, who was one of the key figures in the Democratic Russia movement in Moscow in the early 1990s.
[22] Aleksandr Livshits, *Ekonomicheskaia reforma v Rossii i ego tsena* (Moscow: "Kul'tura," 1994) p. 31.

ruble is freely convertible internally. Most loans are at market rates, and subsidized government lending has practically disappeared (if for no other reason than that the government is too poor to lend). Money, in the form of campaign spending, budgetary politics, bribes, and much else besides, has become the numeraire and the central preoccupation of politics, as it never was in the Soviet era. In short, Russia has become very largely not just a money economy, but a money society and a money polity as well.

Yet the penetration of money into the Russian economy is still incomplete; indeed, since about 1994 it has been partly reversed. The center of resistance is industry. Most industrial transactions-an often-quoted figure is 70% – are settled by barter or through complex chains of promissory notes called "wechsels" (in Russian, *vekselia*). In some provinces local pools of wechsels form virtual local currencies. Increasingly, taxes are paid in barter and wechsels as well. Much of the gas and electricity consumed in the country is paid for (when it is paid for at all) in the same way. When money is offered, it is always accepted in preference to barter; but more often businesses hide their money assets whenever they can, and pay in the lesser numeraire-a classic case of Gresham's Law, in which funny money drives out the real thing.

The reasons for the incomplete victory of money are many and complex.[23] Russian managers themselves complain that there is simply a shortage of money, which they blame bitterly on the "monetarist" market reformers. Careful Western analyses show that this is not so; the real problem goes much deeper.[24] The answer lies in a tangle of Soviet legacies and post-Soviet constraints. The Soviet concept was that value was created by the production of a good, not by its sale. Once an object was produced, manufacturers expected to be paid for it as soon as it moved out of the factory. The fact that there is no longer any demand for many of the goods produced in Soviet-era factories has been understandably difficult for managers to adjust to. They are typically loath to reduce their prices, which are traditionally set on a cost-plus basis and are thus unrealistically high. But in addition most industrial companies are actually barred by Soviet-era rules from lowering their prices below cost. Barter and wechsels allow a partial way out, by enabling buyers and sellers to pretend they are selling their goods at the high official price. Hence many factories are sustained – albeit at a low bare-survival level-by maintaining closed circuits of physical exchange and quasi-money, trading goods at make-believe prices, supported by local banks and orchestrated by local governments.

[23] David Woodruff, *Money Unmade* (Ithaca, N.Y.: Cornell University Press, 1999).
[24] Brigitte Granville, *The Success of Russian Economic Reforms* (London: Royal Institute of International Affairs, 1995).

These circles of unreality can only be sustained, however, if someone else is supporting them. What keeps the whole system going is that the essential inputs – energy and raw materials – are provided below their actual value, while two of the principal partners – workers and the national government-are paid in barter or in promises. The reasons the losers continue to play the game are ultimately political: energy producers supply the domestic market at a loss under a variety of threats (particularly the threat of being denied export revenues); workers are unable to demand their wages because they are unorganized; while the national government is too weak to enforce tax collection against the resistance of local enterprises and regional governments. Finally, to the list of "donors" must be added foreign investors and international financial institutions, which have involuntarily helped to sustain this virtual economy with securities purchases and loan programs that the Russian government has been too weak to honor.[25]

Yet Russia on balance has become a money-based economy just the same, in which de-facto prices are set by negotiation between buyers and sellers. The fact that the numeraire used is not necessarily the ruble – i.e., the official currency of a weak national government – is a grave problem, but it does not change the fundamental importance of the change that has occurred. Barter and wechsels are debased forms of money. They have the effect of obscuring real prices and costs, but they are money just the same, in the fundamental sense that they are not planners' commands. That is a world of difference.

As a result, there are two "informal" economies in Russia today. The "shadow" economy is the world of underground business, unregistered and unreported. The "virtual economy" is the world of Soviet-era manufacturing, which has attempted to shelter itself from market pressures by retreating from it. The "shadow economy" is at the opposite pole from the "virtual" economy. The basis of the shadow economy is strictly cash, while that of the virtual economy is barter and IOUs. The shadow economy lives by its wits; the virtual economy by subsidies (in the hidden form of unpaid taxes and wages). The shadow economy produces services for which there is a market; the virtual economy produces physical goods for which there is none – at least at Soviet-era cost-plus pricing. The shadow economy, until the crash of August 1998, accounted for perhaps 40% of Russian GDP; the virtual economy – essentially the manufacturing and defense-industrial rump – barely 25%.

Both the "shadow economy" and the "virtual economy" are rational (if

---

[25] Clifford G. Gaddy and Barry W. Ickes, "Russia's Virtual Economy," *Foreign Affairs*, September-October 1998, pp. 53–67.

defective) responses to the irrational environment of the 1990s. But they are both forms of money economy.

From state property to private property

The second revolutionary event was the massive transfer of wealth from the state into private hands. In the space of a few years – roughly beginning in 1988 – literally hundreds of billions of dollars flowed from state properties to private entrepreneurs and companies, most of them connected in some way with the previous state enterprises and ministries. A class of super-wealthy individuals and conglomerates sprang up overnight. Never in human history, perhaps, has there been such a dramatic and sudden transfer of wealth, other than through military conquest.

This massive change of ownership – which the Russians call *peredel*, the great redistribution – is at the core of both the "transition" and "takeover" narratives. From the transition standpoint, the important thing is the transfer itself; after all, there can be no capitalism without capitalists. How it happens and who profits are secondary. The real questions are, How are the rights of private property protected, and what do the new owners choose to do with their property? But from the takeover perspective, the *peredel* was fatally flawed because both the process of transfer and the beneficiaries were corrupt. Therefore, their gains could only be protected through further corruption. And this insured that they would not behave like true market capitalists, but rather like rent-seekers.

Both sides are right; but it is the combination of the two stories that gives it its true revolutionary significance: the fact that the property of the country has passed into private hands, and that those hands are precisely those of the newly powerful and well-connected (including, if truth be told, many opposition politicians) means that it will never be handed back to the state, no matter who comes to power. What happens next is still wide open, but the change is irreversible.

The creation of the new private wealth came in three overlapping waves; all three were the result of the weakening of the Soviet state. The first, beginning in 1988, was caused by the collapse of the State foreign-trade monopoly. The second, beginning after 1990, was driven by financial speculation catalyzed by inflation and a weak ruble. The third, from 1992 on, was based on a privatization policy hurriedly put together to head off a massive "wildcat" privatization from below. For a brief time – roughly from 1988 to 1995 – the conditions were right for energetic people with connections and daring to make fabulous fortunes.

Why did foreign trade lead the way? Prior to 1988 the Soviet government's most jealously-guarded monopoly was control over foreign trade and hard currency. All exports of oil, gas, gold, timber, and natural resources of all kinds, were under the sole command of the Soviet government. The Ministry of Foreign Trade negotiated all deals. The USSR State Bank oversaw the transfer of hard-currency revenues to the state. The division of the proceeds was big politics, as powerful officials of the rank of deputy prime minister or above, each representing a potent economic lobby group, did battle for hard-currency allocations. It was big business, but it was state business.

Beginning in 1986 Gorbachev began dismantling the state monopoly over foreign trade. Other ministries were given the right to make deals abroad and handle foreign currency. Then the same right was extended to enterprises, and finally to individuals. Suddenly, the race was on. Anyone with access began exporting practically anything that was not nailed down.[26]

The key to the whole business was that Russia in 1988–1992 was in a no-man's-land between two systems. State controls over trade and exports were disintegrating, but domestic prices remained controlled, frequently at absurdly low levels. Anyone who could acquire oil, diamonds, or metals for rubles at controlled domestic prices, and then sell them abroad for dollars, was rich overnight. This required the connivance of state officials, who issued the necessary licenses and smoothed the way to the borders. But as the Soviet system disintegrated, the borders became practically non-existent. According to a favorite joke in Moscow around 1988, a want ad appeared one day in the daily *Izvestiia*. It said, "The 'Shining Path' cooperative wishes to rent three meters of state border." It hardly needed to bother – the border was already virtually wide open.

The second phase was financial speculation. The ruble was collapsing – but state credits remained available at nominal interest rates. In the runaway inflation of 1991–93, it was easy to borrow money for a month or two, use it to finance export deals, and repay the loan in depreciated rubles. Fortunes made in exports now bankrolled much larger ones from banking. Politicians went along for the ride, lending funds from city and province budgets to the new bankers. (This phase is described in detail in chapter 4.)

Finally, beginning in 1992, the third phase was privatization. Over the following five years most state-owned companies were turned over to private hands, either free or at nominal prices. Trading and banking fortunes were now applied to the purchase of vouchers and shares in privatized companies. This phase lasted through 1996, when the last giant

---

[26] A perceptive analysis is Jean Farneth Boone, "Trading in Power: The Politics of Soviet Foreign Economic Reform, 1986–1991" (PhD thesis, Georgetown University, 1998).

companies in energy and telecommunications were handed over to the new financial – industrial conglomerates that had sprung up in the previous decade.

By the end of 1996, the window for easy windfall gains began to close. Inflation declined, narrowing the opportunities for quick fortunes from financial manipulation. The ruble began to stabilize; this made exports less phenomenally profitable than they had been.[27] There were still ways to get rich, by importing consumer goods or trading in government debt, but these required capital, and it became much more difficult to get started. Beginning in about 1994 the great door of opportunity began to close. The new rich could still multiply their wealth, but the historic chance to get in at the bottom and rocket to the stars was ending.

The key point about the *peredel* is that it was caused by the weakness of the state, and as a consequence private ownership came without rights and without responsibilities. One may fault the reformers for taking a narrow view of private property as simple possession, and for neglecting legal and regulatory reforms to protect it. But in the end it would not have made much difference. The Russian national government was (and is) too feeble, divided, and corrupt to provide effective legal protections for property rights and contracts, or to implement effective regulations for corporate governance and bankruptcy. As a result, the new property owners looked for protection where they could find it – from politicians and from the mafia.

This brings us to the third part of the new Russian revolution – rethinking the state.

Rethinking the state

Building a market economy in Russia involved more than creating new private-sector institutions; it also required a massive rethinking of the state's roles. The Soviet state owned practically everything in the economy and managed it by hands-on controls.[28] But a privately-owned economy needed a different kind of state. The new state would be an

---

[27] Indeed, in real terms the ruble appreciated steadily against the dollar between 1992 and 1996. The "real" exchange rate measures the relative buying power of two currencies. It is calculated by correcting the "nominal" exchange rate (i.e., the current quoted rate) for inflation in the two countries concerned.

The differences between the two rates are striking. In nominal terms, the dollar rose from 37 rubles in April 1991 to over 6,000 at the end of 1997, when the last three zeroes were dropped. But in real terms (i.e., in terms of relative purchasing power), the dollar *fell* against the ruble from 338 to 19 over the same period (assuming June 1992 = 100). Source: *Russian Economic Trends*, various issues.

[28] Ed A. Hewett, *Reforming the Soviet Economy: Equality VS. Efficiency* (Washington, D.C.: Brookings Institution, 1988), chapters 3 and 4.

arbiter and referee instead of an owner, setting and enforcing the rules of the game, but watching and intervening from the sidelines.

Rethinking the state's economic roles was just part of a larger reflection about the state that began in Russia at the same time as Gorbachev's reforms. Western ideas of divided and limited government were in the air from the late 1980s, and Gorbachev himself was much influenced by the concept of the "state of laws," which the democratic reformers under Yeltsin soon expanded to the more demanding Western standard of the "rule of law." But there was relatively little discussion of the state's economic roles in a market economy until market reforms actually began, probably because few seriously believed until the final months of 1991 that they would actually be tried. One must also remember that until the second half of 1991 the Russian government – as a republic-level entity beneath the Soviet level – was merely a shadow government, with no real responsibility for economic management.

When the Soviet state collapsed, the process of rethinking new economic functions had to compete with the much more pressing business of day-to-day survival. In early 1992 the government was in shock, state agencies became virtual empty shells, police vanished from the streets, and demoralized officials left state service in droves for the new private sector. Most of the reformers' early work consisted of putting out fires. For a year or two the central government practically ceased to exist, although local governments in most places continued to function.

By now that extreme state of shock is long past, but the post-Soviet state is fundamentally weaker than its predecessor. The state no longer owns most of the economy, and its direct control over the main economic levers – prices, taxes, investment, and ownership of property – is much reduced. Most prices have been freed, except for some dwindling controls at local levels. The share of GDP raised in taxes by the state at all levels is half of what it was in the Soviet system, and much of that is paid in barter and quasi-monies. (See chapter 9.) The central government plays practically no role in investment, and most of its meager resources are spent on social programs. Privatization has transferred over 70% of large enterprises into private hands, and most small businesses have been privatized as well. The state is still a large shareholder in tens of thousands of enterprises, but it plays virtually no role in their management.

However – and this is the key point-this massive scaling down of the state's economic roles was only partly the result of conscious reform. The early reformers did take a number of significant steps to create a new kind of state. They established an antimonopoly committee to regulate the behavior of the new private corporations; and later on they set up watchdog committees for securities and utilities (see chapter 3). The Russian

Central Bank was reshaped to perform the functions of a modern central bank in a largely private banking system (see chapter 4). The reformers disbanded most of the vast apparatus of state committees and ministries that ran the command economy, leaving much weaker bodies with mainly coordinating functions. And they passed an impressive body of new laws that provided a legal foundation for the new roles of the state (see chapter 7).

But much more of the withdrawal of the state was due to attrition. As a result, the Russian state has not really been rethought or restructured. Like the private-sector economy, it is stuck half-way to the market. It is no longer the owner, but not yet the referee. Its current powers over the economy are mostly of a negative kind – i.e., the power to block, to delay, to withhold permits and permissions, all to the greater profit of the officials concerned, who extract tribute in exchange for their approval. Much of the active rethinking of the state's functions remains confined to good intentions and unimplemented programs. Not only is this a weak and unhelpful kind of state power, but such as it is, it has continued to waste away throughout the decade.

The regions have gained some of what the central government has lost. Half of the total revenues of the state now go to the regional and local levels, and their share is growing steadily. While the number of federal state employees in the central government has declined sharply (including military officers), employment by regional and local governments has actually grown. In short, the balance of power has shifted in less than a decade from a lopsided dominance of the central state (a Russian characteristic in all but the most troubled times) to something quite new in Russian experience, a roughly equal division of power between the center and the regions.

But it is a balance of the weak, not of the strong. The regions, by themselves, cannot create a strong national market economy; they can only accelerate its disintegration into weak regional sub-economies. Moreover, most regional governments still have a rather "Soviet" concept of their economic role: they are co-owners of local businesses; they support local cartels; they intervene in pricing and allocation; they orchestrate the local circuits of quasi-monies. In short, while some may be pro-market in their rhetoric they are nearly all anti-market in their actions. Thus, paradoxically, the weakness of the national state, which initially opened the way for the privatization of wealth and the rise of the market, is also what prevents the market economy from developing on a sound basis.

The captured revolution

Thus the three key features of the Russian revolution are the penetration of money into a previously demonetized economy, the transfer of state wealth into private hands, and the sudden end of the state-as-owner. Yet after a decade all three processes are distorted, unsettled, and incomplete. Both the transition and the takeover narratives offer essentially the same explanation: further change has been blocked by conservative opposition. The only difference between the two is that in the takeover perspective, the time of revolutionary change is over. In the transition view, it has merely stalled, but could resume quickly with the right policies under the right reform-minded leadership. Which is right? The answer is, neither one.

The central event for both views is the early political reconsolidation that took place in 1993 and after. The collapse of the Soviet Union, did not destroy the entire Soviet edifice to ground level. The top blew off, but much of the underlying regional and local structure survived, and remained dominated by people from the middle and lower ranks of the Soviet administrative class. The collapse of 1991 was more thorough at the top of the system than at the bottom, and in the formal institutions than in the informal networks and practices.[29] It left behind much the "hard wiring" of the Soviet economy, in the antiquated technologies frozen into the factories, the roads and public housing built into the enterprises, the one-industry towns, and the mindset of Soviet industrialism.

As a result, within two years after the Soviet collapse in 1991, a conservative political order had begun to consolidate. In most of the regions, local elites based on the Soviet nomenklatura squeezed out or co-opted the handful of democrats who had managed to enter the administration, and created governments based on executive power. In some places, most notably in Moscow, former democrats and the former nomenklatura joined forces and governed together in a pragmatic alliance.[30]

This consolidation did produce one significant result: it restored basic stability to a country that between 1991 and 1993 had seemed on the edge of anarchy. After 1993, the more apocalyptic scenarios widely predicted for Russia – a military coup, or a restoration of communist rule, or the breakup of the country – became increasingly improbable.

The crash of August 1998 reinforced in some respects this apparent consolidation. It forced the remaining reformers off the political stage,

---

[29] David Stark, "Recombinant Property in East European Capitalism," *American Journal of Sociology*, vol. 101, no. 4 (January 1996), pp. 993–1027.
[30] Interview with Ilya Zaslavskii, general director of LARIS, and Moscow deputy Alevtina Nikitina, July 11 1996.

and fatally weakened their one remaining political support, President Yeltsin. The crash also weakened the banking oligarchs and made them even more dependent on the state than before. The Primakov government, even more than the Chernomyrdin government that preceded it, symbolized the desire of the winners to govern by pragmatic consensus.

There has been a tendency in Western discussions to demonize the agents of this consolidation as backward-looking, rent-seeking, value-destroying, and so forth. But much of their behavior is in fact a rational response to the stress and disorder around them. It is not so much aimed against transition and the market economy as it is an attempt to address other problems – to reknit a frayed social fabric, to rebuild the state, and to salvage something of the achievements of the Soviet era. It is all too understandable, and altogether human.

The problem with this apparent consolidation, however, is that it is neither politically stable nor economically viable, and therefore it cannot endure.

Russia today is *politically* unstable, because there is as yet no agreement over the basic design of the state or the fundamental basis of society. Whether the Russian political system will be federal or unitary, presidential or parliamentary, democratic or authoritarian, is entirely unresolved and will shortly be subject to powerful challenges. But the deeper flaw is that the present political system and the people within it are largely rejected by a sullen population that believes it is worse off than a decade ago and sees no salvation from its political class.

Russia is *economically* unstable, because the present halfway economy cannot produce growth or generate investment. The one sector that has generated wealth in the last decade, the commodity-exporting industries, is spending its inheritance and not renewing it. No significant investment is going into education, science, environment, or health. Even the "virtual economy" is bound to wind down as its capital stock continues to deteriorate.

Even now, the consolidation is more appearance than reality. The new elites share a superficial Soviet coloration and language, but that is about all. Competing economic and political interests have formed "clans," which fight one another bitterly for access to the state and its dwindling favors. Government and opposition duel over economic policy, while "have" and "have not" regions struggle for tax breaks and subsidies. The new Russian elites differ sharply on every major political and economic issue, and the result is conflict and paralysis.

To give it its due, the new Russian political system is more open than the old. First, it is a genuine (if still fragile) democracy.[31] The key posi-

---

[31] Stephen White, Richard Rose, Ian McAllister, *How Russia Votes* (Chatham, New Jersey: Chatham House Publishers, 1997).

tions in the system are elective, and elections are competitive. Second, a far wider array of people and resources are involved in politics than formerly. Previously, only one's official rank counted, and politics was limited to a handful of senior players. Now anyone with money, fame, or any other resource can turn them into political resources and enter politics. Third, there is no dominant party or official ideology, and most political contests are fought over concrete issues and personalities, especially at the local level.

Yet the new Russian political system is virtually unaccountable to the voters. It hovers above the electorate, practically without connection. Parties and civic groups are underdeveloped. Instead, Russian politicians respond to other forces, particularly the money and media power of the newly rich and powerful. The relative consolidation that took place after 1993 did not freeze change. The new political system is open enough to admit new players with new resources, and to respond to new forces arising from society (even if at present these are transmitted more often through the backroom than through the ballot box). The political system may be weak and divided; it may be corrupt and intrusive – but it is not an insuperable bar to social and economic change.

Still, the present system is not yet the "synthesis" of old and new that marks the end of a revolution. It is not yet a stable or viable political and economic order. More change, perhaps violent change, lies ahead.

Summing up: revolution or reaction?

The central argument of this book is that a revolution has indeed taken place in Russia, and that the processes of change unleashed by it have not yet run their course. Yet its main legacy so far is a weak state, a private sector deformed by the manner of its birth, an economy stuck halfway between the command economy and the market, and an unsettled, ambivalent relationship between state and society.

This situation could evolve in three directions. The first is a recovery of the financial-industrial "oligarchies" and a reinforcement of their cozy and corrupt intimacy with the state at all levels – essentially a return to the Russian Nineties. But "crony capitalism" was temporarily viable only thanks to high commodities prices and easy access to short-term capital. The power and wealth of the oligarchs was badly weakened by the August crash, and the mechanisms that caused their tremendous concentration of wealth in the late 1980s and early 1990s are now gone. The oligarchs are unlikely to regain their former heights.

The second is authoritarian backlash, if Russians reject the embryonic market economy and the new capitalist class and return to the values and methods of a police state. Sadly, the example of Belarus shows that this outcome is all too plausible. For the many Russians whose only experience of the market has been lower living standards, disorder, and corruption, a strong hand and reassuring slogans may be tempting. In the last chapter of this book, however, I suggest some reasons why this may not be the most likely outcome.

The third is continued democratic and market-oriented reform. In the wake of the August crash it initially appeared as though Russia's experiment with the market was over, but that is clearly not the case. The slogans of "state control" and "industrial policy" now dominate the Russian political class, and regardless of who Russia's next leader turns out to be, more state-oriented policy-makers will have their turn. But a return to state control is unlikely to work, and after a time market reform may return to the fore. If the world economy remains prosperous and dynamic, it will continue to be the dominant model for much of the Russian educated class.

Will a "second generation" of market reforms succeed better than the first? To judge that question, one must understand what was achieved in the first decade and what went wrong. The chapters that follow describe the rise of private property, the creation of new private-sector financial and legal institutions, and the impact of revolutionary change on Russian society. Two themes run throughout the book. The first is the creative energy and resourcefulness of Russian society. The second is the destructive and distorting effect on society of the weakness of the state.

The experience of Russia's first post-Soviet decade has been a vivid reminder that there is no strong market economy without a strong national state. It is the strong state that creates a single market space with a single national money. It is the strong state that provides the essential protections for property rights and contracts, enforces corporate governance and maintains competition, and offsets the imperfections of the market. If these maxims have a familiar ring, it is perhaps because they take us back to an earlier generation of political economists, those of the 1940s and 50s, whose central concern was the construction of regulated and "civilized" markets in the West.

Thus the central condition for the next generation of market reform in Russia is the resolution of the political conflicts that impede the rebuilding of the state. In short, there will not be a market economy in Russia – or any other kind of viable economy – until the post-Soviet political revolution is over.

Nothing will happen in this country until all the state property has been stolen and . . . the bureaucrats, the merchants, and the bandits have divided it among themselves. Then things will settle down.

column in *Moskovskii komsomolets*, March 17 1994

Privatization actually began rather than ended the struggle for private property. Joseph Blasi et al., *Kremlin Capitalism*[1]

2 Creating owners: insider privatization and its consequences

January 1993:

While traveling in West Siberia, I was invited by a friend to attend a company stockholders' meeting. The company was the Tiumen' Shipbuilding Factory, formerly a closed defense plant. Defense orders had vanished and it was on the verge of bankruptcy. Its workforce of 5,000 had melted down to 2,500. They had not been paid in six months.

The Tiumen' plant had privatized quickly in 1992, somehow hoping for a miracle. Two groups began jostling for control. One was said to represent the "insider" nomenklatura. Its rival was a group of outsiders (although no less nomenklatura) who had gotten their start in Tiumen' by trading oil on the first private commodities exchanges. Both groups canvassed the plants' workers one by one, buying up their shares. By the time of the stockholders' meeting, workers and managers began to fear they had sold off control in their own company.

As people assembled in the plant's auditorium it was 30 below outside, but inside the mood was steamy. In the audience, several hundred agitated workers faced a bare stage, on which sat the representatives of the two rival investors. At first the scene seemed straight out of a Soviet movie. Workers shouted at the men on the stage. "Why haven't we been paid?" "When are we going to get back to work?" The audience began to shift and grumble.

Then one of the men on the stage stood up. He calmly announced that the two rival groups of investors had joined forces, and between them now controlled two-thirds of the company's stock. They intended to vote out the old management and take over.

The hall exploded into bedlam. But then another of the investors strode to the rostrum, and the audience grew quiet again. He was well

---

[1] Joseph Blasi et al., *Kremlin Capitalism: Privatizing the Russian Economy* (Ithaca, New York: Cornell University Press, 1997), p. 11.

known to everyone in the hall – he had been the plant's chief engineer before resigning to join the outsider group. "Ladies and gentlemen," he began, pointedly avoiding the word, "comrades." "How long has it been since this plant has gotten any orders? How many of you will still be here in another six months unless something is done? We ask for your confidence. You have nothing to lose."

Those were the magic words. In a moment the workers' mood seemed to swing from revolt to resignation. Silently, they lined up to vote. When the ballots were counted, the new management had won by near-unanimity. The old managers were dismissed on the spot. In the space of a few hours, the Tiumen' Shipbuilding Plant had gone from socialism to capitalism.

As we filed out into the freezing night air, I talked to a local newspaper correspondent, who had formerly been a secretary in the plant. "So now we're capitalist," she said. "But will that really save the plant?"

Privatization has been the trademark of the Russian market reforms. Whereas East European countries such as Poland and Czechoslovakia led off with programs of macroeconomic stabilization, Russia began with privatization. Within less than three years, an economy that had been almost entirely owned by the state had passed largely into private hands.

In round numbers the scorecard of Russian privatization is remarkable. Between 1992 and 1996 the number of state-owned companies was reduced from 205,000 to about 91,000, and it is still declining, although more slowly since 1997[2] But the privatization of companies was only the most visible part of a tidal wave that has changed the life of every Russian citizen. 75% percent of urban families now own garden plots outside Russian cities. One-third of all urban apartments have been transferred to their occupants,[3] and a growing number of commercial buildings are being privatized. A boom in private housing construction has spread across the suburbs of the main cities. Privatized enterprises account for three-quarters of the market share in retail trade and services and two-thirds in catering.[4] Perhaps as much as 90% of Russian industrial production is in private hands.[5] The only major remaining resource that private property has yet to conquer is land, especially farmland, where privatization has hardly made more than a symbolic start.

As a result, there are actually two private economies in Russia today. The first is made up of businesses that were "born private" – that is, that sprang up in the late 80s and early 90s and never belonged to the state (or evolved quickly out of state-owned ancestors). These companies make up

---

[2] *Russian Economic Trends*, No. 2 (1997), p. 95. Most of the remaining state-owned enterprises, about 30% of the initial total, are located in sectors that were excluded from privatization. This group includes major defense facilities and plants, schools and universities, hospitals and laboratories, prisons, and the like. (*Izvestiia*, May 20 1993).

[3] *Russian Economic Trends*, vol. 4, no. 4 (1995), p. 103.

[4] *Russian Economic Trends*, op. cit., p. 96.   [5] Blasi et al., op. cit., p. 50.

a large part of the new service sector, providing finance, insurance, trade, advertising, and the like. The other private economy consists of the former state enterprises which have been fully or partly privatized since 1992. They dominate the "old" industrial economy – extraction, manufacturing, and light industry, as well as the conventional service businesses such as restaurants and shops. They include many companies that are still technically "state-owned," in the sense that the state retains a controlling block of shares in them, even though in most cases it is only a passive absentee owner. The "born private" group is discussed in the chapter on entrepreneurship. In this chapter we focus on the large and medium-sized former state enterprises. It is in this group that much of the "virtual economy" is located.

No aspect of the Russian transition to the market has been more controversial. For the reformers, privatization of the large and medium-sized industrial enterprises was the magic means to create an overnight constituency for private ownership and to make sure that communism would never return. But the way they went about it became for many Russians the very symbol of deceitful insider-dealing, and "large privatization" has tainted the market reforms as a whole.

Many Western observers are equally critical, but on economic grounds: for them Russian privatization has failed to create the efficient property rights that will foster investment and growth. The main issue is insider control. The big winners from the privatization program were the former Soviet-era managers. But once in control of their new properties, most have done little with them. Apart from scaling down their output and letting go a few workers, few enterprise managers have tried seriously to restructure their companies to adapt them to a market economy.[6] They routinely disregard the voices of their shareholders, and internationally accepted standards of corporate governance are observed mainly in the breach.[7] Most of the managers of the newly-privatized companies still look to the state for the solutions to their problems. As Anatolii Chubais, the chief architect of Russian privatization, wrote in a characteristically caustic phrase, "There remain the same instincts, habits, and connections, and the same bend in the spine. It's a rare director that does not rush off to the government, that doesn't seek connections with high-placed officials, that doesn't beg for subsidized credits, tax breaks, quotas, and privileges."[8]

[6] In the most extensive survey of corporate restructuring to date, Joseph Blasi and his associates constructed a scale of 69 "restructuring activities" and measured an extensive sample of Russian privatized companies against it. They found that the average score was 20 and that no company scored higher than 41. Most companies' efforts to restructure were short-term, defensive, and cosmetic. Blasi et al., op. cit., pp. 139–140.

[7] Blasi et al. also conducted surveys of corporate governance, and found that practically none of the companies in the survey met an acceptable standard. Blasi et al., op. cit., pp. 96ff. and Table 9.

[8] Anatolii Chubais, "Peremena uchasti," Otkrytaia politika, No. 2 (1994), p. 16.

It is certainly not the case that privatization has had no impact at all; on the contrary, privatization began having an effect on some companies' behavior almost immediately. A survey in 1994 by the Privatization Center in Moscow, barely two years after privatization began, showed that more than half of privatized companies had already made some changes in their product mix and their wage structure. In Nizhnii Novgorod, in the first year after privatization, nearly 15% of all shareholder meetings threw out their old managers and replaced them with new ones. A survey conducted in Moscow and Vladimir in late 1993 for the World Bank concluded, "About a quarter of the firms showed promise and were easy to spot. . . . Their managers were making strategic shifts in their operations, cutting back on loss-making activities, and expanding into profitable private-sector markets. . . ." But the same report also cautioned, "Serious restructuring had yet to begin in most firms."[9] At the end of the decade, that is still broadly the case.

Privatization, then, has proven to be no magic formula. Taken by itself, it is simply a new institutional form superimposed on an old structure. The fundamental question, then, is what it takes to make privatization effective. Will it turn out that privatization "Russian-style" has permanently scarred the Russian economy – both economically, by creating weak businesses that cannot be efficiently managed, and politically, by making private property (at least, large-scale private property) illegitimate in the eyes of the population? If so, then the results of the privatization of the early 1990s could be repeatedly challenged in coming years, weakening Russia's progress toward secure property rights and strong investment.

This chapter takes another look at Russian privatization. After reviewing why the privatization campaign was designed as it was, we look again at the behavior of the managers of privatized companies. How much of it is actually a result of the way privatization was carried out? How quick are they to respond when favorable opportunities come along? Has there been more adaptation in some sectors than in others? What are the forces for change?

The chapter's key finding is that given the circumstances of Russia in 1991–94 insider takeover was inevitable, and that there is little alternative to insider control today. As for the behavior of the insider-managers, it is on the whole a reasonably sensible response to an environment that still discourages change in most sectors (but not all) of the economy, and the mode of privatization is only partly to blame.

[9] Leila Webster et al., "Newly-Privatized Enterprises: A Survey," in Ira W. Lieberman and John Nellis, eds., Russia: Creating Enterprises and Efficient Markets, World Bank Studies of Economies in Transformation, No. 15 (Washington, D.C.: The World Bank, 1995), pp. 171–183.

But market pressures are mounting on all managers, insiders and outsiders alike, to alter their behavior.

The implication is that Russian privatization, whatever its flaws, has not foreclosed the future. Arguably, the new owners' origins as insiders or the manner in which they gained control will turn out to matter less than the speed with which market conditions evolve and the new owners respond to them. This in turn will determine their ultimate acceptance by the people. Privatization, in sum, is only the first chapter in what promises to be the much longer saga of reallocation and restructuring of property and of adaptation to the market. The struggle for efficient private property has only begun.

How insider privatization happened

Insider privatization was not the result the Russian reformers had in mind when they set out in 1992. Their initial hope had been to use the privatization process to sell off Russian industry to outside bidders who would provide new management and capital. But that original vision was abandoned almost immediately, for three imperative reasons:

1 *To build a coalition of stakeholders*: For the reformers in 1992 the primary goal was to break the traditional dominance of politicians and bureaucrats in the central government. Their experience had taught them that the greatest enemy was the ministries, and they were determined to cut them out.[10] In contrast, the industrial managers and the local politicians had gained a great deal of influence over the previous decade, effectively becoming "stakeholders" in the state enterprises. Any successful coalition would have to deal them in.

2 *To move fast before support melted away*. In 1991–92 the reformers believed they had only a brief window of opportunity, and that they had to use it to make private property legitimate and irreversible. They faced twin dangers: the spontaneous "wildcat" privatization that had begun in 1988 and was gathering speed by 1991,[11] and growing political opposition

[10] This was also the point of view of their Western advisers, some of whom were former Soviet citizens. "Excessive political control rights over assets," wrote Harvard economist Andrei Shleifer, for example, "are the principal source of economic inefficiency in the world." Andrei Shleifer, "Establishing Property Rights" (Paper presented at the World Bank's Annual Bank Conference on Development Economics, April 28–29, 1994, Washington, D.C.), p. 12.

[11] In his historic speech of October 28 1991, which launched the post-Soviet reforms, Yeltsin called attention to the problem. "For impermissibly long, we have been debating whether private property is necessary. In the meantime, the party-state elite has been actively engaged in their personal privatization. The scale, the enterprise, and the hypocrisy are staggering. Privatization in Russia has been going on for a long time, but wildly, spontaneously, and often on a criminal basis. Today it is necessary to grasp the initiative, and we intend to do so." (*Sovetskaia Rossiia*, October 29 1991, p. 1.)

to market reforms, especially in the legislatures, by the spring of 1992. With the wave of illegal privatization in back of them and the conservative opposition looming they had to move fast.

3 *To keep it simple*: Privatization was unfamiliar to all the Russian players, the assets of the state enterprises could not readily be measured, and the government was in extreme disarray. Whatever procedure was devised had to be simple enough to be implemented quickly by a weak and inexperienced bureaucracy, and accepted by a novice population.

The first phase of privatization, 1992–1995

These constraints led the reformers in 1992 to make a series of pragmatic compromises, which set the stage for the first phase of the insider privatization that followed:

Give away rather than sell off: It was soon clear to the reformers that only foreigners and underground entrepreneurs had the capital to bid for assets in a sell-off. Both of these were politically unacceptable, especially since the assets were undervalued and would have been acquired for very little outlay. The alternative was to give the assets away to the workers or to the public, the approach favored by the legislatures. The reformers tried to preserve some room for cash sell-offs, but in the end most enterprises were virtually given away, mostly to their workers and managers. About 20% of the assets of the state enterprises were handed out in the form of "vouchers," distributed free to every Russian citizen.

Privatize first, restructure later: There had initially been strong sentiment for breaking up the unwieldy Soviet-era giants, many of which held monopolies in their sectors and were too large to be managed efficiently. But restructuring would have taken valuable time and political capital. In the end, most enterprises were allowed to design their own privatization plans and were privatized as they were.

Concede a controlling share to the state in key sectors: For the sake of building rapid consensus it was agreed that certain sectors would not be privatized at all, while in others privatization would be postponed until a later stage. As a result, there are still several tens of thousands state-owned companies, and tens of thousands more with a large state stake. In addition, the state owns an average of one-third interest in the 50 largest companies and between one-third and one-half in the next 250. Regional and local governments frequently have major stakes in local companies, both directly and indirectly.

Thanks to these three compromises the reformers succeeded in building initial popular support for privatization and neutralizing the principal sources of opposition – chiefly the federal ministries, the more conservative local politicians, and above all, the increasingly hostile legislatures. As an example of artful political design and execution, the first phase of the privatization program was an extraordinary achievement, which surprised even the reformers themselves. Anatolii Chubais, who as head of the State Property Committee led the team that designed the privatization program and saw it through, wrote in July 1994:

I will admit now that when we came into the government in the late fall of 1991, I could not have imagined in my sweetest dreams that we would achieve the results we have today. It's not that we didn't believe we could succeed, but we didn't think that success would come . . . in our time.[12]

Reformers stoutly defend the compromises that led to insider privatization: "Imagine for a minute," writes liberal economist Vladimir Popov, "that the enterprises had been sold to anyone who could pay a high price. Given our poverty and the bad investment climate, most of them would have fallen into the hands of 'new Russians' and foreigners. It's not hard to imagine what accusations that would have provoked."[13]

These three compromises created a coalition of stakeholders in favor of privatization. Then, to get privatization off to a fast start, Chubais and his team made the key decision in 1992 to distribute vouchers to the population, exchangeable for shares in privatized companies. This produced an early wave of popular enthusiasm for privatization that helped to disarm opposition and gave the reformers the momentum they needed, but it also sowed the first seeds of disillusionment.

Each voucher had a face value of 10,000 rubles (initially a little over $30), and could be exchanged for stock in any privatized Russian company. The idea was to make every citizen an owner. In the end, the results fell short of that lofty goal, but they were impressive just the same. 21 million Russians (14% of the population) acquired shares in privatized businesses, and another 44 million (30% of the population) became indirect owners through investment funds.[14]

I caught something of the initial popular excitement over voucher privatization when I witnessed the good fortune of my friends Rafael and Tamara in West Siberia. For them voucher privatization turned into an

---

[12] Anatolii Chubais, "Peremena uchasti," *Otkrytaia politika* (monthly journal of the Demokraticheskii Vybor Rossii party), No. 2 (1994), p. 13.
[13] Vladimir Popov, *Ekonomicheskie reformy v Rossii: tri goda spustia* (Moscow: Rossiiskii nauchnyi fond, 1994), pp. 39–40.
[14] Russian State Property Committee, cited in Anders Aslund, *How Russia Became a Market Economy* (Washington, D.C.: The Brookings Institution, 1995), pp. 255–256.

unexpectedly good deal, because it made them shareholders in Russia's richest and most successful company, the gas giant "Gazprom." Tamara, who until the previous year had been teaching courses in "scientific communism," worked in an institute that was taken over by the oil and gas industry. "By the time Gazprom held its voucher auction," she recalled, "most of my coworkers had already disposed of their vouchers. But the rector kept whispering to me that something might be afoot, so I held on to mine. In fact, we went out to the local bazaar to buy more vouchers, just in case. It was amazing: there were ladies selling vouchers from stalls, just like carrots or cabbages. In the end we had enough vouchers to trade for 2,000 shares of Gazprom."

But after an initial wave of enthusiasm popular opinion turned sour. The main reason was a wide gap between the publicity and the reality. In principle, people could use their vouchers to bid for any company's shares at public auctions. But the auctions were as a rule hard to reach and underpublicized. Most people who traded vouchers directly for stock could only acquire shares in their own workplace. Overall, shares acquired for vouchers ended up accounting for less than 20% of the equity of privatized companies.[15]

Many people sold their vouchers for cash. This produced a large secondary market in vouchers. Some of the buyers were ordinary individuals who bought vouchers in markets and on streetcorners. But many were acting as brokers for banks and investment companies. A vast flow of vouchers converged on Moscow and other big cities, and were thus concentrated into a few hands. In 1993 and 1994 most of the paper traded on the nascent financial exchanges of Russia consisted of vouchers. In retrospect the chief importance of vouchers is that they provided a means for outsiders to build up a stake in a handful of the most solvent companies.

By 1995 it was clear that for the average Russian voucher privatization and the reformers' enthusiastic promotion had failed to mask the reality of insider privatization. From 1992 to 1994 surveys showed steadily declining public support (see table 2.1).

These poll results show that most respondents increasingly believed that privatization benefited mainly the nomenklatura and the mafia. The reformers had hoped to create a formula that would win lasting popular acceptance for privatization. But in that vital task they failed.

---

[15] Aslund, op. cit., p. 255. Bidders were mostly clustered in northwest and central Russia, and tended to favor smaller enterprises in the retail consumer market. Hotels and restaurants, middle-sized food and tobacco companies, companies in publishing, communications, and trade, were special favorites with Russian voucher investors. For a valuable review, see PlanEcon, Inc., "Voucher Auctions in the First Phase of Russian Privatization and the Emergence of Voucher Investment Funds," *PlanEcon Report*, vol. 10, No. 33–34 (October 4 1994).

Table 2.1 *In whose interests has privatization taken place?*

	1992	1993	1994
In the interests of working people	7.3	3.8	1.4
In the interests of the former nomenklatura	15.4	16.1	26.2
In the interests of entrepreneurial people	18.9	21.6	21.4
In the interests of the "democratic nomenklatura"	21.3	23.8	9.9
In the interests of people from the "shadow economy"	28.7	21.1	49.2

Source: M.K. Gorshkov, A.Iu. Chepurenko, F.E. Sheregi, eds., *Rossiia v zerkale reform: khrestomatiia po sotsiologii sovremennogo rossiiskogo obshchestva*, Russian Independent Institute for Social and National Problems (Moscow: "Akademiia," 1995), pp. 96–97.

The second phase of privatization, 1995–1998

Public disapproval deepened even more in 1995–1998 when the government sold off its remaining stake in some of the country's largest and most profitable export industries, mainly to a handful of politically well-connected banks. The government's decision in late 1995 to turn over controlling shares in key export industries such as oil and metals, marked the beginning of a second phase of privatization.

The second phase was quite different from the first. The pace of privatization slowed and its focus changed. The number of enterprises privatized each year has dropped below 5,000 a year, compared to over 40,000 in both 1992 and 1993.[16] The government's priority shifted from simply shoveling state property out the door as quickly as possible to a more selective strategy of selling off the largest and most valuable and profitable properties, in order to maximize revenues to the state budget. In the process, the government backed away from the policy of turning over shares to workers and managers: whereas in 1993 47% of all shares in privatized enterprises had been distributed to "insiders," by 1996 the share had dropped to 31%, and continued to decline thereafter.[17]

This evolution reflected the growing determination of the government to sell off its remaining large assets, and the inability of the opposition to do anything about it. The shift was particularly striking for industries previously regarded as "strategic," such as oil or telecommunications. In 1995, the Russian government was so nervous about selling off strategic properties that it resorted to the fiction of turning them over "in trust" in exchange for "loans" from the Russian banks. Some of the country's most valuable properties were thus sold off for a fraction of their real worth,

[16] *Russian Economic Trends*, No. 2 (1997), p. 95.   [17] Ibid, p. 97.

since a year later the "loans" turned out to be permanent and the shares remained in the hands of the trustees.

The initial "shares-for-loans" auctions in 1995–96 were so transparently rigged in favor of the large banks that served as the state's agents that they became a major issue in the 1996 presidential campaign. If the communist candidate Gennadii Zyuganov had won, the results of the privatization program would certainly have been challenged on a broad front.

In response to the outcry, the government became more careful. It restructured the privatization process to make it more transparent and genuinely competitive, and it widened the circle of eligible players. By 1997–98, most of the successful bids for the remaining state shares in strategic companies included foreign players, who had previously been excluded. As a result, the prices of auctioned state properties rose rapidly. Along the way, the government restructured the terms of sale so that the privatized companies themselves received some capital infusion in the form of investment commitments.

But the government's belated efforts to make the privatization auctions more open and honest had little success. The main bidders were the "oligarchs," i.e., the heads of the powerful financial-industrial groups that had arisen in the first phase of privatization. They had built powerful media empires, which the losers used to denounce the outcomes of the auctions, reinforcing the public's conviction that the whole process was rotten. Meanwhile, the government failed to win the support of the legislature. A law on privatization, passed in the summer of 1997, sidestepped most of the controversial questions, while the companion "program on privatization" which implemented it remained bogged down in controversy.[18] If an opposition candidate wins the presidency in 2000, there will probably be a challenge, if not to privatization across the board, at least to the largest and more controversial cases, such as the privatization of the oil companies.

Still, for all the noise and conflict, private property is here to stay. The reformers may have lost their bet to make "large" privatization popular in the eyes of the population, but they may have won in a deeper sense. In the poll cited earlier, only 32.6% approved of the way privatization had been carried out, but a large majority of the same respondents – 61.3% – approved of private enterprise in general. Perhaps coincidentally, that was also roughly Yeltsin's majority in the 1996 presidential election. Behind the controversies over the big state enterprises, private property

---

[18] The 1997 law on privatization notably bans – retroactively – "loans for shares" auctions and investment tenders. It also authorizes the government to reclaim privatized property, without going through the courts, if the winning bidder fails to meet investment commitments.

itself has quietly become a fact of life, especially in the larger cities. People's discomfort over "large" privatization is over the procedure, not the principle.

Yet the deed is done, and insider privatization is a fact. How serious are the consequences?

The economic consequences of privatization

The design of the privatization campaign has had far-reaching economic consequences. The newly-privatized companies are starved of capital, since they received no infusion of funds when they were privatized. Their ownership status is ambiguous and potentially unstable, since the managers in most places share legal ownership with their workers. And since privatization raced ahead of the creation of a legal framework for corporate governance and bankruptcy, the new owners still find it all too easy not to pay their bills, their wages, and their taxes. The failure of most managers to restructure their companies since privatization, or to listen to their shareholders, is the logical result.

Might things have been different under any other approach to privatization, or even no privatization at all? On closer examination, it appears that the privatization policy is only partly to blame.

1 *Capital starvation* Since most of the state property in the first phase of privatization was either handed over free or at practically nominal prices, neither the government nor the companies received any significant revenue from privatization. Consequently, most of the newly-private companies started out their new life starved of new capital. "We sold off a herd of elephants at rabbit prices," says one Russian economist, "and now the new class of owners is trying to feed them at the rate of a carrot a day."[19]

Yet it is hard to imagine what procedure or source of capital would have produced a rapid and massive infusion into over 100,000 companies. Countries around the world that have carried out cash privatizations have typically managed to process no more than 200 companies a year. At that rate, Russian privatization would have taken over one hundred years, and most of the proceeds would have been eaten up in consulting fees.[20]

In the second phase of privatization the picture improved slightly. After 1996 sales of state shares were organized as commercial tenders, which obligated the buyer to make specified additional investments in the

---

[19] Economist Oleg Pchelintsev, in *Nezavisimaia gazeta*, May 30 1994.
[20] Maxim Boycko, Andrei Shleifer, and Robert Vishny, *Privatizing Russia* (Cambridge, Mass.: MIT Press, 1995), Chapter 4.

company at the moment of purchase. As a result, the largest and most attractive Russian companies finally started to gain some capital infusion from privatization. Significantly, most of these were still concentrated in the export-oriented extractive sector, mainly energy and metals.[21]

The real question about capital infusion is what the new managers would do with it if they had it. By and large, the handful of companies that had access to capital either invested it in short-term treasury notes or other financial instruments, or used it to pay their workers' back wages or bank loans. Only a very small minority actually invested in new plant or new products. This leads to the conclusion that if by some miracle Russian privatization had produced a massive infusion of capital in the newly-privatized enterprises, it would not necessarily have been productively invested in the companies themselves.

2 *Unstable ownership* The majority shareholders in most places are the employees. The top managers, mostly Soviet-era insiders, do not as a rule own a majority of the shares in their companies (indeed, across the board, their share is fairly modest). Yet they are in control in most cases.[22] Even when companies are nominally owned by outsiders, the outsider-owners do not necessarily challenge the established management. The larger and more important the company, the less likely it is to be actively controlled by outsiders: in 1996, of the top 50 companies in Russia only 5 were clearly owned and controlled by outsiders.[23]

It is clear enough why the insiders came up winners in the mass privatization of 1992–94. What requires explanation is that their dominance has continued with so little challenge since. Despite the coverage given to a handful of spectacular takeover battles in the Russian and Western media, there is no clear trend toward an increase in outsider takeovers and ownership across the board.

The outsiders with the largest private stakes in Russian enterprises were the banks and the handful of large financial-trading conglomerates, which used their large profits in the early 1990s to invest in export-oriented companies (such as fertilizers and metals), in construction materials (for example, cement), or food producers. But after 1995 the profitability of the Russian banks declined sharply and they no longer had the same resources to pursue acquisitions on a large scale, except for

---

[21] *Russian Economic Trends*, No. 1 (1997), p. 135; No. 3 (1997), p. 103.

[22] This is the major conclusion of Blasi et al., op. cit., especially pp. 61–67. The authors are understandably cautious about the exact size of the managers' stake in the privatized enterprises, but they appear to be on solid ground in arguing that the managers did not succeed in taking over controlling shares in most enterprises. In particularly, senior managers do not appear to own a majority of shares in any of the top fifty privatized corporations in Russia.   [23] Blasi, op. cit., p. 70.

a handful of "crown jewels" such as oil companies (and here they increasingly required help from foreign backers).[24] As early as 1996–97 some banking groups began divesting themselves of portions of the holdings acquired earlier, and after August 1998 this process of divestment accelerated.[25]

The largest outside stakeholder by far is the state, which continues to hold nearly half of all the shares in privatized enterprises.[26] But the state in most cases has been a silent partner, seldom interfering in day-to-day management or challenging the managers' control.

Insider managers have been resourceful in finding ways to prevent employees from selling off their shares to outsiders. In some cases, they have required employees to surrender their shares upon leaving the company; in others they have set up dummy insider-controlled companies to buy up shares in their own companies. For example, Gazprom, the giant gas monopoly, long refused to recognize secondary transactions in its stock unless approved by its own management. Thanks to such measures, there appears to be no net trend toward accumulation of shares by outsiders.

The main reason there have not been more outsider takeovers, one suspects, is that most Russian companies have not been worth taking over, except in the handful of cases where there are immediate profits to be made, usually from exports. Then the contest often boils down to which side has the most potent political protection. Outsiders are typically backed by the big Moscow financial-industrial groups, with political support from influentials at the federal level, while the insiders look to the local politicians. In some highly-publicized cases (such as the takeover of Norilsk Nickel by Oneksimbank in 1996) the support of federal-level agencies was decisive. But with the growing political power and autonomy of the regions, local politicians have been able to fight off Moscow-based outsiders, or even to reverse earlier outsider takeovers.

Since August 1998 the balance of power has shifted even more in favor

[24] No precise figures are available on the share of privatized companies owned by banks prior to August 1998. A 1996 survey sponsored by the Russian Federal Securities Commission showed that banks owned sizable blocks of shares (i.e., between 20% and 50%) in only 3% of the privatized medium to large companies in the sample. But this was almost certainly an underestimate even then. (See *Russian Economic Trends*, vol. 5, no. 3, 1996, p. 119–120.)

[25] For an example of such consolidation, see the interview with Oneksimbank president Vladimir Potanin in early 1998, "Reforma oligarkhov," *Ekspert*, No. 10 (March 16 1998), pp. 14–15. See also Inkombank's divestiture of its stake in aluminum processor Sameko (*Ekspert*, No. 9, pp. 40–41).

[26] *Russian Economic Trends*, No. 1 (1997), p. 136. This figure is in sharp contrast with the data cited in Blasi, et al., who report that in 1996 the state owned only 9% of the shares in their sample of large and medium-sized enterprises. I am unable to reconcile the difference.

of the insiders. The Moscow banks have weakened; foreign investors have mostly vanished; and there is no cash available to support takeover bids. But most companies have debts aplenty, and most takeover bids now seek equity in swap for various forms of debt. One of the few outsiders still rich enough to play this game is Gazprom, the Russian gas giant, which is turning its mountain of unpaid gas bills into ownership of chemical plants, oil refineries, and many other valuable properties. But most of the post-August takeover activity has been local. Regional politicians are trading back taxes for a controlling share of equity, either directly for the local government or for favored local interests. In this way a certain reverse *peredel* has taken place, as local interests fight to regain control of the handful of properties that remain lucrative, such as some of the smaller oil-producing companies that had been absorbed by bank-owned holding groups in 1995–96.

Still, for most privatized companies the threat of outsider takeover has been more potential than real. Most insider-managers suspect that their hold over their companies is due less to their own strength than to the weakness or indifference of the other players, particularly their own workers. This sense of insecurity distorts the managers' own behavior: Instead of developing long-range strategies to restructure their companies and adapt them to new markets, they spend their time strengthening their defenses instead. Their concern may be justified: in a quarter of all medium-to-large privatized companies, the stake of outsiders ranges from 30 to 50%. In other words, it would take only a slight strengthening of shareholders' rights and a little increase in the companies' profitability and attractiveness for a cascade of takeovers to result.[27]

3 *The continuation of the "soft budget constraint"* In a market economy, if companies live beyond their means, they go bankrupt. But in the Soviet-style command economy state enterprises did not go bankrupt; they enjoyed what economists call a "soft budget constraint." Soviet managers were rewarded for meeting output targets, not financial bottom lines. They routinely spent beyond their means – and the state wrote off the difference.[28] Through tax breaks, privileges, subsidized and non-returnable credits, debt write-offs, price adjustments, free investment funds, guaranteed markets for output – the list was practically endless – the command economy tempered the wind to its managers.

[27] Blasi, p. 155.
[28] The classic article on the "soft budget constraint" is Janos Kornai, "The Soft Budget Constraint," *Kyklos*, vol. 39, no. 1 (1986), pp. 3–30. The major points are summarized in Janos Kornai, *The Socialist System: the Political Economy of Communism* (Princeton NJ: Princeton University Press), pp. 140–145.

With the end of the Soviet system, the most blatant forms of "soft budget constraint" have now disappeared. Prices are largely decontrolled (with some remaining exceptions, such as some forms of energy).[29] The Russian Central Bank has eliminated most low-interest loans. The number of sectors that are explicitly subsidized (and at a much more modest level than before) has been cut to three: the coal industry, the farms, and a handful of the very largest manufacturing enterprises, mostly in the defense sector. But above all, the entire mechanism of central planning and distribution has disappeared, and enterprise managers no longer live in a world of state targets and supply orders and guaranteed markets.

Yet in reality the "soft budget constraint" is still present. Russian managers are still not truly accountable for their bottom line, because of the weakness of legal instruments to enforce payments, contracts, and bankruptcy. As a result, managers routinely fail to pay their bills and taxes or repay their loans, or they pay them in barter or wechsels, and yet it is difficult to force them out of business.[30] The number of bankruptcy cases is only about 3,000 a year, although a new law on bankruptcy may make it easier to take action against scofflaws and debtors.[31] Taxes are the most glaring illustration: the state's systematic failure to force large enterprises to pay amounts to a massive subsidy to those powerful or resourceful enough to negotiate amnesties and settlements.

Is insider domination really the problem?

Capital starvation, unstable ownership, and non-payment are cited as the chief consequences of insider privatization. The symptoms are real and serious. Yet insider privatization is not by itself a sufficient explanation. It would be more accurate to say that all these are symptoms of a deeper ailment, the halfway state of the Russian market economy. All of the problems just discussed are rooted in the unstable soil of a transitional economy.

Arguably, the same symptoms would have appeared under any system of privatization – and also if there had been no mass privatization at all. There was little capital infusion because there was little capital available

---

[29] *Kommersant-Daily*, August 23 1995, pp. 1 and 2, carries a discussion of the remaining restrictions on prices, mostly at the regional and local levels.

[30] The one major exception to this is the banks. In this area the Russian Central Bank has pursed a tough policy of lifting licenses from insolvent banks. See Chapter 4.

[31] For an analysis of the bankruptcy law, which went into effect in March 1998, see *Ekspert*, No. 5 (February 9 1998), pp. 19–33. Data on bankruptcy cases that come before the commercial courts can be found in *Vestnik Vysshego Arbitrazhnogo Suda RF*, no. 3 (1999), pp. 11–13.

on politically or economically acceptable terms. "Soft budget" behavior is universal, and companies owned by outsiders behave exactly the same way as those owned by insiders. The hit-parade of the largest tax evaders (approximately 80 large companies account for nearly 40% of the tax arrears)[32] consists largely of highly profitable commodities exporters, some of which are dominated by insiders but others not. With banks reluctant to lend, the vast majority of Russian enterprises, regardless of formal ownership, resort to holding back on paying wages, receivables and taxes to raise working capital.[33]

In short, most of the "consequences of Russian privatization" are in reality consequences of depression, inflation, and disorder. The weakness of contract and bankruptcy laws means that Russian managers do not yet face true financial discipline or accountability to owners, and there are many tempting opportunities for easy or illegal gains.

In these circumstances it is not surprising that many Russian managers do better by standing pat than by trying to change. Add to that that many managers have found ways of making personal profits from loss-making enterprises. One popular device is to spin off private "daughter companies," owned by a narrow circle of managers and their allies, through which the output of the enterprise is siphoned off. The "mother enterprise" takes the losses, accumulates debt, delays wages and payments, holds back taxes – while the profits go out the back door. This too is an entrepreneurial response to privatization, if a perverted one. Outsiders, when they take over, do not necessarily behave differently.

It follows that simply changing the mode of ownership, by making it easier for outsiders to take over privatized enterprises, will not by itself change the pattern of managers' behavior. Replacing insiders with outsiders, to have a positive effect, requires that they bring with them new people and fresh capital. This will work in a handful of cases, but not for the Russian economy as a whole. There is not enough capital or managerial talent available in Russia to take over more than a handful of the most attractive enterprises. Therefore, for the foreseeable future the Soviet-era insiders are here to stay.

But the speed and vigor with which they adjust their business strategies and restructure their companies – or not – will depend on the sum of incentives and pressures they face as the Russian economy revives. Those incentives and pressures turn out to be very different from sector to sector, and the responses to Russian managers have been equally diverse.

[32] *Russian Economic Trends*, No. 1 (1997), p. 142.
[33] In 1996, three-quarters of the working capital used by enterprises was derived from deferred payment of wages, taxes, pension and social security, and receivables. (*Finansovye izvestiia*, April 22 1997, p. 5.)

Different environments, different responses

What causes one enterprise to retreat into defensive lethargy, while another responds vigorously and transforms itself? Plausibly, the answer has less to do with the type of ownership than with the conditions of the market itself. Where there is money to be made, competition is high, capital is available, and solutions are ready at hand, then Russian managers, even classic Soviet nomenklatura insiders, can and do respond with far-reaching innovations. By way of illustration we look briefly at four contrasting fields: natural monopolies, food and beverages, automobiles, and natural-resource exporters.

Foods

In the first half of the 1990s imported foods quickly conquered over half of the Russian market. Domestic producers were slow to rebuild distribution and retail networks after the Soviet collapse, and in the prime urban markets, particularly Moscow, consumers turned to foreign goods. But after about 1995 the share of imports began to recede, as Russian producers learned to compete. The sharp decline in the ruble since August 1998 has given Russian producers a further advantage, since imported foods are now prohibitively expensive for all but the wealthiest Russian consumers. But today's "Russian" producer is frequently a subsidiary of an international group. Western companies, finding it more profitable to produce through local plants than to import, have invested heavily in the Russian food sector, buying up scattered Russian plants and consolidating them into larger conglomerates. In the food industry "outsider takeover" has become routine, and the result is a growing concentration of production around a few leading producers.

Insider managers, to survive and compete in this environment, have had to adapt. Two examples are chocolate and beer. Russia's oldest chocolate manufacturer, "Red October" (*Krasnyi Oktiabr'*), still under its Soviet-era management, has managed to hold off foreign competitors and suitors, by modernizing its plant and concentrating on its traditional Moscow market. But "Red October" has also boldly expanded into the provinces, where it had never been present before, and has held its own against powerful foreign groups such as Mars or Cadbury-Schweppes – no mean feat in a market in which per-capita chocolate consumption had dropped by almost half before turning around in 1996.[34]

If chocolate has been a shrinking market, beer has been a booming one.

[34] Interview with "Red October" general director Anatolii Daurskii, *Ekspert*, No. 6 (February 16 1998), pp. 26–30.

Per capita consumption has recovered after a sharp drop in the early 1990s. Imports are being rapidly displaced by domestic production, and the beer business is highly profitable but fiercely competitive. Outsider takeover has become the norm: dozens of local producers have been absorbed by four foreign-led groups, which now hold more than half of the Russian market and are relentlessly cutting costs by integrating vertically, acquiring local producers of barley and hops. One of the few "insider-controlled" brewers to have held its ground is the "Ochakovo" plant, Russia's second largest, which like "Red October" serves mainly the Moscow market. To compete and stay independent, Ochakovo's insider management has had to run hard, investing in new plant, cutting costs, and expanding production.[35]

Thus the emerging pattern in the food sector is vigorous competition, foreign investment in domestic production, frequent outsider takeovers, and the rise of a new generation of foreign-backed Russian managers. To survive, the remaining insider managers have had to develop the same entrepreneurial qualities as their competitors.

Oil

In the initial years after the Soviet collapse, the oil sector seemed the ultimate example of state-managed insider privatization. The Gaidar government took an industry in which every step of the production and processing of oil had been controlled by a separate specialized ministry, and restructured it into vertically-integrated companies, each one under the leadership of a West Siberian "oil general," the Soviet-era name for the general directors of the upstream producers of crude oil. Each of the new oil giants was assigned its own market sector, thus excluding competition. The state retained a controlling bloc of shares in the new companies.

But events soon departed from this carefully-scripted scenario. Exporting oil was so profitable that a whole crowd of new players, previously strangers to the oil business, was soon attracted. Private oil traders, bankers, mafia dons, and big-city mayors and regional governors began to challenge the oil generals for control of exports, service stations, and refineries. The integrated companies began to poach on one another's distribution markets. Here and there, local crude producers rebelled against the mother companies and tried to go it alone. Finally, between 1995 and 1998, as the government divested itself of its remaining stake in the oil companies, several of the integrated oil companies fell into the

---

[35] A profile of the brewing industry appears in *Ekspert*, No. 2 (January 19 1998), pp. 42–43; and No. 10 (March 16 1998), p. 49.

hands of the large banks, which promptly displaced the oil generals and began putting in new managers. The collapse of the large banks in August 1998 has set off a fresh round of battles for control of the oil industry.

Thus in the Russian oil sector insider privatization has given way to a highly diverse and fast-moving pattern, in which insiders and outsiders (including a growing number of foreigners) compete vigorously for ownership and market share. Some of the most innovative entrepreneurs have been the insiders. The most successful Russian oilman today is Vagit Alekperov, founder and president of Russia's leading oil company, Lukoil. Alekperov in 1991 was first deputy minister of the Soviet oil industry, and thus on one level he qualifies as the ultimate "nomenklatura capitalist." But Alekperov is also widely recognized in the international oil business as a world-class entrepreneur. Ahead of anyone else, Alekperov sensed the coming breakup of the state-owned oil sector and moved to seize the opportunity. He quickly assembled a producing company from three of the best oil properties in West Siberia (where his own career had begun), matched them with two refineries, then moved ruthlessly to take control of the cash flow generated by his companies' oil exports. Almost from the start Alekperov began shifting his base from the declining base of West Siberia into Azerbaidjan, Central Asia, and the Middle East. Today Lukoil is a partner with the largest Western companies in some of the most prospective oil regions in the world.

Thus the lesson of the oil sector is that even the most elaborate scheme of insider privatization soon gave way to the forces of competition and opportunity. Even the barriers to foreign players, initially more fobidding in the oil industry than in any other part of the economy, have begun to yield to the Russian players' growing need for technology and capital. In the resulting free-for-all, many new leaders have come to the fore, including several of the insiders themselves.

"Natural monopolies"

Four basic industries constitute much of the framework of the Russian economic infrastructure: railroads, gas, telephones, and oil pipelines. In Russian parlance this group is referred to as the "natural monopolies." Two of the four, gas and telephones, have been privatized or quasi-privatized; the other two, railroads and pipelines, are still state-owned. But whether private or state, the natural monopolies as a group are still run by Soviet-era insiders.

What is interesting about this sector is that competition and opportunity have caused a variety of responses, even among holdover Soviet-era officials, ranging from extreme immobilism or rent-seeking opportunism to highly innovative and entrepreneurial behavior. The answer in each case depends, first, on whether opportunity simply falls into the lap or must be actively courted; and second, on what pressures arise from competitors and customers.

The extreme case of opportunity falling into the lap is "Transrail," the company that serves as shipper and freight agent for half the transit traffic that crosses Russia by rail. Transrail is technically a private company, which was created in the late 1980s as a Swiss-based joint venture between the Soviet Ministry of Railroads and a group of European shippers; today it remains half-owned by the Soviet ministry's Russian successor. Until recently Transrail enjoyed a privileged status as the ministry's quasi-official shipper. It supplied the Ministry with hard currency for key investment projects; and in exchange it received preferential rates on the Russian railroads. By 1996–97 this cozy relationship came under attack, partly reflecting the fact that in the intervening years several hundred private shipping companies had sprung up. Retreating under a barrage of accusations of unfair practice and corruption, the Ministry ended its special treatment of Transrail, forcing the company to compete on more equal terms. Critics note, however, that Transrail remains half-owned by the Ministry and still handles half of the ministry's lucrative transit business.[36]

If the rail transit business comes knocking by itself, so to speak, on Russia's door, the European gas market is an entirely different sort of opportunity, a fast-moving and competitive environment which must be conquered. In this venture a group of Russian inside managers, the leaders of the Russian gas giant, "Gazprom," has been spectacularly entrepreneurial.

Gazprom is far and away Russia's richest and most powerful company. It is the direct descendent of the Soviet gas ministry, and remains partly owned by the Russian government, although the government has turned over its stake in trust to Gazprom and for all practical purposes the company runs its own affairs. The top managers of Gazprom are all gas veterans, who had held leading positions in the Soviet gas ministry and passed smoothly into the top echelons of the new company when it was privatized in the early 1990s.

Gazprom has two faces – its export face and its domestic one. In its export operations Gazprom quickly became one of the most aggressive entrepreneurs in Europe. Teaming up in the late 1980s with a German partner, Gazprom's leadership took on the powerful European national gas monopolies in a bid to penetrate their markets. It was a risky and

[36] Dmitrii Sivakov, "Sviazannye odnoi tsel'iu," *Ekspert*, No. 9 (March 9 1998), pp. 30–33.

unprecedented step, bitterly opposed by powerful interests, but Gazprom has won its bet. Riding the wave of European gas privatization and decontrol, Gazprom established itself as one of the most powerful players in the European gas market. Yet the chief author of this strategy, Gazprom chairman Rem Viakhirev, was a classic Soviet functionary, the lifelong protege of former prime minister Viktor Chernomyrdin. In a remarkably short time, Viakhirev came to be at home with the sophisticated concepts of corporate strategy and high finance, and applied them successfully to his foreign operations.

On the domestic side, Gazprom was slower to change. In exchange for a virtual carte blanche on the export side, the Russian government expected Gazprom to keep Russian homes and factories supplied with gas, whether consumers paid or not. In the early 1990s Gazprom could afford to ignore the resulting losses, since they were far outweighed by its export profits. But as the 1990s went on and the ruble appreciated in real terms, the profitability of Gazprom's dollar flow diminished. Beginning in the mid-1990s Gazprom began to apply its entrepreneurial energy to its domestic market. No longer content to subsidize Russia's virtual economy of unpaid gas bills and barter, Gazprom created an aggressive collections agency (called Mezhregiongaz), which cuts out middlemen, duns solvent customers, and takes over large debtors through debt-for-equity swaps.

Gazprom's evolution as a company is the single most spectacular example of the ability of insider-owners to become aggressive modern managers. Abroad, Gazprom is Russia's most significant player in international markets. At home, though it is still – unwillingly – thrust into the role of the chief supplier of unpaid raw materials for the virtual economy, its fight to extract value from its domestic gas – though still a losing battle – is potentially a significant force pulling Russia into the money economy. The point is that Gazprom has not sat idly by.

Automobiles

The Russian automotive industry has been under heavy challenge, combined with niche opportunities. On the one hand, demand for heavy gasoline-powered trucks, which were the core business of the Soviet-era industry, has practically vanished. The market for Russian-made luxury cars has been wiped out by foreign competition. But at the same time the rise of a new private economy has created fast-growing new niches for light trucks and inexpensive cars. Most of the Russian automotive industry remains in the hands of insiders. But there have been wide differences in the way managers with similar pasts have responded to the mix of crushing pressures and inviting opportunities in their industry.

The most dynamic automotive company in Russia today is also a classic case of insider management. If you've taken a taxi in Moscow, chances are you've ridden in a "Volga." For over three decades the Volga has been the stand-by of Russian taxi drivers and lower-ranking officials. The Volga is produced by the "Gor'kii Automotive Factory" (*Gor'kovskii avtomobil'nyi zavod*) in Nizhnii Novgorod, known to Russians as "GAZ." Nikolai Pugin, the president of GAZ, was the last Soviet minister of the automotive industry. (Pugin had been general director of GAZ once before, on his way up the ministry ladder in the early 1980s.) Under him, the Soviet-era management has retained control of GAZ.

Yet GAZ has been a surprising success story. Faced with a collapse of government orders for its main product – mid-sized trucks for the military and the collective farms – GAZ cut back its output of trucks and threw all its resources into expanding production of its "Volga" passenger car. Squeezing its costs to the minimum (mainly by deferring payment on all its obligations), GAZ was able to keep prices down below the inflation rate.

Buyers came in droves. While overall output of Russian passenger cars sank lower and lower – from 1,100,000 in 1990 to under 800,000 in 1994 – GAZ's Volgas were booming, from 70,000 in 1990 to nearly 120,000 in 1994 and 1995.[37] To keep up with demand, GAZ put its Volga assembly lines on 24–hour shifts, six days a week. Meanwhile, using its profits from the Volga and taking advantage of new imported equipment acquired at the end of the 1980s, GAZ launched a new model of light truck, the "Gazelle," which immediately proved popular with Russian buyers. After selling 10,000 of the new light trucks in 1994, GAZ upped production to nearly 58,000 in 1995.[38]

The "Gazelle" was such an immediate hit because it filled an empty market niche: it met the need of the many small businesses springing up all over Russia for a cheap light truck for short hauls. The most popular model was an all-road version, advertised at the 1995 Moscow Automotive Salon as "perfect for three people and two cows."[39] The closest Western competitors cost many times more than the Gazelle's rock-bottom $5,500.[40]

The Russian automotive industry turned around sharply in 1997. Output of passenger cars passed the million mark for the first time since 1991,[41] and truck and bus production revived as well. The Gazelle con-

---

[37] *Kommersant* (weekly), No. 16 (May 2 1995), p. 17. The description that follows is drawn from an extended profile of GAZ on pp. 14–24. Final 1995 numbers from *Finansovye izvestiia*, March 12 1996, p. 2.   [38] *Finansovye izvestiia*, March 12 1996, p. 2.

[39] *Kommersant-Daily*, August 31 1995, p. 10.   [40] *Kapital*, June 30 1995, p. 16.

[41] Russian passenger car production bottomed out in 1995 at 835,000, turned around in 1996 at 868,000, and soared to 1.05 million in 1997. (Source: "Ekonomicheskoe razvitie otraslei promyshlennosti RF," *RED*, via Internet Securities)

tinues to be a roaring success,[42] but the sale of Volgas stagnated, as Russians begin to look for higher quality. To meet the growing competition, GAZ has created a new joint venture with Fiat to produce 150,000 Italian-model passenger cars – benefiting from a conveniently-timed presidential decree which exempts Russian auto producers who attract large foreign investors from customs duties on imported parts. Thus Nikolai Pugin and his insider colleagues have been able to innovate and compete as well as any capitalist, but they have also not forgotten their way around the corridors of power.[43]

These brief snapshots of some key sectors all point to much the same conclusion. The form of ownership of privatized Russian companies is less important than the business environment in each specific sector. Many former Soviet executives are turning out to be fully able to switch from production to marketing, and from engineering to economics and finance. This is not altogether surprising: after all, the Soviet managerial class was the cream of the crop of an advanced engineering culture. The Viakhirevs, Pugins, and Alekperovs could be successful CEOs anywhere in the world.

The implication of this argument is that the pace of restructuring and adaptation of the privatized Russian companies in the future will depend above all on the speed with which new opportunities and competitive pressures penetrate the various sectors of the Russian economy, and the extent to which constraints and rent-seeking opportunities fade away. Among the new institutions most critical to changing the economic environment are the new capital markets and banks, to which we turn now.

[42] *Delovoi ekspress*, January 20 1998, by Internet.
[43] Aleksei Khazbiev, "Ukaz po 'FiGAZ'," *Ekspert*, No. 6 (February 16 1998), pp. 36–38.

The basis has been created for the formation of a civilized stock market in Russia.

Andrei Kosogov, Chairman of the Board, Alfa Capital[1]

The [Russian stock] market remains a secretive, back-alley business.

The Wall Street Journal[2]

3 Wall Street comes to Moscow: the rise of private capital markets

Spring 1992, Moscow:

A Russian friend of mine and I had decided to visit a special art exhibit at the Manezh, near Red Square. There was a line, as there still was in 1992 for anything worth waiting for. But the line got longer and longer, and it didn't move. My friend grew suspicious. "Something's wrong," he said. "I'll go inquire." A minute later, he was back. "We're in the wrong line," he said. "This is a line for buyers of shares in some new private bank. Something called Menatep."

So we walked away – missing our ticket to become Russian millionaires. Within three years Menatep had become one of the ten largest banks in Russia and the center of a powerful industrial and trading conglomerate. As an old Soviet saying went, "If you see a line, go stand in it." But you have to know what to do when you get there. Yet as later events proved, we were luckier than we knew. By 1999, Menatep was out of business.

Russia's chances for economic recovery and growth depend on investment. In the Soviet system, the state was the investor. But in post-Soviet Russia the state is too weak to invest, and that is likely to remain true for the foreseeable future. "If you believe in the economic transformation of Russia," says a Moscow-based financier, "then you have to believe that domestic savings will be channeled through intermediary institutions into fixed capital formation. If reform is to work, the government has simply got to get out of that business."[3]

In other words, the most important challenge to the private sector in Russia is whether it can build financial institutions and capital markets

---

[1] *Financial Times*, November 3 1994.   [2] *The Wall Street Journal*, January 19 1995.
[3] *Financial Times*, December 5 1994.

that will attract domestic savers and foreign investors and put their funds to the highest value uses.

But will the Russian capital markets be up to the job? In this chapter we look at the brief but tumultuous history of the Russian equities market. In less than a decade enterprising Russians built all the basic structures of stock markets in the West: banks, trading systems, exchanges, brokerages, share registries and custodial services, and the rudiments of securities regulation. The bad news is that those structures have proved unable (so far) to attract capital on a large scale and allocate it efficiently to the best uses. In short, it remains an open question whether equities can play a constructive role in Russian capital formation.

Two models for Russia

Different countries raise and allocate capital in different ways. In the United States, companies raise money mainly through stocks and bonds, and only about one-third through banks. In Japan, stocks and bonds represent less than 10% of corporate finance, while banks play the dominant role. In Germany, companies obtain finance mainly from internal funds, principally their own pension funds.[4]

These varied models have different consequences for corporate ownership and governance. In the United States, corporate ownership is broadly diffused: on the average, the five largest shareholders of a large American company own only about one-quarter of the shares; in Japan they own one-third; but in Germany over 40%. Indeed, in Germany, ownership is far more concentrated than these numbers suggest. In Germany large firms are organized into successive layers of pyramid-like holding companies; many of these are ultimately controlled at the top by a wealthy family or a large bank.[5]

Exposure to open capital markets makes the management of US companies more vulnerable to outside takeovers than in Germany or Japan. In the United States, mergers and acquisitions account for over $1 trillion of business every year (amounting to over 40% of total market capitalization), but only about $60 billion in Germany and $4 billion in Japan. In the United States, hostile takeovers by outside investors are frequent. Almost 10% of the companies listed on the Fortune 500 in 1980 were acquired over the following fifteen years in a hostile or quasi-hostile transaction. But in Germany, as of the mid-1990s, there had been only 4 successful hostile takeovers since World War II, although this is now changing.[6]

---

[4] Peter Dittus and Stephen Prowse, "Corporate Control in Central Europe and Russia: Should Banks Own Shares?" Policy Research Working Paper 1481 (Washington D.C.: The World Bank, June 1995), pp. 3–6.   [5] Dittus and Prowse, op. cit., pp. 4–5.
[6] Dittus and Prowse, op. cit., p. 7.

For Russians, then, there are two broad models of capital formation and corporate governance – the American and the German-Japanese. In the American model, the market is king, and management is insecure. In the German-Japanese model, the banks are the key intermediaries – and also major owners. They mobilize savings, provide capital to companies, and play a large role in their management. The result is large financial-industrial conglomerates, elaborately linked by interlocking directorates and share stakes, the whole system topped by the large banks.

Both systems have their defenders. Americans believe their system produces more responsive, efficient, and innovative companies. Germans and Japanese believe theirs is better-suited to long-range planning and investment. To judge from the performance of the three economies over the decades, it would be hard to argue that there is a single best way.

The German-Japanese model is undoubtedly the one Russian investors and managers would find the most congenial, particularly the large commercial banks, which emerged briefly in the Nineties as the most powerful private institutions in Russia. But Russian banks, even at their height, were not large enough to be the main source of capital for Russia, nor did they mobilize capital from small savers. Until recently, Russian banks made their money by making short-term loans and speculating on inflation and currency exchange, and later by investing in government debt. A handful of the largest banks bought up controlling interests in the most lucrative export-oriented companies, but they invested little new capital into them. In other words, the new private banks never became a major instrument of capital formation or corporate restructuring, and since the August 1998 collapse their future role is, to put it mildly, undefined. Meanwhile the source of most Russian corporate investment, such as it is, is retained earnings.

That leaves the American path, that of the equities markets. Russian privatization turned millions of Russians into shareholders, and a secondary market in equities sprang up almost immediately. (Indeed, one might say the stock market preceded the stock, since Russians began trading privatization vouchers as early as 1992.) In a very short time, the basic institutions of a stock market had been created. Thus a potentially important vehicle for capital formation via share offerings exists and can be developed further. As Andrew Balgarnie of Morgan Stanley's Moscow office put it, "If the banks will not act as they should by getting the funds to the businesses, then the only route is via share offerings. That's why this market is so important, and why it's so important to regulate it properly."[7]

---

[7] Quoted in *Financial Times*, August 2 1994.

Boom and bust: two market cycles compared

But the Russian stock market was never for the faint-hearted. In its brief existence it has already been through two cycles of boom and bust. The first cycle, which ran from early 1994 to early 1996, showed clearly the weaknesses of an embryonic market: thinness and illiquidity, inadequate sell-side structures, low levels of shareholder protection, and the absence of domestic investors. Most of the early buyers were Western hedge funds, attracted by what appeared to be incredibly low asset valuations placed on major companies.

In contrast, the second cycle, which ran from early 1996 to the summer of 1998, showed how much the Russian stock market had matured in three years' time. Liquidity was higher; the range of buyers and sellers was broader; and the sell-side structures had become sufficiently transparent and reliable to keep the market operating even through a sharp market decline. After the bust in 1994, the Russian equities market virtually ceased to exist for about a year; but during the second drop in 1997–98, the market remained functional, even though trading volumes dropped sharply. Many investors lost money in the fall of 1997 and the winter of 1998 – but the market itself passed an important milestone in its development.

By the late summer of 1998, however, the Russian stock market had lost so much value that for a time it effectively ceased to exist. Most of the structures that had evolved since the early 1990s either went out of business or into hibernation. Yet even so, a tiny volume of trading persisted, like the thin pulse of a patient in a coma. By early 1999, when international investors had recovered somewhat from the scare of the Asian crisis and the Russian crash, some tiptoed back into the Russian stock market, which began a modest revival.

The first small-scale trading in Russian securities began quietly in 1992. At first most of the trading was in privatization vouchers. In 1993 stock issues multiplied and trading accelerated, as tens of thousands of newly-privatized state enterprises issued stock. Enterprising Russians, plus a few far-sighted Westerners, began traveling to the sites of the newly-privatized companies, circulating among workers and managers, purchasing shares in ones and twos, and reselling them to Moscow-based brokerages, banks, and investment funds, which were springing up rapidly at the same time.

Thus from all over the country shares began to flow toward Moscow. What had begun as a highly dispersed pattern of share ownership was rapidly concentrated into much larger blocks, which were repackaged and made available for resale, mainly to foreign buyers.

In the spring of 1994, "emerging markets" were hot. Fed by foreign demand and the sudden availability of shares, the Russian stock market swelled rapidly. By September 1994 the flow of foreign money had turned into a flood. Foreign portfolio investment was running at nearly $500 million a month, whereas for all of the preceding year the total had been only $300 million. Share prices in the leading sectors – aluminum, oil, electric power, and telecommunications – were rising at 30% a month. The first Russian stock index, the "ROS Index" of 19 Russian stocks created by CS First Boston, rose 1,500% from December 1993 to September 1994. By some estimates, nearly $2 billion in foreign capital flowed into the Russian stock market in the first nine months of 1994.

But in the fall of 1994 the ruble crashed, and brought the young Russian stock market down with it. CS First Boston's ROS Index, which had started 1994 at 116, peaked on September 15 at 1,706 and slid sharply for the next four months. By January 1995 it had dropped to 600. Foreign shareholders discovered they had paid over $2 billion for pieces of paper that gave them no rights, no registry, no custody, and no recourse. But they had no choice but to hang on, because they could also find no buyers. Just what their investment was worth was anyone's guess.

Foreign buyers retreated to the sidelines. The problem wasn't just Russia; the collapse of the Mexican stock market in January 1995 and the failure of Barings, a respected specialist in emerging markets, the following month, caused investors worldwide to pull out of emerging markets and retreat to lower-risk investments at home.

Ironically, if the Russian stock market had been a normal stock market it would have fallen much farther, possibly clear back to the levels of early 1994. But the Russian market was so illiquid that foreign shareholders could not unload their holdings. Trading simply slowed to a crawl. "It's like a swamp," said a Russian trader, Oleg Mamonov of C.A. and Company, one of the largest Russian brokerage houses. "Ripples move through it slowly."[8] Illiquidity acted like a circuit-breaker.

But the impact on the flow of foreign money into Russia was dramatic. Monthly inflows of foreign portfolio investment dwindled to $20 million in January 1995. What little activity there was on the Russian stock market in the winter of 1995 consisted mostly of bottom-fishing by Russian investors, who scooped up stocks in aluminum and telecommunications.

As the foreign investors drew back and the market froze up, the new Russian investment funds suddenly found themselves in trouble. None of them had ever experienced a bear market before. "Nobody realized that

[8] *Wall Street Journal*, January 30 1995.

the foreigners had left," recalls Mikhail Kharshan, chairman of the largest Russian Investment Fund, "First Voucher Fund." "When the first signs appeared and 'Iuganskneftegaz' started to fall, we said, 'Well, OK, somebody's brought in more shares from the regions.' But before long the Russian investment funds found they were sitting on mountains of equity, but had no cash. "How much is an enormous block of 'Uralmash' stock worth?" asked Kharshan. "Nothing. If the stock is absolutely illiquid – then it's worth nothing."[9]

The Russian market stagnated until March 1996, three months before the presidential election. It was then that Boris Yeltsin started his remarkable turnaround in the opinion polls, and a few daring investors took a risk that he might win. By June 1996, Yeltsin triumphed in a landslide, and the Moscow market, after a brief post-election profit-taking, took off again.

The second time around

The second market cycle was even more spectacular than the first. The RTS Index, now the leading Russian market measure, bottomed out on March 18 1996 at 66.7, then began a steady climb over the next year-and-a-half, reaching a peak of 571.7 on October 6 1997, an increase of over eight-and-a-half times. In 1997 the Russian stock market was the most profitable emerging market in the world.

Even more impressive was the growth in daily volumes on the Russian Trading System, Russia's equivalent of the NASDAQ (described below). From levels of 2 or 3 million dollars a day, RTS trading volumes reached a record high of 216 million dollars on October 3, and in the summer and fall of 1997 trading days of over 100 million dollars were not uncommon.

But just as three years before, a combination of foreign and internal troubles brought the boom to an end. The "Asian flu" caused foreign investors to retreat from emerging markets, just as the Mexican "tequila effect" had done in 1994–95. At home, the Russian reformers lost position due to scandals and political infighting. In late October 1997 the Russian market crashed for the second time, and over the following nine months Russian shares lost over three-quarters of their value, reaching a low of 134.8 on July 8 1998. Yet daily trading volumes remained high, typically hovering between 50 and 100 million dollars. In other words, unlike the fall of 1994, the market did not simply freeze up.

But there was worse to come. With the government's devaluation and default on August 17 the market crashed again, bottoming out at 38.53

---

[9] *Kommersant* (weekly), No. 14 (18 April 1995), p. 46.

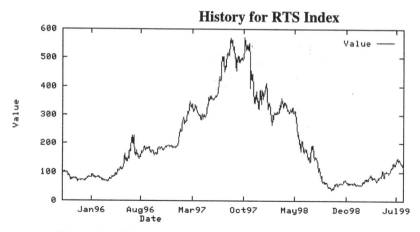

Figure 3.1 The Russian stock market, 1995–99 (September 1, 1995 =100)

Note: * Russian Trading System (RTS) Index: September 1, 1995–July 30, 1999 (Source: Internet Securities.)

on October 5. Daily trading volumes on the RTS plummeted, dropping below $10 million for the first time on August 19, then below $1 million on September 9, finally reaching a low of only $163,000 on September 25. Throughout the fall and winter, trading in Russian stocks was limited to a handful of "blue chips," with volumes on most days hovering between one and two million dollars.

But spring brought a fresh surge of interest. By May 1999 the RTS topped 100 again, yielding good profits for those who had come in at the bottom, and by the summer of 1999 Russia's market was once again the world's most profitable stock market, although it is too soon to say whether a third cycle has begun.

Meanwhile, what of the market's structure? The Russian equities market is no longer a back-alley business. A substantial structure of brokerages, index-makers, analysts, and regulators has grown up around it in a very short time. Much of what was achieved may turn out to have lasting value later on.

The stockbrokers

Along with the first Russian stocks came the first stockbrokers and the first of several spectacular success stories. In 1992 Credit Suisse-First Boston hired a self-confident 25-year-old American of Russian descent, Boris Jordan, to open an office in Moscow. Jordan not only looked for opportunities, he also helped make them. Serving as an unpaid advisor to Anatolii Chubais and the fledgling Russian State Property Committee on the eve of voucher privatization, Jordan made valuable contacts throughout Russia. When Russia's first stock market boom took off in 1993 and 1994, Jordan was ready.

Working for Western clients and CS First Boston's own account, Jordan swooped down on the voucher market and eventually acquired 17 million vouchers – nearly 12% of the privatization program's total buying power.[10] He then cashed them in for shares in Russian companies, attending voucher auctions all over the country. Two-thirds of the flood of Western portfolio investment in 1993–94 went through CS First Boston. In the *annus mirabilis* of 1994, the Moscow office of CSFB reportedly earned $66 million, and Boris Jordan garnered a bonus of $4 million.[11] By then, Boris Jordan was known as "The Tsar."[12]

But Jordan was not alone. Western and Russian banks, voucher investment funds, oil companies and industrial manufacturers, and above all enterprising individuals, saw the opportunity. Some were Russians, such as Oleg Tsarkov and Andrei Orekhov, who founded Grant Financial Center. "MFK-Moskovskie Partnery," formed by a group of former Vneshekonombank traders under general manager Sergei Osiniagov, carved out a more specialized niche, buying stocks in aluminum and nickel companies for Western banks.[13] Some, like Jordan, were of Russian descent, such as Peter Derby, an early founder of the Russian-American Troika Dialog brokerage.[14] Some Western pioneers started their own, such as the two Swedes who founded Brunswick, which soon became one of the largest of the Moscow-based brokerages.[15]

A booming stock market required investment research and an index, providing an opportunity for entrepreneurs like Sergei Skatershchikov, who at the age of nineteen founded the Skate-Press Consultancy Agency and turned $100 into a $500,000–a-year company in less than four years.[16] Today Skate-Press, Credit Suisse-First Boston, RTS, the

---

[10] *The New York Times*, September 20 1995, p. D1.

[11] *Institutional Investor* magazine, cited in *The New York Times*, September 20 1995, p. D1. See also similar reports in *The Wall Street Journal*, May 8 1995, p. A13.

[12] *Financial Times*, February 6 1995.

[13] *Kommersant-Daily*, October 12 1994. p. 5. MFK-Moskovskie Partnery was founded in 1993 by a group of bankers including the then-powerful import-export bank, ONEK-SIMBANK. It played a major role as a dealer in hard-currency bonds issued by the Ministry of Finance and VEB Eurobonds.

[14] *The Wall Street Journal*, August 2 1995, p. A5.

[15] Michelle Celarier, "Russian Risk," *Global Finance*, January 1995, p. 34. See also *The New York Times*, September 20 1995, p. D1. Author's interview with Martin Andersson, Brunswick director, Moscow, March 8 1996.

[16] *The New York Times*, July 23 1995, p. 12.

Moscow Times and many others, all provide Russian stock market indexes. A Moscow based company, AK&M, founded in 1990, also rates brokers, issuers, and other players in the Russian market. Most of these indexes and ratings now appear on the Internet.

The shock of the first market drop in 1994 and the year-long stagnation that followed caused a shake-out among the original market players. Russian brokerages and investment companies began looking for Western partners, many of them seeking to diversify into fixed-income securities and direct investments.[17] The Russians brought their knowledge of the local scene and their access to local investment opportunities, while the Westerners brought their connections to world capital markets. "First Voucher Fund" led the way in April 1995, selling a 30% interest to an American company, the Pioneer Group, for $20 million.[18] In May 1995, Boris Jordan and most of his team left CS First Boston to form a new Russian-Western investment bank, called Renaissance Capital, backed by a Russian banking giant, International Financial Company (MFK), affiliated with Oneksimbank.[19] Other major brokerages, such as Troika-Dialog, Rinako-Plus, and Grant, soon followed suit.[20] Brunswick became Brunswick Warburg. By early 1997, foreign companies and mixed Russian-Western partnerships handled over half the turnover in Russian stocks.

The second crash brought all this effervescence to an abrupt end. This time the Western banks and brokerages cut back their Moscow operations and most of the expatriates went home, causing a sharp crash in Moscow real estate prices. A handful stayed in Moscow but moved on to other jobs, such as the perennial Boris Jordan, who became chairman of an oil company. Tens of thousands of young Russians who had become traders and analysts were abruptly on the street. Yet most of the companies created to serve the equities market continue to exist, if largely as empty shells, but ready to revive quickly with any return of demand, as indeed they did in the spring of 1999.

How the Russian stock market works

Most Russian stocks do not trade on an actual "Russian Stock Exchange," in the sense of a large trading floor devoted to trading stocks, like the New York Stock Exchange. Most trading in equities is conducted by telephone and computer among a few dozen brokers, located in Moscow and a handful of Russian cities. Minimum lot sizes accepted by

---

[17] Natasha Miliusnik and Aleksandr Gubskii, "Brokeram stanovitsia tesno na rynke Rossii," *Kapital*, February 28–March 5 1996, p. 5.   [18] Ibid.

[19] *Kommersant-Daily*, December 26 1995, p. 6.

[20] *Kommersant-Daily*, February 23 1996, p. 6.

brokers are very large by the standards of most Russian investors – $15,000 and up – and the spreads (the gap between bid and ask quotes) are very wide by Western standards. In short, buying and selling equities is not a game available to the Russian small saver.[21]

When trading in stocks began in 1992, it seemed at first that exchanges (*birzhy*) would play a major role. Literally hundreds of *birzhy* had sprung up overnight in 1991, mostly specializing in commodities but eager to branch out into anything tradable. Some of these have survived (sometimes after spectacular false starts), mainly by specializing in particular types of commodities, such as the Moscow Interbank Currency Exchange. But exchanges in Russia have never lived up to their early promise, mainly because of punitive tax rates that have driven transactions underground.

By mid-1995 only a dozen exchanges handled equities at all, and the volumes traded were small – between $600,000 and $3 million per week country-wide.[22] A regional commodities exchange might make a market in the stock of a local company, such as Sverdlovsk Power (*"Sverdlovenergo"*) on the Ekaterinburg Commodities Exchange, or the Far Eastern Steamship Line on the Vladivostok Exchange, or even "Moscow Power" (*"Mosenergo"*) on Moscow's principal commodities market. But for these exchanges stocks are only a sideline. Only the Moscow Interbank Currency Exchange (MICEX) has emerged as a significant trading floor for equities, especially since the 1998 crash.

The Russian stock market of the future is likely to look less like the New York Stock Exchange and more like NASDAQ – an electronic exchange linking brokers. In the spring of 1994, a group of fifteen Moscow-based brokerages formed the Professional Association of Stock Market Participants (PAUFOR). With help from NASDAQ and an American computer company, the Russian brokers began to lay the basis for a NASDAQ-like over-the-counter network.[23]

The new network faced one major problem at the outset: existing telephone lines were so bad that they could not communicate with one another at reasonable speed. Unless they could overcome that, RTS would remain a collection of isolated pools. To by-pass the regular telephone system, RTS gained access to former government "specialized lines."[24]

[21] Michael P. Claudon and Andrey F. Yakushin, "The Sell-side of the Russian Securities Market," in *Investing in Russia's Securities Market: an Independent Assessment of the State of Play* (Middlebury, Vermont: Geonomics Institute, December 1996), pp. 34–45.

[22] Dmitrii Grishankov, Svetlana Lokotkova, Andrei Shmarov, "U vlasti – krupnooptovaia partiia," *Ekspert*, No. 12 (October 31 1995), pp. 18.

[23] *New York Times*, August 5 1994.

[24] Moscow Conference on Financial Technology, reported in *The Moscow Times*, June 22 1995, p. 13.

In September 1994, the first computerized trading system, called Portal, went on line, linking 33 brokerages trading stock in 83 companies. By the spring of 1995 some 15% of all stock transactions in Russia were being handled through Portal, and a second generation system, called RTS (Russian Trading System) was installed. With the new network in place, the Russian over-the-counter market linked Moscow with the three largest stockbrokers' assocations in the provinces, Ekaterinburg, St. Petersburg, and Novosibirsk. Using RTS, Russian brokers could get current quotations, but also negotiate with one another on-line and get help in reregistering shares.

In November 1995, PAUFOR went national: the major regional associations joined their colleagues to create a national brokers' association called NAUFOR (National Association of Securities Market Participants).[25] In the last couple of years RTS has been extended to include the regional members as well. RTS is open to any brokerage that joins NAUFOR, and by the end of 1997 the association had grown to over 600 members, who used RTS to handle over 90 percent of the trades on the Russian equities market.[26]

Reality still falls somewhat short of the press releases. RTS can post offers to buy and sell, but actual transactions have to be executed off-line by telephone. In 1997 NAUFOR launched a pilot program with Russia's largest depository to create a computerized settlement system. Centralized settlement is making progress in Moscow, but it has been slower to spread to the rest of the country.[27] The Russian Trading System at first distributed trading results only once a day, after 6:00 p.m., but is now updated every hour. The system is still dominated by the Moscow brokerages who founded it, and who do half of their trading through the system.[28]

Yet the brokers' achievement is remarkable. In a few short years they have produced the basis of a modern trading system. Equally significant, NAUFOR represents the most striking example of a self-governing professional association in the new Russian economy. Through its tough membership rules and tight discipline, NAUFOR has established an impressive level of contract compliance and transparent reporting, which have been a major factor in the improvement of the Russian stock market.

[25] *Kommersant-Daily*, December 2 1995, p. 6. For background, Dmitri V. Ponomarev, "Self-Regulation of the Securities Market in Russia," in *Investing in Russia's Securities*, op. cit., pp. 50–55.

[26] Timothy Frye, "Governing the Russian Securities Market," *Post-Soviet Affairs*, vol. 13, no. 4 (1997), p. 384.   [27] *Russia Portfolio*, vol. 3, no. 1 (January 6 1997), p. 1.

[28] Grishankov et al., op. cit.

In addition, NAUFOR is one of the few examples of incipient partnership with a state regulatory body, the Federal Securities Commission.[29]

Registrars and custodians

Part of the "Wild East" image of Russia in the early 1990s came from stories like this one, which made headlines in the Western press: In November 1994, two associates of UK-based Trans World Metals traveled to the Siberian city of Krasnoyarsk to participate in a stockholders' meeting of the Krasnoyarsk Aluminum Smelter, one of the world's largest aluminum producers. The visitors thought they owned 20% of the company. But at Krasnoyarsk they discovered their names had been removed from the register of stockholders.[30]

Such incidents of outright stock fraud by Russian enterprise managers have mostly been limited to industries with large export revenues, where there have frequently been bitter battles for control. But the Krasnoyarsk episode pointed up serious weaknesses in the Russian mechanisms for share registration and custody. Early Western buyers discovered that the only register of shareholders was usually in the possession of the company's managers or a "pocket" registrar owned by the company. Re-registration of shares to a new owner typically required a trip direct to the enterprise.[31] This could be time-consuming and expensive. The registrar could take up to three days to make the changes, and charge a fee of up to 5% of the value of the sale. Or the registrar could decide some key document was missing and refuse to make the entry. Or the company could exercise a right of first refusal and buy the shares back for a nominal price. Indeed, in the case of the Russian gas giant "Gazprom" the right of first refusal was written right into the company's corporate charter.

Many Western investors discovered – too late – that what they held was not actually a stock certificate but a forward contract to buy the certificate later. Many who had thought to cover themselves by buying an extract from the official share register learned that some Russian businessmen in the provinces ran thriving businesses supplying fake extracts, known as "dead souls," from the nineteenth century novel by Nikolai Gogol. As one Western banker in Moscow commented acidly, "If you are willing to pay for an extract, you can get as many as you like."[32]

The good news is that there have been major improvements. Since early

[29] The best description of NAUFOR and its operations is Frye, op. cit., especially pp. 383–389.
[30] *Financial Times*, November 16 1994; *Kommersant-Daily*, November 25 1994.
[31] *Izvestiia*, August 30 1994.   [32] *Financial Times*, November 19 1994, p. IX.

1996 the Federal Securities Commission has begun auditing and licensing registrars,[33] and beginning in 1997 it began turning over cases of unlicensed registrars to the police. A majority of Russian enterprises still ignore the requirement that they must maintain registers with independent registrars (if they have one thousand shareholders or more). But the larger Russian enterprises are moving to comply. The very largest companies – the ones most likely to be of interest to investors – can now use the services of an international independent registry built with Western technical assistance funds, the National Registry Company, which uses world-standard procedures and largely eliminates shareholder record-keeping risks.[34] In short, Russia is moving toward a modern registrar industry.

There are similarly positive developments in other key parts of the capital-markets infrastructure. Specialized depository companies have appeared, with Western banks leading the way in providing custodial services on behalf of foreign investors. The movement toward improved custodial services is being driven so far by the requirements of the Western regulatory agencies. But the Russian Securities Commission has also begun to license specialized depositories, which are required before Russian mutual funds are allowed to operate.[35]

Improvements in the capital-markets infrastructure showed a powerful virtuous circle at work: Western bankers and brokers, under pressure from foreign investors and regulators back home, create Western-standard institutions that then serve as models for Russian regulators and brokers. The resulting increase in confidence generates increases in share prices and turnover, which then draw in more Russian companies, which adopt the new standards in order to participate. By the end of the market's second cycle in 1998 much of the basis for a civilized equities market had been created.

Regulating the securities market

Alongside these impressive strides in self-regulation by the private sector, the Russian government too gradually developed mechanisms to oversee and regulate the securities markets. The key to success in this case was cooperation between the private sector and a state agency.[36]

---

[33] Holly Nielsen, "Infrastructure Develops in the Russian Securities Markets," in *Investing in Russia's Securities Market* . . . op. cit., pp. 56–68. Holly Nielsen is deputy executive director of the Resource Secretariat of the Russian Federal Securities Commission.

[34] Nielsen, op. cit., p. 61.   [35] Nielsen, op. cit., p. 68.

[36] Timothy Frye's pioneering book, *The State and the Market: Governing the New Russian Economy* (Ann Arbor, Michigan: University of Michigan Press, 1999), explores several cases of government regulation of private institutions in the Russian capital market. Frye explains convincingly why in some cases the state-private relationship was successful, in others not.

Efforts to provide securities regulation began even before there were securities to regulate. As early as December 1991 the Russian government created a skeletal structure of rules governing disclosure, licensing, and exchange operations. Over the years, the government's regulatory regime grew steadily, culminating in 1996 with the passage of a major framework law on securities markets and an expanded regulatory body, the Federal Securities Commission (FSC).

But the growth of the market soon raced ahead of the regulators, and government regulation faces several basic weaknesses. The first is overlapping jurisdictions. Initially the Ministry of Finance was the principal government body with authority over the securities markets. But the rapid growth of the private sector soon drew in other agencies as well. The State Property Committee, charged with overseeing the privatization program, has a role in enforcing sound corporate governance and protection of shareholders' rights. Several other state agencies share jurisdiction over securities markets, including the Central Bank and the Anti-Monopoly Committee, as well as various committees of parliament. Because banks were major players in the equities market, the Ministry of Finance claims a role as a regulator as well. The Federal Securities Commission tries to coordinate the roles of all these state agencies, but competing jurisdictions remain a problem.

The second problem is enforcement. In the first years there was no legal basis for civil or criminal penalties for securities violations, and more often than not they were simply ignored. Regulators were helpless to deal with investment scams and recalcitrant enterprise directors. The 1996 Law on the Russian Securities Market provided for civil penalties, but Russian legislation is still largely silent on criminal offenses. The new Criminal Code does recognize several new categories of business crime (see Chapter 6), but it will be several more years before the Criminal Code has been fully fleshed out with detailed penalties. In theory the FSC has considerable powers: it can bring civil lawsuits and it can invoke criminal sanctions. However, FSC has no power to levy fines, and to enforce criminal penalties it must rely on the uncertain cooperation of the police and the tax inspectorate.[37]

Given these weaknesses Russian investors and brokers try to fend for themselves, bypassing the formal regulatory system. Some groups operate their own private mediation system: thus NAUFOR has its own "arbitration court" (although it prefers to call it a "disciplinary committee," to avoid the suggestion that it is by-passing the official court system)

---

[37] The activities of the Federal Securities Commission can be conveniently followed through its Internet web site, at http://feast.fe.msk.ru/infomarket//fedcom, which features news in both English and Russian.

and tries to settle disputes within its own ranks. The Russian Securities Commission encourages the private players to organize themselves into professional associations and to keep their own houses in order.

In sum, the regulatory framework for the securities industry is still insufficient, but it is making progress. Technical assistance groups, Western regulators, and financial companies have all given active assistance, providing funds, personnel, practical models, and experience. Securities regulation is starting to have an impact.

Five targets for reform

The Russian stock market, considered as a private-sector institution and as an example of cooperation with the state, was one of the genuine success stories of the 1990s. Yet it was also defective at its core, because it was mainly a vehicle for foreign speculation. Five main issues must be addressed before the Russian equities market can play a role as a mobilizer of capital and a source of market signals about corporate performance:

1 *New issues* The Russian equities market is still essentially a secondary market trading in the first-generation shares created by the mass privatization of 1992–94. As foreign money poured into the Moscow stock market, the consequence was not an injection of capital into Russian enterprises, but a windfall capital gain for the existing shareholders. Few Russian companies have issued new shares (except as a defensive maneuver to maintain insider control), and fewer still have brought new issues to the market. The same is not true, incidentally, of debt financing: many Russian companies use promissory notes (*vekselia*) that are tantamount to corporate bonds, but they serve as a substitute for money, not as a vehicle for financing investment. Practically all Russian companies finance new investment from internal funds, mostly from depreciation deductions.[38]

2 *Small savers* If private demand for capital largely bypasses the capital markets, so does Russia's meager private capital supply, especially popular savings. By some estimates, the amount that ordinary savers could put into investments today is somewhere between $7 billion and

---

[38] G. Kasatkin, "Investitsionnyi klimat v Rossii: luchshe ne stalo," *Rynok tsennykh bumag*, No. 12 (1995), pp. 28–31. In 1996, as a result of the continuing decline in state investment, the share of investment from enterprise funds was above 70%. (*Russian Economic Trends*, vol. 5, no. 3, 1996, p. 88.)

$20 billion.[39] But Russians are not putting that money into stocks and corporate bonds. Many Russians now own a few symbolic shares of stock, but they received those shares free, either at their workplace or in exchange for vouchers. If they happen to put their savings into a bank, it is likely to be the government-owned Sberbank. But for the most part they either convert their rubles into dollars and keep them under the mattress, or they spend them as fast as they can on consumer goods and foreign tourism.[40] In short, very little of ordinary people's savings ends up in the legitimate private capital market.

3 *Valuation* If the Russian stock market is ever to become more than a vehicle for speculation, investers will need more reliable ways of assessing the value of Russian shares. But valuation is a problem. First, Russian accounting methods are in flux. Traditionally, Soviet accounting methods were designed to detect misuse of state funds, not to provide information about company performance. Now more and more Russian companies are switching to international accounting standards, and the major Western accounting firms are actively helping them provide more accurate information to investors. The result has been some gain in transparency, but not yet enough.

Valuation of Russian equities, as one leading Western analyst puts it, "remains more of an art than a science."[41] The problems have to do with the transitional Russian economy itself. Trying to evaluate a Russian company's cash flow, for example, requires making subjective judgments about the enormous sums of "quasi-money" in the system – barter, wechsels, and unpaid receivables – which are difficult to account for on a company's books.[42] There are also continuing uncertainties about the value to be placed on company assets. For example, should a Russian enterprise's "social assets" – housing, roads, day care centers, etc. – be counted as assets or liabilities? As a result of such difficulties in valuation, different methodologies and assumptions produce widely different price-to-earnings ratios for the same stock.

---

[39] Estimates from Russian government sources, quoted in *Finansovye izvestiia*, February 23 1995.

[40] In 1996 Russians purchased approximately $20 billion in dollars. However, most of that went to finance foreign travel and purchases of foreign goods by shuttle traders. In 1995 there was no net increase in hard-currency holdings outside of banks. Source: *Russian Economic Trends*, loc. cit.

[41] Address by John-Paul Smith, Russian equity strategist at Morgan Stanley Group, London, before the Symposium on US-Russian Investment, Harvard University, January 9–12 1997.

[42] Iulia Latynina, "Den'gi po-rossiiski," *Izvestiia*, January 30 1997, p. 4.

4 *Competition from government debt* Beginning in 1995 the Russian government became a heavy borrower on domestic capital markets to finance its deficits. Initially, this was a positive innovation. Previously, the federal government financed its deficits by borrowing from the Central Bank of Russia – tantamount to printing money.

But the Russian government borrowings became a formidable competitor to the private capital market for Russia's scarce funds. By offering high interest rates, the Russian government was able to outbid the private sector, as government paper became the investment of choice for Russian banks and many Russian enterprises. (In 1996, for example, Russian banks typically held five times more money in government securities than in equity shares.)[43] In effect, the government became a giant vacuum cleaner, sucking capital out of the private sector to finance its debt. This system came crashing to the ground in August 1998, but the lesson is clear: capital markets will not develop normally if they have to compete with the government's deficit spending.

5 *Investment fraud* Russian small savers have been repeatedly scalded by fraudulent investment schemes, with names like "Svetlana," "Tibet," "Vlastilina," "NB Trust Office," and "Telemarket." The biggest of all, and the most spectacular investment bubble of the early 1990s until its collapse in the summer of 1994, was "MMM." MMM was a classic pyramid scheme. Early investors bought "tickets" (MMM carefully avoided calling them shares), and cashed them in a few months later at fabulous profits. MMM kept the pyramid going by using the cash flow from new buyers to pay off old ones. Like all pyramids, it worked beautifully – except for those left holding the bag at the end.

In the first half of the 1990s investment fraud spread like a contagious disease. By one estimate, the public was bilked of over $2 billion.[44] No one knows how many people have lost money; guesses run between 5 and 24 million people.[45]

One major reason the fraudsters were so successful was that the equities market was reserved for large players, and there was no legitimate avenue open to small savers. One possible solution for the future is mutual funds. The Russian Securities Commission has issued the necessary decrees and about 20 equities funds began operating in 1997–98, catering mainly to Western investors.[46] But Russian small savers have

---

[43] *Russian Economic Trends*, vol. 5, no. 3 (1996), p. 114. The share of equities increased in 1997.

[44] Financial Information Agency news release, Moscow, April 27 1995.

[45] *Izvestiia*, April 27 1995, p. 2.

[46] *Russkiii telegraf*, March 11 1998, by Internet. For a review of the mutual funds' performance as of early 1998, see Dmitrii Grishankov et al., "Seans pifoanaliza," *Ekspert*, No. 7 (February 23 1998), pp. 24–33.

grown wary. It will be a long time before mutual funds catch on with them.

If not the Russian stock market, then what?

The Russian equities market, even at its height, was miniscule by international standards. On a good trading day in 1997, perhaps $100 million in stocks changed hands over the RTS system, and another $30 million through direct trades among Russian-based brokers. The offshore market accounted for roughly $40 million in daily trades in Russian ADR's in New York and London. All told, trading in Russian stocks totalled no more than $170 to $200 million a day.

The strongest future direction of growth, when the Russian economy turns round, may be Russian stocks trading in Western capital markets. By 1997 over a dozen Russian companies had gained first-stage approval to sell their shares in the US market, and the number was growing rapidly. By 1999, much of the trading in Russian equities had shifted offshore. Russian ADR's traded in foreign centers such as Frankfurt and quoted over Internet services were typically 4 to 5 times the shrunken volumes of the Russian Trading System in Moscow.[47]

On the whole, this is a beneficial process, because to gain access to foreign capital markets Russian companies must meet stringent Western standards of accounting and disclosure. If more Russian companies line up to sell equities in the west, this will bring further improvement in corporate transparency inside Russia, at least among the handful of Russian "blue chips."

But selling equity to foreign investors can only go so far before foreigners begin to gain control of Russia's richest and most strategic companies. So for this is not politically acceptable, at least in the so-called "strategic industries," such as metals and oil. In addition, the list of attractive Russian companies with immediate "blue-chip appeal" is short, especially so long as Russia remains suspect. Consequently, although foreign portfolio investment will be an important source of capital for a handful of "have" companies, it will not be the solution for the many thousands of "have-not" companies that make up the bulk of the investment problem in Russia.

As for capital markets inside Russia, an equities market based largely on foreign capital is bound to be unstable, as global capital flows react to crises outside Russia, such as the Latin American crisis in 1994 and the "Asian flu" in 1997–98.

If the equities markets do not play the lead role in capital formation,

---

[47] Author's interview with Georg Kjollgren and Peter Boone, Brunswick Warburg, Moscow, March 9 1999.

then what will? Insurance companies, pension funds, and mutual funds, which play so large a role in capital formation in the West, are still embryonic in Russia. That leaves one last private-sector institution, the banks, to which we turn now.

The first half of the 1990s will go down in history as the
"golden age" of the Russian banking system. . . . The
private banks appropriated most of the "inflation tax"
levied on the Russian economy, practically without
opposition.　　*Russian Banks at the End of the Golden Age*[1]

"We built our hut on chicken legs, and it was bound to be
blown down, not even by a storm, but by the first wind."
　　– *Sergei Leont'ev, president of Probiznesbank, October 1998*[2]

4　　The rise and fall of the private banks

Yuzhno-Sakhalinsk, July 1998:
There it stood, gleaming reassuringly in the hotel lobby – an ATM cash
machine, courtesy of a leading Russian bank. It was the first modern object I had
seen on arriving on Sakhalin Island, eight time zones east of Moscow and one of
most neglected places on earth. Yet with the discovery of oil, new money was
starting to bring the first signs of change – a remodeled hotel, a new business
center, and even a cellular telephone company, all within a stone's throw of
Lenin's statue on Revolution Square. And an ATM machine.
　　Cautiously I stepped up and inserted my card. Amazingly, it beeped and
whirred, and out popped a sheaf of fresh ruble notes. It worked! But not for long:
within less than a month that Russian bank had collapsed, the cash machine stood
cashless, and anyone on Sakhalin who wanted ruble notes had to fly to Moscow to
get them.

Until the summer of 1998, banking was the headline story of Russia's
nascent market economy. More than any other post-Soviet institution,
the new private banks symbolized the vast transfer of wealth from state to
private hands and the return of money to center stage in the Russian
economy. The private banks were born in the late 1980s from the break-
up of the Soviet banking monopoly, and they grew rich on the opportunities for trade and arbitrage that opened up as the Soviet state weakened.
They were then the chief beneficiaries of the high inflation and the weak
ruble of 1991–95. They spawned vast conglomerates ranging from insurance to trade, which took control of many of the country's largest and
most profitable industries and private media. They were the core of the

---

[1] Mikhail Dmitriev and Dmitrii Travin, *Rossiiskie banki: na iskhode zolotogo veka* (St.
Petersburg: "Norma," 1996), p. 7.
[2] Quoted in *Ekspert*, No. 39 (October 12 1998), p. 53.

"oligarchies" that dominated the country's politics and finance. In the space of one decade the private banks grew into the largest, richest, and politically most powerful institutions in the new Russian economy.

Then in one day, August 17, 1998, the government's surprise devaluation and default hit the private banks like a bomb. The top twenty commercial banks, which had held two-thirds of the assets of the new banking sector, were instantly reduced to empty shells. Hundreds more teetered on the edge of insolvency. The wealth and power of the oligarchs appeared to evaporate overnight. Suddenly what had seemed the most spectacular achievement of the Russian marketization was exposed as a hollow pretense. Behind their grand buildings with their imposing grecian columns and the gold letters there was only a rickety scaffolding of bad loans and dodgy practices. Like the "Potemkin villages" built by Catherine II's favorite on the path of her official visits, the assets and capital of the Russian banks turned out to be little more than fronts.

This was no ordinary bank failure. The shock wave of the banking collapse ripped through the economy, paralyzing the financial system throughout the country. The private banks had been responsible for the bulk of transfer payments between companies; they provided most of the short-term finance for exports and imports; they stored the working funds of state agencies and local governments and businesses; and most important, they forwarded tax remittances from taxpayers to the treasury. The devastating economic impact of the banking crisis demonstrated, as the private banks went down, the essential functions they had gained in the space of a decade – and also how far money had penetrated much of the Russian economy.

Why did the Russian banks prove to be so vulnerable? The government's August default and devaluation was itself a terrific blow. But the stage had been set for the collapse much earlier. The banking crisis actually began in the fall of 1997, when the "Asian flu" hit Russia. Commodities prices fell worldwide and global capital began withdrawing from emerging markets. Borrowers defaulted; interest rates soared; the interbank loan market dried up; and the crisis was on.[3]

But even that is only part of the story. The Russian banks had already been weakening for several years as a result of the government's policies. From 1994 on, the government's increasingly tight money policy had closed off the banks' previously lush profits from speculation and arbitrage. In response, in 1995–97 the larger banks had turned to the last

---

[3] Russian Federation, Russian Central Bank, *Programma neotlozhnykh mer po restrukturizatsii bankovskoi sistemy Rossiiskoi Federatsii* (October 19 1998 draft), by Internet. For background analysis, see *Russian Economic Trends: Monthly Update*, November 1998, by Internet (http://www.hhs.se/sit/ret/ret.htm)

remaining source of profit, the government's own borrowing, which grew rapidly from year to year, drawing capital from the banks, companies, and individual savers throughout the country, finally building into the tidal wave of debt that crashed in August 1998. In other words, the deeper irony of the banking collapse is that it was a by-product of the government's own flawed macroeconomic stabilization.

Yet the bankers themselves contributed mightily to their own downfall. In the autumn of 1998, surveying the wreckage, a committee of experts in the Central Bank drew up a harsh indictment.[4] The private banks were riddled with conflicts of interest. Their directors lent freely to their friends, to themselves, and to powerful politicians. They misspent their depositors' funds, including those of state agencies. They built up vast structures of bad loans, which they carried from year to year. They depended on cheap funds from state agencies and on close ties with politicians, whom the banks in turn supported. They carried huge staffs, paid themselves lavish salaries, and built palatial offices. The Russian banks, in other words, had never been "normal banks." They were quasi-banks in a quasi-market, and badly run to boot.

The collapse of the banks was also a failure of state regulation. Ironically again, the Russian Central Bank had created the closest thing to a real regulatory structure of any sector in the Russian economy. By 1997–98 the Central Bank was weeding out dozens of the weaker banks each month, and imposing steadily tougher capital and reserve requirements. Yet as the crisis proved, the Central Bank proved helpless to deal with the core of the problem – the free-wheeling ways of the larger banks and their political protectors.

But the wreckage also revealed something else. Alongside the failed giants were hundreds of smaller banks that had not bought government debt or piled up bad loans. These were the survivors amid the rubble, badly damaged but still viable. In coming years, as the Russian banking sector is rebuilt, this tier of smaller banks may be the breeding-ground for a second generation of private banks, more soundly based than the first.

This chapter tells the ten-year saga of the Russian private banks, from the late 1980s to the collapse of 1998, exploring the reasons for their rise and fall, then the consequences for the Russian market economy. In long-range perspective, the most serious failure of the "first generation" of the Russian private banks was that they never developed into private-sector intermediaries between households and businesses, mobilizing popular savings and supporting investment. Their collapse leaves a legacy of mistrust that will prevent their successors from performing for a long time to

[4] "*Programma neotlozhnykh mer...*" op. cit.

come that most essential function of normal banks in normal market economies. How then will Russia save or invest?

How the Russian private banks got their start

The Soviet command economy was based on physical output and relegated money to a minor role. Russian policy-makers hardly gave a thought to the money supply or its impact on economic growth or stability. Nor did they need to: in a system that largely rejected the role of money and markets as guides to economic decisions, money served a passive function, it was a mere unit of account.[5] This left the banks with little power or significance. The State Bank's major functions were to process payments and to account for monies spent.[6] As the perennial chairman of the Russian Central Bank, Viktor Gerashchenko, once put it, the Soviet banking system was "little more than a settlement house."[7]

Ironically, in its last years the Soviet banking system proved increasingly unable to ensure even the one thing it had been created for – financial control. Under pressure from all sides, the USSR State Bank extended credit to farms and state factories virtually on demand, and loans were seldom repaid. State managers diverted credits to their own purpose, granted unauthorized wage increases to their workers, and piled up illegal inventories. The budget ran a chronic (if officially unacknowledged) deficit from the mid-1970s on, and there was a steady (also unacknowledged) inflation rate of about 5% a year, which gradually accelerated after the mid-1980s. In other words, the Soviet state had begun to lose control of money and credit long before the collapse of 1991.[8]

The Soviet banking system breaks up

The beginning of the end came in 1987. The Gorbachev government, seeking to reform the economy by decentralizing it, broke up the USSR State Bank into five specialized banks (for agriculture, foreign trade,

[5] For overviews of the Soviet financial system, see Gregory Grossman, "Gold and Sword: Money in the Soviet Command Economy," in Henry Rosovsky, ed., *Industrialization in Two Systems* (New York: John Wiley and Sons, 1966); and Robert Campbell, *The Socialist Economies in Transition* (Bloomington, Indiana: Indiana University Press, 1991), chapter 5.

[6] One exception to this point was the portion of the Soviet banking system that served foreign operations. A minor part of the system in Soviet days, it provided an important reservoir of skills and experience as private foreign trade emerged as the chief engine of the Russian marketization after 1988.

[7] Quoted in *Financial Times*, March 22 1990.

[8] Gregory Grossman, "Monetary and Financial Aspects of Gorbachev's Reforms," in Christine Kessides et al., eds., *Financial Reform in Socialist Economies* (Washington, D.C.: The World Bank, 1989).

industry, housing, and household savings).[9] But once started, the process did not stop there. The following year, the banking system divided and divided again, and hundreds of new banks appeared overnight. By the end of 1991, when the Soviet Union broke up, there were already over 1,600 private banks in Russia,[10] and the number grew steadily over the following years. The state retained control of central-banking functions, gathered into a newly-renamed Russian Central Bank modeled along the lines of European central banks, and of the main savings bank system, Sberbank. Most of the rest passed quickly into private hands.

Just where the initial capital and entrepreneurial energy for the new Russian banks came from has been the subject of a good deal of sensational speculation, but in most cases the answer is straightforward: most of the new private banks were created by Soviet state bureaucrats, acting in their own interest as the regime weakened. The best Western study of the origins of the Russian banking system sums up the story: "Ministries, state committees, large state enterprises, government organs, state financial institutions, the Communist party and its affiliates – these were the entrepreneurs of the new banking sector."[11]

These state players needed private banks because they were already doing business on their own account. As the command economy weakened, the state monopoly on foreign trade disappeared, and along with it the state's tight controls over hard currency.[12] Anyone with access to exportable commodities seized the opportunity – and required a bank.

Some commercial banks, such as Promstroibank, were the direct descendants of the Soviet state banking system. More numerous were the commercial banks that grew out of the Soviet state industrial enterprises. "Our company needed a bank, so we created one," was a commonly-heard story. One of the greatest success stories of the nineties, Oneksimbank, was created by a consortium of foreign-trade companies descended from the Soviet foreign-trade ministry. Tokobank (which was Russia's sixth largest private bank when it went bankrupt in the spring of 1998) was created by the state supply system, Gossnab. Banks with more-or-less direct state origins are still today the single most powerful block within the new banking sector.

In a class by itself, but in the same broad category of direct

[9] This brief account is drawn mainly from the excellent analysis of the post-Soviet banking system by Joel S. Hellman, "Breaking the Bank: Bureaucrats and the Creation of Markets in a Transitional Economy" (Ph.D. Dissertation, Columbia University, 1993)

[10] International Monetary Fund, *IMF Economic Reviews: Russian Federation* (Washington, D.C.: International Monetary Fund, June 1993), p. 24.

[11] Hellman thesis, op. cit., p. 155.

[12] An excellent account of the break-up of the state monopoly on foreign trade and hard currency is Jean Farneth Boone, "Trading in Power: The Politics of Soviet Foreign Economic Reform, 1986–1991" (PhD dissertation, Georgetown University, 1998).

descendants of the Soviet banks is Sberbank, the giant savings bank. With more than 34,000 branches throughout Russia, Sberbank is the one truly national bank in Russia, and dwarfs all others in assets and capital. Its biggest shareholder is the Russian Central Bank, which oversees Sberbank and sets its policies. In effect, Sberbank is the savings arm of the Russian Central Bank, an arrangement also used in several European countries.[13]

Only a handful of the largest banks sprang from the quasi-private cooperatives that proliferated after 1987, but even these had close ties to Soviet institutions. One of them was Stolichnyi Bank (now known as SBS-Agro), founded by a consortium of Moscow construction cooperatives that worked on city contracts. A variation on the same theme was the cooperatives founded by young entrepreneurs with backing from the Communist Party youth organization, the Komsomol. The Komsomol's many quasi-private ventures in entertainment, travel, and even high-tech consulting, starting in the early 1980s, provided entrepreneurship and funds for many of Russia's new companies (see chapter 5). Both Menatep and Most, two of the largest banks originating outside the state sector, drew their original capital from Komsomol-sponsored businesses.

A third source of initial capital was the criminal underworld. For obvious reasons, much less is known about it. Attracted by the easy profits to be made in banking, organized crime clearly made determined efforts to penetrate the banking sector; the main evidence is the grisly tail of bank presidents' bodies left by contract killers over the years. It would be surprising indeed if capital originating from organized crime did not make up a substantial part of the Russian banks' capital. Yet for what it is worth, none of the top Russian banks has been linked with organized gangs. The kind of financial operations gangsters would be most interested in – money laundering, export of capital, embezzlement and fraud, etc. – would best be performed by smaller banks, and among these the proportion of "mafia" banks may be large.

Whatever their origins, the early ties of the largest Russian banks were soon loosened. As the banks grew, the more entrepreneurial of the young bankers who at the outset had been staked by Soviet institutions quickly outgrew their backers and many of the banks that had been closely tethered to industrial founders gained their freedom. The banks' shareholders, whoever they might be, soon discovered they had little control over management. In short, the thesis that the bankers were nothing more

[13] For two contrasting portraits of Sberbank, see Rustam Narzikulov, "Neestestvennaia monopoliia," *Nezavisimaia gazeta*, April 1 1997, by Internet; and Elena Starostenkova, "Kontrol'nyi paket Sberbanka ostanetsia v rukakh Tsental'nogo Banka," *Finansovye izvestiia*, June 3 1997, by Internet.

than the "authorized" representatives of unnamed powerful interests that stood behind them – a view that is perennially popular in Moscow – needs to be examined carefully.[14]

But the banks' origins still matter: on the whole, the banks founded by banking professionals and originating within the state banking system or large state companies have tended to hold up better than the ones founded by outsiders, many of which flamed out after brief spectacular careers even before the crash of August 1998. One reason, as we shall see presently, is that the insiders had better connections with government and access to government funds, and especially lately, better protection from the Russian Central Bank.

Spontaneous products of the decaying command economy, the Russian private banks were deformed from birth. They grew out of a system in which the skills and structures of conventional banking hardly existed. Then, from 1988 on, the opportunities for quick gain lay everywhere for the daring and the unscrupulous.

At first, the emerging banks performed mainly two kinds of functions, which might be called "defensive" and "opportunistic." The defensive functions were responses to the break-up of the Soviet system of payments and transfers. Traditionally, a Soviet enterprise was automatically paid for its output as soon as it left the factory gate, by a simple transfer of funds from the account of the buyer to that of the producer. As this system shattered in 1990–91, enterprises needed to find new sources of funds to maintain liquidity. One of the main defensive functions of the new private banks was to funnel state credits to cash-starved enterprises.

But the private banks also enabled their founders to get around the remaining restrictions of the Soviet system and to mobilize short-term capital to take advantage of the new opportunities opening up, mainly in foreign trade. The banks bankrolled commodity trading and import-export operations, or participated directly as players; they helped their clients convert their state-controlled assets into cash; they conducted illegal foreign-currency exchange; they transferred profits abroad through illegal correspondent accounts. It was only gradually that they began taking deposits and making loans.

Thus the period 1987–91 could be called the era of "pre-banking." It was then followed by the "golden era" of 1991–95, when the Russian

---

[14] The relationship between bankers and their principal backers is a complex question that goes beyond the present study. The answer is clearly different from case to case. Even some of the largest banks, such as Gazprombank and Natsional'nyi Rezervnyi, remain tightly subordinated to their principal shareholders, in this case Gazprom. Others never quite gained independence from their backers; Imperial Bank, for example, passed from Gazprom's control into that of Lukoil. Still another question, even more tangled, is the relationship of the banks to their parent holding companies.

banks multiplied manifold the capital they had accumulated in the previous phase. This was the time in which the banking giants grew and the financial base for the "oligarchies" was built. But how did they do it?

How the Russian banks made money in the "golden age"

The chief source of the bonanza was inflation. In contrast to the leading economies of Eastern Europe, which put the fight against inflation at the top of their list from the start, the Russian government delayed implementing a program of macroeconomic stabilization until 1994, and even then did not apply the screws consistently until 1995. The worst year of the Great Inflation was 1992, when the growth in the price index topped 2500%. Overall, between 1991 and 1995 prices increased roughly 10,000-fold.

Inflation is a powerful redistributor of fortunes: in inflationary times, anyone who holds cash and can't put it to work is sitting on a wasting asset; but anyone who can borrow money cheaply, move it quickly, and convert it to other values makes a killing. In 1991–95 the Russian banks found themselves in the "sweet spot." By one estimate, their profits from inflation in those years may have amounted to as much as 10% of the Russian GDP.[15]

The way they did it was straightforward: they converted low-interest ruble deposits into dollars, then lent the dollars at high interest rates to finance short-term commodity exports. The banks made money from every link in the chain, first by charging high interest rates on the dollar loans, then converting the dollars back into depreciated rubles, which they returned to their depositors' accounts.[16]

Making this profitable business work required a source of low-interest rubles. The very best source was state enterprises and government agencies, which tended to keep their ruble accounts in commercial banks, usually free of interest. Individual depositors were a minor source of funds (except for Sberbank), but their ruble deposits too received interest at rates well below inflation.

It is a fascinating question why depositors allowed themselves to be used in this way. Why was there so little demand for indexation, which would have matched interest rates to the prevailing inflation? There were three reasons. The banks had captive (or accomplice) customers. They were in a sellers' market. And Russians initially had little understanding of the way inflation affected them.

---

[15] Mikhail Dmitriev and Dmitrii Travin, op. cit., pp. 74–75.
[16] The description that follows is based on Dmitriev and Travin, op. cit., pp. 67–87.

The captive customers were mostly large state-owned (or recently privatized) industrial enterprises. They typically kept their working funds either in a local branch of one of the so-called *spetsbanki* that arose from the break-up of the USSR State Bank, or in one of the "pocket banks" which they founded themselves.[17] The shareholders in the pocket banks were frequently the top managers of the enterprises; thus they were one of the mechanisms through which the managers put the resources of their enterprises to work for their own private gain.

In a normal banking system such funds would not be a useful source of revenue for banks: though they receive little or no interest they can be withdrawn by the client at any time. But in the highly speculative environment of Russia in the early 1990s, if the banks could hold on to such funds for even a few days or a few weeks, they could make money from them; they supplied the bulk of the overnight interbank loans that banks used to lend to one another.

Government agencies were another group of captive clients. In Russia there is no state treasury system to handle the revenues and payments of state agencies, and governments at all levels use the commercial banks instead.[18] Tax receipts, customs duties, and pension payments, for example, are typically used as "free loans" by banks, who hold on to them for as long as several months before passing them along to the treasury. At the time of the August crash up to 90 percent of all government funds were processed through "authorized" commercial banks.[19] (This, incidentally, explains why tax payments and government services were so severely disrupted by the banking crisis.)

Russia had not experienced high inflation since the 1920s, and depositors took a while to understand that with prices growing at 2,500% a year, a bank account paying less than that was a loser. Even after they had grown more sophisticated, many depositors discovered that they had little choice. Outside Moscow, most cities had only a handful of banks; many enterprises were tied to a single bank. Few banks anywhere were interested in attracting individual savings. The government placed no limits on interest rates or loan conditions. In short, the banks enjoyed a sellers' market, and they were free to set whatever terms the emerging market would bear. Not only could they keep interest rates low, but they charged

[17] Author's interview with Leonid Grinfeld, chairman of Zapsibkombank, an early descendant of the USSR Promstroibank, Tyumen, January 1992.

[18] Aleksandr Smirnov, the head of the Federal Treasury, estimated in the spring of 1997 that state funds were distributed among some 170,000 bank accounts. About half of those accounts were in the Central Bank, 6% in Sberbank, and 44% in commercial banks. (RFE/RL Newsline, No. 55, Part I, 18 June 1997)

[19] Denis Cherkassov and Iaroslav Skvortsov, "Upolnomochennye banki – ukazy na vyzhivanie," *Kommersant* (weekly), April 29 1997, by Internet.

exorbitant transaction fees and commissions. Most of their clients, at least initially, could do little about it.[20]

Yet even in this favourable environment not all of the commercial banks managed to make money. On the deposit side, the banks with the best access to low-cost funds tended to be the ones that had been first off the mark in the late 1980s. A Moscow location was a powerful advantage, bringing good connections with the federal and the city government. These advantages reinforced the heavy concentration of Russian banking wealth in the top twenty Moscow banks.

Newer entrants or local banks had to use more costly sources of funds. In order of desirability, these were interest-bearing ruble deposits, hard-currency deposits, or overnight loans obtained through the interbank system. The more the bank had to pay for the money it used, the higher the returns it had to seek, and the greater the risk of losing everything. Consequently, up to the time of the August 1998 crash the smaller Russian banks were always more vulnerable than the larger ones, and as the opportunities for gain dried up after 1995, they were the most severely squeezed. (Ironically, the Moscow banks' privileged access to federal funds turned into a fatal liability in 1998, whereas the smaller banks, in the end, turned out to be less exposed.)

On the loan side, the most important thing was a quick return. The one mistake to avoid was tying up one's money in longer-term loans. Yet many banks failed to follow this rule, or for a variety of reasons were unable to do so. Some made the mistake of investing in construction projects with long payback periods, and this frequently proved fatal. Another common mistake was to build sumptuous corporate headquarters, and to pile on overhead through conspicuous consumption and overstaffing.[21]

Other banks tied up money because they could not help themselves: a bank belonging to a large industrial corporation, for example, might be forced to lend money to cover the parent's payrolls. This was particularly a problem in the early days of the commercial banks, since many of them originated as subsidiaries of state industrial enterprises, and essentially operated as "pocket banks." Over time, the larger commercial banks managed to distance themselves from their initial sponsors and gain better control over their own lending. But pressure to please a large share-holder or a local politician remains a common problem for most middle-sized and small banks.[22]

---

[20] Dmitriev and Travin, op. cit.

[21] This was one reason for the demise of Kredobank, one of the largest Russian banks, in 1996–97.

[22] According to the then-chairman of the Russian Central Bank, Aleksandr Dubinin, most Russian banks remained tied to one of a handful of powerful clients, who were the chief source of their business and their funds. (*Finansovye izvestiia*, June 10 1997, by Internet).

Yet on balance most Russian banks prospered enormously between 1991 and 1995. As a result, both the banks themselves and the entire financial sector became distorted. The banks grew accustomed to a fast-and-loose style that was closer to loan-sharking, currency speculation, and arbitrage than to the more conventional banking skills required in a stable economy. Their reliance on government accounts as a source of cheap funds encouraged a cozy, frequently corrupt relationship with state officials. In short, the private bankers proved to be highly rational entrepreneurs in an irrational environment – but the skills they learned then were the wrong ones in a more normal setting.

The "golden age" of the banks also had consequences for the growth of the Russian financial sector as a whole. Inflation favored the banks, but constrained or distorted the growth of other financial institutions, particularly insurance companies and pension funds. In most Western countries such non-banking institutions are the main source of investment finance. In Russia, by contrast, banks were the only private institutions large enough to serve as investment intermediaries.

With their destruction, it is the future of investment in Russia that is in question.

Giants among pygmies, pygmies among giants

The media liked to portray the Russian banks at their height as all-powerful giants, whose tentacles reached into every government office and every corner of the economy. But myth far outstripped reality. By world standards even the largest Russian banks were small, and their impact on the Russian economy was modest. On August 1, 1998, on the eve of the collapse, the total assets of the approximately 1,600 Russian banks (state and private combined) were generously estimated at $125 billion, of which nearly two-thirds were held by the top 20 banks. In 1997 60% of Russian banks had capital of less than $1 million, and 90% had less than $3 million. Only 124 banks (about 6% of the total number) had capital greater than $5 million.[23]

By world standards, the Russian banks were still pygmies. Ten years after the start of private banking, 12 of the largest Russian banks had broken into the list of the 1000 largest banks in the world, but none of them ranked very high. The two largest, Sberbank (134th place) and Vneshtorgbank (279th place), were still state-owned. It was not until the 346th place that one found the first new "commercial" bank, Oneksimbank.[24]

---

[23] *Finansovye izvestiia*, April 22 1997, p. 5.
[24] *The Banker*, July 1997, quoted in *Finansovye izvestiia*, July 17 1997, by Internet.

Russia's top banks measured against the world's 1,000 largest (end-1997)

World rank	Name of bank	Capital(*) ($millions)	Assets ($millions)	Profits ($millions)
134	Sberbank	2,752	29,764	759
279	Vneshtorgbank	1,023	3,126	97
346	Oneksimbank	826	3,779	72
536	SBS-Agro	466	5,201	56
670	MFK	320	1,299	115
683	Rossiiskii Kredit	314	2,135	60
697	Menatep	305	3,433	41
720	Tokobank	287	1,219	2
761	Inkombank	261	5,102	115
852	Imperial	210	1,110	65
919	Mosbusinessbank	183	1,509	82
993	Promstroibank	155	1,196	26

Note: Capital refers to Tier One Capital.
Source: The Banker (UK), July 1998, p. 196.

Before August 1998 the Russian banks played a minor role in the Russian economy. Their total deposits amounted to about 12% of GDP (compared to, say, 69% in the Czech Republic).[25] They held only a small share of the population's savings: the average Russian household had financial assets equal to only 2.5 months' income, of which less than half was held in banks.[26] The banks played an equally minor role in investment: barely more than 1% of the banks' loans were for more than one year,[27] and lending to the business sector was equal to only 11% of GDP (vs. 82% in the Czech Republic)[28] Mortgages were practically non-existent, and the banks played practically no role in the household construction boom of the 1990s. The banks' role was especially modest in the provinces: only one of Russia's top twenty banks, the St. Petersburg Bank, was based outside of Moscow; and among the country's top 200 banks, Moscow-based banks held 88% of the assets.[29]

[25] Source: International Monetary Fund, reprinted in *The Banker*, July 1998.
[26] Russian-European Center for Economic Policy, *Russian Economic Trends*, No. 1 (1997), pp. 84–89. This estimate is based on a revised methodology, which scales down substantially the official estimates of the Russian household savings rate as calculated by the Russian Goskomstat. Whereas the official statistics estimate household savings at 24% of income for 1996, the Russian-European Center estimates 8.9% is closer to reality. The Center also dismisses as myth the Goskomstat estimate that the population's holdings of hard currency total over $108 billion; $11 billion is a more likely figure.
[27] *Finansovye izvestiia*, April 22 1997, pp. 4 and 5.
[28] International Monetary Fund, reprinted in *The Banker*, July 1998.
[29] *Finansovye izvestiia*, August 14 1997, by Internet.

Nevertheless, where the myth of the all-powerful Russian banks had a basis in fact was in takeovers of industry and the media. The banks invested heavily in the stock of Russian companies, targeting mainly two sectors: the producers of exportable commodities (the main source of profits in the Russian economy over the last decade) and the producers of construction materials and foods (which by 1996–7 began showing a profit in the better-off regions, where the local economies had turned around).

Banks started picking up shares in companies from the very beginning of privatization in 1992, first buying large bundles of privatization vouchers and exchanging them for equity shares. After voucher privatization ended in 1994, the banks continued to build their holdings, acquiring blocks of shares through cash auctions, investment tenders, and purchases on the secondary market. Their equity, as a rule, was cheaply acquired, and until 1996 involved little cash outlay. In 1996–97 growing competition for the more valuable remaining state assets forced the banks to pay more, although still well below the assets' real value.

It is impossible to say just how much of the Russian economy was owned by the banks at the height of their power, or how much they still own today.[30] The "commanding heights" were easy enough to catalog, and it was an impressive portfolio. Cement, steel, nickel, and copper were largely dominated by banks, as well as roughly half the major oil companies, including such giants as Yukos and Sidanko. Aluminum, another profitable export industry, was divided among banks, local entrepreneurs, and foreign investors. Outside these sectors, the pattern was much more difficult to track, because the companies were smaller and more scattered, and because the banks frequently operated through a thicket of subsidiaries.

Only the largest banks had the financial resources and the political connections to take over large companies, let alone whole sectors of industry. Much less is known about the equity holdings of medium-sized banks, especially in the provinces. From anecdotal evidence it appears that banks frequently accepted shares in lieu of repayment of loans. Regional bankers were also typically part of the circle of local notables who sit on boards and own blocks of shares. Thus the stake of banks in enterprises throughout the country was probably substantial. But the

---

[30] Various attempts to survey the extent of ownership by banks produced estimates that were clearly too low. For example, a survey in 1995 by Joseph Blasi and Andrei Shleifer for the Federal Securities Commission showed that the average stake owned in large enterprises by banks and financial-industrial groups was about 5%. (Joseph Blasi and Andrei Shleifer, "Corporate Ownership and Corporate Governance in the Russian Federation," Research Report of the Federal Commission of the Capital Market, Moscow 1996)

medium-sized banks' ownership share in enterprises was usually modest, and rarely amounted to a controlling block. Thus in equity ownership as in every other aspect of Russian banking, there was a widening gulf between the top two dozen giants and all the rest.

The August collapse set off a fresh scramble for industrial assets, as the larger banks were frequently forced to turn over shares in payment for bad debts, or sell them off at bargain prices. Broadly there were three trends. Better-off banks bought shares from worse-off ones. Parent holding groups distanced themselves from their banking subsidiaries, sometime abandoning them as empty shells. And at the regional level local governments and financial-industrial groups attempted to regain control of assets that had previously fallen into the hands of the Moscow-based giants. How far this second redistribution of property will go, and how substantially it will change the distribution of ownership of private industry, remains to be seen.

At their height, the financial-industrial groups founded on the the banking fortunes of the "golden era" appeared to create a mechanism for channeling capital productively into longer-range investment, once economic and fiscal conditions were right. The large banks were the major exception to the prevailing pattern of "insider privatization." As "outside" investors, they were the main potential force for corporate takeovers and restructuring. But very little restructuring actually took place, even in 1997 and early 1998, after inflation had temporarily subsided and the ruble had stabilized. The main reason is that by that time the banks were in serious trouble, as we shall see now.

1995–1996: the game changes

Inflation began to drop in late 1993, as the government began applying an increasingly strict tight-money policy. By the end of 1996 annual inflation rates had subsided to the 20% range and continued to decline steadily through mid-1998.[31] In parallel with the easing of inflation, the ruble stabilized. Macroeconomic stabilization, as it gradually took hold, changed dramatically the environment in which the private banks operated.

The government's main tool in the fight against inflation was strict controls over the rate of growth of the money supply and credit. The Russian Central Bank clamped down hard on credits granted to the government or the banks. Instead of financing its deficits by borrowing from the Central Bank, the government began selling debt on the open market, a non-inflationary device.[32] As we shall see in chapter 9, this policy ulti-

[31] *Russian Economic Trends*, No. 1 (1997), pp. 40–47.
[32] For background see Brigitte Granville, *The Success of Russian Economic Reforms* (London: Royal Institute of International Affairs, 1995)

mately paved the way to the collapse of 1998, since it led to a rapid build-up of short-term debt. But the fault was not with the policy *per se*, but with the government's chronic inability to control its spending and balance its budget.

Whether wrestling inflation down to single digits was the right policy for the Russian government at this stage is a controversial question. But there is no doubt about its impact on the private banks: it eliminated their chief source of profits. As inflation began to drop and the ruble stabilized (in fact actually appreciated in real terms), converting ruble deposits into dollars and using them to finance exports became risky. Banks could no longer automatically assume that exports would make money and that exporters would repay their loans, or that the ruble would necessarily depreciate. Thus the banks could no longer count on repaying their depositors in depreciated rubles. The banks were stuck in a middle ground that was no longer profitable. As early as 1996, according to Aleksandr Khandruev, first deputy chairman of the Russian Central Bank, nearly half of the loans on the books of the commercial banks were overdue,[33] and the share continued to mount over the next two years.

The government's tight money policy had other effects. Industrial enterprises reacted by conducting more of their operations on a barter basis, and these non-money transactions bypassed the larger banks (although after a time local banks developed a profitable business undewriting local networks of wechsels, or promissory notes).[34] As the ruble stabilized, Russians put less of their money into foreign currency, and consequently the exchange business also shrank. As interest rates dropped and banks attempted to pass on the lower rates to their depositors, depositors became choosy and began shopping around. Interest rates on loans dropped faster than interest rates on deposits: over 1995–96, the "spread" between the two (which is one major source of the banks' profits) dropped by over 140 points.[35] In these and other ways, the banks' profits came under severe pressure. This was new territory for the Russian bankers, and it found most of them unprepared.

The "stabilization shock" of 1995–96 was widely expected to bring a tidal wave of bank failures. But the great banking shakeout that nearly every expert predicted did not happen for another two years. Why? The answer varied with the type of bank. Local banks in the provinces served local governments and managed chains of IOUs of local enterprises.

---

[33] Cited in *Kapital*, July 10–16, 1996, pp. 1–2.

[34] David Woodruff, *Money Unmade* (Ithaca, N.Y.: Cornell University Press, 1999), Chapters 4 and 5.

[35] At least, this was the case for ruble loans and deposits; dollar loans and deposits were less affected. See "Cherez prizmu informatsionnoi otkrytosti," *Ekonomika I zhizn'*, No. 25 (June 1997), pp. 4–5, based on a survey by the Central Mathematical Economics Institute (TsEMI) of the Russian Academy of Sciences.

Medium-sized banks based in big cities switched from financing exports to financing imports. But for the largest banks the biggest source of profitable new business was the government itself.

The government's poisoned chalice: GKOs and OFZs

Salvation for the larger banks came almost by accident in 1995–96, as a by-product of the government's stabilization policy. Searching for a non-inflationary way to finance its deficits, the Russian government turned to the private capital market and began selling debt, mostly in the form of three-month and six-month treasury notes, called GKOs and OFZs.[36] These paid very high interest rates, because of the political uncertainties connected with the elections of December 1995 and June 1996, yet the Ministry of Finance redeemed them like clockwork, never once defaulting.[37] By 1995–96 government debt offered the most attractive combination of high return and low risk available in Russia, and banks bought GKOs with enthusiasm.

Political uncertainty also boosted interest rates on ruble loans generally, counteracting the effects of lower inflation. Consequently, at least until President Yeltsin was re-elected in mid-1996 and political conditions stabilized, the banks continued to enjoy a wide spread between the low rates they paid for their ruble funds and the high rates at which they could lend them. The downside was that as borrowers paid higher rates, they also tended to default more often. Consequently, during this period the banks' potential profits remained high, but their risks also went up.

Thanks to these developments, the large banks were partially shielded from "stabilization shock" until mid-1996. Once again the big Moscow banks had an advantage over the smaller provincial ones. They had easier access to the GKO auctions. (Indeed, Moscow banks with networks of branches in the provinces, especially Sberbank, were able to siphon funds toward the GKO market in Moscow, while the local banks could not.) The Moscow banks could get cheaper funds, because they relied less on time deposits from physical persons and more on interest-free transaction accounts from state bodies. On the whole, then, the Moscow banks emerged in better shape from the stabilization shock of 1995–96 than their colleagues in the provinces.

[36] GKO (*Gosudarstvennye kratkosrochnye obligatsii*, or Short-Term State Treasury Notes) were issued in 3-month and 6-month maturities, while OFZ (*Obligatsii federal'nogo zaima*, or Federal Bonds) came in longer maturities.

[37] Indeed the Ministry of Finance's record through the spring of 1996 was flawless. As the IMF's deputy managing director, Stanley Fischer, observed, "In 1995 and through April 1996 the Ministry of Finance met all its targets. Russia during this period was literally the best client the IMF had ever had." (Address to the U.S.-Russia Business Council, December 11 1998)

But these were short-term adjustments, not fundamental adaptations. Russian banks still lent very short money. A survey of the Moscow banks at the beginning of 1997 showed that out of their total loan portfolio of some $20 billion, only 1.2% of loans were for more than one year. Most Russian bank loans still went to finance trade, transportation, to pay wages, or to buy government securities. Almost none financed investment projects in industry.[38] This reflected a combination of things: the banks' lack of experience in lending longer money, the difficulty of telling a good risk from a bad one, the problems in collecting bad loans. But above all, the banks' reluctance to lend long reflected their dependence on unstable ruble deposits and their mistrust of the government's monetary policies.

Meanwhile, after the 1996 elections the government toughened its stabilization policy even more. Inflation continued to decline, and the Central Bank steadily lowered the interest rates on government debt. Returns on GKOs dropped from annualized rates of nearly 200% in the spring of 1996 to below 20% a year later.[39] With politics more stable, spreads between interest rates on ruble loans and ruble deposits continued to drop. Thus the pressure on the banks' remaining sources of profits continued to mount.

As a result, the banks' financial shape actually worsened even as the political and economic outlook improved. By 1997 half of the banks in Moscow were considered to be "problem banks," with heavy portfolios of nonperforming loans.[40] The banks in the provinces were in even worse shape.[41] For one-fifth of Russian banks, representing 10% of all deposits, overdue loans were greater than the banks' own capital.[42] Despite the Russian Central Banks' growing reserve requirements (in themselves a source of pressure on the banks' liquidity), the volume of problem loans in the banking system as a whole exceeded the reserves set aside to cover them.[43] Indeed, these data understate the true picture, since loose reporting requirements enabled the banks to carry nonperforming loans longer than their Western counterparts, thus masking their vanishing profitability.[44]

---

[38] *Finansovye izvestiia*, April 22 1997, pp. 4 and 5.
[39] *Russian Economic Trends*, monthly updates by Internet.
[40] Vladimir Efremov, head of public relations for the Moscow Directorate of the Russian Central Bank, *Finansovye izvestiia*, April 22 1997, p. 4.
[41] "Cherez prizmu . . ." op. cit.
[42] Interview with Sergei Panov, head of the RCB's workout department, *Finansovye izvestiia*, June 10 1997, by Internet.
[43] Sergei Egorov, president of the Association of Russian Banks, *Finansovye izvestiia*, April 22 1997, p. 3.
[44] For a bleak assessment of the loan structure of the Russian banks on the eve of the August crash, see Michael S. Bernstam and Alvin Rabushka, *Fixing Russia's Banks: a Proposal for Growth* (Stanford, California: Hoover Institutiona Press, 1998).

Thus by the summer of 1997, the Russian bank's were already severely weakened. When the "Asian flu" hit Russia, it found a ready victim.

Fall 1997: the Russian banking crisis begins

Starting in the fall of 1997 the worldwide decline of commodities prices, especially oil, cut into the revenues of Russian exporters, forcing them to delay repayment of trade credits to the banks. Meanwhile, the market reformers, who had returned to influence that spring, began restricting the banks' access to low-cost funds from government agencies, forcing the banks to turn for funds to the more expensive and unstable interbank loan market. Pumping up the banks' profits, however, was the government's ever-growing volume of sales of short-term debt. As the Asian economic crisis worsened and international lenders retreated to safer markets, the Russian government was forced to offer ever-higher interest rates on three-month and six-month money. In effect, the larger Russian banks were back where they had been two years before – making money by financing the government's deficits – but in a far riskier environment.

The failure of Tokobank in the spring of 1998 was the first tremor of the coming earthquake. Tokobank, then Russia's sixth largest private bank, had been one of the most respected. Rumors about its financial health began circulating in late 1997, and by February 1998 Russian banks began refusing to lend to Tokobank through the interbank market. By May the Russian Central Bank confirmed the worst when it appointed a temporary receiver and began trying to put together a consortium to take over the bank.[45] As the weeks went by, the picture grew worse. Inspectors combing through Tokobanks's books discovered a tangle of insider loans, fictive collaterals, and suspicious transfers of funds to offshore accounts. One loan was secured by bulldozers, which turned out to be parked in a remote wilderness in East Siberia, and had already been committed as collateral in another loan.[46] By July the known total of Tokobank's bad loans and trading losses topped half a billion dollars. The Russian Central Bank invited one major Russian bank after another to take over Tokobank, but after sniffing the mess they all refused.[47] Shortly before the August crash, the Central Bank lifted Tokobank's license.

In retrospect, the failure of Tokobank signaled that the banking crisis was entering its acute stage. The government's failure to rescue one of the country's largest banks caused the interbank loan market, a major source

---

[45] *Ekspert*, No. 18 (May 18 1998), pp. 36–37.
[46] *Ekspert*, No. 46 (December 7 1998), pp. 30–32.
[47] *Ekspert*, No. 26 (July 13 1998), by Internet. See also *Segodnia*, July 16 1998; *Russkii telegraf*, July 14 1998;

of overnight credit for many banks, to dry up. From that point on, the banks were highly vulnerable to any shock. It was not long in coming. The government's finances had deteriorated steadily throughout the spring and early summer. Lower export earnings, declining tax receipts, a rapidly growing debt service burden, and rising interest rates put growing pressure on the ruble, forcing the government to defend the currency with a rapidly-shrinking supply of dollars. By May and June 1998, investors began betting against the ruble, and devaluation began to seem all but certain. Even a last-minute rescue package in July by the International Monetary Fund could not stem the tide.

But when the blow finally came on August 17, it was devastating, because it combined a devaluation far larger than even the most pessimistic had predicted with the bankers' worst nightmare-a moratorium on debt repayments that abruptly rendered the banks' holdings of government paper worthless. Government debt accounted for 11–12% of their total assets[48], but it was concentrated in the top twenty where the share of GKOs and OFZs was 20% and more. Suddenly the largest banks' prime asset and the main source of their revenues had vanished.

For most banks the devaluation proved more damaging than the debt moratorium, because few banks below the top twenty had large holdings of government debt. But hard currency was a different matter. On the eve of the August crash, hard-currency loans by foreign banks represented nearly 13% of the liabilities of the Russian banks; when the ruble lost two-thirds of its value overnight, the burden of servicing these loans became crushing.[49] The icing on the cake was some 88 billion rubles (over $14.4 billion at the pre-devaluation exchange rate) in forward contracts committed by Russian banks to Western investors, amounting to 86% of the total capital of all the Russian commercial banks combined-but concentrated, once again, in the top twenty banks.[50]

A failure of state regulation

The August collapse was not only a banking failure, it was a failure of state regulation. Yet ironically, over the course of the decade the Russian Central Bank had done a creditable job of adapting to the new reality of a largely private banking sector and developing the necessary regulatory functions. Indeed, there had arguably been more progress in developing state regulation in the banking sphere than in any other sector, with the

---

[48] Russian Central Bank, "Sovremennoe sostoianie bankovskoi sistemy Rossii," by Internet (http://www.cbr.ru/system/overview.html), December 1998. This number does not include the Russian Sberbank, which was the largest single holder of government debt.
[49] "Sovremennoe sostoianie," op. cit.   [50] "Sovremennoe sostoianie," op. cit.

possible exception of the securities markets. Unlike the securities market, in which the private sector, with abundant help from foreign advisers and the Russian Securities Commission, largely regulated itself, in the banking sector the chief driving force was the Russian Central Bank.

Yet the Central Bank failed to deal with the deeper diseases of the banking system. The major question in the years ahead is whether it will be able to take advantage of the banking crisis to promote constructive reforms and lay the basis for a sounder "second generation" of private banks. At this writing, the initial returns are not encouraging.

But first, some history. Nowhere was the collapse of the state more extreme in the late 1980s and early 1990s than in the banking sector. In the first two or three years after the break-up of the USSR State Bank's monopoly over the banking system and the rise of the commercial banks, the core functions of central banking – processing payments, managing exchange rates, enforcing banking laws, regulating the money supply and interest rates – virtually disintegrated. Today's Russian Central Bank, which succeeded the USSR State Bank in 1990–91, was rebuilt on the ruins of the Soviet system.

To the casual observer the Russian Central Bank looks much like its predecessor. Inside the massive buildings of its eighty-four branches throughout Russia, the Central Bank's 45,000 employees carry on the Soviet traditions of centralization, bureaucracy, and secrecy. Yet like every other post-Soviet institution, the Soviet Central Bank has had to develop new roles in a changed world.[51]

When it first emerged from the ruins of the USSR Gosbank, the Russian Central Bank inherited two contradictory functions: on the one hand, to maintain a sound financial system; on the other, to suppport production, where necessary by providing credits to the government and to industry. In the early years the credit role clearly dominated. Under its first two chairmen, Georgii Matiukhin and Viktor Gerashchenko, the Central Bank channeled credit to enterprises at increasingly negative interest rates – meaning well below inflation, tantamount to subsidies – to keep them open and operating.

Reinforcing this basic policy was the fact that until 1993 the chairman of the Central Bank answered to the parliament. During this period the executive and legislative branches were locked in bitter battle, and competed with one another in using state credits to bid for local support. Gerashchenko, as an experienced Soviet official, did what was expected of him and doled out the money. This stance made Gerashchenko hugely

---

[51] For a portrait of the Russian Central Bank through early 1996, see Juliet Ellen Johnson, "Banking in Russia: Shadows of the Past," *Problems of Post-Communism*, May–June 1996, pp. 49–59.

unpopular with Russian reformers and their allies in the West. "Viktor Gerashchenko may be the worst central-bank governor of any major country in history," Harvard economist Jeffrey Sachs once said of him.[52] In actual fact, Gerashchenko was an experienced international banker; but his view of the function of a central bank – like that of most other Russian leaders at the time – was that of the Soviet era.[53]

In October 1993 the conflict between the executive branch and the parliament was resolved by tankfire, and the Russian government embarked on a tight-money policy that it pursued for the next five years. Gerashchenko, perhaps not entirely fairly,[54] had become the symbol of loose money and was removed in the fall of 1994. His successors, Tatyana Paramonova and Sergei Dubinin, were strong supporters of low inflation and a stable currency. The conflict between the Central Bank's two competing roles – credit-giver vs. regulator – was resolved decisively in favour of the latter.

The Central Bank also rid itself of other legacies of the Soviet past. By 1994 it had severed the monetary connections between Russia and the other former Soviet republics and created an independent Russian ruble. It established a foreign-currency auction system, making the ruble internally convertible. Through its sales of currency, the Central Bank kept the ruble within an exchange-rate corridor that helped to maintain stability after 1996. And by requiring the banks to submit regular accounts and other reports, the Central Bank began nudging the Russian banking system toward international reporting and accounting practices.[55]

The Central Bank played the key role in the government's stabilization policy, by sharply curtailing credits, especially to the Russian govern-

---

[52] Quoted in *The Economist*, October 16 1993, p. 90.

[53] Born in 1937, Viktor Vladimirovich Gerashchenko graduated from the Moscow Finance Institute in 1960. He then rose through the ranks of the USSR Foreign Trade Bank (VEB). From 1965 to 1967 he was a director of the Moscow Narodny Bank in London. From 1967 to 1971 he directed the Lebanese branch of the VEB, and from 1974 to 1975 its Singapore branch. From 1977 to 1981 he was chairman of the board of the Ost-West Handelsbank in Frankfurt am-Main. In 1983 Gerashchenko was appointed deputy chairman of the USSR VEB, and in 1985 he became first deputy chairman. In 1990 he was named chairman of the management (*predsedatel' pravleniia*) of USSR Gosbank. (Source: *Kommersant*, July 29 1992, and *Izvestiia*, October 29 1994)

[54] David Woodruff, in his valuable book, *Money Unmade*, provides a detailed picture of the reasons for this policy and the mechanisms through which it operated, and modifies the picture of Viktor Gerashchenko as a "loose-money" man previously drawn by Western scholars.

[55] But not without a fight. The Russian Central Bank has gradually been stiffening penalties for banks that do not submit reports on time (*Kommersant-Daily*, August 1 1997, by Internet), and has been extending the reporting rules to include non-banks that conduct bank-like operations (Ivan Zhagel', "Bank Rossii pytaetsia usilit' kontrol' za finansovymi strukturami," *Finansovye izvestiia*, June 3 1997, by Internet) All of these moves have been surrounded by objections from the commercial banks.

ment, and thus slowing the emission of money.[56] Instead, after 1993 the government financed most of its deficits (that is, what IMF and other foreign loans did not cover) through the sale of short-term treasury bills. These changes actually began under Gerashchenko, but most of the spadework was done by reform-minded deputies, such as Dmitri Tulin, then RCB deputy chairman, with the assistance of Western advisers. The government's reliance on short-term debt came back to haunt it five years later, as debt-service costs soared to one-third of the government's revenues, but at the time the shift to treasury bills was hailed as a positive innovation. Dmitri Tulin compared it to the Soviet Union's "first space shot,"[57] and it was indeed a revolutionary step forward in bringing order to Russia's finances by halting the long-standing practice of borrowing from the Central Bank to finance the state's deficits.

But the most daunting task facing the Central Bank was to bring order to the commercial banking system. From 1993 it steadily raised reserve requirements (especially on foreign-currency accounts, to "dedollarize" the economy) and made it more difficult to obtain banking licenses. It stiffened the limits on the level of savings deposits banks were allowed to carry relative to their capital, curtailed the volume of letters of credit (*vekselia*) that could be issued by any one bank, and raised the minimum capital banks were required to hold.[58]

The Central Bank's most effective weapon was removing licenses. From 1994 on the RCB lifted several hundred banking licenses every year, gradually winnowing out the weakest banks, while sharply limiting the creation of new ones. By August 1998 the number of authorized commercial banks had dropped from a peak of 2,500 to around 1,550.[59] But most of the banks that lost their licenses were small ones, many of them already inactive. When large banks got into trouble, the Russian Central Bank tried to restore them to health by appointing a temporary administrator to straighten out their affairs. On the other hand, the RCB watched without apparent regret the passing of smaller, fly-by-night commercial banks, such as Chara, "LLD-Bank," "Favorit," "Kapital," and "Gornyi Altai," which became household names – as they went under. To critics, the Central Bank's policy amounted to "selection of the largest,"[60] which made sense, perhaps, from the standpoint of efficiency, but gave the

---

[56] Granville, *The Success of...*, op. cit.   [57] *Wall Street Journal*, September 23 1993.

[58] The basic document in RCB's campaign to extend regulation and reduce banking risks is the so-called "Instruktsiia No. 1," which sets a wide range of basic requirements for the banking system. (*Finansovye izvestiia*, April 22 1997, p. 6.)

[59] Russian Federation, Russian Central Bank, *"Programma neotlozhnykh mer..."* Current information on the number of banks in Russia can be obtained from the Russian Central Bank's website, at http://www.cbr.ru.

[60] *Finansovye izvestiia*, May 8 1997, by Internet.

impression the RCB unduly favoured the Moscow-based fraternity of former Soviet bankers.[61]

In short, the Central Bank made many of the right moves, but its efforts proved wholly inadequate. The key weakness, as so often in Russia in the Nineties, was implementation. A critical banking function is processing settlements, that is, interbank transactions in which banks reconcile claims against one another. Matters improved compared to the dark days of 1992, when mountains of transfer slips piled up in the Central Bank's basement. But the Central Bank failed to create a fast and efficient nationwide system, and by 1998 it still took weeks for claims to clear. Instead, individual commercial banks, such as SBS-Agro, built private payments networks that competed with the Central Bank.[62] This is why the collapse of the larger private banks in August 1998 caused payments to freeze all across the country, including tax remittances, which were processed through the private banks.

The Central Bank also failed to create a deposit insurance system to protect small savers. The Bank feared – correctly, as it turned out – that given the fragile condition of the system, a deposit insurance fund would be overwhelmed by a massive bank failure.[63] Indeed, a deposit insurance program was seen as an invitation to fraud, since there was little to prevent unscrupulous bank directors from lending out their banks' capital to friends and cronies, knowing in advance the loans would never be repaid.[64] All these were real problems. Yet the Central Bank essentially washed its hands of the insurance issue, arguing that it was the commercial banks' responsibility to band together to create a private insurance system. Thus the problem was left unattended.[65]

Even the Central Bank's strongest single weapon – the power to lift licenses – was blunted by problems with implementation. The RCB discovered that it was not enough to remove a bank's license to put it out of business. First a "liquidation commission" had to review the bank's operations and balances. But the Russian Central Bank did not have the resources to appoint commissions in more than about one-third of the cases in which it removed licenses, and even then the review process dragged on for months. This gave a defunct bank's officers an easy opportunity to conceal assets from creditors. The next step, to declare a bank

[61] Aleksandr Bratko, "Regiony i denezhnye potoki," *Nezavisimaia gazeta*, August 7 1997, by Internet.   [62] *Finansovye izvestiia*, April 22 1997, p. 4.

[63] Dubinin interview in *Finansovye izvestiia*, June 10 1997, by Internet.   [64] Ibid.

[65] For the sake of perspective, it is worth noting that few of the banking systems involved in major crises and subsequent restructuring programs elsewhere in the world had deposit insurance systems. In that respect Russia was hardly different. (See William E. Alexander, et al., *Systemic Bank Restructuring and Macreonomic Policy* (Washington, D.C.: International Monetary Fund, 1997).)

formally bankrupt and have it removed from the official registry of "juridical persons," took even longer. According to the Central Bank, out of the
800-odd banks whose licenses had been lifted as of the beginning of
1998, only 52 had actually been "de-registered" as legal entities.[66] In
other words, even before the August crisis the banking landscape was lit-
tered with "dead souls," with obvious potential for fraud.

But in the end the Bank's greatest failing was that it could not cope with
the two problems that proved fatal for the banking system: the government's insatiable need for credit to meet its mounting deficits, and the
excessively cozy relations of the largest commercial banks with powerful
politicians. The Central Bank wrote rules for the banking sector, but
could not prevent the largest banks from ignoring them. They were
simply too well connected for the Central Bank to trifle with.

This, then, was the legacy of the first decade of private banking in
Russia: a profusion of weak banks, the larger ones excessively dependent
on lending to an insolvent state, the smaller ones vulnerable to default by
private borrowers engaged in foreign trade, the whole loosely regulated by
a weak Central Bank. It was, as one Russian banker put it, a system built
on "chicken legs."

Yet the Russian Central Bank made impressive progress between 1991
and 1998 in adapting to its new roles of regulator of a largely private
banking sector and manager of the money supply. Its ultimate test will be
its success or failure in overseeing the restructuring of the Russian banks
after the crash.

Picking up the pieces: responses to the collapse

Following the August collapse three main responses developed. In the
initial weeks, the Russian Central Bank sought to restore a minimum of
activity to enable the country to function. Then, over the following two
months, it developed a plan for restructuring the banking system. But
throughout this period, there was a parallel response from the private
banks themselves: many bankers, shareholders, and large customers
feverishly stripped the remaining assets from the insolvent banks.
Ironically, the Central Bank's efforts to restore liquidity accelerated the
asset-stripping. As the Bank pumped new money in, the unscrupulous
pumped it right back out again.

Fortunately, that was not the only response of the private sector. Many

[66] Panov interview in *Finansovye izvestiia*, June 10 1997, by Internet. For data as of early
1998, see *Ekspert*, No. 21 (March 23 1998), p. 21. It is widely expected that the process of
liquidating fantom banks will accelerate thanks to a new bankruptcy law which went into
effect in March 1998.

smaller banks survived the crash in viable condition and set to work to rebuild a "second generation" banking system. Which response will prevail? It will probably be several more years before the answer is clear.

Phase One: Emergency measures

The August crash caught tens of billions of rubles in transit inside the banking system – tax and pension payments, settlements between banks and companies, and other funds processed by the private banks. In September and October 1998 the Russian Central Bank ran a series of emergency meetings of banks throughout the country to disentangle who owed what to whom. These meetings enabled banks to compare liabilities and to offset mutual debts. In this way the Central Bank quickly unblocked some 30 of the 40 billion rubles stuck in the banking pipeline, freeing 20 billion rubles in tax and pension payments. The process worked best at the regional level, where most of the banks were still more or less sound. But at the same time the *rasshivka* ("disentangling") revealed the enormous net debts of the large Moscow banks.[67]

The Central Bank also helped to restore the payments system by lowering reserve requirements and allowing the banks under some circumstances to use their frozen GKOs as collateral for further emergency loans. In effect, such measures amounted to pumping liquidity into the banking system, swelling the money supply. In addition, the Bank granted direct stabilization credits to a handful of favored banks, notably SBS-Agro and Most-Bank, which it defined as essential to the functioning of the country's financial system. In all, according to RCB chairman Viktor Gerashchenko, in the first three months following the crash the Central Bank injected 55 billion rubles into the banking system (then equivalent to over $3 billion at post-crash exchange rates).[68]

Thanks to these measures, by November the banking system had returned to a semblance of normality. A limited number of the large banks banks resumed servicing their depositors and (from time to time) stocking their ATM machines with rubles, and even began advertising for new depositors. Smaller banks did a booming business picking up corporate accounts from companies shopping around for new banks. Millions

---

[67] Russian Federation, Russian Central Bank, "*Programma neotlozhnykh mer…*,"

[68] *Russian Economic Trends*, Special Report, "Resolving the Banking Crisis" (November 1998), by Internet (http://www.hhs.se/site/ret/ret.htm). More than half of this total had been allocated in the immediate wake of the August crisis by Gerashchenko's predecessor Sergei Dubinin. In the two following months, according to Viktor Gerashchenko, a further 13 billion was injected in the form of lowered reserve requirements, and 14 billion in direct stabilization credits to a selected handful of banks. (*Kommersant Daily*, November 3 1998, by Internet)

of smaller depositors switched their ruble accounts from the private banks to Sberbank, the state-owned savings bank, and were able to recover at least a portion of their savings.

But in reality the bulk of the hard work still lay ahead. The largest banks had no capital to cover their bad debts. Lending had slowed to a trickle, while interbank credit was practically nonexistent. Small savers had retreated (where they could) to the safety of their mattresses, and the flow of foreign capital had ceased for all but the most secure export-backed loans.[69] Only a massive restructuring could bring the banking system to new life.

Phase Two: Restructuring

Banking crises are not uncommon around the world. Over the past twenty years some 30 countries, ranging from Argentina to Sweden, have had to restructure their banking systems following a major crisis. Both the diseases and the cures are by now reasonably well understood, and there are a clear guides to what works and what does not. Broadly, the chances of success are high when action is comprehensive and prompt (with most of the restructuring completed within one year); when the worst banks are closed down quickly; when those responsible for losses are made to bear them; and when a specialized independent agency, not the central bank, is in charge.[70] How will the Russian restructuring measure up?

Within two months after the August crash the Russian Central Bank had worked out a plan for restructuring the banks that followed most of the usual prescriptions.[71] The core of the plan was to separate the wounded from the dead and to nurse the viable back to health, by rein-jecting them with capital, reshaping their ownership, sanitizing their balance sheets, and cleaning up their operations. So far, so good.

The next step was to determine which banks needed help and which could survive on their own. The preliminary verdict confirmed the picture of widespread devastation: Only some 600 banks, representing 15% of total private assets, were rated stable. At the other extreme, 700 banks, with about 35% of assets, were in critical condition and would probably not survive. The most important group lay in-between: some

[69] "Luchshe men'she da luchshe: obzor kreditnogo i depositnogo rynka," Analiticheskoe obozrenie (korporativnye finansy), Agenstvo ekonomicheskoi informatsii Praim-TASS (Moscow, December 15 1998), by Internet. This source provides a good overview of the state of the banking system at the end of 1998.

[70] William E. Alexander, et al., Systemic Bank Restructuring and Macreonomic Policy, op. cit. The most successful recent illustrations of good practice in bank restructuring have been the Philippines, Poland, Spain, and Sweden.

[71] Russian Federation, Russian Central Bank, Programma neotlozhnykh mer . . . op. cit.

200 banks, with about half of total assets, might still be saved by a systematic restructuring program.[72] The viability of this middle group was hard to assess precisely, however, because it included most of the large banks, which resisted revealing their full balance sheets and the details of their loans.

After the initial triage came the creation in December 1998 of an independent agency, called ARKO (or "Agency for Restructuring Credit Organizations"), to manage the restructuring. Such a body, theoretically free from political and insider influence, is the key to the whole process. ARKO is intended to take over the shares, assets, and management of the largest bankrupt banks, and perform the hard work of collecting or writing off bad loans, attracting new capital, cutting costs, and replacing managers. Unfortunately, at this writing (spring 1999), ARKO has not yet begun to operate. Its success or failure will depend on two things that are not yet known: whether it will have the autonomy to make the tough decisions; and whether it will have enough funds to recapitalize the banking system.[73]

Asset-stripping vs. reorganization

Even before the August crash, some of the bankers and their backers had begun stripping assets. Old loans stopped being serviced or repaid; unscrupulous bank officers extended new "midnight loans" to their senior shareholders or to dummy companies they set up themselves. Hard currency was transferred to offshore accounts. After the crash, a substantial share (it is impossible to be more precise) of the money initially injected by the Central Bank was converted into dollars and vanished from the banks. Some of it went abroad, but probably most of it was simply transferred to the banks' founders and senior shareholders. In a few cases, the banks were simply gutted and allowed to fail.[74] But most of the larger banks were left standing as empty shells.

At the level of the smaller banks, particularly in the provinces, the picture in the months after the crash was mixed. The local branches of the big Moscow banks frequently went under (ironically, many of them were

---

[72] *Rossiiskaia gazeta*, December 3 1998, by Internet.

[73] Gleb Baranov, «Milost' k padshim,» *Kommersant-Den'gi*, December 9 1998, by Internet; Irina Yasina, "Russia's Default Left Banks in Crippled State of Survival," *Moscow Times*, February 23 1999; Jeanne Whalen, "Central Banks Loans Missing Their Target," *Moscow Times*, February 13 1999; see also *Kommersant-Daily*, January 26 1999, p. 7; Segodnia, February 19, 1999, p. 4.

[74] The two major examples are Imperial and Inkombank, previously the ninth and tenth largest banks respectively. For a detailed account of the end of Imperial, which points an accusing finger at its principal shareholder, see Nikolai Nikolaev, ". . . I razgovarival s nimi, vspominaia ikh imena," *Neft' i Kapital*, No. 10 (1998), pp. 21–23.

previously independent banks that had only recently been absorbed by the Moscow giants). In contrast, independent banks enjoyed a temporary burst of new business, as companies transferred their accounts to them.[75] However, few local banks were actually healthy, and in some provinces the local governments began talking of consolidating the largest local banks into pools under local government control. This was a worrisome prospect from the standpoint of the Central Bank, since it could lead to a regionalization of the financial system and a further disintegration of the monetary system into local fiefdoms.[76] One of the unanswered questions about the implementation of the Central Bank's restructuring plan, therefore, is how much priority it will give to recapitalizing the stronger regional banks.

The future of the banking system

August 1998 brought to an abrupt end a ten-year chapter that seemed drawn from a picaresque novel. Starting from nothing in 1988, the Russian commercial banks constructed towering pyramids of wealth, based largely on asset-stripping, speculation, and government debt. By the end of the decade, they were brought down again, ironically by the weakening of some of the very forces that had built them up. It was a rollicking tale, filled with swashbuckling entrepreneurs, brass and arrogance, and an ambiguous moral ending.

We shall not see its like again. The extraordinary opportunities for enrichment that existed in the late 1980s and early 1990s are no longer present. There are no longer vast fortunes to be made from arbitrage between a dying Soviet system and the world economy. There will be no more mass privatization, and therefore no more industrial properties to be picked up for a song. Inflation and a weak ruble, though they are likely to be once again chronic features of the scene in coming years, will no longer be as profitable for banks as they were in 1991–95, because large depositors (chiefly corporations and state agencies) have become smarter and choosier, and they will demand higher interest rates and indexation. International lenders, badly burned by the Russian defaults on public debt and private forward contracts, will not return soon in large numbers.

These differences imply that the next generation of Russian banks will not be as rich or as powerful as those of the last decade. Even the survivors of the larger first-generation banks will likely be smaller and less free-

---

[75] "Regional'nye banki: kazhdyi vyzhivaet kak mozhet," *Vremia*, November 30 1998, by Internet.

[76] Petr Rushailo, «TsB raionnogo masshtaba,» *Ekspert*, No. 42 (November 3 1998), pp. 26–27.

wheeling than they were before. But just what the second generation will look like turns on two questions: How will they make money? What will be their relationship to industry and government?

If the great opportunities for speculative enrichment are gone, then the banks could earn their money through more conventional banking. That means attracting more stable long-term deposits and making longer-term loans. But that will not be any easier in the coming decade than it was in the last. The Russian banks face several fundamental obstacles:

On the funds side, there are two broad sources of cheaper and more stable money: Russian small savers and foreign capital markets.

The commercial banks initially made no effort to attract household savings. Only in the second half of the 1990s did some of them begin to reach out to small savers. But they never made much of a dent in the near-monopoly position of the giant Sberbank.[77] Compared to Sberbank's 19 trillion rubles[78] in individual deposits in 1997, the next two largest holders of household accounts, Inkombank and SBS-Agro (formerly Stolichnyi), held only 0.56 and 0.23 trillion respectively.[79] But the few small savers who took a chance on the commercial banks were badly burned in August 1998, and it will be a long time before they will return in any numbers.

The other potential source of funds is the international capital market. In 1995–98 the Russian banks had learned how to tap international sources, either directly through syndicated loans and Eurobonds, or indirectly as intermediaries for Western loans to Russian corporate borrowers. Many Russian bankers had begun to see such "international intermediation" as their principal future source of growth, and strove to develop higher levels of skill and sophistication in international operations.[80] But that avenue has been largely closed off, at least for the foreseeable future, by the August collapse and its aftermath. International capital will still be available to the most reliable borrowers – chiefly the commodity exporters-but it will be neither abundant nor cheap.

Consequently, the one remaining source of funds for the banks will be the government, both at the provincial and federal levels. Commercial banks will continue to serve as a repositories and transfer agents for government receipts such as taxes and customs duties, and as lenders of last resort. But this will expose the banks to the same temptations as in the past.

---

[77] *Finansovye izvestiia,* August 14 1997, by Internet.
[78] In January 1998 the Russian government "redenominated" the ruble by lopping off the last three zeroes. Here and elsewhere, ruble amounts prior to January 1998 are given in "old rubles."
[79] *Russian Economic Trends,* No. 1 (1997), p. 112.
[80] For a thoughtful analysis, see Lev Makarevich, "Konkurentosposobnost rossiiskikh bankov budet prirastat' proizvodstvom," *Finansovye izvestiia,* April 22 1997, p. 7.

On the loans side, the two main problems are valuation and risk: the banks must figure out which applicants to lend to and how to recover if they default. The obstacles are many: Legal mechanisms for recovering bad loans or forcing delinquent borrowers into bankruptcy will remain weak for the foreseeable future. Government guarantees will be unreliable so long as the government itself has so few resources. The mafia exacts a high price for its enforcement services, and in any case is too blunt an instrument. What is left?

The formula that is likely to re-emerge as the dominant one is "pocket banking," that is, banks lending primarily to companies or groups that own them. This was the way many commercial banks began at the end of the 1980s. As the banks grew rich in the 1990s, they frequently gained independence from their corporate founders and in some cases even became the dominant partner. But August 1998 shifted the balance of power back to the holding groups.[81] In the coming generation the banks are more likely to be the servants of the big industrial groups than their masters, and consequently even less able than in the past to control the quality of their loans. The same will be true of loans to governments, which will keep the banks on a shorter leash than in the 1990s.

In sum, the second generation of Russian commercial banks will find it difficult to obtain cheap long-term funds and to place them independently in safe long-term investments. Consequently, only a handful of niche players will be able to evolve toward conventional Western-style banking. The rest will fall into three broad groups. The first will be the "pocket banks" controlled by industrial groups. The second will be the more-or-less restructured descendants of the larger banks, operating under the supervision of the Central Bank. The third will be consortia of regional banks subordinated to local governments.

A successful bank restructuring is essential to the future of the entire financial system. In a healthy market economy money and credit must flow freely, both within and outside national borders, and a healthy banking system is essential to both flows.

There are two principal dangers:

(1) *International Isolation*: if the bank restructuring does not produce an acceptable rescheduling of the banks' debts to foreign creditors, then Russia runs the risk of being isolated from world capital markets for many years to come. Not only will Russian banks be unable to borrow abroad, but they will be unable to operate or invest abroad, because their assets

---

[81] There are only a handful of exceptions, such as Alfa-Bank, which had avoided investing in the companies of its parent group, building up instead a broad portfolio of holdings in unrelated companies. (Interview with Alfa-Bank managing director Alexander Knaster, *Ekspert*, No. 43 (November 16 1998), pp. 32–33.)

will be subject to seizure. In effect, Russia could end up behind a financial iron curtain.

(2) *Internal Disintegration:* the August collapse strengthened the motivation of regional politicians to create their own subnational banking systems, based on individual provinces or regional associations. Such local banks support chains of *vekselia* and other quasi-monies that sustain the barter-based virtual economy – in effect, local submonies supporting local subeconomies. Maintaining a single "monetary space" throughout the country requires a network of strong banks operating at the national level. Without such a network, the result will be continued disintegration and demonetization.

Thus a successful restructuring is crucial. But the government's dilemma is that it does not have the resources both to compensate the foreign lenders and at the same time to recapitalize the banking system. Its initial response to this dilemma is unfortunate: it has, in effect, held the foreign lenders at arm's length while feeding favors to the best-connected domestic creditors. That tactic, if continued much longer, will dissipate the government's limited resources without creating the basis for a healthy banking system.

I seen my opportunities and I took 'em.

George Washington Plunkitt, in William L. Riordan,
Plunkitt of Tammany Hall

A freshwater fish cannot live in salt water. But Russian
businessmen can move from one kind of water to another.
Their main characteristic is their ability to adapt.

Russian sociologist Vladimir Gimpel'son[1]

5   No capitalism without capitalists: entrepreneurship in the new Russia

April 1991, London:

The young Soviet deputy oil minister, Vagit Alekperov, was modest in
manner, but quietly self-assured. He had come to London on a tour of
oil companies and government offices, but also, intriguingly, of banks.

His delegation was strangely low-ranking compared to Alekperov
himself. As the Soviet group took their chairs across the long table,
Alekperov took in his group with a broad wave of his arm. "Allow me to
introduce my colleagues," he said. "Mr. Maganov of the Langepas Oil
Company, Mr. Putilov of Urai, and Mr. Safin of Kogalym."

Little did we realize at the time that the first letters Langepas, Urai,
and Kogalym spelled LUK. In front of us was the beginning of Lukoil,
today the leading oil company in Russia – and a name becoming known
around the world.

June 1996, Moscow:

On Moscow's busy Leningradskoe Shosse we stopped at an unmarked
door and entered a dark, deserted hallway. Stepping over trash and
construction debris, we passed through a hole in a wall into an adjoining
building, as gray and tumble-down as the first. I was beginning to
wonder what I had gotten myself into, when my companion knocked on
a steel-reinforced plate and we heard the sound of a police lock sliding
aside.

From the gloom we stepped into a brightly-lit and ultra-modern
workshop. Computer-driven printing presses rumbled, large computer
screens shone brightly, young people bustled purposefully about, carry-

---

[1] Vladimir Gimpel'son, "Novoe rossiiskoe predprinimatel'stvo: istochniki formirovaniia i strategii sotsial'nogo deistviia," *Mirovaia ekonomika i mezhdunarodnye otnosheniia*, No. 7 (1993), p. 35.

ing four-color proofs. Stacks of brightly-printed calendars and posters were piled high, ready for shipment. An elegant, well-dressed woman greeted us with a smile, "Welcome to Raster. What you'll see here is as state-of-the-art as you'll find anywhere in the world."

Entrepreneurship – the crucial ingredient

Russia has immense natural resources, a highly educated population, and – if it ever straightens out its financial system – access to considerable capital. But these alone are not enough to produce sustained growth. The essential extra ingredients are entrepreneurial energy and managerial skill.[2] The promise of a market economy is that it opens the way for entrepreneurial talent. But fulfilling that promise is anything but automatic. Building the right environment for entrepreneurship is essential for Russia if it is to be competitive in the next century.

The greatest surprise of post-Soviet Russia, in the eyes of the outside world, has been the explosion of entrepreneurial energy that followed the break-up of the Soviet economy. Yet long-time students of Russia were aware of the powerful creative energies present there. In the initial decades of its existence, the Soviet regime tapped those energies to build industry and military technology.[3] But as the system aged it increasingly failed to reward creativity and innovation, and much of the entrepreneurial energy of Russians was forced underground, into the "second" economy. Ironically, it was precisely this fact that created the basis for the quick reemergence of open private business, as soon as the grip of the Soviet state weakened.

But the surge of Russian entrepreneurship that began in the mid-1980s and ran through the mid-1990s was highly distorted. Initially, much of it was the underground economy coming to the surface, in response to the opening created by Gorbachev's reform policies. Then, as the Soviet system disintegrated, the energy of the emerging class of new Russian businessmen was mostly devoted to seizing the assets of the state economy and taking advantage of the disintegration of state borders. In

---

[2] All theories of economic growth stress this point, whether classical theory, with its emphasis on specialization and the division of labor; neoclassical theory, which stresses capital formation; or modern theory, in which the build-up of knowledge is the essential driver. But the most striking statement of the importance of entrepreneurship and innovation in capitalist systems is still Joseph Schumpeter's description of the "creative destruction" caused by innovation and competition, in his classic, *Capitalism, Socialism, and Democracy* (London: George Allen and Unwin, 1944)

[3] There is a rich literature on Russian technological innovation and entrepreneurship before and during the Soviet period. One of the best works on the subject is Kendall E. Bailes, *Technology and Society under Lenin and Stalin* (Princeton NJ: Princeton University Press, 1978)

the years of high inflation and weak currency that followed the Soviet collapse, much of Russian entrepreneurship consisted of arbitrage and speculation. In addition, throughout the decade private business was held back by government restrictions, high taxes, scarce and expensive capital, inadequate laws, and crime. In short, the reborn Russian entrepreneurship emerged lusty but deformed.

Now the time of easy gains is over. The financial crash of August 1998 decimated the small-business sector that had grown up in the previous decade, and in the depressed environment that followed it became almost impossible to start new businesses. Small-scale credit, never abundant to begin with, practically vanished. Much of the demand for services, which had been fed during the Nineties by revenues from commodities exports, slowed to a trickle. And the competitive advantage created by the devaluation of the ruble mostly benefited larger established companies. It is a bad time for small business, despite the competitive edge provided by the recent devaluation.

But in actual fact Russian entrepreneurship had been on the decline for several years before the August 1998 collapse. On the face of it, this is a mystery. The stabilization of the Russian economy between 1995 and 1998 had created a more orderly setting for business. Interest rates were lower, and Russian banks were beginning to look for a wider range of borrowers. Popular attitudes had evolved from suspicion of private business to growing acceptance. The domestic market was reviving, and Russian businessmen were learning to compete against imported products and services. In theory, these changes should have created favorable conditions for a new generation of more conventional small businesses, more oriented toward innovation in products and services, as in other market economies.

Yet Russian entrepreneurship, far from responding to these favorable conditions with a blossoming of new businesses, declined instead – at least to judge from the official statistics. The number of new small companies officially registered each year declined from 1994 on. Small business in 1997 accounted for barely 12% of Russian GDP, whereas in advanced market economies the figure is closer to 50%. The actual share may have been larger, since new businesses frequently avoided registering with the authorities, but indirect evidence on the unofficial economy did not suggest any great wave of underground entrepreneurship.

These signs of weakness raise tough questions for the future. What was the source of the initial wave of new businesses in 1985 and after, and why did the wave then subside? Were the new Russian businessmen of the first decade really "entrepreneurs," as the West would understand the term, or were they essentially "rent-seekers," profiting from the unique conditions of the time? Will their skills and experience, molded in that distorted environment, be transferrable to the next stage of transition – if there is one – when more normal business knowledge and practices will presumably be required? Can a new generation of Russian entrepreneurs arise, now that many of the niches of the new economy have been filled by people with power and connections?

A pseudo business class?

Most Russians have an unflattering opinion of their new business class. A popular view in Russia is that most of today's private businessmen got their start in the Soviet underground economy, or that they are former members of the Party *nomenklatura* who managed to convert the Party's funds and connections into private capital. Or that they are "red directors" who embezzled state assets and turned them into private fortunes. Russian wags quickly turned the word *"privatizatsiia"* (privatization) into *"prikhvatizatsiia,"* a made-up word based on the verb *"prikhvatit',"* which means to grab.

This negative view is spread enthusiastically by law-enforcement officials, opposition politicians, many intellectuals, and even businessmen themselves. Colonel Viacheslav Seliverstov, deputy director of a research institute belonging to the Ministry of Interior, asserts flatly, "Every fourth businessman has ties to the criminal economy; more than 20% once faced criminal charges at one time or another; and more than 40% accumulated their starting capital in the criminal world."[4] Most Russian law-enforcement officials would probably echo Colonel Seliverstov's view.

Even those Russians who do not quite believe that all the new money is criminal readily accept that it came straight from the spoils of the *nomenklatura*. Olga Kryshtanovskaia is a Moscow sociologist who has become well known in recent years for her studies of the new Russian business elite. Nearly two-thirds of the new businessmen, she asserts, come from the Soviet *nomenklatura*. But Kryshtanovskaia's most provocative finding is that the richest and most successful of the lot were backed from the beginning by state interests. The founders of the powerful commercial banks of the Nineties – Menatep, Most, Inkombank, SBS-Agro, etc. – were little more than the "authorized representatives" (in Russian, *"upolnomochennye"*) of powerful forces inside the state. They all had behind-the-scenes backing from the nomenklatura. As Kryshtanovskaia concludes, "They were never small and they were never poor."[5]

---

[4] *Moskovskie novosti*, No. 17 (12–19 March 1995), p. 29. These numbers are derived from a survey conducted in 1992 by the "Expert Institute" of the Russian Union of Industrialists and Entrepreneurs. The results are quoted in Gorshkov 1995, p. 75.

[5] Ol'ga Kryshtanovskaia, "Finansovaia oligarkhiia v Rossii," *Izvestiia*, January 10 1996, p. 5.

The *upolnomochennye* were never truly independent of the state, Kryshtanovskaia argues. They continued to breathe the "official oxygen" of special relationships with the government. They serviced the government's debts and held its bank accounts. They acted on behalf of the powerful lobby groups who made them what they are today. In short, the *upolnomochennye* were not a true business class; they were the agents of a new financial-political oligarchy that bound state and private interests together. Meanwhile, Kryshtanovskaia writes, the few successful independents, the handful of true "self-made men," were gradually squeezed out.

A broader view, which looks beyond the handful of giant conglomerates to private business as a whole, comes from Moscow economist A. Vilenskii, who distinguishes three generations of private entrepreneurship since 1985.[6] In the first generation, from 1987 to 1991, most small businesses, argues Vilenskii, were barely more than "channels for the transfer of state assets into private hands." The real explosion of entrepreneurship came in the second stage, in 1992–94, when hundreds of thousands of Russians responded enthusiastically to the new freedoms of the post-Soviet era. Yet those were also the years when business conditions were deteriorating dramatically. Inflation wiped out savings and drove up interest rates, while consumer demand collapsed and imported goods drove domestic products off the shelves. Many new businesses, founded more on hope and enthusiasm than on realistic business plans, were quickly wiped out. The survivors turned away from innovation and production and toward trade – hence a lasting distortion in the structure of Russian private business.

By 1995, Vilenskii writes, the gateway of opportunities for massive gains through asset-stripping, contraband, speculation, and trade, had swung shut. At the same time the wave of popular enthusiasm for private business subsided, as people became more aware of the difficulties of running one. A third stage began, characterized by consolidation, as successful larger companies absorbed the smaller ones. The rate of new business formation fell off, while a re-registration in 1995 removed from the official records a large number of businesses that had long ceased to exist. The result was a sharp fall-off in the number of officially registered small companies. Since then the creation of small businesses has slowed.

Both Kryshtanovskaia and Vilenskii, in their different ways, put their main stress on the distorting effects of the environment on entrepreneurship in the decade 1985–95. However, they may be taking a good point too far, by suggesting – Kryshtanovskaia explicitly, Vilenskii in more mea-

---

[6] A. Vilenskii, "Etapy razvitiia malogo predprinimatel'stva v Rossii," *Voprosy ekonomiki*, No. 7 (July 1996), pp. 30–38.

sured terms – that Russian entrepreneurs are not really that, but only quasi-entrepreneurs, capitalizing on the opportunities created by the decay of the Soviet system and the turmoil of the early post-Soviet transition. It was a one-time phenomenon: the opportunism faded with the opportunities.

Yet from the same events one can also draw a more positive view. Entrepreneurship is less a specific behavior than a form of energy. The business entrepreneur, the classic capitalist, has always fascinated philosophers, sociologists, and novelists, because entrepreneurs by definition are people who take risks, who pit themselves against the conventional and create something new. They are typically mavericks, outsiders, driven individuals with a vision. They are destroyers as well as builders. They take pieces of the past as they find them, and recombine them into new structures, amassing capital and building new institutions. In the process they are themselves changed and they change the people around them. In this perspective it matters little where the entrepreneur comes from. Nor does it matter what kind of opportunities are presented to him; the point is that he takes maximum advantage of them in ways that are new. That is what it means to be an entrepreneur.[7]

In this perspective, every stage in the rapidly changing environment of the last decade has provided openings for entrepreneurial energy. All have produced new companies with new skills and capital. The true lesson of the decade 1985–95 is that it revealed tremendous entrepreneurial energy in the Russian people. That energy can now be encouraged and rechanneled – or it can be repressed.

But how plausible is the case that the businessmen who emerged in 1985–95 are true entrepreneurs? Let us take a closer look.

Entrepreneurship before perestroika

The Russian business class that existed before the 1917 Revolution was completely stamped out by the end of the 1920s. Yet entrepreneurship did not die. Within the ranks of the managerial class created by Stalin in the 1930s, there was room for energetic and ambitious people – if they escaped Stalin's prison camps, and sometimes even if they did not. Sergei Korolev, the father of the Soviet space program, was arrested in the purges of the late 1930s, and for a time actually designed warplanes inside one of the secret police's special laboratory prison camps, the notorious

---

[7] Nicolo de Vecchi, *Entrepreneurs, Institutions, and Economic Change: the Economic Thought of J.A. Schumpeter* (London: Edward Elgar, 1995). See also the profile of the "jungle fighter" in Michael Maccoby, *The Gamesman: the New Corporate Leaders* (New York: Simon and Schuster, 1976)

sharagi described in Solzhenitsyn's *The First Circle*. There were many others like him.

Meanwhile, at the other end of Soviet society, a vigorous illegal economy flourished underground. Yet private enterprise as such – legal and free – was limited to a handful of small trades. The low point of legal private enterprise in the Soviet Union came, ironically, in the 1960s and 70s – not under Stalin, but under Brezhnev and Kosygin. As the arteries of the Soviet regime hardened and its growth slowed, official ideologists redoubled their efforts to stamp out the few remaining islands of private trade and small crafts. The number of officially authorized private craftsmen (*"kustari"*) dropped from a modest 110,000 in 1960 to an insignificant 10,000 by 1973.[8] In actual fact, most of these "craftsmen" were old men who repaired shoes on the street, and who finally died out by the end of the 1970s.

But at the very same time the living standards of ordinary Russians were rising, creating a growing demand for consumer goods and services. The result was a vigorous expansion of the shadow economy. From the 1960s on, Soviet citizens increasingly lived in two worlds – the official socialist one, and the underground, illegal one (or as the Russian phrase went, the economy "on the left," *na levo*). Perfectly respectable citizens by the millions hired private tutors for their children, rented private vacation homes, bought privately-made shoes, hailed private taxis, sought out medical specialists in unofficial private practices, or had their apartments painted and repaired by private workmen.

On Saturdays and Sundays Muscovites by the thousands gathered at private markets called *tolkuchki*, which sold home-made wares such as knitted caps, *defitsit* items from state stores resold at hefty markups, or foreign goods brought home by Soviet travelers. In smaller cities such as Kaliningrad or Saratov such markets were the main source of imported goods, and were crowded with young people looking for the latest Western fashions.

In some corners of the economy, such as housing construction, auto repair, dockwork, and truck-farming, private business became more important than the official kind, and in services private enterprise was supreme. The official and the unofficial worlds were intertwined; in wholesale trade every public organization also did business on the side. From perhaps 2% of the Soviet economy in 1960,[9] the world "on the left" came to account for more than 10% of the labor force and up to one-third of

---

[8] V.A. Zevelev, *Malyi biznes – bol'shaia problema Rossii* (Moscow: "Menedzher," 1994), p. 96.

[9] T.I. Koriagina, "Istoriia i opyt analiza," *Tenevaia ekonomika*, Moscow: "Ekonomika," 1991, p. 40.

household incomes by the mid-1980s, on the eve of Gorbachev's *perestroika*. [10]

In some ways the shadow economy prepared the way for the rise of true private business and large-scale entrepreneurship later on. The last generation of the Soviet era became accustomed to private business. The shadow economy created informal networks of business relationships that survived after the official institutions of the command economy collapsed. Many ordinary people learned to hustle to make money, and this helps to account for the otherwise surprising explosion of entrepreneurial energy in Russia after 1985. Above all, the shadow economy created the first small pools of private capital.

A prominent Moscow banker, Ivan Iur'evich (not his real name), whom I interviewed one summer, stressed the continuity from the underground to the cooperatives that followed after Gorbachev first authorized them in 1986:

You mustn't imagine that 1986 was a magic start date. A lot of people like me, who had been working in trade prior to *perestroika*, had accumulated a certain amount of capital even before the green light came to create cooperatives. Even very ordinary street-corner businessmen – "*pirozhochniki*" and the like – had the savings and the energy to take advantage of *perestroika* when it came.

But the shadow economy was in many ways a parasite on the larger command economy, and its illegal, underground status deformed it in ways that proved unhealthy once the command economy disappeared. The high wages paid to private construction crews, known as "*shabashniki*," or the side-payments exacted by distributors and retailers, amounted to rents on goods and services made artificially scarce by the system of central planning. Private craftsmen used free "state" goods, such as bricks and cement lifted from a construction site and delivered with a "borrowed" company truck. Party and state officials became accustomed to bribery. The more-or-less universally condoned larceny, the lack of formal structures and paper documents, the reliance on winks and nods among friends – have left a legacy of conspiratorial behavior, poor management, and sharp practice.

[10] According to Gregory Grossman, the leading Western student of the Soviet underground economy, by the late 1970s private income comprised between 28% and 33% of total household income. [Cited in Vladimir G. Treml and Michael V. Alexeev, "The Growth of the Second Economy in the Soviet Union and its Impact on the System," in Robert W. Campbell, ed., *The Postcommunist Economic Transformation* (Boulder, Colorado: Westview Press, 1994), pp. 221–248.]

The first wave of legal private enterprise (1986–1991): cooperatives and their descendants

In 1986 came the first and most fateful of the Gorbachev reforms – the decision to authorize private "cooperatives." The response was immediate and overwhelming. Young Russians, especially in the cities, rushed to take advantage of the opening. By 1991, there were 135,000 officially registered cooperatives. By official reckoning, they produced nearly 3% of all consumer goods, but an astonishing 18.4% of all services,[11] and the real, unreported numbers were undoubtedly much greater. From the beginning, the word "cooperative" was hardly more than a euphemism. In reality, these were small entrepreneurial businesses, run by a single owner or a small group of partners, hiring wage labor.

Many of the cooperatives came out of the shadow economy: the legalization of cooperatives simply gave them the opportunity to emerge from the undergound. This was particularly the case in trade and construction. By 1991 former *shabashniki* had founded over 50,000 cooperatives, more than one-third of the total.[12] By 1993, most of these had gone on to become joint-stock companies or "limited partnerships", and the number of cooperatives in construction had dwindled to fewer than 20,000. By 1995 practically none was left.

Many cooperatives turned out to be little more than siphons to divert state resources into private hands. A state manager would create a "cooperative," owned by relatives or friends, to sell the output or inventory of his enterprise out the back door, preferably abroad for hard currency. The state enterprise absorbed public credits but secreted private profits.

The initial intent of many of the early founders of cooperatives was to produce consumer goods, computer software, design and research services, and the like. But suspicious government agencies surrounded the cooperatives with restrictions: they could not buy materials wholesale, they found it difficult to rent office and factory space, and unpredictable rules limited their size and the sectors they could work in. Above all, they were heavily taxed.

Squeezed out of manufacturing and technical services, the fledgling private businessmen found opportunities in trade, especially import and export. They diversified, spun off multiple "daughter companies" to stay small and invisible, founded trading and banking subsidiaries. Several of the immense banking and trading fortunes that emerged by the mid-1990s got their start as modest "cooperatives" in 1986–88.

Regardless of origins or motives, successful cooperatives required

[11] Zevelev, op. cit., pp. 102–103. See also L. Nikiforov and T. Kuznetsova, "Sud'ba kooperatsii v sovremennoi Rossii," *Voprosy ekonomiki*, No. 1 (1995), pp. 86–96.
[12] Ibid.

entrepreneurial energy to prosper. The opening provided by the Gorbachev reforms gave many young Russian professionals an opportunity to start legal businesses. Many of the most successful private businessmen came from highly diverse non-business backgrounds, such as research scientists, computer designers, theater managers, or student Komsomol activists. Some of them were genuinely self-made men. One colorful example is Vladimir Dovgan', whose rise and fall personifies the Russian Nineties.

Vladimir Dovgan': pioneer of Russian franchising

Vladimir Dovgan' will go down in history as the man who brought pizza to Russia – or rather, the man who brought pizza franchising. In the late 1980s Dovgan' was an engineer at Tol'iatti's Volga Auto Plant. He had been a member of the Soviet rowing team and had good connections in the elite world of former athletes. Even as a student Dovgan' always had something on the side. "We set up a construction crew, we repaired buildings part-time. I was making four times as much as a regular worker."[13]

The road to pizza, strangely enough, started through karate. Dovgan' had taught martial arts as a hobby in his student days, and published a book on "eastern martial arts." Finding no readers, he borrowed several thousand dollars to run an advertising campaign in *Argumenty i Fakty*, then the widest-selling weekly newspaper in the Soviet Union. Within weeks he had sold 600,000 copies.[14] The profits from the book bankrolled Dovgan''s first business, a small cooperative that made potato-chip machines. That was in 1990. The venture proved profitable, and Dovgan' and his partners decided to branch out into pizzerias.[15]

Dovgan' was first exposed to franchising during a trip to the United States. As recently as 1992, says Dovgan', "even Russian economists had never heard the word, 'franchising.'" My partners and I, in Tol'iatti, founded a small company, called "Doka-Pizza," to make pizza ovens. In 1993 we launched a TV advertising campaign to find franchisees."

Almost overnight Doka-Pizza had a chain of 400 franchise cafe-pizzerias throughout Russia. But they did not do well. "It was our Russian mentality," says Dovgan'. "The franchisees made junk. They messed up the recipes, they stole the ingredients, the cafes were dirty. . . . By cheating the customers, they were destroying themselves and killing the brand name. All the money we spent on advertising was thrown to the winds."[16]

---

[13] Interview with Vladimir Dovgan' in *Kapital*, 28 February–5 March 1996, pp. 24–25.
[14] *Kapital*, loc. cit.   [15] *Delovye lyudi*, No. 47, July–August 1994, pp. 12–13.
[16] *Kapital*, loc. cit.

So Dovgan' branched out again. Noting that Russian bakeries were antiquated and inefficient, he decided to franchise mini-bakeries, using baking equipment manufactured in factory space that Dovgan' leased from local defense plants in the Tol'iatti area. The new venture was financed by issuing bearer shares.

Little is left of Dovgan''s early franchising ventures today, except the occasional empty kiosk with the sign, "Doka-khleb." Faced with growing competition from foreign franchisers, Dovgan' moved into vodka, marketing "Dovgan' Vodka" in smart bottles featuring his own portrait. But Dovgan' did not manufacture the vodka himself; he redistributed it. His company was briefly one of the most successful of a thriving category in Russia, the "shell company" (*obolochechnaia firma*) that buys products from smaller producers and redistributes it under its own brand.[17] But like many business pioneers, Dovgan' once again proved better at thinking up new concepts than at managing them profitably. By 1999 Dovgan' had left the franchising business and was trying his hand at politics.[18]

Today few of the first generation of entrepreneurs are still in business, and practically none is engaged in manufacturing. But after 1990 new fields opened up for new businesses – chiefly foreign trade and banking, but also insurance, advertising, tourism, and the media. Foreign trade led the way. Trading in oil, timber, and metals was the basis for some of the earliest large fortunes in 1990–92.

Then, after 1993, as the ruble firmed somewhat and dollar-denominated goods became cheaper in real terms, new Russian businessmen moved into imports, selling foreign products and representing foreign brands inside Russia. The import boom produced yet another wave of spectacular success stories, in fields such as consumer electronics, retailing, and computers.

The people who were in the best position to take advantage of the new wide-open environment were those who started out with good connections and some initial capital and experience. The most important source of all three, curiously enough, was the youth organization of the Communist Party, the Komsomol.

The Komsomol: training ground for private enterprise

As early as the 1970s private enterprise was flourishing within the Communist establishment, all with the blessing of the orthodox Party leadership. The main source of "communist businessmen" was the youth arm of the Communist Party, the Leninist Youth League

---

[17] *Ekspert*, No. 1 (January 12 1998), p. 75.
[18] Kommersant-Daily and Vremia-MN, May 17 1999, by Internet.

(Kommunisticheskii Soiuz Molodezhi), known to three generations of Soviet citizens as the Komsomol.

Young people joined the Komsmol as a way station between the Pioneers (the Soviet boy scouts) and adult membership in the Communist Party. As the national youth organization, it had its own professional apparatus, which paralleled the senior Party apparatus at every level. Ambitious young men aspiring to political careers, like Mikhail Gorbachev in the 1950s, typically moved up through the apparatus of the Komsomol before switching over to the Party ladder. Westerners snorted over these "youth" leaders in their 30s and 40s, but the Komsomol apparatus was one of the main roads to success in the Soviet system.

From the 1970s on, the Komsomol was also a business empire. It ran a far-flung network of organizations that started out as "youth activities," but which by the 1980s had turned into valuable properties and lucrative businesses. Through its "Committee of Youth Organizations" (known by its Russian acronym KMO), the Komsomol had a major role in tourism for young people, both domestic and international. The Komsomol also ran summer construction brigades, which sent college students all over the Soviet Union to build housing. It was active in show business, organizing rock concerts and producing television programs. The Komsomol was a major sports sponsor, and owned and managed sports clubs, gyms, fields, and stadiums. The Komsomol even formed consulting groups in scientific research and computer software development.

Komsomol entrepreneurship became an important training ground for a generation of private businessmen, as well as a source of capital and property. Unlike the Communist Party apparatus, which was systematically dismantled in 1991–92, the Komsomol's business organizations survived the transition smoothly. The property and assets of the Communist Party (where they could be identified) were confiscated by the Yeltsin government, amid huge media publicity. Not so the Komsomol, which hung on to its property and stayed in the shade. It helped, of course, that most of the middle-level players in the Komsomol apparatus supported Yeltsin.

Even as the Soviet system began to fall apart, the Komsomol's businessmen repositioned themselves to go private, with help from key democratic politicians, especially in Moscow. Gavriil Popov, the first post-communist mayor of Moscow, actively supported the Association of Young Entrepreneurs, a Komsomol-backed organization which helped new private businesses get started. The leaders of the Association subsequently became the core of the so-called "Moscow Group," which included some of today's leading businessmen and politicians, such as Duma deputy Konstantin Zatulin, founder of the Moscow Commodities

Exchange. The most significant member of this group was Iosif Ordzhonikidze (grandson of Sergo Ordzhonikidze, one of the earliest Bolshevik leaders). As secretary of the Komsomol Central Committee, Ordzhonikidze oversaw the Komsomol's business enterprises. Moscow mayor Popov made him deputy mayor of Moscow and put him in charge of land privatization. Today Ordzhonikidze is one of the three most powerful men behind Moscow mayor Iurii Luzhkov, and plays a key role in managing the city government's relations with the new private business sector – many of whose leaders once worked for him. The Moscow group is the most visible and influential example, but Komsomol networks flourished in the provinces too; the former prime minister, Sergei Kirienko, was a Komsomol activist in Nizhnii Novgorod and recalled with nostalgia his start in the organization.

Today the alumni of the Komsomol are the most important single group within the Russian business elite. To that extent there is indeed some basis for the charge that today's businessmen are drawn from the *nomenklatura* and benefited from Komsomol connections. But the Komsomol connection provided mainly a means to get started. The rest was a matter of individual talent and energy. The best example is the story of Mikhail Khodorkovskii, the founder of Menatep Bank and now president of Russia's second-largest oil company, Yukos.

Mikhail Khodorkovskii: from Komsomol activist to businessman

Menatep, until recently one of the largest banks in Russia and the financial arm of the giant Rosprom holding group, originated as a café-discotheque sponsored by the Young Communist Youth League. Its founder, a 23-year-old chemistry student in Moscow's Mendeleev Institute, Mikhail Khodorkovskii, was the secretary of the institute's Komsomol committee. When the Communist Party issued a decree in 1986 authorizing amateur groups and clubs, Khodorkovskii and a group of friends from the institute leapt at the opportunity.[19] Shortly after, when the Komsmol authorized youth groups to create "Youth Centers for Scientific Creativity" (NTTM), Khodorkovskii and his friends turned their business into an R&D consulting group whose main activity was importing computers.[20]

A profitable contract with the High Temperatures Institute of the Academy of Sciences netted the group's first modest capital, which Khodorkovskii used as seed money to expand his business, though still

[19] I.M. Bunin, ed., *Biznesmeny Rossii: 40 istorii uspekha* (Moscow: AO "OKO," 1994), p. 170.   [20] Inna Luk'ianova, "Chelovek," *Profil'*, No. 43 (November 1998), p. 74.

under Komsomol auspices. By this time Khodorkovskii had graduated from the Mendeleev Institute and served briefly as deputy secretary of the Komsomol for Moscow's Frunze district. But by 1987 he was working full time as director of the network of NTTM Centers, with 5,000 people working for him on over 500 R&D contracts for state industrial enterprises.[21]

Khodorkovskii's move into banking came two years later, when a government decree forbade his clients from paying advances for contracts. Suddenly Khodorkovskii needed working capital. With support from Komsomol alumni in the Moscow city government Khodorkovskii founded his own bank. In 1990 he bought out his partners in the Moscow city government and renamed his bank Menatep-Invest.[22]

By this time Khodorkovskii was beginning to move away from direct dependence on the Komsomol. In 1991 Menatep began the first of several public stock issues, which provided it with capital for expansion. The timing was perfect: the break-up of the Soviet system was opening up glittering new opportunities. In its first years Menatep did little actual banking; instead, the group imported computers and exported raw materials. In 1992 Khodorkovskii began providing export credits to the oil industry.[23] In that same year, as Russia began the voucher privatization program, Menatep began picking up shares in industrial enterprises, and soon Menatep had assembled an impressive portfolio of industrial properties in which it had controlling stakes.

A critic might discount Mikhail Khodorkovskii as an entrepreneur, because of his initial ties to the Komsomol and his subsequent backing from Komsomol alumni in the Moscow city government. Indeed, for a brief time he combined his business in Menatep with service in the government, initially as adviser to the prime minister and then briefly, in 1993, as deputy minister of fuel and power. Menatep, along with other Russian banks, serviced government accounts and processed payments to and from the state. By these yardsticks Khodorkovskii is a classic *nomenklatura* capitalist. Even today, as a symbolic reminder of the past, his holding company, Rosprom, is located in the former headquarters of the Moscow Komsomol on Kolpachnyi pereulok.[24]

But by any reasonable definition Khodorkovskii is a true entrepreneur. When he began he was in his early twenties, and he had no apparent high-level backing. His first ventures were modest and clearly self-started, not

---

[21] *Natsional'naia sluzhba novostei*, by Internet.
[22] The name Menatep is an acronym for "Interbranch and Scientific-Technical Programs" (*Mezhotraslevye i Nauchno-tekhnicheskie Programmy*)
[23] Author's interview with Khodorkovskii, spring 1992.
[24] Luk'ianova, op. cit., p. 74.

"authorized" by some powerful group behind the scenes. Indeed, Khodorkovskii's first efforts to get credit for his business were rejected by the established banks of the day, forcing him to found his own bank from unconventional sources. He took risks; he left the beaten path; and the empire he has built is quite unlike what existed before. Banker Ivan Iur'evich comments:

It's a mistake to believe that most of the money for the new private sector came from the nomenklatura. What came from the nomenklatura was not money, but connections, and mostly at the more junior levels. The more senior Soviet officials, for the most part, did not have the energy or the daring to take advantage of the new opportunities. They were conditioned by decades of training in the Soviet system, and they were afraid (especially since the memory of Andropov was still fresh in their minds). They were afraid – and they missed the train.

Most of the other major new Russian bankers likewise started very young from junior positions in the *nomenklatura*. Nearly all of them came from outside the Soviet banking system. For example, Vladimir Vinogradov, founder of the (now-bankrupt) Inkombank, graduated in 1979 from the prestigious Moscow Aviation Institute, then went to work at Atommash, a manufacturer of nuclear powerplants where he was secretary of the plant's Komsomol organization, suggesting that he was more active as a political organizer than as an engineer. In 1985–87, at the beginning of the cooperative era, he was a post-graduate student in economics at Moscow's Plekhanov Institute, and simultaneously he served as economist at Promstroibank in Moscow, rising to senior economist by 1988. It was here that Vinogradov chose to take a different path, when he left to found Inkombank in 1988.[25]

Today's big bankers [continues Ivan Iur'evich] were not high officials under the Soviet system. Rather, they were younger people on lower rungs of the ladder, who combined their own energies with higher-level connections. Good examples are Rodionov of Imperial (he actually comes from a banking family), Smolenskii of SBS Agro (Smolenskii was in construction for the city of Moscow), Zurabov of Konversbank (who came from a high-ranking family in the nuclear weapons industry), and Potanin of Oneksimbank (formerly a junior foreign-trade official).

Right behind the bankers came a host of entrepreneurs in a wide variety of service fields. They resembled the bankers in that they were generally junior-level members of the *nomenklatura* and benefited from connections. Nevertheless, they broke away from secure jobs and founded their businesses outside the state structure, occupying niches that the Soviet system had left unfilled or underdeveloped. Thus they too qualify as genuine entrepreneurs. Until recently such companies played

---

[25] *Natsional'naia sluzhba novostei*, by Internet.

leading roles in media, finance, commodity markets, insurance, real estate, advertising, auditing and consulting, and other services.[26] Unfortunately, many such companies were also among the chief victims of the crash of August 1998.

1991–1992: entrepreneurs from within the system

By 1992, with the beginning of the Gaidar market reforms, the pattern of entrepreneurship changed. The first generation of Russian private businessmen (1986–1991) may have originated at the edges of the system or at the junior rungs of the *nomenklatura*, but to start their businesses they had to break with the still-existing order. In 1992 and after, a second generation of entrepreneurs emerged, many of whom came from inside the Soviet system, and for whom the move to the private sector was less a break than a transition. By early 1992 the move to private companies had become such a migration that *Izvestiia* could ask sarcastically, "Who will be the last to become an entrepreneur?"[27] Among educated young Russians, private enterprise became the fashion. A survey in early 1993 showed that 45% of all Russians between 16 and 25, 40% of college graduates, and 45% of middle-level managers all wanted to start their own businesses.[28]

As a result, by the early 1990s the origins of most new entrepreneurs became more conventional. A survey of private businessmen in 1992 showed that over 60% had come from enterprises and institutes. Within this group some 15% had come from ministries and other state agencies.[29] Many of these new businessmen also benefited from connections and financial support, but instead of Party, Komsomol, or state sponsorship, the new private sector itself was already emerging as a source of support.

Does this post-Soviet generation of businessmen also qualify as "entrepreneurs"? One must use a different yardstick. The question no longer turns on their origins but on their strategies and their vision. By the early 1990s private businessmen were no longer mavericks; many moved smoothly from the top of the Soviet system to the top of the new business elite. But the businesses some of them built were radically different from the Soviet institutions they started with. Arguably, this group has been as genuinely entrepreneurial as those who previously broke with the system.

---

[26] V.A. Lepekhin, *Obshchestvenno-politicheskie protsessy v srede predprinimatelei.* Issue No. 5 of the "Seriia obozrenii k pervomu kongressu rossiiskikh predprinimatelei," general editor A.S. Orlov (Moscow: Kruglyi stol biznesa Rossii, Akademicheskii tsentr 'Rossiiskie issledovaniia,' 1994), p. 6.   [27] *Izvestiia*, February 19 1992.
[28] *Izvestiia*, July 31 1993.   [29] Gorshkov, p. 76.

Two examples are Igor Malashenko of Independent Television and Vagit Alekperov of Lukoil.

Igor Malashenko: "truth is our profession"

Until the early 1990s, Igor Malashenko's job was arms control. A senior researcher at the prestigious Institute of the USA and Canada in Moscow, Malashenko was well known to Western colleagues as a leading expert on strategic weapons and US defense policy. But by the mid 1990s Malashenko had launched a post-Soviet career, as founder and director of the second most-watched television station in Russia, NTV Channel 4. Something of Malashenko's first career occasionally shows through. To Western visitors he hands out coffee mugs inscribed with NTV's motto: "Truth is our profession." "You recognize it, don't you?" he says with a smile. "I adapted it from the US Strategic Air Command."[30]

After serving for a time in the apparatus of the Central Committee of the Communist Party, Malashenko became an assistant press secretary to Soviet leader Mikhail Gorbachev. In 1991 he moved over to television, rising by 1992 to become the head of "Ostankino," the main government channel. In 1991 he conceived the idea of a purely private television station, and by 1993, when he lost a battle for control of Ostankino, he decided to act. At first, he could find no backer that would take the idea seriously. But through a friendship with the increasingly powerful founder of the MOST Group, Vladimir Gusinskii, Malashenko found the support he needed. A consortium of three Russian banks – MOST, Stolichnyi (now SBS-Agro), and National'nyi Kredit – lent Malashenko $32 million for the first 15 months – an unusually large and long-term loan at a time when most lending was limited to three months or less.

Malashenko wrote a business plan and lobbied the Russian government to issue the necessary license. As Malashenko says discretely, "MOST provided the money. I did the publicity." Using leased equipment and a borrowed facility, plus shared space on Channel 4, Malashenko started broadcasting in January 1994.[31] NTV's star program is "Itogi," anchored by Russia's leading television news personality Evgenii Kiselev, but NTV's core formula is mass entertainment, a business formula successfully developed by Malashenko.

Malashenko and NTV faced a complex challenge. Russian television sets were antiquated and ill-adapted to modern satellite or cable broadcasting. The existing satellite and relay system was in the hands of his competitors. Meanwhile, all across Russia hundreds of local television

---

[30] Author's interview with Malashenko, July 1995
[31] *Itogi*, January 19 1998, by Internet.

stations were springing up, competing for advertising revenues. Malashenko and Most-Media built a business formula combining Western programming and networking, access to Moscow advertisers, and alliances with local broadcasters, that enabled NTV to extend its reach across the country. The potential market was enormous. "There's a boom in television advertising in Russia," Malashenko told me in 1995. "There is no national press left. The only way to reach a nationwide audience is through television."[32]

Malashenko subsequently played a major role in the consortium of bankers, media managers, and advertising men who banded together in 1996 to finance and manage the publicity campaign for Yeltsin's re-election. Today he heads the holding company, "Media-MOST," that controls the media empire of the MOST Group.[33]

Igor Malashenko is clearly a variation on the theme of the "post-Soviet entrepreneur," in the sense that he moved smoothly from the corridors of power in the Central Committee of the Communist Party and the General Secretary's office to private enterprise. His moment of risk-taking came in 1993, when he left Ostankino to create NTV, but he was solidly backed from the beginning by a private banking consortium that had already grown strong. Yet Malashenko proved himself a builder and a bold thinker, devising a business strategy for Most-MEDIA that used technology and Western models to extend NTV beyond the range of conventional television into the new fields of cable television and network management.

The Lukoil story is different. The founder was a senior Soviet official, the ultimate insider – yet in several key respects a maverick and a visionary, a true entrepreneurial outsider.

A Rockefeller from Baku

Vagit Alekperov was born in the Azerbaidjani capital of Baku, one of the historic cities of the oil world. In Baku the smell of oil is everywhere, and nearly everything and everyone there is connected with oil. Until his late twenties Alekperov worked in the offshore oil industry in Azerbaidjan, then migrated to West Siberia. Soviet oilmen in West Siberia were a multinational breed, and among them there was a large Azerbaidjani contingent. Alekperov rose quickly through the ranks. He was smart and tough, and didn't hesitate to cut corners. The story goes that when he was still the young head of a local production team, he was faced with a leaking pipeline. His welders were afraid to go near it; they worried it

[32] Author's interview
[33] Interview with Igor Malashenko in *Nezavisimaia gazeta*, January 17 1998, by Internet.

would blow up. Alekperov lay down next to the pipe and ordered, "Now weld it."[34]

By 1983 Alekperov was promoted to head a new oil company located in the frontier region of Kogalym, today the linchpin of the Lukoil organization. Backed by a team of fellow oilmen from Bashkiriia (Muslims like himself, incidentally, although it was better not to make a point of this in the old Soviet days), Alekperov turned Kogalym into the fastest-growing oil producer in West Siberia. By 1989 Vagit Alekperov, then not yet 40, became deputy USSR minister of oil and moved to Moscow. Within another year he moved up to first deputy, just one chair away from the top of the Soviet oil industry.

The idea of creating a private integrated oil company must have come to Alekperov some time in 1990. An early version of Lukoil was registered with the Moscow City Soviet in February 1991.[35] By the spring of 1991 he was touring the West with a retinue of Soviet executives from his home base in West Siberia, men who subsequently became the top command of Lukoil. As the Soviet Union broke up, Alekperov cobbled together three Siberian oil producers, two refineries, and a trading company, and Lukoil was in business.

On the surface, this too is a classic case of nomenklatura privatization. But other Soviet-era "oil generals" tried to follow his example, and few of them have survived. Alekperov demonstrated the skill and toughness to keep control of his empire and make it grow.

There were several keys to his success. He succeeded early in gaining control of the cash flow of his subsidiaries. He was the first post-Soviet Russian oilman to move into the Caspian Sea. He pioneered the first strategic alliance with a Western oil company. He developed the first successful network of retail gasoline stations. In all of these "firsts" Alekperov demonstrated the same combination of vision, innovative energy, political skill, and ruthlessness.

Alekperov's successful career in the Soviet oil industry might seem to stamp him as an "insider," but Alekperov is also an outsider. As a non-Russian, he always had to struggle against a barrier of prejudice and suspicion from Russian oilmen. Russians describe his style as "eastern," and indeed Alekperov plays by different rules from his Russian colleagues. Instead of managing by consensus and negotiation, the usual Russian approach, Alekperov created a team of mostly non-Russians who answer to him personally. To establish secure control over his organization, especially the rebellious refiners and distributors, Alekperov set up a subsidi-

---

[34] Cited in Paul Klebnikov, "The seven sisters have a baby brother," *Forbes*, January 22 1996, pp. 70–75.
[35] Interview with Alekperov in *Kommersant-Daily*, February 6 1996, p. 10.

ary called "Lukoil-Finance," headed by a young Chechen who made sure that the company's receivables got paid.

But above all, what marks Alekperov as a true entrepreneur is that he has a vision of the future. In a country in which most people were fighting for the spoils of the Soviet system and few thought more than three months ahead, Alekperov formed a long-range plan to build the future of Lukoil on the oil riches of the Caspian basin. His core market in the next century could be the reviving economies of south Russia and Ukraine, and he will export his oil to the world through a network of pipelines to the Black Sea and the Mediterranean. If he survives the turbulence of the next decade, Alekperov will go down in history as one of the most talented oil executives in the world.

The example of Alekperov underscores a key point about the first decade of Russian entrepreneurship: *nomenklatura* connections may have provided the start; but it has taken true entrepreneurship to survive.

The life stories sketched in this chapter – of Dovgan, Khodorkovskii, Malashenko, and Alekperov – are certainly not representative of the majority of Russian managers today. In any population the percentage of true entrepreneurs is small. Yet these are not unique cases. They show that a substantial number of today's private businesses were founded by people who took risks, showed vision, and built something new. It is this fact, and not their origins or their initial connections, that marks them as a creative force in the new Russian economy.

But for the Russian economy to grow new creative forces will be needed. We look now at the next generation of entrepreneurs.

Russian entrepreneurship today: tough to get started, even tougher to survive

Will there be a "third wave" of entrepreneurship, once the long post-Soviet depression bottoms out? Entrepreneurship, as we have seen, can blossom anywhere, in businesses both large and small. But the classic place to look is small business. In advanced market economies small businesses account for half or more of all economic activity and for much of the innovation in new products and technologies. The future growth and wealth of a market-based Russia depend on whether the same thing happens there.

The picture is not encouraging – indeed, it was not encouraging even before August 1998. As the government's austerity policy took hold in 1995, bringing with it lower inflation and interest rates, the growth of small business slowed. After a fast start in 1991–93, the number of reported small businesses peaked at about 900,000 in 1994.[36] It then dropped by more than 100,000 over the following two years, partly because of a re-registration in 1995–96 that winnowed out a large number of "dead souls" that had gone out of business but had never been removed from the rolls. By mid-1997 the number of officially registered small businesses had recovered to 838,000 and a modest growth trend had resumed.[37] But the share of small business in the Russian economy remained modest. Small business employed perhaps 9 million workers (some 16% of those officially employed), accounting for between 7 and 9% of industrial output.

Yet these figures – which come from government statistics – always understated the true importance of small business to the Russian economy. Small business was the one sector that had grown continuously throughout the great Russian depression. By 1996–7, when the Russian economy looked ready to turn around, the small-business sector led the way, with annual growth rates of more than 30% a year. Small business, by some accounts, actually accounted by then for some 12% of Russian GDP.[38] The true figure could have been even greater since many small businesses are unregistered and even the official ones underreport their actual turnover. Indeed, in trade and services small private businesses are the dominant players. In Moscow, on the eve of the 1998 crash, small companies employed one-third of the work force and paid nearly one-half of Moscow's taxes.[39]

Russian reformers, from President Yeltsin on down, speak of "building the middle class" as a prime objective of reform policy and tie it in to support for small business.[40] In 1997 President Yeltsin named a prominent liberal politician, Irina Khakamada, to head the small business

---

[36] Source: Russian Federation Statistics Committee (Goskomstat RF), *Rossiiskii statisticheskii ezhegodnik 1997*, by Internet. Just what qualifies as a "small enterprise" varies with the type of business and the structure of ownership. An enterprise qualifies as "small" if it employs fewer than 100 full-time people (if it is in industry or construction) or 50 people (if it is in trade or restauration). Similarly, a state agency, a social body, or a large enterprise may not own more than 25% of a "small" enterprise. Despite this requirement, many "small" enterprises are still owned by state bodies, mostly at the municipal level.

[37] Sergei Khoroshev: "Predprinimatel'stvo: problemy razvitiia malogo biznesa," *Delovoi ekspress*, December 23 1997, by Internet.

[38] Then first deputy prime minister Boris Nemtsov, quoted in *Delovoi mir*, November 6 1997, p. 4. Other sources, such as the *Delovoi ekspress* article cited in the previous footnote, give lower figures in the range of 9 to 11%.

[39] *Delovoi ekspress*, loc. cit. See also Ivan Sas, "Podarki biznesmenam ostaiutsia nevostrebovannymi," *Segodnia*, December 10, 1997, by Internet. Viktor Ermakov, head of the Russian Agency for the Support of Small and Medium-sized Business, cites Samara as another city where small business is well developed, providing up to 30% of the city's revenues. (Radio *Maiak*, January 17 1997, by Internet) But just how "small business" is defined in these sources is unclear; it may include "middle-sized" businesses as well.

[40] Radio address by Boris Yeltsin, reported in *Izvestiia*, November 29 1997, by Internet.

agency.[41] First deputy prime minister Boris Nemtsov, then still a rising star in Russian politics, adopted small business as part of his portfolio,[42] and gave frequent speeches about the importance of middle-class enterprise.

But the talk was never matched by action. After the August crash Nemtsov and Khakamada left the government, and now even the talk has died away. There have been three dozen laws and decrees on small business since the beginning of market reforms in 1992, all of them dead letters. Funding for small business in the state budget is miniscule, and the government's small-business agency, the grandly-named State Committee for the Support and Development of Small Enterprise, goes largely unnoticed on the bureaucratic landscape. Small wonder that small businessmen dismiss government policy as "declarative."

Anyone who starts up a small business in Russia runs a gauntlet of confiscatory taxes, criminal extortion, scarce credit, thin services, and obstructive bureaucracy. The obstacles are so numerous that reformers wonder where to start. But small-businessmen themselves answer without hesitation: taxes are the worst problem; bureaucracy comes next.[43] Crime they say they can handle themselves.

Taxes

Small businesses must pay a bewildering array of taxes. At the top of the list come levies on profits, value added, and property. But that is just the start; next comes a gaggle of regional and local taxes. Unlike large enterprises, small businesses have little defense against the arbitrary powers of tax inspectors. The only significant relief the government offers is a two-year holiday on profits taxes for new businesses.[44]

Since 1995 the government has debated simplifying the tax system for small entrepreneurs, by having them pay a single flat tax. The latest concept is a so-called "imputed" tax (*vmenennyi nalog*). In the minds of reformers like Boris Nemtsov, the imputed tax was meant to be a single

---

[41] Irina Khakamada, Moscow-born daughter of a prominent Japanese communist, was one of the founders of the Russian Commodities Exchange with Konstantin Borovoy, then served as secretary of Borovoy's Political Freedom Party. Before her appointment to the government, Khakamada was a deputy in the State Duma. (Source: *Natsional'naia sluzhba novostei*, by Internet)

[42] Interview with first deputy prime minister Boris Nemtsov, *Izvestiia*, January 20 1998, by Internet.

[43] Iulia Latynina, "Malyi biznes v Rossii: meniaem svobodu na bezopasnost'," *Segodnia*, July 27 1996.

[44] A. Arkhipov, G. Batkilina, and V. Kalinin, "Gosudarstvo i malyi biznes: finansirovanie, kreditovanie i nalogooblozhenie," *Voprosy ekonomiki*, No. 4 (1997), pp. 141–151.

flat charge, in effect a one-time payment for a license to do business.[45] But what emerged instead from the bureaucracy was a cumbersome plan to calculate the "imputed" tax on the basis of a long list of indicators – the type of business, its location, its floor space, etc. Tax officials would reckon the tax from these indicators on the basis of the profit the business "should" make, regardless of whether the business was actually profitable or not. Mikhail Motorin, deputy minister of finance for tax matters, commented acidly on the mess that would result: "If you sell ice cream, you'll pay one level of taxes; if you sell beer, another; and vodka, a third."[46] The new system has not yet been implemented, and perhaps that is just as well.[47]

Whether small businesses would even respond to tax reform is another matter. Over the last decade small entrepreneurs have adapted to the world of high taxes by evading them. A common arrangement is for small businesses to pay 10% of their gross revenues to their local mafia "shelter" (in Russian, *krysha*, or "roof"), which then protects them from the tax inspectors.[48] Irina Khakamada, the former head of the government's small business agency, said that when she talked to small businessmen about tax reform, they told her bluntly, "Don't change anything; it's fine as it is. We evade all taxes, from profits taxes to VAT. We've learned to bypass all social charges. No problem. The government won't get our money anyway."[49]

Bureaucratic obstacles

For the small businessman, dealing with local government is a constant headache. Just registering a small business is itself a major achievement. The would-be entrepreneur must make the rounds of 20 or 30 local government agencies for permits and approvals. These are typically in no hurry to give their blessing. The local offices of the Ministry for the Protection of Nature, for example, may take three months to mull over a request for a building permit for a small addition, when the mandated review time is three days.[50]

---

[45] Interview with first deputy prime minister Boris Nemtsov, Radio *Maiak*, January 13 1998.
[46] Mikhail Motorin, cited in *Kommersant-Daily*, January 14 1998, by Internet.
[47] Statement by Stanislav Smirnov, chairman of the Russian Chamber of Trade and Industry, *Prime-TASS*, December 23 1998.
[48] *Izvestiia*, November 5 1997, by Internet. Interview with Irina Khakamada, then newly appointed chair of the State Committee for Support and Development of Small Business.
[49] Interview with Irina Khakamada, Radio Mayak, "Voprosy k vlasti" program, December 19 1997, by Internet.   [50] Sas, op. cit.

Once a small business is up and running, it faces a stream of government inspectors, ranging from fire wardens to sanitation workers, any of whom can shut down its operations or impose fines. Compared to their counterparts in Warsaw, one survey discovered, Moscow small entrepreneurs face twice as many inspections and fines.[51] The only defense is to pay bribes and to cultivate useful friends in the city government.

Removing obstacles such as repressive taxes or bureaucratic deterrents is half the battle. The other half is to supply the missing services and support that small businesses have access to in the West. The most important is credit. Russian banks lend to large customers, not small ones. For credit small businesses are obliged to turn to private savings – or underground lenders. The result is to bias small enterprise toward activities that require little capital and produce fast results.

There is no lack of good ideas, such as creating a network of "collateral centers" in smaller cities, to which would-be small businessmen could bring their valuables and obtain cash advances against them. Another idea is leasing. Large enterprises with tens of billions of dollars' worth of underused equipment and inventories could lease them to small businesses, who can put them to work faster and more profitably than the large plants. (This would merely formalize a relationship that has long existed underground.)

But in the end, nothing beats having good friends in the right places, and even the most energetic entrepreneurs need an opening. One illustration is the story of "Raster," the graphics company described in the vignette at the beginning of the chapter.

"Raster" is the creation of Marina Pereverzeva, a former staffer of *Kommersant* magazine, who is already well started on her third successful venture as a private businesswoman. Raster was the first printing and graphic design company in Russia to switch to contemporary computer-driven image setters and offset printers, the foundation of today's colorful, slick-paper advertising and publishing. The work that Russians used to send out to Finland or Austria now gets done at home.[52] Raster is especially busy at election time, because Raster prints the slick political posters and four-color campaign literature for practically all of the political parties in Russia, government and communists alike.

The chief secret to Raster's creation is politics. Until the fall of 1995, Russian tax laws made it impossible for a modern printing company to operate: imported printing equipment was slapped with heavy taxes, while Russian paper was exported to foreign competitors tax-free. But in

---

[51] Timothy Frye and Andrei Shleifer, "The Invisible Hand and the Grabbing Hand," *American Economic Review*, vol. 87, no. 2 (May 1997), pp. 354–358.

[52] Author's interview, March 1996.

the fall of 1995, as elections approached, Russian politicians needed a good printer – fast. A new tax law, exempting imported printing equipment, flew through the parliament in record time, buoyed by a united coalition of all parties, communists and liberals alike. Raster was on its way. Pereverzeva smiles, "In Russia, politics is both direct and indirect, but it is everywhere."

The most difficult thing for businessmen to deal with is the constantly changing playing field of taxes and customs duties. Within a single year government bureaucrats may raise or lower excise taxes or import duties on sugar, cars, or beer, or any other commodity – and thus at a single stroke turn an entire sector of business from a money-maker to a loser.[53] The unpredictability of politics and state policy makes rational market analysis and corporate strategy practically impossible. Large businesses can defend themselves, but small businesses cannot, unless they vanish underground. Until the state becomes more predictable, small business cannot prosper.

Conclusions

There are two ways to read the story of entrepreneurship in Russia so far. The first is the pessimistic reading. The burst of enterprise that took place between 1985 and 1995 was for the most part an opportunistic response to the disintegration of the Soviet system. Much of it consisted of asset stripping and arbitrage. As a result, business empires were created that have effectively occupied all the major niches in the new Russian economy and are closely tied to political interests at all levels. It is now practically impossible for new businesses to get started, except in the informal economy. The surest sign of this is the stagnation of officially registered small businesses. Entrepreneurship in Russia has been practically stifled.

But there is a more optimistic reading. Entrepreneurship is a trait that Russians have long shown in abundance, and under circumstances far more difficult than those of today. There is no reason why this source should abruptly dry up. If the Russian market continues to develop, it will provide openings for a new generation of managers who are equipped to deal with it. On this reading, the recent signs of revival of consumer goods and food processing after August 1998, especially in the provinces outside Moscow, suggests that there is already a strong entrepreneurial response to the cheaper ruble and the edge it gives Russian players against imports.

---

[53] Dan Medovnikov, "Ozhivshie rynki," *Ekspert*, No. 1 (January 12 1998). pp. 74–75.

On the eve of the August crash, entrepreneurship was still flourishing in some sectors, such as computer software. A senior executive of the Russian software giant IBS commented to me, "I don't see a crisis of entrepreneurship in this country. In the software field, I see many more companies than there were five years ago." They're mostly middle-level managers from companies like mine. They're pragmatic people, very tuned to the bottom line. They're different from the first generation of entrepreneurs, who had original ideas but couldn't manage."[54]

Yet it will be a long time before the effects of the Russian Nineties fade away. The lasting legacy of the first phases of entrepreneurship – the underground, the cooperatives, the "siphons," the arbitrageurs and speculators – is a style of business oriented toward near-term opportunism, cozy ties with the state, location in Moscow, and large size.

[54] Vera Krasnova and Anastasia Matveeva, "Nastuplenie 'chernykh vorotnikov,'" *Ekspert*, No. 1 (January 12 1998), pp. 76–78.

A criminal revolution is taking place in this country. Or rather, it is already nearing completion. And its final victory will be the building of a criminal-mafia state.

Stanislav Govorukhin, Russian film-maker and
nationalist politician[1]

Sure, it's all true. But my children will be honest.

Otari Kvantrishvili (1948–1994), late Moscow godfather[2]

6   Russia's epidemic of crime

Spring 1998:

Walking down the neat paths of Moscow's grimly fashionable Vagankovskoe cemetery, a visitor will find in the rows of freshly-dug graves a distinguished company of Russia's new business and criminal elite. There Ivan Kivelidi, lately chairman of the Russian Business Roundtable, and Vladislav Listev, ex-general director of ORT Television, rest in peace not far from Otari Kvantrishvili, one of the most flamboyant of Moscow's dons until he was gunned down outside his favorite steambath in 1994. Watching over them all is Vagankovskoe's most famous resident, the bard Vladimir Vysotskii, who died in 1980. Vysotskii would have mined rich material for his ballads from today's scene – not least from the fact that Vagankovskoe itself has become a market commodity. So great is demand lately that getting buried there requires some of the heftiest bribes in Moscow.[3]

A tidal wave of crime

From one of the world's most tightly-policed and well-ordered societies only twenty years ago – at least, so it seemed to the outside world and to most Russians themselves – Russia has become one of the most criminal and corrupt. Recorded crimes have more than tripled since the mid-1970s.[4] And those numbers are well short of the true mark, since even the

[1] Stanislav Govorukhin, *Velikaia kriminal'naia revoliutsiia* (Moscow: "Andreevskii flag," 1993), p. 34.
[2] Iurii Shchekochikhin, *Literaturnaia gazeta*, quoted in *The New York Times*, April 14 1994, p. A3.   [3] *The New York Times*, November 15 1994, p. A3.
[4] These numbers, which originate from the Ministry of Interior, are reproduced in *Izvestiia*, October 18 1994, p. 1; and V.M. Rybkin, ed., *Prestupnost' v Rossii v devianostykh godakh i nekotorye aspekty zakonnosti bor'by s nei* (Moscow: "Kriminologicheskaia Assotsiatsiia," 1995), pp. 4–5. Goskomstat, the Russian government statistical agency, publishes annual updates, which are available by Internet.

police acknowledge that at least half of all crimes go unreported. In some categories the share of reported crimes may be as a low as 10%. Crime has ballooned in all its forms, from ordinary burglaries and assaults to sophisticated computer scams, massive embezzlement and fraud, bribe-taking, international drug traffic, and organized violence.

What makes Russian crime different?

Russia, of course, is not the only industrial country with a serious crime problem. Violent crime in the inner cities of America is arguably worse than in downtown Moscow or St. Petersburg, although the overall homicide rate is higher in Russia than in the United States.[5] The underground economy of the United States, consisting of unreported and/or illegal activities, is variously estimated at between 6 and 8% of GNP.[6] In the European Union, the estimated size of the informal economy ranges from 2 to 7% of official GDP in the Scandinavian countries to as much as a quarter or even one-third in Italy and Greece.[7]

Crime and corruption were certainly not unknown in the old Soviet system. Just underneath the surface of the centrally-planned economy there was a thriving underground. It grew steadily in the last decades of the Soviet regime, and by the mid-1980s, on the eve of the Gorbachev reforms, may have accounted for as much as 20% of the Soviet GNP.[8]

But the key point about Soviet crime is precisely that it was under the surface. An article in *Izvestiia* sums up nicely the difference between the Soviet past and the Russian present: "Crime was never able to gain

[5] Former interior minister Anatolii Kulikov cites 29,000 homicides in Russia in 1997, vs. 22,000 in the United States. (*Nezavisimoe televidenie*, January 28 1998, by Internet). But official statistics in the two countries are not directly comparable. The homicide rate in the United States runs at about 10 per 100,000, while in Russia the category of recorded "murders and attempted murders" in 1996 was about 20 per 100,000.

[6] For two approaches, one from the income side and the other from the production side, see Morton Paglin, "The Underground Economy: New Estimates from Household Income and Expenditure Surveys," *Yale Law Journal*, vol. 103 (1994), pp. 2239–57; and Harry I. Greenfield, *Invisible, Outlawed, and Untaxed: America's Underground Economy* (Westport, Connecticut: Praeger, 1993).

[7] European Union Commission, as reported in *Financial Times,* April 8 1998, p. 2. See also James J. Thomas, *Informal Economic Activity*, LSE Handbooks in Economics (Ann Arbor, Michigan: University of Michigan Press, 1992).

[8] Vladimir G. Treml and Michael Alexeev, "The Growth of the Second Economy in the Soviet Union and its Impact on the System," in Robert W. Campbell, ed., *The Postcommunist Economic Transformation* (Boulder, Colorado: Westview Press, 1994), pp. 222–224. Treml and Alexeev estimate that by the late 1970s the second economy accounted for between 15 and 18% of total economic activity in the USSR. By the mid-1980s it had presumably grown even larger. Cf. p. 115, fn. 10 above for estimates by Gregory Grossman.

See also Konstantin M. Simis, *The Corrupt Society: the Secret World of Soviet Capitalism* (New York: Simon and Schuster, 1982)

enough strength to compete with the state's law enforcement system. The criminal world had ties with the police, but it was all kept deeply hidden. Money had influence, but it was not all-powerful. Laundering the profits from crime was difficult, and spending them equally so. There were millionaires, but they were underground. There were gangs – but to get weapons they had to run enormous risks. We had it all. But it was all under the surface."[9]

So just what makes the new Russian crime wave different from the past or from other countries? How does it affect the new Russian market economy? And how may it shape Russia's capitalism in the future?

If crime was endemic in the Soviet system, it became epidemic in the 1990s. For an epidemiologist, an epidemic is different from an endemic disease in three ways: it strikes when society is weakened, it rapidly builds to a peak in which a large part of the population is infected, and then it subsides.

What turns an endemic disease into an epidemic is opportunity. The Russian state is weak, yet obstructive. Society is in disarray and many people have been cut loose from their moorings. An inexperienced private sector is unable to manage its own affairs. And the opportunities for gain have been tremendous. Russia is like an organism whose immune system has broken down, and which succumbs to opportunistic infection by a microbe that previously lived more or less quietly in its gut. The breakdown of the Soviet system and the turmoil of transition have overwhelmed Russia's defenses, making it an easy victim.

But the key point is that epidemics eventually subside, and the same thing will likely happen to the Russian crime epidemic, provided its three principal causes abate. As Russian society settles into a new order, as relations between the state and the private sector evolve and stabilize, and as the massive transfer of rent and property is completed – then crime in Russia will settle into less virulent and violent forms.

Yet Russian crime in its endemic form may turn out to be no less insidious and no less damaging to the prospects for a healthy market economy. Ultimately, the answer to the question, "What makes Russian crime different?" is the lack of clear line – both in law and in people's minds – between legal and illegal. That is why the most serious forms of crime in Russia are not crimes of violence but of money.

---

[9] The quote comes from a two-part series on crime that appeared under the title of "Ugolovnaia Rossiia" in *Izvestiia* on October 18 and 19, 1994, pp. 5 and 6 respectively.

The Russian "trademark" crimes: extortion, fraud, and bribery

Murder gets the headlines, but the Russian "trademark" crimes are extortion, fraud, and bribery. "Economic crime" is a catch-all category used in Russian law-enforcement statistics to cover an assortment of crimes against property, ranging from theft, embezzling, and fraud to counterfeiting, falsifying documents and contracts, and concealing income.[10] The epidemic of economic crime broke out as soon as there was new private money to steal. According to the Russian business weekly *Kommersant*, as early as 1994 economic crime in all its forms represented $30 billion in stolen or falsified assets.[11] By 1997 it was estimated that economic crimes were doubling every two years.[12]

Seventy to eighty per cent of all Russian private enterprises and commercial banks, according to a presidential report,[13] pay protection money to criminal rackets, amounting to between 10 and 20% of their turnover, or roughly half of their profits. Practically all small consumer businesses, such as kiosks, restaurants, cafes, and small shops, pay tribute in this way. Extortion has also spread into the countryside, strangling the small class of private farmers even before they get started.

Organized gangs know whom to shake down and how much to demand, because an army of police officers, bank officials, and undercover agents serve as tipsters. Traffic police stopping cars at checkpoints radio ahead to gang accomplices when they discover something valuable in the trunk. Bank officials are pressured into opening their account lists to gangs, revealing the balances of private businesses. (This is one reason why bank officials have been the special target of contract killers.) Criminal groups infiltrate companies with moles who gather information about illegal activities or personal scandals, which is then used to blackmail the company's officers.[14]

Extortion is tough to fight because nearly everyone has something to

---

[10] A wide-ranging survey of "economic crimes" appears in *Kommersant* (weekly), No. 22 (June 13 1995), pp. 17–24. In addition to the crimes listed in the text, this category includes illegal exports of strategic goods, unlicensed trade, sale of debased goods, illegal privatization, false declaration of bankruptcy, and creation of fictitious companies and false bank guarantees.

The definition of "economic crimes" excludes, however, illegal trade in criminal goods and activities, such as narcotics, prostitution, arms traffic, and the like. Also excluded are crimes committed in Chechnya and Ingushetiia, since the police have no statistics from those areas.   [11] *Kommersant* (weekly), op. cit., p. 17.

[12] Elena Kudriavtseva, "Ekonomicheskaia bezopasnost' v Rossii," *Delovoi ekspress*, January 27 1998, by Internet.

[13] The report, written by then-presidential adviser Petr Filippov, is summarized in *Izvestiia* (January 26 1994) and in *The New York Times* (January 30 1994).

[14] *Kommersant* (weekly), No. 20 (May 30 1995), pp. 44–48.

hide. Victims will not report crimes to the police, for fear of revealing their incomes to the tax inspectors or to corrupt officials who will tip off the gangsters. One Russian source estimates that 80% of robberies and 90% of frauds are never reported.[15]

The epidemic of money crimes is the rough underside of the new Russian revolution, a by-product of the return of money to center stage and the overnight transfer of Russia's wealth into private hands. But why has it become so universal? The answer is the weakness of the defenses against it, in both the private sector and the state.

The hapless private sector

Russian private business has had to learn from scratch how to protect itself. The enemies outside are violence, extortion, and corruption; those inside are fraud and theft. Russian private companies have had to learn to survive in a jungle, in which, initially at least, there was no way of telling a good loan from a bad one, an honest partner from a crook, or a legal act from a crime.

Embezzlement and fraud are frequently committed by owners and managers themselves. Internal shadiness then invites external aggression. A typical sequence goes like this: a disloyal employee (or a plant) informs local ganglords of illegal goings-on inside a company. The gang then blackmails its way into control of the company. If the management refuses to cooperate, it is eliminated. Many private banks have been penetrated in this way.[16]

This is the cycle that leads to murders of businessmen and bank presidents.[17] Business leaders are learning the hard way that the best way to keep a hired killer off their trail is to run a tight ship and avoid attracting unwelcome notice in the first place. Vladimir Lutsenko, a former KGB counterterrorist officer and now the head of a private security agency named "Stealth," comments, "When businessmen start getting threats, they run to us, crying, 'For God's sake protect me!' But they don't understand that it's already too late. They should have begun thinking earlier."[18]

---

[15] *Finansovye izvestiia*, No. 24 (May 26–June 1 1994).

[16] Georgii Shvyrkov and Boris Klin, "Agent mafii," *Kommersant* (weekly), No. 20 (May 30 1995), p. 45.

[17] According to the Association of Russian Banks, 97 bank presidents and high-ranking bank officers were murdered in the five-year period between 1992 and 1997. (Source: Vitalii Sidorov, executive director of the Association of Russian Banks, cited in Kudriavtseva, op. cit.)   [18] *Kommersant* (weekly), No. 10 (March 21 1995), p. 44.

The deficient state and its consequences

The next major cause of the Russian crime epidemic is the state. There are three problems. First, the state has become too weak to provide basic law and order – to protect citizens' lives and property rights, and to enforce contracts. Second, the state has not yet developed the legal framework and the regulatory functions needed to keep markets open and honest. Indeed, the laws and the judicial system are so deficient that much of the time it is simply not clear what is legal and what is not, and in any case it is difficult to gain redress through the courts. Third, what powers the state does retain are more often "negative" than "positive," i.e., they consist of obstructions and prohibitions – the result of incomplete liberalization of the economy – which officials at all levels exploit to levy tribute.

The main direct cause of the state's weakness is its inability to bring in tax revenue (this is discussed in detail in Chapter 9). This problem is especially difficult to combat because it is self-reinforcing. For lack of money, the police, the customs, and the tax collectors are underpaid, undertrained, and underarmed. Not surprisingly, many of them have streamed into the private sector, to work for private security services. Among those who remain, morale is low and corruption is rife.

Where ordinary Russians see it most is on the roads. "The traffic police pull you over to the side of the road," says a young trucker, "and you'll stay there for one or two days, because one of your headlights is out. You'll pay a 'lemon' (*limon* – slang for 1 million old rubles, then worth about $160) just to get away."[19]

The state is weak, but it is still ever-present. Despite the reforms since 1992, the economy has been only partly liberalized. Regional and city governments require a host of licenses and permits before private businesses can operate. Whatever the original intentions, these restrictions turn government offices into tollbooths for bribery. Even the reformers' efforts to create new regulatory structures for the market economy, such as anti-trust legislation or foreign-trade controls, become new opportunities for bureaucrats to claim turf and levy tribute.[20]

The result of such official corruption is that many markets and

[19] *Rossiiskaia gazeta*, June 22 1995, p. 8.
[20] Anders Aslund, *How Russia Became a Market Economy* (Washington, D.C.: Brookings, 1995), p. 155. See especially Chapter 5 for a discussion of problems of liberalization. The sources of corruption are discussed at length in Georgii Satarov, M.I. Levin, M.L. Tsirik, "Rossiia i korruptsiia" (Report sponsored jointly by the Council on Foreign and Defense Policy and the "Information for Democracy" Fund), published in *Rossiiskaia gazeta*, February 19 1998.

transactions which should be legal behave instead like illicit markets – unpredictable, insecure, and inefficient. Such markets force otherwise honest businessmen to skirt the law, and attract criminals to run them.[21]

The most striking example of this is the management of oil exports. Fearing that domestic industries would be deprived of cheap oil, the federal government until 1995 restricted oil exports through licenses and quotas. As a result, domestic oil prices remained so low that many Russian oil producers operated at a loss.[22] But the difference between the domestic price and the world price created a huge incentive to cheat, and oil leaked out of the country through every available pore. A barrel of oil leaving the wellhead could get "lost" in countless ways: flow meters in the pipeline system undercounted actual volumes shipped; oil travelling by rail and small river tankers bypassed official controls; exports to Ukraine and Latvia at low subsidized prices ended up in the West. But the main loophole in the system was officialdom itself, as traders and producers lined up outside government offices to obtain special export licenses, deferments of export taxes, and quotas "for state needs." The oil trade soon became one of the most lucrative sources of illegal profits in the Russian economy.

Russian gangsters quickly muscled into some part of the oil trade, buying crude and refined products from oilmen and reselling them through networks that stretched to Cyprus and New York. One of the legendary figures in this business was Sergei Timofeev, a former tractor driver from Novgorod Province, who under the name of "Sylvester" became one of the most notorious of the Moscow dons. Sylvester had a talent for business, and was one of the first to set up offshore companies in Cyprus to launder his profits. He fought ruthlessly for control of the illegal oil flow, reportedly hiring professional killers to rub out his rivals. But in September 1994 Sylvester's enemies caught up with him. On a busy street in downtown Moscow his Mercedes 600 blew sky-high, taking Sylvester with it.[23]

In the space of ten years, Russia has gone from a closed economy to one of the world's most open ones. This is partly the reformers' design, but

[21] On the properties of "illicit markets," see Diego Gambetta, *The Sicilian Mafia* (Cambridge, Mass.: Harvard University Press, 1995), p. 226.

[22] Eugene M. Khartukov, "Russia's Oil Prices: Passage to the Market" East-West Center Working Papers, Energy and Minerals Series, No. 20 (Honolulu, Hawaii: East-West Center, September 1995). For background see Organization for Economic Cooperation and Development, International Energy Agency, *Russian Energy Prices, Taxes, and Costs 1993* (Paris: OECD, 1994), and same, *Energy Policies of the Russian Federation: 1995 Survey* (Paris: OECD, 1995). The evolution of the oil-export system is systematically covered month-by-month in the journal, *Russian Petroleum Investor*.

[23] *Moskovskie novosti*, No. 39 (June 4–11 1995), pp. 1 and 2.

also a result of the state's limited inability to control its own borders. Its frontiers with the other republics of the former Soviet Union, previously only symbolic lines drawn on maps, are now wide open to every kind of commerce. International telephone circuits have multiplied, and Russians are surfing on the Internet. And as Russian travelers and capital stream through the porous borders, they are rapidly connecting the country to the international pathways of finance, trade, tourism, and crime. It is no wonder that the Russian border guards and customs officials have been overwhelmed. Two examples give the flavor: the thriving drug trade through Central Asia and international computer crime from St. Petersburg.

Hundreds of years ago the riverbeds of south Russia and Central Asia were the favorite attack routes of the Mongol cavalry. As dry beds in summer or frozen highways of ice in winter, they allowed fast and undetected movement. Today some of those same channels are being used for a new invasion – a Silk Road of international crime, bringing opium from the vast poppy fields of Afghanistan and Tadzhikistan through Kyrgyzstan and then Moscow to markets in Europe and America. The economics are overwhelming. A brown brick of pure opium gum costs $400 a pound in the market at Osh in Kyrgyzstan, and $5,000 a pound in Moscow, where it is turned into heroin.

It is a fast-growing traffic, helped along by massive bribes to local officials and police. Russian soldiers and border guards play a key role. "If you have enough money," says a Kyrgiz anti-narcotics official, "you can pay Russian border guards to deliver your opium in helicopters."[24] In Europe, the Moscow connection is becoming one of the most important drug arteries in the world.[25]

At the other extreme is international crime by computer. On March 3 1995 a slight, harmless-looking young man with thick spectacles landed at Heathrow Airport on a flight from St. Petersburg. British police, seconded by FBI agents, were waiting for him. They marched him off to London's Brixton Jail, where he awaited extradition to the United States for trial. The charge: 128 counts of computer fraud and illegal entry. Thus ended the career of Vladimir Levin, international hacker extraordinaire.[26]

From June to October 1994, armed with nothing more than a laptop, Vladimir Levin sat in his small office on Malaya Morskaya Street in St. Petersburg and roamed at will through the vaults of Citibank in far-off

[24] *The New York Times*, May 2 1995, p. A10.
[25] International Narcotics Control Board, cited in *The New York Times*, ibid.
[26] The Levin affair was widely covered in the Russian press. See *Izvestiia*, August 23 1995, p. 2; August 24 1995, p. 2; September 7 1995, p. 5; September 19 1995, p. 5; *Kommersant-Daily*, September 7 1995, p. 14.

New York City. Over the course of five months, he broke in over forty times into Citibank's electronic banking system, and transferred more than $10 million to accounts controlled by his accomplices in banks all over the world.

The main victims of computer crime are more likely to be the Russian banks themselves. Between 1993 and 1997 there have been several hundred attempted computer break-ins into the Russian Central Bank, Sberbank, and the major commercial banks.[27] The banks have had to develop their own private methods for dealing with this form of crime, since public law-enforcement bodies have neither the skills nor the technology to cope with it.

Who are the criminals?

Who are the criminals? In the media folklore they have gang names (in Russian, "*klichki*") like "Baboon," "Globus," "Calistratus, "the Jap," and "Mad Fedor." They are the dons and the foot soldiers of the gangster armies that have taken over Russia in the last few years – some 35,000 mobsters, loosely grouped in over 8,000 gangs throughout the country, a ten-fold increase since 1990.[28] They wage a relentless war against one another and against their victims, for control of drugs, prostitution, gambling, protection, foreign luxury cars, banking, and retail trade of all kinds. In the media they are easily recognized by their tattoos and their baleful stares.

But in reality the ranks of the Russian criminal world are far more diverse than the stereotypical picture. The weakness of the post-Soviet state and the upheaval in Russian society have supplied hundreds of thousands of potential recuits for crime, many of them former KGB and army officers, professionally trained in the arts of war and violence – veterans of Afghanistan, Chechnya, and the border wars of recent years, as well as athletes and members of sports clubs. This sudden influx of manpower helps to account not only for the sharp increase in crime, but also its violent and anarchic character.

The term, "mafia," has a very specific meaning in the West, but Russians apply it loosely to all organized crime, or indeed to the government.[29] In actual fact, there is nothing in Russia quite like the "Cosa Nostra," with its deep roots in rural Sicily, its elaborate rituals, and its tradition of silence.[30] The closest equivalent is the clan-based gangs of the

---

[27] Kudriavtsev, op. cit., based on reports from the Association of Russian Banks.

[28] *Prestupnost' v Rossii*, op. cit., p. 14, based on figures from the Ministry of Internal Affairs.

[29] For an example see Fridrikh Neznanskii, "Mafiia – nash rulevoi!" *Posev*, No. 4 (1993), pp. 25–35.   [30] The best treatment is Gambetta, op. cit.

asteroid-belt republics of the North Caucasus, chiefly Chechnya and Dagestan. The cultures of these mountain peoples are similar in some ways to those of Sicily, notably in their stress on honor and shame, and in their hostility to Russian outsiders and to the government in far-off Moscow. In Russia itself, the closest equivalent to the mafia was the Soviet criminal underworld, whose central figure was the *vor v zakone*, literally "thief in the law," an untranslatable expression meaning a thief who had taken a vow of loyalty to his fellow thieves and their counter-culture. However, if we define the term "mafia" functionally, as some experts do, as a criminal group supplying private "protection," then there are indeed powerful mafias in Russia.[31]

But to a Western ear, terms like "mafia" and "organized crime" suggest a reasonably well-ordered world, in which mafia godfathers divide up turfs and keep the peace, despite occasional break-downs and gang wars. But in Russia in the last decade the world of crime has been a free-for-all. In that sense, the Russian criminal world mirrors the rest of the new Russian economy.

There have been three distinct generations of crime at work in Russia. The first generation, made up largely of Russians and Russianized Caucasians, arose out of the penal system and underground economy of the Soviet Union. The Soviet thieves' code, like other Soviet institutions, weakened in the 1970s and 80s, particularly the ban on material wealth. Many *vory v zakone* had already amassed large amounts of capital by the mid-1980s, and they grew richer still on the opportunities opened up under Gorbachev. As soon as cooperatives became legal in 1987, the thieves' *obshchak* (traditionally a store of money that was a sort of self-help fund for thieves and their families) became venture capital for the creation of private businesses of all kinds, including banks and trading companies. As their fortunes grew, many of the *vory* moved upstairs into the executive suites of the businesses they had created. From behind the scenes they now control large territories of kiosks, casinos, cafés, currency exchanges, and automotive showrooms.

But even as early as the 1970s the older generation of *vory v zakone* began to be challenged by a new crowd of gangsters, mostly from the southern republics. Under Gorbachev's *perestroika* the southern groups, with their keen commercial sense, were quick to put their wealth to work

---

[31] On the differences between Russian criminal groups and "true" mafias, see Federico Varese, "Is Sicily the Future of Russia? Private Protection and the Rise of the Russian Mafia," *Archives Européennes de Sociologie*, vol. 35 (1994), pp. 224–258; also same, "Some Misconceptions Regarding the Russian Mafia," testimony to the United States Senate Committee on Foreign Relations, Washington, D.C. May 15 1995. (Published in A. Van Boren, ed., *Russian Organized Crime: A White Paper Report*. Washington, D.C.: United States Senate, Committee on Foreign Relations, 1995).

in new business opportunities. By 1990 the Caucasians had become a force to be reckoned with in the major Russian cities; and throughout southern Russia.[32]

The Caucasians are desperate and well-armed men, who have managed to displace several of the established *vory v zakone* in the big cities. But both the classic Russian *vory* and the Caucasians have come under fierce attack from a third generation of younger Russian criminals, who have sprung up since 1990. The new Russian toughs reject the codes of the older generation. Many are former soldiers who saw action in Chechnya, or former policemen. Another source is the sports and fitness clubs and self-defense schools in the major cities. These were formerly supported by the state but have now been taken over by gangs, giving a new twist to the term, "organized sports."[33]

The old Russian criminal aristocracy is still dominant only in the quieter provinces.[34] Elsewhere, the more money there is to be made, the fiercer is the war between the generations, and between the Russians and the Caucasians. Moscow is the big time, and therefore the biggest battlefield, but some other locations have recently emerged as prime territory for crime, well worth fighting to control.

In recent years, several members of this first generation have begun the transition out of the thieves' world and into "respectable" business and politics, though keeping one foot in both. The most spectacular example was Otari Kvantrishvili. By the time of his untimely death in 1994 Kvantrishvili had become one of Moscow's leading godfathers, but simultaneously a prominent philanthropist, politician, and television personality. Born in Georgia but raised in Moscow's Presnia district, Kvantrishvili was never strictly speaking a *vor v zakone* – he had not done enough time in prison and he kept steady official jobs – yet he came from the same criminal milieu, initially specializing in illegal card games and racetrack oddsmaking.

Beginning in the late 1980s, Kvantrishvili helped to found a trading company called "Century 21," which soon amassed a fortune exporting oil, timber, and metals (and some say, importing weapons as well.)[35] By 1992 Kvantrishvili had branched out into businesses all over Moscow, including a network of trading companies, two banks (one of them named after Kvantrishvili's old neighborhood, Presnia), and a well-known

---

[32] Galina Sergushina, "Prestuplenie v sotsial'nom rakurse," *Stavropol'skie gubernskie vedomosti* (January 20 1999), p. 1, by Internet.   [33] Kryshtanovskaia, op. cit.

[34] A. Tereshonok and Iu. Adashevich, "Vektor prestupnosti," *Moskva*, No. 11 (November 1992), pp. 119–122.

[35] Ol'ga Kryshtanovskaia, "Mafioznyi peizazh Rossii," *Izvestiia*, September 21 1995.

casino, "Gabriela," located in the Intourist Hotel, where Kvantrishvili also had his main office.[36]

Kvantrishvili became famous for his philanthropy and his sponsorship of sports clubs throughout Russia. Through his charity, the "Yashin Fund," he gave lavishly to veterans' groups, orphans, and elderly athletes. He supported sports clubs and schools, and sponsored sporting events. But philanthropy was also good business. In 1993 Boris Yeltsin signed a decree granting to one of Kvantrishvili's organizations, the Sports Academy, the right to import consumer goods tax-free to support its sporting activities. Thus Kvantrishvili became one of the leading beneficiaries of the billions of dollars of duty-free imports that poured into Russia in the early 1990s.

Kvantrishvili became a unique figure in Moscow – on the one hand a mafia godfather, arbitrating disputes among gang leaders and brokering deals, yet on the other hand a leading man about town, maintaining close friendships with leading politicians and police officials. By early 1994 Kvantrishvili had even founded a political party, "Sportsmen of Russia," and seemed about to take a whirl in the parliamentary elections scheduled for that December. It is no wonder that when he was murdered in April 1994, the cream of Moscow's gang leaders, athletes, businessmen, and politicians showed up for a spectacular gangland funeral. No one had managed quite so well to reach out to all of the diverse worlds of the new Russia. As Kvantrishvili himself used to say, in words that summed up his career, "I have a good feel for horses and people." As usual, his killers were never found.

Disorganized Russian crime: "in this environment, who can do any business?"

Thus three generations of crime have been busy slugging it out in Russia. The gangsters themselves understand this is bad for business, especially their own. Intergang warfare raises costs and cuts into profits. Host businesses are squeezed too hard and fold up. Illegal goods are oversupplied, and total revenues go down. The biggest crime problem in Russia is not organized crime, but disorganized crime.

The difficulty, as economists would say, is controlling market entry. A good example of the problem is on the highways, where it is easy for beginners to get started. A trucker sighed for the good old days: "It used to be quite clear. People would pass the word along the road: 'Vaskin's

---

[36] Kryshtanovskaia, op. cit.

team is working the Penza area. Get 200 rubles ready.' And when you got to Penza someone would come up and say, 'I'm from Vaskin.' And we'd settle with him. But today the serious bandits don't come out on the highways. They have their own offices. Now the small fry are working the roads."[37]

The "serious bandits" (meaning the ones with the most to lose) have been working to solve the problem by regulating the crime market themselves. Police accounts speak of endless meetings among criminal groups, obviously attempts to work out more stable territories. This is easier to achieve in the smaller cities than in Moscow, where the potential gains from crime are the most enticing and the oversupply of gangsters is the greatest. But in Yekaterinburg, for example, it is reported that the city has been divided up into three more or less stable zones, each one under the control of a separate gang: the Uralmash group, the Central, and the Sky-Blue (so named because of the tattoos covering their bodies).[38] Similar reports come from Krasnoyarsk, Penza, Yaroslavl', and even Moscow Province, where seven *vory v zakone* are said to preside over 49 "stable" criminal groups.[39]

But it is doubtful that true stability can be achieved in this way. As sociologist Diego Gambetta points out, peace among gangs is almost always unstable. After all, mistrust is precisely what the criminal world feeds on, and illicit markets are by definition disordered markets.[40] It is only in places like Sicily, where mafia gangs share a common rural culture and a suspicion of outsiders, that some basis for solidarity exists.[41] A strong and closed urban ethnic neighborhood, as in some cities of the United States, can produce the same result. Clearly, in today's Russia, where criminal groups come from widely different backgrounds and have little in common, mutual trust is all the more difficult to attain.

Yet the key factors to watch, as in any market, are supply and demand. Over time, as Russian society stabilizes, the supply of criminal recruits will dwindle. And as the market economy matures, the gains from what one might call "windfall crime" – the opportunities created by the transitional economy – have already faded.   In their place is already emerging the next generation of crime – economic crime, insider fraud and embezzlement, armed with computers. It is quieter and less violent, and far more difficult for the authorities to deal with. Indeed, as the criminal world stabilizes inside Russia, it may become even more dangerous outside. As a senior FBI official in charge of tackling Russian organized

---

[37] *Rossiiskaia gazeta*, June 22 1995, p. 8.
[38] *Izvestiia*, June 30 1995, p. 5; October 19 1994, p. 5. See also Govorukhin, op. cit., pp. 23–31.   [39] *Izvestiia*, October 19 1994, September 21 1995.
[40] Ibid, p. 226ff.   [41] Gambetta, pp. 246–247.

crime in the US commented in early 1999, "It's a growth industry, and we're still losing."[42]

The most spectacular example to date is the incredible odyssey of the YBM Corporation, a Philadelphia-based manufacturing company that turned out to be a money-laundering front for a powerful Russian criminal boss. Until the company was exposed in mid-1998, it boasted a blue-ribbon board, had its books audited by the best accounting companies, gained a listing on the Canadian stock exchange, and sold its stock throughout North America. To its shareholders it appeared to be a respectable producer of industrial magnets. But unbeknownst even to some of its directors, the company's real business was laundering the profits of Russian mobsters from prostitution, extortion, arms-dealing, and drug-trafficking throughout the former Soviet empire.[43]

The impact of crime

In the 1990s Russians have had to adapt to crime as an everyday reality. At all levels of society, crime has changed the social landscape and the psychological climate. The wealthy can afford bodyguards, but the new middle classes must find other strategies for self-defense. They have learned to keep a low profile and to strengthen their front doors. But as crime has seeped into the fabric of Russian society, it has become less visible, more routine. For many smaller businessmen, "protection" these days literally comes with the rental lease.

What is the impact of crime on the Russian economy? The question is difficult to answer precisely, because most nonviolent crime is not reported – and anyway, it is hard to draw a clear line between what is criminal and what is not. But it is clear enough that crime is a major drain on the new Russian economy. Its overall effect is to aggravate the new economy's two most central problems, non-payments and disinvestment.

There are six negative effects. The first is aggravated inflation. Many forms of organized crime have the effect of creating money and increasing its velocity. False letters of credit and payment orders, embezzlement, forgery of money and financial paper, all amount to uncontrolled emission of money. In addition, businesses that lose money from crime pass their increased costs on to their customers.

The second effect is distributional. Crime robs the have-nots by reducing tax receipts, thus cutting into government spending for welfare and other social programs. To offset the inflationary effect of crime, the

[42] Presentation to the U.S.–Russian Business Council, Washington D.C. (January 27 1999).   [43] *The New York Times*, July 25 1999, pp. A1 and 4.

government is obliged to lean harder in the other direction with harsher deflationary policies, chiefly by delaying payment of wages and pensions and withholding other government funds. In short, crime reduces public goods in favor of private ones.

Third, crime reduces investment as against current consumption, thus robbing the future in favor of the present. Because it cannot collect its taxes the state invests less – notably in future-oriented programs such as education and scientific research. The private sector invests less because its profits are siphoned off. Crime-induced inflation causes individuals to save less. In addition, crime adds to the general insecurity of life, causing people to spend their money instead of saving it – which in turn adds further to inflationary pressures. All of these effects together produce high interest rates, which also discourage investment.[44]

Fourth, crime contributes to capital flight and the "dollarization" of the economy, thus weakening the ruble and fueling inflation still more. More capital has flowed out of Russia since 1991 than has come in, amounting to a massive disinvestment in the Russian economy. Criminals themselves, for obvious reasons, prefer to export their booty rather than invest at home. But legitimate businessmen, too, seek to safeguard their assets against crime by moving them abroad. Ordinary people, also looking for safe havens, put their money into dollars rather than invest them in vulnerable ventures.

Fifth, a criminal economy is an inefficient economy. Penetration by gangs turns some otherwise legal markets into illicit ones, and illicit markets are disorderly markets. Insecure or fraudulent property rights are inefficient property rights. Lack of investment means no new technologies and therefore no efficiency gains from innovation. Corruption and extortion amount to double taxation, adding to costs. Moreover, the lure of corruption discourages bureaucrats from removing barriers to the free movement of resources, thus increasing the overall "friction" in the economy. The threat of extortion favors large cartels that can defend themselves – but these then lobby the government for special favors, thus encouraging inefficiency rather than the opposite.

Last, and perhaps most important, crime creates attitudes and expectations that threaten the very basis and survival of a market economy. Fear and distrust pervade relations between people, discouraging the free movement of goods and people, and creating a "demand for trust" that criminal elements are quick to provide.[45] Expecting to be cheated, people

---

[44] From the economist's perspective, interest rates represent the price of money, but they also express the "social rate of time preference" between the present and the future. An economy that does not invest is, in effect, discounting the future.
[45] Gambetta, pp. 255–6.

cheat first – and thus a downward cycle is created, in which everyone comes to expect the worst. Above all, pervasive crime breeds popular disgust and rage, which undermine the legitimacy of both the government and the private sector.

The future of Russian crime

The extent and nature of crime, anywhere in the world, are symptoms of the state of society. In Russia in the 1990s, epidemic crime has been a by-product of collapse and shock. Indeed, the financial crash of August 1998 brought new hardship and instability, perhaps accounting for a sharp upturn in reported crime in 1998.[46]

The crime epidemic will only begin to pass as the shock does. The era of easy plunder and overnight fortunes is already ending, as inflation slows and the ruble stabilizes. The state will gradually gain greater control over tax revenue, which would enable it to pay decent wages to soldiers and policemen. More important, as the post-Soviet "coercive elites" stop shrinking, the flood of trained new recruits for crime may be diminishing. Disorganized crime is becoming more organized, as criminal *avtoritety* divide up their turfs and close out new entrants. Hired killings may decline, as private businessmen figure out more efficient ways to collect debts and enforce deals, and also learn how to protect themselves. Today's bloody battles for control will subside as the vast Russian redistribution of property and rents, the *peredel*, comes to an end.

But perhaps organized crime has taken such deep hold in Russia that its grip cannot be broken? Not necessarily. The new mafias in Russia may be weaker than they appear. The non-Russian gangs are especially vulnerable. Unlike America, there are no large and well-defined ethnic enclaves in the major Russian cities. Non-Russian gangs cannot simply melt away from the police into friendly neighborhoods. That makes them more exposed than ethnic gangs in the United States. (On the other hand, on their home turf in the North Caucasus, such groups are proving all the more difficult to deal with.)

Second, organized crime in Russia cannot hide behind the law. Criminal justice in Russia, when it chooses to be, is still swift and summary, and defendants' rights are weak. Most arrests lead to convictions, there is no plea-bargaining, and sentences are long. Administrative detention is still the norm. If the authorities begin making a determined effort to crack down on organized crime, the "mafias" will have few legal

---

[46] Annual report by acting General Procurator Iurii Chaika, *Nezavisimaia gazeta* (February 4 1999), by Internet.

defenses. Ironically, the low level of legality that helps to breed crime in the first place also deprives organized crime of one of its defenses.

Yet the deeper causes of endemic crime will remain for a long time, particularly the weakness of the laws and the lack of any clear distinction between legitimate business and racketeering. So long as all private business lies in a twilight zone between legality and illegality, it is suspect. Dirty money cannot be laundered (except abroad), since no money is indisputably clean. Businessmen and racketeers alike will require political protection, and will buy politicians to get it. Both businessmen and racketeers will continue to use private enforcers so long as there are no strong legal mechanisms for the execution of contracts.

Consider the contrast between the United States and Russia. In the United States, criminal money can become "clean" as soon as it is invested in a legitimate business. This leads to a typical American pattern: the mob money of one generation can become respectable in the next. But this is possible so long as the line between legitimate and illegitimate business is clear. In Russia, practically no business is entirely legitimate – not only in the eyes of the population but before the law as well. Consequently, the only way for second-economy profits (whether criminal or not) to become really legitimate is to go abroad. Neither is there any basis for amnesty, except a blanket one that would forgive all sins.

A true decriminalization of Russia will come only when the country has filled in a long list of needs: more effective laws and courts, better state protection for private property and contracts, better-paid and more competent law-enforcement officials, a less intrusive state with fewer opportunities for bureaucrats to levy tribute, a tax system that can be obeyed without ruin. But the most important deterrent to endemic crime will come when there is a clear line between legal and criminal, and businessmen can survive and prosper by abiding by the difference. That is why the evolution of the law and the judicial system is central to any transition. Can the law and the courts ever cope with the epidemic of crime? That is our next topic.

We are being asked to solve complex equations in multiple unknowns without so much as a multiplication table to guide us.

Veniamin Iakovlev, chairman of the Higher Commercial Court[1]

S sil'nym ne boris', s bogatym ne sudis'. (Don't fight the powerful and don't sue the rich.) Russian saying

7 Toward the rule of law?

On a spring day a few years ago Aleksey Liubchik, a 36-year-old unemployed man from Tomsk, brought his wife and young son from Siberia to the offices of MMM, a notorious investment pyramid, on Moscow's Varshavskoe Shosse. There he opened a canister of gasoline, poured it over himself, and threatened to set himself on fire. It turned out that Liubchik had sold his apartment the previous year for $25,000 to buy shares in MMM. The shares were now worthless and the Liubchiks had no place to live. For months Liubchik and his family had been wandering from one official to another to get his money back. They had been to the mayoralty of Moscow, to the parliament, to the police – all to no avail.[2]

One place Liubchik did not bother to go was the courts. That would have been hopeless. The judicial system has been overwhelmed by thousands of cases brought by the victims of fraudulent investment companies and insolvent banks. The law has been helpless to counter the epidemic. Most of the culprits are not actually bankrupt, but have simply closed their doors and removed their shingles, ignoring the long lines outside. It is suspected that they still own property and have foreign bank accounts, but their assets are beyond the reach of the courts. In some cases, well-organized plaintiffs have been able to obtain judgments and get them enforced. But these are the lucky exceptions.

Such weaknesses in the courts and the laws affect all Russians, in their dealings with the state and with each other. Legal protection for private property and contracts is still embryonic. Most Russian citizens avoid the courts, and businesses largely bypass them, resorting to personal connections and private arbitration and enforcement to protect their interests.

---

[1] *Izvestiia*, July 3 1993, p. 4.   [2] *Kommersant-Daily*, April 13 1995, p. 14.

Among both individuals and businessmen awareness of the law, especially of the new laws written since the Soviet period, is low.[3]

Part of the blame lies with the Russian government, which has given legal reform a low priority in its reform program. The weakness of the judicial system is the most glaring example of the state's failure to supply a crucial public good – legal order – thus undermining the efficiency and the legitimacy of the post-Soviet order.

Yet it is not true, as the Western media so frequently write, that Russia is a "legal void" or a "judicial black hole." What Russian jurists and judges have achieved since 1991 is in many respects highly impressive. But the process has a long way to go.

This chapter examines the reasons for the weaknesses of the legal system and the prospects for improvement. The first part of the chapter deals with the problems of the system and their causes. The second part analyzes the rise of the commercial courts – arguably the most promising development for the protection of private property and contracts. At the end, we look at some of the implications for the future of the Russian economy.

Weaknesses of the Russian legal system

The Soviet inheritance

The collapse of the Soviet system in 1991 left a legacy of laws unsuited to a civil society and a market economy, a tradition of judicial dependence on the state, and popular suspicion of the courts.

Many Westerners are surprised to learn that Russia inherited an elaborate legal system from the Soviet era. The Soviet judiciary had a well-developed structure of courts and judges. There were law schools and legal scholars; state institutions and enterprises maintained legal staffs; and citizens involved in private disputes over property or various torts could seek (and sometimes obtain) redress through the courts.

But the Soviet legal system was unique by Western standards. Jurists and police officials in the 1930s turned Leninism, European civil law, and Russian tradition into a legal amalgam that was designed to serve the state and its leaders.[4] Formal statutes were often mere window-dressing, and in any case they were only the tip of a largely invisible iceberg of so-called

[3] Kathryn Hendley, "Legal Development in Post-Soviet Russia," *Post Soviet Affairs*, vol. 13, no. 3 (1997), pp. 228–251. See also Kathryn Hendley, Barry W. Ickes, Peter Murrell, and Randi Ryterman, "Observations on the Use of Law by Russian Enterprises," *Post-Soviet Affairs*, vol. 13, no. 1 (1997), pp. 19–41.

[4] Harold J. Berman, *Justice in the USSR* (Cambridge, Mass.: Harvard University Press, 1963)

"sub-laws" (*podzakonnye akty*), i.e., implementing directives issued by any number of government agencies, and mostly secret. The laws themselves were the least important part of this system: without the necessary directives to implement them they remained a dead letter, yet the directives frequently contradicted the laws. (In this Alice-in-Wonderland system, a plaintiff could sue on the basis of a sub-law if he could prove its existence in court!).[5]

Soviet judges were anything but independent. They knew that in cases involving important persons or sensitive issues they were to check with the local headquarters of the Communist Party apparatus before deciding on a verdict. This practice came to be known as "telephone justice." Criminal proceedings were dominated by the state prosecutors, who prepared the cases against the accused. Judges were reprimanded if their rulings were "incorrect," and thus the whole system was biased toward conviction.[6]

The Soviet legal system was highly politicized in every sphere, but where the interest of the state was directly engaged, even the semblance of due process went out the window. From the show trials of the 1930s to the prosecution of dissidents in the 1970s and early 1980s, the state refused to be bound by its own laws. The Russian people understood this very well and avoided the courts whenever they could.[7] Today's widespread "law aversion" has deep roots.

The tradition inherited from the Soviet period is that of a legal system opposed to private interest. With this kind of background, today's jurists and judges have a lot of ground to make up. "The legacy left by Soviet power," writes a leading Western scholar, "did not include legal order."[8]

The concept of "legal order" implies two things: (1) uniform and universally binding legal rules; and (2) enforcement by independent courts and legal services. But can a system that was slavishly devoted to the service of the state now become the neutral arbiter between state and society, the defender of the constitution, the protector of civil liberties, contracts, and private property rights? And is that what Russian politicians, entrepreneurs, and the common people really want and will support?

Building a legal order in Russia will not happen overnight; it is more

---

[5] Dietrich A. Loeber, "Legal Rules 'For Internal Use Only,'" *International and Comparative Law Quarterly* (January 1970), p. 80.

[6] Peter H. Solomon, Jr., *Soviet Criminal Justice under Stalin* (Cambridge: Cambridge University Press, 1996)

[7] Peter H. Solomon, Jr., Legality in Soviet Political Culture: A Perspective on Gorbachev's Reforms," in Nick Lampert and Gabor T. Ritterspoon, eds., *Stalinism: its Nature and Aftermath: Essays in Honor of Moshe Lewin* (London: Macmillan, 1992)

[8] Peter H. Solomon, "The Limits of Legal Order in Post-Soviet Russia," *Post-Soviet Affairs*, vol. 11, no. 2 (1995), pp. 89–114.

likely the work of a generation or more. A country's judicial system is a large and complex affair involving millions of people. It is bound to its past by its accumulated rules and structures, which are necessarily slow to change. To change its fundamental orientation from servant of the state to even-handed defender of both state and society is a revolutionary change indeed. It will take a long time to accomplish-if it can be accomplished at all. The evolution of the Russian legal system is the most vivid illustration of what is really at stake in post-Soviet Russia: not only the transition to market-oriented institutions, but also the rebuilding of the state and its relationship to society.

We look first at the *capacity* of the Russian legal system to support the rule of law. That turns on four questions: (1) the quality and coherence of the laws themselves; (2) the implementation of them; (3) the independence of the judges and courts; and (4) the professional quality and the impartiality of judges and lawyers, as well as their numbers. Then we look at the *demand* for legal order by the population, the politicians, and the state.

What laws to write?

In the early years of market reforms Russian jurists still operated with Soviet-era laws. The result was a jungle of contradictions, a cover for corrupt bureaucrats. For example, even as foreign-currency exchange offices sprang up all over Moscow and the main Russian cities, the Russian Criminal Code still defined all private currency operations as criminal.[9]

A massive revision of criminal, civil and procedural statutes has been under way since 1991. But writing laws is not some obscure scholarly exercise. It is one of the highest-stakes games of power. Competing interests fight some of their hardest battles to codify their advantages in law. Consequently, the new Russian legislation written since 1991 is a tangled array of acts, written at different times, by varied players with shifting interests.

Russian legal purists complain that the result is a hodge-podge. Most of the new laws, they say, were written by on the run, by people with little understanding of legal procedures or Russian legal traditions. Much has been borrowed from Anglo-American ideas and practices based on common law, which have been grafted awkwardly on a system derived from Roman and continental European law.[10] Russian lawyers in the

---

[9] Commentary by Iurii Feofanov, *Izvestiia*, July 6 1994.

[10] A.D. Boikov, "Sudebnaia reforma: obreteniia i proschety," *Gosudarstvo i pravo*, No. 6 (1994), p. 14.

Soviet period never had to develop real expertise as legal drafters, and it shows today, in the poor technical quality of the laws being written by legislatures at all levels.

Typically, the new Russian laws contain both too much and too little. They attempt to regulate the entire political, economic, and social life of the country, and thus they overburden the law. At the same time, sometimes through the inexperience of the drafters but more often because the subjects themselves are politically explosive, Russian laws are vague or silent on key points, or are mutually contradictory. Contributing to the latter problem since 1990 has been the so-called "war of laws" among legislatures at various levels, all claiming sovereignty over the same subjects.

Even where the new laws have been carefully and systematically drafted, they tend to reflect the concerns of the reform-minded legislators and their Western advisors, not those of the Russians to whom they will apply. Russian businessmen frequently find the new laws incomprehensible or irrelevant, and in most cases neither they nor their legal staffs have made much effort to acquaint themselves with them.

It is an old debate, whether an effective system of law can be imposed from above or must grow "organically" from below. In the Russian case most of the new laws have come from above, and there is a clear danger that many of them will simply be ignored because they depart from common understandings and established practices.[11]

The new civil and criminal codes

Yet despite these problems a fundamentally new post-Soviet body of laws is gradually being created. The biggest steps forward have been the adoption of new Civil and Criminal Codes.

The new Civil Code, adopted in pieces beginning in January 1995, covers all the main forms of property, buying and selling, contract relations, and obligations. It eliminates many of the restrictions of the Soviet-era Civil Code of the RSFSR, which dated from 1964 and was designed to protect and regulate socialist property.

Some topics are not yet covered by the new Civil Code. The status of land, especially farmland, remains a hugely sensitive issue in Russia. Russians of all political views share a visceral sense that farmland is a special form of property and that there should be a preferential place for collective property in agricultural land. The Russian parliament, when it debated the Civil Code, voted that in this area the Civil Code should be subordinated to the Land Code – much to the frustration of legal

---

[11] Hendley et al., op .cit., and Hendley, "Legal Development," op. cit., pp. 236–237.

reformers, who had wanted the Civil Code to be clearly established as the "second law of the land" – a superlaw second only to the constitution.

Only time will tell whether the new Civil Code will achieve such "superlaw" status. Its creators clearly hope that the Civil Code will be superior to all forms of "sub-laws," including presidential decrees.[12] But turning the new Civil Code into the basic law of the land will require many years of further legislation to flesh it out, as well as many court cases and rulings.

The new Russian Criminal Code, which went into force at the beginning of 1997, likewise fills many of the holes in the patchwork of laws inherited from Soviet-era legislation. Its most valuable contribution, from the standpoint of the market economy, is that it covers several types of economic crimes that the previous Criminal Code of 1960 failed to define. Without laws to invoke, law-enforcement officials were frequently unable (or unwilling) to act.[13]

Thus the new Criminal Code covers several types of fraud, including obtaining loans with false information (Article 176), as well as deliberate failure to repay (Article 177). The Code establishes criminal liability for securities fraud (Article 185), for false bankruptcy (Article 197), money laundering (Articles 173 and 174), illegal disclosure of confidential banking or commercial information (Article 183), operating an unregistered business or bank (Articles 171 and 172), and tax evasion (Articles 198 and 199). All of these crimes have been common in Russia since the beginning of marketization in the late 1980s, but had not been systematically treated as criminal until the new Criminal Code was adopted.

At the same time, the Criminal Code also decriminalizes certain activities that were forbidden by Soviet-era laws, notably currency trading. And it reinforces the position of the private sector, by defining as criminal certain acts of state officials, such as corruption and bribe-taking (Articles 290 and 291), abuse of authority (285), and unjust denial of registration or issuance of licenses (Article 169).

More criminal prosecutions and convictions, by themselves, are not the answer to the wave of economic crime that has gripped Russia. Russia, with 800 convicts behind bars for every 100,000 people, shares with the United States the distinction of having the toughest penal system in the

---

[12] V.F. Yakovlev, "O novom grazhdanskom kodekse Rossii i ego primenenii," introductory essay to the text of the Civil Code, *Grazhdanskii kodeks Rossiiskoi Federatsii*, Parts I and II (Moscow: "Kontrakt," 1996), p. IX.

[13] Alla Kazakina and Alexander Dneprovski, "The New Russian Criminal Code Battles Economic Crimes," *CIS Law Notes* (bimonthly newsletter of the law firm of Patterson, Belknap, Webb, and Tyler).

world (the incarceration rate in Western Europe, by contrast, averages 50 per 100,000).[14] Russia hardly needs tougher laws or more prisoners.

But the key contribution of the Criminal Code is to establish, for the first time, a clearer line between what is legal economic behavior and what is not, thus shrinking the huge gray zone within which everyone and no one was criminal. It is only a first step, all observers agree. Like the Civil Code, the Criminal Code will need to be fleshed out and corrected through application. But it is an essential beginning.

Executing the laws

Implementation is the next hurdle. Good courts require independent and well-trained judges, but good judges are in short supply and their independence is still shaky. In addition, the court system faces two powerful competitors – state officials and private businessmen, who bypass the judicial system.

Russian governmental agencies still continue the practice of issuing unpublished rules and regulations,[15] even though the practice is clearly forbidden by the 1993 Constitution. Many violate the letter and spirit of the laws they supposedly spell out. There is still no Russian equivalent of the *Federal Register*, where the daily output of such agency actions is published, although the situation has improved since Soviet times.[16] The notion of a public hearing is still exotic to Russian bureaucrats' ears, and the accountability of Russian agencies to the public, or even to another branch of government, is only weakly established, even in theory. The spirit of the system remains resolutely statist, and the odds remain stacked in favor of the bureaucrat.

---

[14] Figures drawn from a three-year study of the Russian prison system by "Novyi Dom," a Russian human-rights organization, and by the UK-based Penal Reform International Group.

[15] For background see Eugene Huskey, "Government Rulemaking as a Brake on Perestroika," Eugene Huskey, "Government Rulemaking as a Brake on Perestroika," *Law and Social Inquiry*, vol. 15, no 3 (Summer 1990), pp. 419–432. See also William E. Butler, "Pravovaia reforma nakanune XXI veka," in Tat'iana I. Zaslavskaia, ed., *Kuda idet Rossiia? Sotsial'naia transformatsiia postsovetskogo prostranstva.* (Proceedings of the third annual international symposium held under the auspices of the Interdisciplinary Academic Center for the Social Sciences, January 12–14 1996 (Moscow, "Aspekt Press," 1996), pp. 143–144.

[16] The standard source, the *Biulleten' normativnykh aktov*, has been expanded, and many agency regulations are published in the government daily newspaper, *Rossiiskie vesti*. In addition, some government agencies issue their own bulletins, and a few, such as the Russian Securities Commission, maintain web sites. Increasingly, ordinary Russian companies routinely subscribe to on-line legal information services such as *Konsultant-Plius*.

Half-way to independence?

As for the independence of Russian judges, in theory it is much improved, but in practice less so. With the collapse of the communist apparatus, much of the basis for "telephone justice" disappeared. A fundamental law passed in 1992, "On the Status of Judges in the Russian Federation," made Russian judges independent – at least on paper – for the first time in Russian history. In theory, Russian judges have been granted life tenure to age 65 (although they must first pass through a five-year probationary period). They are no longer hired and fired by the Ministry of Justice. The Law on Judges of 1992 provides that judges may be removed only upon the assent of "qualification boards" composed of their peers.

But the real independence of Russian judges is still uncertain. The first question is who appoints them. The presidential administration has taken advantage of a loophole in the 1993 Constitution to claim the right of appointment to all courts.[17] The judicial branch and the local governments have been fighting back; and as a result further legislation on the court system has been held up.

The second threat to judicial independence is the courts' lack of control over their own administration. Judges' salaries and budgets, their perquisites, their housing, their automobiles, all come from the federal Ministry of Justice or from the province administration. The judiciary is still vulnerable to pressure from the other two branches.

Lately another threat to the judges' independence has emerged – pressure from their own superiors within the judicial system. Thus in criminal cases local judges are frequently told by higher judges what sentences to impose.[18] In the commercial courts judges face strictly mandated schedules that force them to expedite cases at a brisk pace.[19]

Most of Russia's 15,000 judges work outside the big cities in local towns and counties. The backbone of the Russian judicial system is the network of district judges, the so-called *rayonnye sud'i*. They are all-purpose judges, who handle civil, criminal, and administrative cases all at once. Their case load is heavy – 2 or 3 cases a day on average – and they work practically without staff. "The inside of the courtroom," says one local judge, "is squalid and stinking, with cockroaches everywhere."[20] But there is no money from local budgets to keep up the courthouses.

---

[17] Solomon 1996, op. cit.

[18] Todd Foglesong in Peter H. Solomon, Jr., ed., *Reforming Justice in Russia, 1864–1994: Power, Culture, and the Limits of Legal Order* (Armonk, NY, and London: M.E. Sharpe, 1997).

[19] Katharina Pistor, "Supply and Demand for Contract Enforcement in Russia: Courts, Arbitration, and Private Enforcement," *Review of Central and East European Law*, vol. 22, no. 1 (1996).   [20] *Obshchaia gazeta*, July 29–August 4 1994, p. 6.

The judges get little cooperation from the local police, who "could spit on the court," says the same local judge. The police have to be coaxed even to bring the accused to court, much less reluctant witnesses. "Who am I supposed to send?" he asks. "My secretary? The cleaning lady? Or should I go myself, with fixed bayonet? I don't even have a bayonet."[21]

Too few judges, and too few good ones

The Russian legal system is far smaller than that of a free market civil society. There are about 15,000 judges, 20,000 prosecutors, 36,000 "lawyers" (*advokaty*), and some 5,000 notaries. Compared to the United States, with one lawyer for every 300 people (admittedly the high end of the scale), Russia has one lawyer for every 4,000 people. These numbers suggest that the legal profession will have to grow before it can serve a free market economy and a "government of laws, not of men."[22]

The quality of the Russian judiciary is more elusive to define. The most important quality is impartiality, which means being removed from politics and respecting procedure over result. But Russian judges and prosecutors are often not impartial: some are corrupt, some are deep into politics, some are impatient with procedures that would diminish their prerogatives, some are so used to their role as defenders of the state's interest that they cannot adopt a more neutral position. Many Russian judges and officials in law-enforcement bodies are sincerely ambivalent about the law; they may respect it, but only as one of several social values. Since 1990, as wage scales have fallen behind inflation, many judges have left the bench; but even though younger judges have replaced them, it is not clear that they bring with them more liberal attitudes toward the law.

Corruption, abuse of power, and self-regulation

Ironically, for a growing number of Russians, the problem is not too little judicial independence, but too much. Honest judges are not yet

---

[21] *Obshchaia gazeta*, loc. cit.

[22] Statistics on admissions to higher educational institutions suggest that the numbers of the next cohort are growing, although the Russian educational system remains strongly biased toward engineering. For the academic year 1991–92 the number of students admitted into the catchall category "Economics and Law" was 6.5% of the 565,900 admissions that year (compared to 37% for "industry and construction). By 1996–97, five years later, the percentage had increased to 10.0% of 674,300. Yet the share of "industry and construction" remained steady, at 37% (Source: *Rossiiskii statisticheskii ezhegodnik 1997*, by Internet)

Unfortunately, there has been little growth in the number of judges, which remains at about 15,000. The main reason is lack of funding. In 1998 over 1,000 judgeships remained unfilled, and a proposal to create a new system of justices of the peace was frozen for lack of funds.

adequately protected from outside pressures; but corrupt or tyrannical ones now enjoy virtual immunity from removal.

Under the 1992 legislation on the status of judges, a criminal case against a judge can be brought only by the federal Procurator General, with the concurrence of a local "qualifications collegium," a sort of internal review board in which the local judges review cases against their own colleagues.[23]

Meanwhile, the temptations are strong. "We get offered plenty of bribes, and big ones too," says one local judge.[24] The internal disciplinary system enables judges to protect their own. In 1993 the qualifications collegia removed 69 judges for all causes; in 1994, 56. (The judges like to point out that in previous years, when the Ministry of Justice had the power to hire and fire judges, the removal rate was far smaller, perhaps 8 to 10 per year.) The leading cause was drinking, followed by unreasonable delays in bringing cases to trial.[25] There was only one removal for corruption – and even that case was still under investigation.

By 1995 corruption and malfeasance in the courtroom had become a growing public scandal, as the public, rightly or wrongly, became convinced that judges were on the take. Fearing that popular anger could lead the Duma to weaken judicial immunity, the judges reluctantly moved to cooperate with the procuracy to deal with at least the more obvious cases. A judge in Mordovia was removed for sexual blackmail, another for freeing prisoners in exchange for menial services.[26] Finally, in Moscow came the first bribery case. A district judge was removed for taking a $1,500 bribe to lessen the charge against a man accused of concealing a homemade firearm – the first removal of a Moscow judge on corruption charges in fifteen years.[27]

But the larger issue in many Russians' minds is whether judicial immunity has gone too far. In 1996 a group of lawyers and human rights' advocates brought suit before the Constitutional Court, hoping to get the immunity rules declared unconstitutional. On that occasion the Constitutional Court rejected the suit and left the immunity rules standing. But it is clear that judicial independence is still a fragile concept, not securely anchored in Russians' minds.

---

[23] *Izvestiia*, March 7 1996, p. 2. Decisions of the local qualifications collegia can be appealed to a Higher Qualifications Collegium, on which sit 32 judges drawn from local courts around the country. The final court of appeal is the Supreme Court. (*Kommersant-Daily*, January 21 1998, by Internet) Anatolii Zherebtsov, chairman of the Higher Qualifications Collegium, provides useful background in *Nezavisimaia gazeta*, December 23 1997, by Internet.   [24] *Obshchaia gazeta*, op. cit.

[25] Interview with Anatolii Merkushov, deputy chairman of the Russian Federation Supreme Court, *Literaturnaia gazeta*, No. 31 (1994), p. 13.   [26] *Izvestiia*, July 8 1995.

[27] *Kommersant-Daily*, July 5 1995, p. 14.

Meanwhile, the judges' qualifications collegia have stepped up the pace of their work – but not by much. In 1996 96 judges were removed for cause, and in 1997 about the same, although only a half-dozen each year on criminal charges. When in 1998 the Higher Qualifications Collegium removed a judge in Rostov for accepting a $1,000 bribe – the crime was even recorded on videotape – it was such news that the media were called in to witness the decision.[28] Still, prosecutors concede that the collegia are gradually becoming less defensive.[29]

In sum, the legal system has serious flaws, in both the laws and the court system. But all is not bleak; there is also a distinct trend toward improvement. One of the most significant, from the standpoint of a market economy, is the evolution of a system of commercial courts.

Progress in building a new legal order

The commercial courts

Some of the busiest places in Russia today are the commercial courts (known in Russian as *arbitrazhnye sudy*), which hear disputes over privatization, tax issues, delinquent loans, broken contracts, bankruptcy, and other civil matters. The commercial courts make up a parallel network alongside the regular courts (known as "district" or "people's" courts). With over 2,200 judges located throughout Russia's provinces and republics, the commercial courts have their own independent hierarchy (reinforced in 1995 with 10 regional commercial courts to hear appeals) and a Higher Commercial Court (*Vysshiiy Arbitrazhnyi Sud*) which oversees the entire structure.[30] (Thus Russia has not one but three supreme courts – a Constitutional Court, a Supreme Court proper, and a Higher Commercial Court.) Over two-thirds of the commercial judges are women. Most are young, under 45. They are appointed for life. Interestingly, in contrast to the regular courts, where turnover has been high and vacancies are a problem, there has been little turnover among the commercial court judges.[31]

The commercial courts are not actually new. They are carried over from the Soviet system of "arbitration courts," which existed throughout the Soviet period. But their function under the command economy was

---

[28] *Kommersant-Daily*, January 21 1998, by Internet. For the 1996 figure, see *Kommersant-Daily*, November 28 1997, by Internet.

[29] "Kto vyvedet piatna na sudeiskoi mantii?" *Izvestiia*, August 6 1997, by Internet.

[30] Veniamin F. Iakovlev, "On the Resolution of Commercial Disputes in Russia," *Rule of Law Newslatter*, No. 2 (July–August 1995), p. 2.

[31] Keith Rosten, "The Commercial Judiciary in the Russian Federation," *Rule of Law Newsletter*, No. 1 (June 1995), p. 6.

completely different. The Soviet arbitration courts were intended to resolve disputes between state enterprises. The idea was that any disagreement between two arms of the state should be settled amicably through negotiation.[32] Their common aim, after all, was to meet the plan.

But no longer. Now that most state property has been handed over to private owners, the role of the commercial courts has been transformed. They are up to their ears in disputes over property rights, suits over money damages, cases involving unpaid loans, and claims and counterclaims over taxes. As Russia develops a new body of civil law to govern private contracts and property and the relations between society and the state, the commercial courts are becoming a crucial battlefield.

The work of the commercial courts covers mainly two kinds of cases, disputes between private parties and cases involving the state. (The commercial courts are restricted to cases involving "juridical persons," i.e., companies and organizations; "physical persons" use the ordinary courts.) A typical week's docket may include a private business suing the Tax Inspectorate (or the other way around) over a tax-related fine, or two government agencies involved in a dispute over improper privatization, a private bank or an enterprise trying to recover an unpaid loan or an overdue payment, or perhaps an action by the procuracy against a fraudulent bankruptcy.[33] New legislation in effect since July 1 1995 has broadened the jurisdiction of the commercial courts to include disputes involving foreign companies, and has expanded the opportunities for appeal.[34]

Many of the cases before the commercial courts involve privatization. Mass privatization moved so fast between 1991 and 1995, and with so little legal basis, that it will take years to resolve the many disputes it has left. A few examples give the flavor. A newspaper in Vladivostok is evicted from its new building by its parent publishing house. Who has the right to the property, which was completed on the eve of the Soviet collapse? The newspaper, for which the building was built in the first place? Or the publishing house, to which the building was assigned, almost as an afterthought? At stake, of course, is not just the right to property but also the

---

[32] William E. Butler, *Soviet Law*, 2nd edition (London: Butterworths, 1988), pp. 121–126.

[33] Until 1997 summaries of cases decided by the commercial courts were published every Tuesday by *Kommersant-Daily*, and in occasional surveys by *Kommersant* (weekly). This is still a useful source. According to Hendley et al., "Observations on the Use of Law . . .," op. cit., p. 26, debt-collection cases constitute between two-thirds and three-quarters of the total case load of the commercial courts.

[34] Veniamin F. Yakovlev, "On the Resolution of Commercial Disputes in Russia," *Rule of Law Newsletter*, July-August 1995, p. 2. Over 2000 foreign companies used the commercial courts in 1998. See also Veniamin F. Yakovlev, "Tendentsiia k povysheniiu roli arbitrazhnykh sudov sokhraniaetsia," *Vestnik Vysshego Arbitrazhnogo Suda RF*, No. 4 (1999), p. 9.

basis for the freedom of the press, since without a place to work a newspaper does not exist. In this case, the Higher Commercial Court found in favor of the newspaper.[35]

One major category of privatization involves so-called "strategic" sectors. In an odd case, the Moscow Commercial Court recently found itself reviewing the privatization of the company that made astronauts' diapers. In 1991 the diaper manufacturer, delicately named the Special Design Bureau for Experimental Equipment, went private, and started making Pampers instead. But organizations connected to the space program may not be privatized, claimed the General Procurator in a suit before the Moscow Commercial Court. The court agreed, and ordered the diaper-maker returned to its parent organization, the even more aptly-named Federal Administration for Microbiological and Emergency Problems.[36]

Some of the privatization cases involving the commercial courts are multi-billion dollar disputes. The aluminum industry is a prime example. In 1995 the commercial court of Moscow threw out the results of an investment auction at which 20% of the shares of the Bratsk Aluminum Plant were sold to private bidders, on the grounds that two potential bidders had been unfairly disqualified from taking part in the auction. Thus by decision of the court a huge block of shares, in which the winning bidders thought they had acquired a secure stake, would have to be auctioned off all over again.[37]

In cases such as these the commercial courts are stepping into the middle of the highest-stakes battle in Russia, the redivision of Russia's property – such a historic process that Russians apply to it the word *peredel*, the same word they used in the nineteenth century to describe the all-important redistribution of land following the end of serfdom. But are the commercial courts, squaring off against powerful interests, really able to make the law prevail?

The record is mixed, but the general view among Moscow lawyers and entrepreneurs is that the commercial courts are becoming increasingly significant, particularly as defenders of private property against arbitrary actions by the state.[38] Through their daily decisions the commercial courts are gradually establishing some simple but essential points. Privatization can be reversed if proper procedures are not followed – but

---

[35] *Izvestiia*, May 27 1994.   [36] *Kommersant-Daily*, September 19 1995, p. 15.
[37] *Kommersant-Daily*, March 21 1995, p. 15.
[38] There is some suggestion that the lower courts are more enthusiastic defenders of private property than the Higher Arbitration Court, which frequently reverses lower-court decisions and finds for the government, particularly in tax cases. See Sergei Stepanov, "Arbitrazh stal po-gosudarstennomu interesnym delom," *Kommersant* (weekly), No. 7 (February 25 1997), pp. 30–31.

should stand if they are. Tax authorities must have proper evidence before seizing private assets. Leaseholders' rights must be respected. Banks and other agents must execute their clients' instructions. Trademarks are a form of property and can be defended against encroachment. Loans must be repaid. Contracts matter.

This last point is crucial. Private contracts have assumed a new and critical importance as the key tool of the economy. Millions of private entities enter into contracts in Russia, and the contracts themselves are increasingly based on new models drawn from Western practice.[39] In the words of two leading US attorneys with long experience in Russia, "Those who claim that in Russia 'there is no contract law' or 'no commercial law exists' are opining without knowledge."[40] On the other hand, interviews with enterprise managers disclose that for most of them contracts are still a secondary formality, useful as a bargaining tool but commonly not implemented.[41] The status of contracts, like so much of the rest of the economy, is still in transition.

Three main problems of the commercial courts

The commercial courts face three major problems: a growing case load and tight deadlines; limited power to enforce their decisions; and a severe challenge in upgrading the judges' skills to keep up with the rapidly changing laws.

The new commercial courts handle fewer cases than their predecessors the arbitration courts – just under 400,000 cases in 1998, compared to over 700,000 in 1981.[42] But today's commercial cases are far more involved and lengthy than the old arbitration cases were, and the judges are hard pressed to make it through their docket, especially since they are required to hear cases within two months.[43]

Initially, from 1991 to 1994, the number of decisions issued by the commercial courts dropped sharply, suggesting that plaintiffs were avoiding the courts. But since then the number of decisions has picked up, indicating that the earlier decline may simply have been a reflection of the shift in the courts' functions, from Soviet-era disputes over contracts to a much broader array of commercial cases.[44]

---

[39] Randy Bregman and Sarah Carey, "Contracting in Russia: Not Perfect, but it Works," *Russia Business Watch*, vol. 3, no. 1 (Winter 1995), p. 1.

[40] Bregman and Carey, op. cit., p. 42.

[41] Hendley et al., "Observations on the Use of Law . . .," op. cit., p. 24.

[42] Butler op. cit., p. 123, for the 1981 figure. For 1998 data, see *Vestnik Vysshego Arbitrazhnogo Suda Rossiiskoi Federatsii*, No. 3 (1999), p. 8.

[43] Interview with Veniamin Iakovlev, chairman of the Higher Commercial Court, *Izvestiia*, September 21 1995, p. 2.

[44] Katharina Pistor, on the basis of numbers available through 1994, saw an insufficiency of

Table 7.1 *Civil cases decided by Russian commercial courts,*
1991–98

Series A:	Disputes arising from civil matters
1991	358,000
1992	330,000
1993	264,447
1994	190,471
1995	213,662
1996	244,467
1997[a]	–
Series B:	**All cases decided**
1995	237,291
1996	290,094
1997	341,537
1998	398,622

Note:
[a] There is a break in the series in 1997, when the Higher Arbitration Court
stopped reporting records of "civil cases" and switched to "all cases."
Nevertheless, even though the two partial series given here are not compatible,
they show a clear pattern of growth.
Sources: For 1991–94 Pistor 1996; for 1995–1997: *Vestnik Vysshego*
Arbitrazhnogo Suda, Nos. 3–1996, 4–1997, 4–1998, and 3–1999.

The case load could become much heavier, especially if the commercial
courts come to be seen as the place where the private sector can successfully defend its interests. Even now, the local commercial courts are facing
a growing number of privatization-related suits from local governmental
agencies seeking to reverse the privatization of state properties, alleging
either violations of privatization procedure or improper activities by the
newly-privatized businesses. In recent years cases between private parties
have grown only slowly, while cases involving the tax authorities are
booming, often with the state as plaintiff.[45]

The next problem is clout. The hardest part of the arbitrators' job is
getting their decisions enforced. There is a system of bailiffs (*sudebnye*
ispolniteli), but these are subordinated to the courts of general jurisdiction
and are not usually available to the commercial courts. In theory, the

demand for law. In a broader sense, that is certainly true, but in the case of the commercial courts the more recent numbers suggest that demand has bottomed out. See "Supply
and Demand for Contract Enforcement in Russia: Courts, Arbitration, and Private
Enforcement," *Review of Central and East European Law,* vol. 22, no. 1 (1996), p. 71
[45] Veniamin F. Yakovlev, "Tendentsiia k povysheniiu...," op. cit., p. 9.

police will act to enforce the courts' rulings. But the police are frequently met at the door by well-armed people, and in any case the local police are commonly corrupt. A glaring example is MMM, the investment pyramid mentioned at the beginning of the chapter. Dozens of plaintiffs have brought civil cases against MMM's founder, Sergei Mavrodi, hoping to recover some of their lost property. They invariably win – but the courts are unable to locate MMM's assets, and so the judgments are without effect.[46]

To deal with this problem, a law has been passed creating a system of court officers to enforce commercial court decisions. But the law has not been implemented, except for tax-related cases, for which the Tax Police has been instructed to serve as court officers.[47] Existing law-enforcement agencies are opposed to such measures, seeing them as duplication. In addition, there are powerful interests that find weak courts to their liking. Some of the biggest culprits are local governments. The commercial judges complain that they are constantly pressured and harassed by local politicians who happen to be interested parties.

The courts' third major problem is legal competence. The new private sector has arisen so quickly, and the legal problems it poses have become so complex, that they far outstrip the meager skills of the commercial judges. Increasingly, cases before the commercial courts are argued by well-trained young Russian corporate lawyers, who must sometimes instruct the judge on the points of law involved.

These problems discourage potential litigants, driving them to solve their problems outside the legal system. In 1994 the money involved in cases before the commercial courts totalled 6.2 trillion rubles (then about $3.1 billion); the courts' judgments involved about half that amount.[48] Those are tidy sums, but even if actually collected they are only a tiny fraction of the total at stake in commercial disputes in Russia. And in reality, only a small part is collected.

In addition to the uncertain justice they dispense, the commercial courts initially charged very large trial fees – up 10% of the total claim, payable in advance.[49] Filing fees have dropped in recent years, but there is still a widespread perception that court costs are high.[50] Access to the courts is restricted in other ways. For example, before being allowed to bring suit against the tax authorities in an commercial court, the plaintiff

---

[46] In just one unique case, a particularly determined plaintiff was able to locate a building belonging to Sergei Mavrodi and to obtain a court order to put up the building for auction. See *Izvestiia*, December 26 1996, pp. 1–2.

[47] *Moskovskie novosti*, No. 45 (July 9 1995), p. 16.   [48] *Moskovskie novosti*, op. cit.

[49] Interview with Iurii Platonov, chairman of "Moscow Legal Center" (the presidium of the college of defense lawyers), in *Delovoi mir*, August 5 1994, p. 4.

[50] Hendley et al, "Observations on the Use of Law . . .," op. cit., p. 27.

must first take his case through a lengthy appeals procedure in the tax service itself. Only after such internal remedies have been exhausted can a suit be brought.[51]

Consequently, many Russian businessmen do their utmost to avoid the courts, and those who do use them do not consider the courts their main source of remedy. Interestingly, interviews with managers suggest that it is not the courts' weak enforcement powers that deter managers from using them more than they do. A more serious obstacle is that most of the managers' business dealings involve no paper documents, while the commercial courts will only act on the basis of written evidence.[52] Instead, most Russian businessmen have their own ways of resolving disputes. The preferred method is still to appeal to political patrons and well-placed friends.

There is also a growing resort to private arbitration. In many areas of business the leading companies have set up their own arbitration courts and try to settle their disputes among themselves. These are called *treteiskie sudy* and they have a recognized if modest place in the official legal system.[53] For example, the National Association of Stock Market Participants (NAUFOR), the successful Russian counterpart to NASDAQ, maintains its own arbitration court, which issues decisions that are binding on its members.[54] These are not the only "alternative courts." Criminals have set up their own commercial courts, complete with lawyers arguing the fine points of the law. Veniamin Iakovlev, chairman of the Higher Commercial Court, refers to these as "thieves' courts" (*vorovskoi arbitrazh*), and fears that they will compete with the regular commercial courts for the business of the private sector.[55]

But the greatest threat comes from people who simply take the law into their own hands, hiring a private enforcer to recover a loan or to settle a dispute over goods. Such cases then show up, if at all, in the criminal courts. One case that came before the Moscow courts in 1996 involved a trading company trying to recover the value of 16,000 pairs of imported shoes. After two years of unsuccessful negotiations – none of which went near the courts – the trader finally lost patience and hired a professional to kidnap the other party.[56]

---

[51] Platonov, op. cit.   [52] Hendley, "Legal Development . . .," op. cit., p. 244.
[53] Pistor, op. cit., pp. 68–74.
[54] Timothy Frye, "Governing the Russian Equities Market," *Post-Soviet Affairs*, vol. 13, no. 4 (1997), pp. 366–395.
[55] Competition from the alternative courts can be real enough. In March 1998, for example, the NAUFOR threatened to expel a brokerage in St. Petersburg for having litigated a case in arbitration court, instead of submitting it to NAUFOR's Disciplinary Committee as the organization's rules require. (*Kommersant-Daily*, March 7 1998, by Internet)   [56] *Kommersant-Daily*, December 18 1996, p. 19.

Conclusion: how much justice is enough?

In developed market-based societies there is a fine balance between the legal order maintained by the state and private mechanisms of making and enforcing agreements. In such economies relatively few disputes actually go to court; indeed, relatively few deals involve formal contracts. But the existence of an effective legal system acts as backstop, reinforcing private sanctions and norms. In short, in a healthy system there is a balance between public and private conflict resolution.[57]

There is also a fine balance between personal and impersonal relationships. In mature market economies people learn to trust other people they have never met, because of institutions that provide credit ratings, certify standards, manage risk – and, when all else fails, resolve disputes through the authority of the courts. If the institutions work, habits of trust are reinforced, and people come to expect compliance as the norm.

The problem in Russia is that private and public, and personal and impersonal, are out of balance. People do not trust people they do not know, yet they trust the courts still less. The clearest evidence of this was the way Russians reacted to the high inflation of 1991–95. In theory, one would have expected the "demand" for law – the number of cases brought before the courts – to rise dramatically, as rapidly changing prices increased the temptation to renege on contracts. Such a "legal boom" occurred in Germany, for example, in the 1920s. But in Russia it did not happen. On the contrary, through 1995 the number of cases brought before the commercial courts declined. Even though the number of disputes mushroomed during those years, most of them bypassed the state's legal system.[58]

Instead, Russian managers and citizens rely on the mechanisms they know. These are essentially patron-client relations inherited or adapted from the Soviet period. Russia has made remarkable progress since 1991 in writing new laws, laying the basis for judicial independence, and adapting its judicial system to the requirements of a market economy. But most Russians still do not perceive the law as a useful or dependable substitute for the defenses they have traditionally resorted to. Good friends still matter more than good contracts.[59] A particularly telling datum is that since 1991 the legal staffs of most privatized Russian enterprises have shrunk, not expanded, and that the surviving staffers (and their bosses) are still largely unfamiliar with post-Soviet laws.[60]

This matters for two reasons, one economic and the other political.

[57] Katharina Pistor, "Supply and Demand," op. cit., pp. 55–57. The seminal article on this theme is Stewart MacAulay, "Non-contractual Relations in Business," *American Sociological Review*, vol. 28 (1963), p. 55.   [58] Pistor, op. cit.

[59] This is the central argument of Hendley et al., op. cit., based on extensive interviews with a broad sample of Russian managers in 1995 and 1996.

[60] Hendley et al., "Observations on the Use of Law . . .," op. cit., p. 22.

The economic reason is that without a better legal system private property and contracts will not be adequately protected. This deters Russian businessmen from making many deals that might be made in the West, particularly more complex ones. In the main, this means that transaction costs remain high, and business and investment are constrained. The political reason is that the lack of a legal order weakens the legitimacy of the entire political system in the eyes of the citizens.

These two reasons reinforce one another. An illegitimate polity is potentially unstable, and instability deters investment and enterprise. A weak economy fails to supply the tax revenue to support government programs, and a bankrupt government cannot supply essential public services – including legal ones. This is the vicious circle with which Russia is still struggling today.

But Russians, ever resourceful, have fallen back on "second-bests." The most important of these is vertical integration in large financial-industrial conglomerates, within which rules are promulgated and enforced internally. The advantage of vertical integration is that it creates "extended families" of people who may not know one another personally but who develop loyalty to the same company and a measure of trust for those who work within it. To be a "Gazprom man" (a *"gazovik"*), for example, is a powerful lifelong tie, and over time the successful conglomerates that are consolidating today may develop equally powerful internal loyalties and cultures.

Yet we should not conclude too quickly that patron–client relations inherited from the Soviet era, or vertical integration, will be Russia's final answer to the problem of building and maintaining trust in business. We do not know how younger people will behave once they reach senior levels. One thing is sure – they will not have the old Soviet networks to support them. Whether they will turn to the courts instead is an open question.

In the meantime, the whole system is in movement: the number of lawyers is growing, caseloads are increasing, the level of legal sophistication is rising, and the writing of new laws continues at a rapid pace. The law is not yet at the center of Russian life, but in the legal sphere as elsewhere, the term, "transition," is more than an expression of hope.

There will not come a magic day when Russians suddenly wake up to find they have become a country of laws. Nevertheless, in all human affairs there are critical "tipping points," when a majority of the people begin to believe that something is happening. As the laws improve, and as more and more lawyers and judges learn to apply them, there may be a day – perhaps not too far off – when parties in a dispute will begin to find the law and the courts a more reliable and less costly mechanism than a *krysha*. When that day comes, Russia will have taken a long step toward legal order.

8   Beyond coping: toward the recovery of Russian society

Lake Baikal, June 1998:
It's a gray, windy day on Lake Baikal, and there's a steady swell from the north as the *Mirage* slices her way through the brooding mass of icy water. Igor steers the boat, while his partner bustles about the cabin, laying out vodka and herring for his guests. Both are *doktora nauk*, senior research scientists with international reputations. But when their institute stopped paying wages in 1991, Igor and his partner turned to their first love, the *Mirage*, a 50–foot cutter they had rescued from the scrapheap ten years before and had lovingly restored, with coat upon coat of gleaming white and blue paint. For years they had sailed Lake Baikal as a hobby. They became authorities on the lake's unique fauna and flora. In 1993 they took the plunge. They resigned from their institute – an unheard-of move in Soviet times – and began a new life as charter captains. "The *Mirage* was our hobby; now it's our livelihood," says Igor. "But we're the lucky ones."[1]

Fili, November 1997:
There is no sign, no gate – but everyone in Moscow knows the place as the *teletolkuchka*, Moscow's outdoor wholesale electronics market. You will find it in an unpaved vacant lot in the Fili district of Moscow's northwest. On Saturday mornings crowds of customers walk down the muddy spaces between solid rows of parked trucks. Fast-talking young men with fat sheaves of rubles in both fists stand at the open back of each truck and hawk their wares – boxes of Aiwa tape players and Toshiba VCR's and everything else under the cybersun, stacked high and moving fast.

I am talking to a man loading boxes of VCR's into his Gazelle pick-up. He's a retailer from a nearby town. "There is a lot of money in Russia," he says. "The statistics may not show it. But you can just smell it."

Russian society has lived through two great shocks in the 1990s. The first was in 1990–91, with the disruption that followed the collapse of the

---

[1] Quoted in Serge Schmemann, "How Can You Have a Bust if You've Never Had a Boom?" The New York Times Magazine, December 27 1998, p. 28.

Soviet Union and the beginning of the market reforms. The second came after August 1998, as inflation returned and the economy resumed its downward slide.

But the impact of the two shocks was very different. The first opened the way to private business, especially in Moscow and St. Petersburg, and led to the emergence of an embryonic middle class, while the rest of Russia lagged behind. The second weakened the new private economy and drove the emerging middle class back toward the common level. Ironically, outside the two major cities, the rest of Russia was somewhat sheltered from the financial collapse of August 1998 by its relative isolation from the money economy. Yet the second shock was damaging for all of Russia, because it cut short a fragile turnaround in economic growth and sent real wages plummeting once more.

Now, with a critical leadership succession impending, Russia's future course will depend above all on the state and mood of Russian society – and the political prize will go to the politician best able to read his countrymen's response. But the story is not easily read. It was not hard, before the August crash, to find stories and statistics of coping and recovery in Moscow.[2] but these are now obviously out of date. Much harder is to make sense of the unreliable and contradictory data from outside the capital, from the *glubinka* ("deep Russia") of the provinces, or for that matter in the poorer neighborhoods of Moscow itself. This is where the statistics fail, the polls thin out, and observers disagree on the most basic questions. Moreover, it is still too soon to know the full impact of the August collapse and its aftermath.

How is Russian society really faring? The disturbing answer is, We really do not know. It is clearly badly damaged, not just by the stress of the Soviet collapse, but also by decades of Soviet misrule. It is deeply divided, not just between rich and poor, but also between young and old, sick and healthy, drunk and sober, employed and jobless. Is Russian society strong enough to move up from its present depressed state and support strong growth? That is the subject of this chapter.

1991–1995: the post-Soviet shock

For most Russians the end of the Soviet Union was a disaster. The worst year was 1992, the first year of the market reforms. Real wages plunged by over one-third, and average personal consumption dropped over 40%. By the end of that year nearly one-third of the population had fallen below

---

[2] For an overview of Moscow compared to the rest of the country, see Boris Dubin, "Rossiiane i moskvichi," *Ekonomicheskie i sotsial'nye peremeny* (*Monitoring obshchestvennogo mneniia*), No. 6 (1997), pp. 14–18.

the official poverty line.[3] Most Russians at that time had no other source of income than their main job – if they kept that – and their savings and pensions melted away under inflation.

Over the following three years living standards kept on sinking, though more slowly. By the end of 1995 real wages were only half of what they had been in 1990, and the average pension had dropped to only 70% of the official poverty level.[4] Wages and pensions were frequently paid late or not at all (as indeed they still are).[5]

But after the initial shock Russians began to rally. People who had a dacha or access to a plot of land or even a small victory garden grew more of their own food. Anyone who took the *elektrichka* out of Moscow on a weekend and walked about the country paths anywhere within a 100-mile radius of the city limits would see city people hard at work raising fruit and vegetables. The same was true of every other Russian city. By 1996 small household plots accounted for half of total agricultural output and an astounding 78% of vegetables and 91% of potatoes.[6]

Millions of Russians traveled abroad to buy goods to sell back in Russia. Tens of millions more hit the streets and markets at home, selling whatever they could. Anyone with a skill looked for odd jobs or went into business as a private contractor. The importance of the "official" place of work declined: by 1997 wages and salaries from the primary workplace had dropped from 70% of household income to less than half,[7] and only 14% of survey respondents said they got by on just their "main" job.[8]

The shift from official wages to outside income was particularly spectacular in Moscow. Industrial output in Moscow and its surrounding province declined by 60% after 1990 and has yet to recover. But money from foreign trade and financial services flooded into the city, creating a host of new jobs. By 1997 Muscovites took home only 10% of the country's official wages, but over 30% of total "other income," that is,

---

[3] *Russian Economic Trends*, various issues. The best summary table will be found in No. 2 (1997), p. 46. The category, "real wages," refers to wages due, not wages actually paid.

[4] Ibid.

[5] Richard Rose, "New Russian Barometer VI: After the Presidential Election," Studies in Public Policy No. 272 (University of Strathclyde, Center for the Study of Public Policy, 1996), p. 6. In surveys over three-quarters of respondents say that they have experienced delays in one or the other

[6] *Russian Economic Trends*, No. 1 (1997), pp. 104–105. In reality the shares of household plots are undoubtedly even higher, since much of the output from them is unreported. According to sociologist Natalya Rimashevskaia, 70–80% of Russian families raise a large part of their own food. (Natalia Mikhailovna Rimashevskaia, "Sotsial'nye posledstviia ekonomicheskikh transformatsii v Rossii," *Sotsiologicheskie issledovaniia*, No. 6 (1997), pp. 56–63)   [7] *Russian Economic Trends*, No. 2 (1997), p. 61.

[8] "New Russian Barometer VI," op. cit., p. 5.

from new private businesses in trade and services, property, and the shadow economy.[9]

Over the course of a decade one Russian in ten rose abruptly to a West European standard of living, and by 1997 two Russians in ten reported that they were better off than under the Soviet system. But Russian society was split in two. By the mid-1990s between 20 and 40% of the Russian population had fallen into poverty, and rates of death and disease soared to levels not seen in any developed country in peacetime.

Inequality in Russia reached levels comparable to third-world countries such as the Philippines.[10] The richest one-fifth of the population got nearly half of the country's money income, compared to less than one-third in 1990, while the share of the poorest fifth dropped from one-tenth to about 6%. A similar split separated the richest regions from the poorest: the top dozen of Russia's 88 regions accounted for nearly half of the GDP.[11]

That's how the the official statistics read, but the real gap was probably much greater, because unreported income accrued primarily to the better-off.[12] The liberal Moscow daily *Izvestiia* summed it up for its readers in a year-end cartoon, showing a man in a tuxedo sitting in an opulent Moscow restaurant, raising his glass in a New Year's toast to a bum in rags standing in the snow on the other side of the window.

For most Russians the first taste of a market economy was bitter. Nearly two-thirds of the population told pollsters they were worse off. 60% said they disliked the post-Soviet economy, while 70% preferred the Soviet system.[13]

On the eve of August 1998: the beginnings of stabilization?

By 1997 and early 1998, there were growing signs that Russian living standards were starting to stabilize and the shock of the Soviet collapse was starting to pass. Statistics and polls suggested that about 60% of the population had managed to stabilize their family incomes, though at

---

[9] *Russian Economic Trends*, No. 2 (1997), p. 127.

[10] Jeni Klugman, "Poverty in Russia: an Assessment." A summary of the report appears in the World Bank's newsletter, *Transition*, vol. 6, nos. 9–10 (September–October 1995), pp. 6–9.

[11] "Special Report: A Statistical Look at Russia's Regions," in *Russian Economic Trends*, No. 2 (1997), pp. 123.

[12] Current statistics on income and income differentials can be found in *Russian Economic Trends*. For a discussion of the statistics' meaning and limitations, see Tat'iana Maleva, "Differentsiatsiia dokhodov naseleniia v usloviiakh finansovoi stabilizatsii," in Anders Aslund and Mikhail Dmitriev, eds., *Sotsial'naia politika v period perekhoda k rynku: problemy i resheniia* (Moscow: Carnegie Endowment for International Peace, Moscow Center, 1996), pp. 45–62.   [13] *Ibid.*

about half the level of 1990. Most families had found ways to cope, and reported they were getting by. By some measures the gap between rich and poor had stopped widening, and had perhaps begun to close slightly, thanks mainly to declining inflation.[14] Fewer people seemed to be falling below the poverty line.[15] Unemployment appeared to have peaked.[16] Between the extremes of wealth and poverty were signs of an as-yet small but emerging middle class, whose presence could be detected by the way they spent their money. People told pollsters they were starting to feel more hopeful about their personal future, even though they remained nostalgic about life in Soviet times and over three-quarters still called their standard of living unsatisfactory.[17]

Statistics on death and disease started to tell the same story. Russian society between 1991 and 1994 seemed to be coming apart at the seams. Birthrates plummeted, while death rates shot up. Infectious diseases like diphtheria and tuberculosis spread rapidly. Suicide rates reached some of the highest levels in the world. But beginning in 1995 the worst trends bottomed out. These early indications – Russians called them *rostki*, little green shoots – suggested that the worst of the shock of the end of the Soviet era was ending. To be sure, there was little sign of a turnaround, either in living standards or in public attitudes towards the post-Soviet economy. Household incomes and consumption remained mired at low levels. And after a brief burst of enthusiasm following the 1996 presidential elections, Russians' political responses to pollsters returned to the same sour levels of earlier years. The most one could say was that public dissatisfaction was at least not growing worse.[18]

---

[14] Maleva in Aslund and Dmitriev, pp. 47ff.

[15] *Russian Economic Trends*, No. 2 (1997), p. 53. The Russian government uses an official "average monthly subsistence level," calculated on the basis of very modest basket of services and food. The official poverty rate is defined as the percentage of the population below the subsistence level. By these government measures about one-fifth of the population was classified as "poor" in the first half of 1997, but the proportion had declined steadily from 1992 through 1996.

Other measures of poverty, such as the "Russian Longitudinal Monitoring Survey" conducted by the Carolina Population Center of the University of North Carolina, show much higher levels of poverty, and suggest that poverty is still growing, especially outside Moscow and St. Petersburg. Natalya Rimashevskaya, a noted sociologist and director of the Institute of Socioeconomic Population Problems, believes the true number of Russians living in poverty is closer to 40%. (Rimashevskaia, op. cit., p. 56)

[16] *Russian Economic Trends*, No. 4 (1997), pp. 81ff.

[17] "New Russian Barometer VI," op. cit., p. 6.

[18] "Monitoring peremen: osnovnye tendentsii," VTsIOM (Russian Center for Public Opinion Research) *Monitoring obshchestvennogo mneniia:Ekonomicheskie i sotsial'nye peremeny*, No. 1 (1998), pp. 4–6. It is striking, however, that most respondents were considerably more optimistic about the prospects for their own immediate families than for society as a whole. Similarly, their responses as consumers were more positive than their responses as citizens.

It is still too early to measure the effects of the August crash. In the initial public opinion polls, not surprisingly, the share of negative answers rocketed up. Yet as the months went passed and the country settled back to a fragile calm under prime minister Evgenii Primakov, the negatives subsided again, and the share of those reporting they were getting by returned to pre-August levels.[19] Consumer spending, which had dropped sharply in the first two months after the crash, stabilized once more, although at a level about 10% lower than the preceding year.[20] Monthly inflation, which had briefly ballooned up into double digits again, subsided once more.

Yet other measures suggested more ominous damage. By the spring of 1999 real wages had plummeted by 40% from the previous summer.[21] The share of the population below the official poverty level, which had stabilized around 20% in 1997 and early 1998, shot back up to the upper 30s.[22] Unemployment, as measured by private surveys, jumped four percentage points to over 18%.[23] 75% of poll respondents said they expected either high inflation or monetary collapse in the year ahead, and prices had become their top concern.[24] In short, as Russia headed into a fateful electoral season, the economic and social barometer offered little cheer.

Beyond coping: positioning for long-term? recovery

But let us take the longer view. Let us assume, for the sake of discussion, that Russia begins the new century with a fresh political leadership of moderate views and with a more favorable economic environment. How well prepared is Russian society to support a longer-term recovery?

The optimistic view is that rich and poor alike will benefit as the economy improves. Before August 1998 there was indeed some evidence for this. Measured in terms of GDP, a recovery had begun, most noticeably in Moscow; and even though it did not last long enough to raise living standards in the countryside, the wave of improvement appeared to be spreading to some other cities and regions. In any case, optimists argue, the picture of poverty and dissatisfaction is exaggerated: Russians make more than they report, and most are better off than they say.

---

[19] VTsIOM nationwide poll results, January 14–28, 1999 (by Internet). The share of those answering, "Our disastrous situation can no longer be tolerated," soared from 46% in July 1998 to 61% in September, but then subsided back to 47% by January 1999.
[20] *Russian Economic Trends*, Monthly Update, January 20 1999, by Internet.
[21] *Russian Economic Trends,* Monthly Update, April 13 1999.   [22] Ibid.
[23] Ibid.
[24] VTsIOM nationwide poll results, January 14–28, 1999 (by Internet). The share of those reporting inflation as their top worry increased from 58% at the beginning of 1998 to 87% in January 1999.

Pessimists counter that the statistics – most of which come from the government – understate the true extent of popular misery. A super-rich upper class, with much of its booty safely tucked away abroad, dominates a mass of new poor, with virtually no middle class in-between. The lack of a middle class is crucial, because that is the group whose spending and saving drive any market economy. For lack of savings and broad-based buying power, a resumption of export-led growth will soon sputter and slow down. Under "crony capitalism," the new society of inequality and privilege is already locked into place. Poverty, inequality, and alienation can only get worse.[25]

Which side is right? To form a judgment we need to ask more fundamental long-range questions. The essential issue is how well positioned Russian society is to support a broad-based economic recovery:

1 What strengths can Russian society bring to economic growth?
 • How large is the Russian middle class and how does it spend its money?
 • What savings are available for investment?
 • How is the job structure adjusting to the needs of a dynamic market economy?
2 How heavy is the long-term "welfare burden" on the Russian economy?
 • How badly damaged is Russian society and how quickly will it heal?
 • How will inequality among regions affect economic growth and welfare?
 • What will be the drag of the welfare burden on economic growth?

A thorough treatment of these questions is beyond the scope of this book, but we can at least form an overall picture. We turn first to the question of the middle class.

An emerging Russian middle class?

If the new Russians consisted only of the rich and the super-rich, the future of capitalist Russia would be bleak. But there was some early evidence in 1997–98 that the gains from marketization had begun to spread beyond the new rich. A larger segment of Russian society – a middle-income group if not yet a middle class – was starting to have an impact on the economy.[26] The term, "middle class," was more and more frequently

---

[25] See for example the essay by Mikhail N. Rutkevich, "Transformatsiia sotsial'noi struktury rossiiskogo obshchestva," *Sotsiologischeskie issledovaniia*, No. 7 (1997), pp. 3–19.

[26] The most persuasive case for the rise of a new Russian middle class is Harley Balzer, "A Shadow Middle Class for a Shadow Economy" (paper presented at the XXIX Annual Convention of the American Association for the Advancement of Slavic Studies, Seattle,

heard on Russian television and in the press, and it had caught on with politicians.

But the middle class proved easier to talk about than define. The most common yardstick was income. Sociologist Natalya Rimashevskaia defined the middle class as the income band between $100 and $1,000 a month; by 1997 20% of the population fell within this zone. Another 15% earned between $1,000 and $3,000 a month; this band Rimashevskaia called the "upper middle class."[27] Another Russian sociologist, Igor' Berezin, defined the middle class as the group earning between $100 and $500 a month in 1996, about 31.5% of the population.[28]

But income was a poor yardstick because there was no accurate way to determine how much people really earned. To avoid this problem, Tatiana Zaslavskaia, perhaps Russia's best-known sociologist, defined the middle class by occupation. She saw three main groups: middle-level managers and state employees; independent professionals; and small and middle-level businessmen. Using this approach, Zaslavskaia called 21% of the population middle class, and another 6–7% upper middle class.[29]

There had arguably existed a "Soviet middle class," based on the leading occupations of Soviet society. It included military and security officers, middle-level bureaucrats and industrial managers, and above all, the armies of intellectuals and scientists supported by the state. It was a class defined by its professional standing in the Soviet order, and by a common educational background and careers in state service. It had little independent property or income, and consequently it was hard-hit at the end of the 1980s. Many members of the Soviet middle class, especially intellectuals and officers, have been among the heaviest losers of the 1990s.

The new middle class overlaps only partially with the old one, and the basis of its income is completely different. Their occupations have little to do with the schools they went to, and are commonly unconnnected to their professions. They have no common outlook or culture, and they still have little property. Indeed, the only thing that unites the middle-income groups, in the eyes of many Russian sociologists, is their common culture of consumerism and tax evasion.[30]

Washington, November 20–23 1997). See also Elena Iakovleva, "Est' li srednii klass v Rossii?" *Novye izvestiia*, March 10–13 1998, a series of informal articles based on work by sociologist Tat'iana Zaslavskaia of the Moscow Higher School for Social and Economic Sciences.

27 Natalia Rimashevskaia, "Sotsial'nye posledstviia ekonomicheskikh transformatsii v Rossii," *Sotsiologicheskie issledovaniia*, No. 6 (1997), p. 60.
28 Igor' Berezin, "Rossiiane nachinaiut bogatet': nishchie stali bednymi, bednye pereshli v srednii klass," *Vek*, No. 2 (January 24–30, 1997), p. 8, cited in Balzer, op. cit.
29 Zaslavskaia, cited in Iakovleva, op. cit.
30 For a summary of sociologists' views, see Boris Startsev, "Nash srednii klass," *Itogi* (April 20, 1998), by Internet.

In other words, what may best define the emerging middle is life style. In the absence of more precise data, one way to track the new Russian middle class is by what they spend. By 1997 middle-class spending was less eye-catching than that of the Russian *nouveaux riches*, but it had become a noticeable force in the Russian economy.

Foreign travel, media advertising, even the growing demand for fur and flowers, all suggested the presence of a growing number of people who had moved beyond the bare necessities. But the best indicator of the rise of middle-income consumers has been the automotive industry.

In Soviet times, most of the traffic on Russian city streets consisted of trucks. But as every resident of Moscow knows, private cars now choke the streets of the capital. By 1995 there were 2 million automobiles in Moscow, and the number was rising by 20% a year. In the country, the number of car owners was growing at 5% a year. Most of the new cars sold were still humble Zhigulis and Volgas, but the fastest-growing category of gasoline consumption in Russia was high-octane, which is used by imported cars, many of which are imported second-hand from Japan. But domestic models also sold well, and as a result the Russian automotive industry turned around in 1995, and by 1997 was growing strongly.[31]

In short, on the eve of the August crash there was a modest but growing middle-income population in Russia, with enough money to be able to afford discretionary purchases. In 1992, at the worst of the post-Soviet shock, Russian households spent most of their income on food. But five years later, the share of food had dropped sharply, and the more fortunate part of the population was expanding its purchases of clothing, furniture, consumer durables, and even luxuries.

The ultimate source of support for this "middle class" was the recycled revenues from commodities exports. When these began to drop in mid-1997, middle-income spending was squeezed hard. Then came the financial crisis of 1998, which wiped out small businesses and private savings and made imported goods unaffordable. But commodities producers responded by boosting exports of oil, gas, and other raw materials to record levels, partially offsetting the decline in world prices. Meanwhile, the ruble lost over three-quarters of its value in the space of six months, making Russian goods highly competitive. Anecdotal evidence at this writing (spring 1999) suggests that spending by middle-income groups did not disappear after the crash, but shifted to Russian-made goods, notably automobiles, which have continued to sell well. In short, the emerging Russian "middle class" may be far from dead,

---

[31] *Rossiia v tsifrakh 1997*, p. 284.

and as world commodities prices improve, its fortunes may revive as well.[32]

But whether this is the nucleus of a true middle class as it is usually defined in the West is another matter. The answer depends on whether it saves money, buys property, creates businesses, moves into new occupations – in short, whether it becomes an engine for growth. We turn now to the question of savings.

Popular savings and investment

Ultimately, the strength of investment in Russia will depend on domestic capital, and that will require domestic savings. There are a lot of myths about Russian savings. The Russian statistical system is responsible for some of them, because its methodology overstates the share of income that Russians save. Goskomstat, the Russian state statistical service, treats all sales of hard currency to individuals as "savings." By that measure, says Goskomstat, Russians currently save about one-quarter of their total income, most of it in the form of cash dollars.

But in actual fact most of those dollars are quickly spent, not saved. Households resell their dollars for rubles; they use them to pay for the "shuttle" trade; and they spend them as tourists. Consequently, the true savings rate is closer to 8–10% of personal income, not one quarter. If the Goskomstat approach were correct, Russians would be sitting on $108 billion in hard currency; but one revised estimate says only $11 billion.[33] Most estimates are in the range of $20 to $40 billion.

In other words, the power of personal savings to contribute to Russia's long-term economic recovery is still small.[34] In 1996 household savings averaged only 2.5 months' income, and 80% of the population had no savings at all – a sharp contrast to 1990, when 70% of the population had some savings, averaging eight months' income.[35] Only about half of that

---

[32] This is the argument of Mariia Golovanivskaia in "Likvidirovany kak srednii klass," *Kommersant-Vlast'*, No. 37 (29 September 1998), pp. 42–44. In the spring of 1999, as the Russian economy revived under the stimulation of the cheaper ruble, reports of the new middle class revived as well. See the view of sociologist Mikhail Gorshkov, general director of the Independent Russian Institute of National and Social Problems, "Est' v Rossii takoi klass!" *Nezavisimaia gazeta*, May 25 1999, by Internet.

[33] This methodological issue is discussed at length in *Russian Economic Trends*, No. 1 (1997), pp. 84–89.

[34] The estimates above do not include the "capital flight" from Russia, which is clearly very much larger. Some of this capital will return to Russia as investment conditions improve, but for all practical purposes it can no longer be considered part of "domestic savings" but rather a species of foreign capital. If it returns it will do so through essentially the same intermediaries as foreign investment.   [35] Ibid., p. 89.

was in banks.[36] The rest was, as Russians say, "in the sock." Ordinary savers were more leery of banks than ever, and with justification. The 10,000-fold decline in the ruble between 1991 and 1995 melted down their nest egg, while banks and other rent-seeking institutions captured much of the value.[37] They are understandably even less enthusiastic about saving today.[38]

The weakness of Russian savings as a source of investment capital is aggravated by the lack of credit instruments. Mortgages are still practically non-existent. A middle-class Russian who wants to build a house or refurbish an apartment must pay cash (although instalments are possible, if paid in advance). This helps to account for the fact that housing construction, which turned around early and was a leader when everything else was in decline in 1993–95, ran out of steam in 1996 and 1997. Housing construction relies more and more on private savings and investments (the share of state and municipal funding is now down to about one-third and is dropping steadily), and the downturn in the sector, even before the August 1998 crash, at a time when other economic indicators were turning around, suggests the shallowness of the middle class's power to invest.[39]

The right people in the right places

How fast the Russian economy will be able to grow, once it turns around, will depend on the availability of people in the right places with the right skills. At the beginning of the 1990s the Russian labor force was poorly fitted to the needs of a market economy. Most of the labor force was employed in industry; and its skills were predominantly those of the factory floor. In addition, up to one-quarter of the labor force was tied up

---

[36] Just how much smaller savers may have lost as the result of bank failures in 1998 is not yet known. Most individual savings accounts are held in Sberbank, which is state-owned and did not fail. Some savings accounts held in commercial banks were transferred to Sberbank in the fall of 1998 and thus were not entirely lost.

[37] Anders Aslund, "Reformy i prisvoenie renty v rossiiskoi ekonomike," in Aslund and Dmitriev, op. cit., pp. 89–104.

[38] Surveys by VTsIOM (Russian Center for Public Opinion Research) support the view that Goskomstat's estimates of popular savings are exaggerated. In the spring of 1997 82% of the population reported having no savings. In addition, the surveys show a declining propensity to save. Upon further inquiry it turns out that about one-quarter of respondents also hold stock; almost invariably these are shares in the enterprise in which the respondent is employed. (Marina Krasil'nikova, "Sklonnost' k sberezheniiam i potrebleniiu," *Ekonomicheskie i sotsial'nye peremeny: monitoring obshchestvennogo mneniia*, No. 3 (1997), pp. 25–30.

[39] *Russian Economic Trends*, No. 1 (1997), pp. 110–111. Monthly updates are available by Internet.

in unproductive agriculture, cut off from the urban economy by long distances and bad roads.

But the structure of jobs and skills is changing. The depression that has gripped the Russian manufacturing and consumer-goods sectors since 1991 has shaken tens of millions of people loose from their former employment. While many are unemployed, the Russian economy has also created new jobs[40] and labor mobility is surprisingly high, given the many obstacles to changing cities or finding housing.

Increasingly, a change of job brings a change of specialty or occupation. Overall, 40% of respondents in a 1997 survey said they had changed their occupation since the beginning of the 1990s. But among those who had held their current jobs for one year or less, over 60% had changed occupations.[41] On the surface, this suggests an encouraging picture of rapidly changing job skills and a vigorous adaptation to the requirements of the market.

But on closer examination the picture is not nearly so promising. Many of those who report a change in occupation have flocked into services and trade, but the largest single growth category is the lower ranks of the local government bureaucracies. Most people were driven by the loss of a previous job, not by the prospect of higher earnings or more interesting employment. They are about evenly split over whether their occupations are better or worse than their old ones. Few have tried to upgrade their skills to take advantage of the new opportunities, and fewer still are attracted by the prospect of starting their own businesses. On the contrary, most respondents say they do not expect – and do not wish – to change jobs again. Surprisingly, on these points young people's answers hardly differ from those of their elders.[42] In other words, the pattern still suggests short-term coping, but not long-term adaptation.

Many people have hung on to their old jobs while they moonlight. They may not actually be working or drawing a paycheck from their former enterprises, but they retain a formal affiliation and continue to receive some minor benefits.[43] At the same time about one-fifth of the workforce

---

[40] But not as many as other post-Soviet economies. According to a 1998 survey, the Russian private sector lags in job creation in every major category. See Simon Johnson, John McMillan, and Christopher Woodruff, "Job Creation in the Private Sector: Poland, Romania, Russia, Slovakia, and Ukraine Compared" (Paper presented at the IMF Conference on "A Decade of Transition: Achievements and Challenges," February 1999).

[41] Zoia Kupriianova, "Real'naia i professional'naia professional'naia mobil'nost' v Rossiiskoi Federatsii," VTsIOM (Russian Center for Public Opinion Research) *Monitoring obshchestvennogo mneniia: Informatsionnyi biulleten'*, No. 4 (July–August 1997), pp. 26–30.   [42] Kupriianova, op. cit.

[43] Recent studies have shown that benefits provided by Russian enterprises have declined sharply in the first half of the 1990s and now amount to a very small share of household

report they have a second source of income, typically one-third to one-half time. In most cases the official primary employer is still a state-owned or a privatized former state enterprise, but the second job, more often than not, is in the new private sector. In other words, many Russians have arranged a sort of bridge, leading from their old world to the new one.[44] Not surprisingly, those who reported the largest earnings from their second jobs in this 1997 survey were young, well-educated males in Moscow or St. Petersburg. These represented perhaps 4 to 5% of the total.

In sum, the adaptation of the workforce to the new economy is still at an early stage. For the vast majority, "secondary employment" still consists of odd jobs, "temping," or in many cases, subsistence farming. Most people report that their second jobs do not really use their skills and that their new jobs are not satisfying. Sociologists speak of "dequalification" (*dekvalifikatsiia*), in other words, the underuse of skills symbolized by the physicist who drives a cab or the chemist who is a shuttle trader.[45]

Yet job satisfaction is not necessarily the same as productivity or contribution to wealth. Many of the highly skilled professionals trained under the Soviet system were underemployed even then – engineers working as skilled workers at the bench, for example, or scientists going through the motions in a state laboratory. Now their energies have been released to the new private sector, creating wealth where previously the command economy created little. In short, the important thing at this transitional stage may not be the quality or productivity of people's new occupations, but simply that they are working in the private sector at all.

What do these early indicators of middle-class consumption, savings, and occupational change tell us? The picture is mixed. The workforce, despite constraints on its mobility, is sufficiently flexible to provide a steady flow of recruits for the growing private sector (in part precisely because of the "bridge strategy" used by many people). There is enough new employment, if at modest wages, to support a rising level of discretionary spending. On the other hand, there has been little retraining into new skills, and people's savings are low.

This pattern suggests that the Russian population is still at an early stage of its adaptation to a market economy. There is a large pool of labor

---

footnote 43 (*cont.*)
income. Organization for Economic Cooperation and Development, Center for Cooperation with the Economies in Transition, *The Changing Social Benefits in Russian Enterprises* (Paris: OECD, 1996).

[44] Eduard V. Klopov, "Vtorichnaia zaniatost' kak forma sotsial'no-trudovoi mobil'nosti," *Sotsiologicheskie issledovaniia*, No. 4 (1997), pp. 29–45.

[45] A good summary is Liudmila Khakhulina, "Povedenie rabotnikov na rynke truda v usloviiakh perekhoda k rynochnoi ekonomike," in Aslund and Dmitriev, *op. cit.*, pp. 13–28.

still loosely employed in traditional jobs and potentially available to the private sector. Since savings rates are low, any increase in income is immediately reflected in consumption. In short, the existing labor force could well support a strong short-term recovery in both production and consumption. Indeed, the signs of recovery that began to be observed in 1997 were driven above all by a revival in household consumption.[46]

It is the longer term that is more open to question. Down the road the failure to adapt the population's education and skills and to remove obstacles to their mobility will act as a brake on productivity growth. In addition, Russian society also inherits severe liabilities – particularly poor health, a heavy welfare burden, and extreme inequalities among regions. We turn to these now.

No precedent outside of war or famine

If anyone doubts that Russian society has been badly damaged, the country's health statistics dispel any illusion. The post-Soviet revolution, outwardly so peaceful by the standards of other revolutions, swept across Russian society in the early 1990s like a scythe, taking a fearsome toll of lives. Death rates soared between 1992 and 1994, from 12.2 per thousand to 15.7.[47] Life expectancy for Russian males dropped from 63.5 years in 1991 to 57.6 years in 1994.[48] Infant mortality jumped from 17.4 per thousand in 1990 to 19.9 in 1993.[49] "There is absolutely no precedent outside of war or famine" for such a stunning decline, commented Judith Shapiro, a leading demographer at the University of London.[50]

But in actual fact the health crisis of the early 1990s only accelerated deep trends that had been under way in Russian society for a generation. Bad food, bad air and water, and an inadequate health system had taken a mounting toll on Russians' health since the early 1970s. As in any classic epidemic, opportunistic infections at a time of crisis preyed on an already weakened population.

Infectious diseases that were considered all but wiped out in the West – measles, typhoid fever, and other killers – came roaring back in Russia in

---

[46] "Special Report on Growth," *Russian Economic Trends*, January 1998, by Internet. In contrast, the rebound that began in early 1999 has been driven primarily by increased exports, favored by the low ruble. See *Russian Economic Trends*, Monthly Report (April 1999).

[47] *Statististicheskoe obozrenie* (monthly publication of Goskomstat), No. 1 (1997), p. 7. For background see Timothy Heleniak, "Dramatic Population Trends in Countries of the FSU," *Transition*, vol. 6, nos. 9–10 (September–October 1995), pp. 1–3.

[48] Rimashevskaia, "Sotsial'nye posledstviia . . .," p. 61.

[49] Natalia Rimashevskaia, Institute for Socio-Economic Studies of the Population, address at Harriman Institute, Columbia University, New York City, February 1994.

[50] *The New York Times*, November 12 1995, p. A1.

the early 90s. Diphtheria, which had practically disappeared from Europe in the 1980s, reappeared in Russia in 1989 and then spread rapidly to the other former Soviet republics. By 1994 there were 40,000 cases in Russia alone, and another 10,000 elsewhere in the Former Soviet Union.[51] By 1995, fortunately, the epidemic began to subside, thanks to an emergency vaccination program. But other infectious diseases, such as syphilis, dysentery and hepatitis, were not so easily countered.[52] Tuberculosis, which had declined from 94.4 thousand new cases in 1970 to a low of 50.4 thousand in 1991, was up to 85 thousand by 1995.[53] Still, by the second half of the decade the rising tide of infectious diseases appeared to have begun to recede.[54]

But if opportunistic infections have peaked, there is a deeper current of chronic social disease that is continuing to build. Rising rates of suicide and alcoholism, to mention only two, show more clearly than public-opinion surveys the depth of popular demoralization. From 26.5 per 100,000 in 1991, the suicide rate climbed sharply to 45 per 100,000 in 1995.[55] In especially hard-hit regions, such as the Russian North, the Urals, or Eastern Siberia, where unemployment is especially high and life seems hopeless, suicide rates are over 50 per 100,000.[56] In bustling Moscow, this toll is little noticed – except when desperate people throw themselves in front of the Moscow Metro, as over 200 did between 1991 and 1995.

Consumption of alcohol, especially vodka, skyrocketed in the 1990s, from 10.6 liters of pure alcohol in 1986 to 14.5 liters in 1993, putting Russia firmly in first place worldwide.[57] Alcohol is the special curse of the Russian male, but in recent years alcoholism has been growing fastest among women and children.[58] Vodka is the only category of Russian con-

---

[51] Massachusetts Medical Society, *Morbidity and Mortality Weekly Report*, vol. 44, no. 10 (March 17 1995), pp. 177–181. Also Goskomstat RF, *Rossiiskii statisticheskii ezhegodnik 1996*, p. 214.

[52] Evgenii Beliaev, chief of the State Committee for Sanitary-Epidemiological Inspection, cited in Reuters, August 14 1995.

[53] Goskomstat RF, *Rossiiskii statisticheskii ezhegodnik 1996*, p. 215.

[54] This is at least the picture that emerges from government statistics, but many authorities dispute it. Tuberculosis specialists, for example, claim that the disease is on a rampage, with no peak in sight. Aleksandr Khomenko of Moscow's Tuberculosis Institute stated in the fall of 1998 that 2.5 million Russians – or one in every 60 – have tuberculosis, and that the number of new cases is still growing at 8.5% a year. (Cited by Paul Goble, in "Promoting Federalism, Fighting Disease," *RL/RFE Daily Report*, October 26 1998).

[55] Rimashevskaia, "Sotsial'nye posledstviia . . .," p. 61.

[56] Aina Ambrumova, *Izvestiia*, September 16 1994.

[57] Aleksandr Nemtsov, Moscow Institute of Psychiatry, quoted in *The Los Angeles Times*, November 12 1995, p. A1. The official statistics are much lower: according to Goskomstat, per capita consumption of pure alcohol is only 6 liters per year.

[58] A.S. Kiselev and A.E. Ivanova, "Mental Illnesses, Alcoholism, and Drug Addiction," in Murray Feshbach, ed., *Environmental and Health Atlas of Russia* (Moscow: "Paims," 1995), pp. 3–8 and 3–9.

sumer goods to have grown steadily throughout the post-Soviet economic depression. In Siberia, alcoholism has become an epidemic. In Krasnoiarsk province, rural people have taken with gusto to drinking *tekhnicheskii spirt*, a vicious near-pure alcohol that killed 800 people in 1994 and maimed many more. Siberian doctors call it "glass cutter" (*steklorez*).[59]

Russian health statistics confirm strikingly that Russia has split into two societies – but they also show that this problem has been building for a long time. The worst environmental and behavioral problems lie outside Moscow and St. Petersburg, in the decaying villages of the Russian northwest, the depressed military-industrial cities of the Urals and the lower Volga, and the vast expanses of East Siberia and the Russian Far East. Economic maps of Russian look like mosaics, with the handful of prospering cities standing out as bright spots, and large splotches of color showing the lagging hinterlands.[60]

Yet even in this second category of non-infectious "chronic" diseases Russian demographers and public health experts believe the worst of the post-Soviet shock may be passing. The death rate peaked at 15.7 in 1994, and has declined steadily since then.[61] Infant mortality has been going down since 1993, although it is still at two to three times the levels of other industrial countries.[62] Life expectancy too has recovered slightly from the low point of 1994.[63]

Still, Russian society will enter the next century badly damaged. Russians point with particular concern to the long-term genetic effects of environmental pollution. Up to 8% of all children are born with serious birth defects, and only one child in five is born free of problems.[64] According to school authorities, only one-tenth of all schoolchildren are fully healthy.[65]

---

[59] *Izvestiia*, April 27 1995, p. 5.   [60] Murray Feshbach, ed., *op. cit.*

[61] *Ekonomicheskoe obozrenie*, No. 1 (1997), p. 7. In 1995 the death rate was 15.0 per thousand, and in 1996 it was down to 14.3.

[62] According to Goskomstat statistics, infantile mortality dropped back from 19.9 per 1000 in 1993 to 17.4 per 1000 in 1996. (Goskomstat, *Statisticheskii ezhegodnik Rossii 1997*, by Internet). But infantile mortality statistics are notoriously tricky. Russian statisticians and public health experts believe that 10% of all infant deaths are never counted, and if standard international definitions of infantile mortality were used, the Russian numbers might be 20 to 25% higher. (I.N. Veselkova et al., "Nekotorye demograficheskie tendentsii v Rossiiskoi Federatsii," *Zdravookhranenie Rossiiskoi Federatsii*, No. 3 (1994), p. 32.)   [63] Rimashevkaia, "Sotsial'nye posledstviia . . .," p. 63.

[64] Iuliia Revazova, professor at the Russian Mutagenic Society, quoted in *Nezavisimaia gazeta*, September 23 1993.

[65] ITAR-TASS World Service in Russian, May 5 1994. See also *Nezavisimaia gazeta*, March 26 1994, p. 6. A "fully healthy" schoolchild is defined as one who qualifies for the "first health group" on the basis of tests that include strength tests, emotional and mental development, as well as physical health.

Meanwhile, the birth rate is continuing to decline, from 10.7 births per thousand in 1992 to 8.8 per thousand in 1996[66] (although there is anecdotal evidence that a turnaround may be occurring among middle-income women in Moscow). The combination of lower birth rates and high death rates has caused a steady drop of 5–6% a year in the natural growth rate of the Russian population, masked only by the high immigration rates of recent years. To thrive, a new market society will need a young and vigorous labor force, but Russia may simply not have it.

The Russian health system is not much help. From the Soviet period it inherited a system of gigantic specialized institutions that serve few patients, vast hospitals with too many doctors and hospital beds but too few nurses and modern medicines, and virtually no preventive medicine. Now that vast bureaucratic machine is winding down for lack of money. Whereas the United States spends 12% of its GNP on health, and Great Britain 6%, Russia budgets less than 1%, a figure on a par with the poorest third-world countries. According to the Russian Health Ministry, half of the country's hospitals have no hot water and a quarter have no sewage.[67] The message for the coming century is clear: Russia is going to have to spend more.

Winners and losers among regions

Regions, not just people, have split into new rich and new poor. In 1995, the top fifth of Russian regions had nearly five times the per-capita GDP of the bottom fifth. On the eve of the August crash, Moscow had far and away the highest per capita income in Russia, over triple the national average.[68] With 7% of Russia's population, Moscow commanded 27% of the country's retail trade, and the growth of its consumer sector was the main factor in Russia's economic turnaround.[69]

The basic explanation was straightforward. Regions with commodities to export did well throughout the 1990s until 1997. Their revenues were then recycled to Moscow banks and brokerages, where they multiplied again, enriching the capital city and generating a consumer boom. In contrast, regions that previously specialized in military industry and other manufacturing remain mired in poverty. The agricultural south is likewise severely depressed, reflecting the lag of reform on the land and the impact of foreign competition in the food sector.[70] Moscow itself is the

[66] *Statisticheskoe obozrenie*, No. 1 (1997), p. 7.

[67] *New York Times*, February 19 1995, p. 12.

[68] "Special Report: A Statistical Look at Russia's Regions," *Russian Economic Trends*, No. 2 (1997), pp. 123 and 126.   [69] "Special Report," loc. cit.

[70] For a review of the state of the agricultural sector see Evgeniia Serova, "Russian Agrarian Sector: Development and Prospects" *Russian Economic Trends Monthly Report* (January 20 1999).

best illustration of the contrasting performance of Russia's two economies: its industrial output declined by more than two-thirds between 1990 and 1996, but the industrial collapse was more than offset until the fall of 1998 by the growth in the new tertiary sector.[71]

Another extreme example is Tyumen Province, West Siberia's oil and gas center, which split in three after 1991. The two northern portions, the Yamal-Nenetsk and Khanty-Mansiisk *okrugi*, achieved a *de facto* secession from the province, taking the bulk of the country's oil and gas wealth with them. Thanks to that bonanza, they have far and away the highest GDP per capita in the entire country. The remaining southern portion, essentially an agricultural rump which also contains the former provincial capital, has less than a tenth of the GDP per capita of its two northern neighbors.

Much of the inequality among regions, as in Tyumen, is a product of differences in natural endowment. But some is due to contrasts in economic policies at the local level. The more conservative governors reacted to Gaidar's 1992 price liberalization by imposing controls on "essential commodities," chiefly food, at the local level. Those same regions tended to oppose privatization and to impose restrictions on the growth of small businesses. The extreme case is the Far Eastern province of Primor'ye, where the local governor has turned his back on the Pacific Rim and together with his cronies divides up a dwindling flow of subsidies from Moscow.

On the eve of the August crash the extreme inequalities among regions appeared to have peaked. After Moscow and the export producers, a second tier of regions was starting to turn around. St. Petersburg and its hinterland were growing, fueled by foreign trade. Several cities in central Russia – Nizhnii Novgorod, Perm', and Samara, for example – started to show increased activity in fields like telecommunicatioins and electrical engineering. Small-scale trade was spreading. More local governments were learning how to promote business. Price controls disappeared almost everywhere.[72]

Whether this positive trend will continue depends largely on how investment flows. During the years of high inflation and high interest rates, money tended to flow from the provinces toward the Moscow banks and financial markets. Sberbank, the country's main savings banks, acted like a pump, drawing household savings from all over Russia and putting them into three-month treasury notes in the capital. Foreign investment likewise went primarily to the Moscow stock market. By late 1997, according to former prime minister Chernomyrdin, out of a total of $20

---

[71] "Special Report," loc. cit., p. 125   [72] Ibid, p. 128.

billion in foreign investment in Russia, only $2 billion had been invested in the provinces.[73] Now it is anyone's guess where new investment will come from.

Inequality among regions would not be so serious a problem if the population were free to move to follow opportunities. But there are restrictions, both official and unofficial. Large concentrations of skilled workers are stuck in places with no future, especially the European north, the industrial Urals, and the villages of the "Non-Black Earth Zone" north and west of Moscow. In the North Caucasus birthrates are high but jobs are scarce. Yet the surplus populations of these regions cannot move readily to the more prosperous areas. The prime location for new jobs, Moscow, still requires residence permits (ignoring court rulings that such permits are unconstitutional), and housing in the capital is short.

Inequality among regions is a source of instability in the new market economy, because the have-not regions are too well entrenched in the political system to be ignored. In the upper house of parliament, for example, the ten to fifteen "donor" regions whose tax revenues support the rest are handily outvoted by the poorer "recipient" regions. Fiscal reallocation is a constant and contentious issue in center-regional relations, and so long as the regions remain as unequal as they are today, the slogan of "taking from the rich" will be a constant temptation for populist politicians.

Yet regional disparities may well soften in coming years. They are due, after all, to the present lopsidedness of the post-Soviet economy. But if the Russian economic recovery broadens and other sectors revive – consumer goods, construction materials, agricultural products, etc. – the pattern of growth may become more balanced, and the dangers of today's inequalities may ease.

The drag of the Russian welfare burden

Compared to the populations of most of the market economies of the world and even to most of the other republics of the Former Soviet Union, the Russian population is older, poorer, and sicker.[74] The main economic consequence is that Russia is likely to face a heavy welfare burden well into the next century.

Statistics on government spending tell an eloquent story. As tax rev-

---

[73] Telecast of former prime minister Viktor Chernomyrdin's meeting with the Advisory Council on Foreign Investment, October 13 1997. "Vstrecha Chernomyrdina s zapadnymi investorami," NTV "Segodnya," full transcript from Internet Securities News.

[74] Ol'ga Dmitrievna Zakharova, "Demograficheskie protsessy v Rossiiskoi Federatsii i stranakh novogo zarubezh'ia," *Sotsiologicheskie issledovaniia*, No. 7 (1997), pp. 60–69.

enues have gone down, the federal and regional governments have tried to preserve social spending. Social programs now account for over half of total state spending, up from about one-third at the end of the Soviet period.[75] Regional governments have borne much of the brunt, as local enterprises have sloughed off their traditional roles as providers of housing and other benefits, while the federal government has shifted down to the local level much of the responsibility for social and welfare spending.[76]

Defense spending is not usually considered a category of "welfare," but in Russia it has become so. More than two-thirds of the Russian defense budget – which itself still accounts for more than 30% of federal spending – is devoted to salaries, pensions, and support of military personnel and their families. Little is left over for development and procurement of new weapons, or even ordinary maintenance of existing ones. "The Ministry of Defense looks like a welfare agency," comments Sergei Regov, a top Russian defense expert. The root of the problem is that the Russian army is too large for the country's security needs, and is overstaffed with officers. But military reform has been slow to get underway, and the drain of military "welfare" on the federal budget is likely to remain high for the foreseeable future.[77]

Russia's welfare spending is made heavier by the fact that much of it is misdirected. Only 19% of Russia's spending on health, unemployment compensation, housing support, and other social programs actually reaches the poor. Most of it goes instead to people with middle and even upper incomes.[78] The largest single item in social spending is subsidies for housing rent and maintenance, which goes indifferently to all tenants in publicly-owned buildings. Gas, electricity, and heat are provided to residences at reduced prices. Monies from the Employment Fund go not to the unemployed but to employers to help bolster payrolls. The Social Insurance Fund still supports enterprise-owned sanatoria and resorts, which benefit mainly the better-off employees. Child support is paid to all families according to the number of children, without regard to their income. In short, most Russian social programs are untargeted (*bezadresny*), or as we say, "categorical" and as such amount to a wholesale subsidy of the middle class.[79]

[75] Mikhail Dmitriev, "Sotsial'nye reformy i biudzhetnyi krizis v Rossiiskoi Federatsii," in Aslund and Dmitriev, *op. cit.*, pp. 105–128.
[76] For background analysis, see Lev Freinkman and Michael Haney, "What Affects the Regional Governments' Propensity to Subsidize?" Policy Research Working Paper 1818 (Washington, D.C.: The World Bank, August 1997)
[77] Sergei Rogov, "Military Reform and the Defense Budget of the Russian Federation" CIM 527 (Alexandria, Virginia: Center for Naval Analyses, August 1997)
[78] Aslund and Dmitriev, op. cit., pp. 133ff.
[79] Ibid. See also the essay by Aleksandr Puzanov in the same collection.

When reformers briefly returned to power in the spring of 1997, welfare reform was at the top of their agenda. Boris Nemtsov, the telegenic former governor of Nizhnii Novgorod, was put in charge. But opposition to change was broad-based and deeply entrenched. Local politicians were quick to rise to the defense of local utilities, gas distributors, municipal contractors, and housing authorities, all of whom have a vested interest in the existing system. Behind these is the mass of the Russian urban population, which is hardly inclined to support the loss of its meager cushion. During their last brief tour in office between 1997 and 1998, the reformers made hardly a dent in the system. Welfare reform is likely to be a slow and arduous process.

Because of the heavy welfare burden, federal and local governments in coming decades will have little left over for investment. This is not entirely bad, at least where industrial investment is concerned, because state technocrats will be prevented from misallocating resources to pet projects. But investment includes human capital – schools, universities, hospitals, laboratories, basic science. These too will be constrained by the pressure of welfare spending. The populist temptation will be to spend the money anyway. Deficit spending and a return to high inflation will be constant dangers in years ahead.

Beyond coping?

The overall finding of this chapter is that by the beginning of 1998 the shock of the Soviet collapse had begun to pass, and most people had found ways to cope. But the second shock, the financial collapse of August 1998 and its aftermath, severely damaged the gains of the most successful element of the population, of precisely those who had gone farthest into the market economy. But even before the second shock, the capacity of Russian society to support vigorous long-term growth was open to question.

This chapter offers two conclusions: Russian society is still at an early stage of its adaptation to a market economy, and its capacity to adapt is slowed by the heavy liabilities carried over from the Soviet era and the lack of systematic investment in health and skills.

The Soviet legacy is heavy. Chronic neglect of environmental and health programs by the Soviet regime has left the Russian population in poor health. The Russian population has few young people and many pensioners. The location and skills of the workforce are still at an early stage of adaptation.

Large parts of the Soviet system did not collapse in 1991, but instead have decayed slowly throughout the 90s. This has been a mixed blessing.

On the plus side, the reluctance of enterprises to lay off their workers out-right has provided a buffer, both psychologically and economically. The survival of state subsidies and benefits – particularly through such vital items as low-cost heat and light – has cushioned the population and helped to stabilize middle-income Russians. But the maintenance of this "Soviet umbilical cord" is now turning into a liability, forcing the state to spend most of its revenue on welfare and delaying the longer-term adaptation of both employers and workers to a new economy.

The second problem is the lingering aftermath of the post-Soviet shock wave. Savings were wiped out by five years of high inflation, and the present savings rate – at least the portion that finds its way into banks – is too low to support strong investment. Incomes remain mired below half of the 1990 level. Much of the secondary employment currently available to the population consists of low-productivity occupations, and the wholesale conversion of the workforce to the new skills required by a market economy has hardly begun.

In sum, the Russian population at present has only limited resources – in savings, in spending power, in health or in productivity – to support an economic recovery beyond an initial rebound. The same is true of the Russian state, whose resources for the foreseeable future will remain lopsidedly committed to social and welfare programs and to the less favored regions, at the expense of investment in physical and human capital in the most promising places. The Russian population is poised to move "beyond coping" – but not at a rapid pace. To judge from the condition of Russian society, there are no economic miracles in the wings.

Speeding the "social transition" to the market will require no less investment in human capital than in industry and commerce. Improving the health, the environment, and the skills, and the mobility of the population are the keys to the long-term success of the transition to the market and its ultimate popular acceptance.

Fantastic grow the evening gowns;
Agents of the Fisc pursue
Absconding tax-defaulters through
The sewers of provincial towns.   W. H. Auden

9 The shrinking Russian state and the battle for taxes

The crash of August 1998 was first and foremost a failure of the central state. The government's inability to balance its budget and its resort to massive short-term borrowing led inevitably to default and devaluation – in effect, bankruptcy on a nation-wide scale. But states, unlike private companies, do not simply go out of business. The Russian government's bankruptcy was only the prelude to what promises to be a long and painful period of insolvency and crisis. That is because the August collapse was only the surface symptom of a deeper and more complex disease.

The Russian state is shrinking. Since the breakup of the Soviet regime there has been a steady decline in the share of Gross Domestic Product collected in revenues by the state at all levels (see table 9.1).

These numbers understate the actual extent of the decline, because up to 40% of the true GDP is produced by the unofficial economy and is not fully reflected in official GDP figures.[1] Allowing for the large share of goods and services generated by the "unofficial" economy, state revenues are less than one-quarter of total GDP – and are still falling. Moreover, since Russian GDP itself has declined by roughly half since 1990, state revenues in absolute terms have dropped by almost three-quarters. And finally, more and more of the government's revenue at all levels consists

---

[1] The methodology for calculating GDP in Russian official statistics has been repeatedly revised in recent years to take greater account of the unofficial economy, particularly by increasing the share attributed to the service and trade sector. At present the official GDP figures estimate that roughly 25% of the total comes from the unofficial economy. However, many experts believe that the true figure should be closer to 40%. See Daniel Kaufman and Aleksandr Kaliberda, "Integrating the Unofficial Economy into the Dynamics of Post-socialist Economies: A Framework of Analysis and Evidence," World Bank Policy Research Paper 1691, Washington D.C., December 1996; and Simon Johnson and Daniel Kaufman, "In the Underground" (Paper prepared for the IMF Conference on "A Decade of Transition: Achievements and Challenges," February 1999).

Table 9.1 *Share of GDP collected in state revenues (%)*

1992	44.2
1993	36.1
1994	36.9
1995	31.2
1996	31.8
1997	33.3
1998	29 (est)

Note: The definition of state revenues used here is that of so-called "enlarged" revenues, i.e., federal and regional, plus the four main "extra-budget" funds.
Source: Russian Economic Trends, various issues.

not of actual "live" money but of barter and various write-offs and quasi-monies.

What is the explanation? The immediate cause is tax evasion. But tax evasion on such a colossal scale as in Russia is the result of something even deeper – a massive "exit" by the population. A culture of tax evasion has taken hold of the country. The result is a downward spiral: the less people pay, the weaker the government gets; and the weaker it gets, the less people pay. The fatal flaw threatening the entire enterprise of building a market-based democracy in Russia is the fiscal crisis and the failure of state-society relations that it represents.

This chapter traces the roots of the Russian tax crisis and offers three conclusions. First, the culture of tax evasion is not new, but is a continuation in "free market dress" of practices, institutional biases, and patterns of behavior that were already deeply ingrained in the Soviet system.

Second, the day-to-day urgency of bringing in revenues competes with the task of long-term reform. The result is a series of dilemmas, which so far the Russian government has not been able to resolve. The danger is that the state will respond to the growing fiscal crisis with more and more repression – to which the population will respond by ever more determined evasion.

Third, Russia's tax problems cannot be understood in isolation from the overall problem of state spending. Russia's taxes are too high because Russia's state spending is still too high, especially at the regional level. Behind that lies a more fundamental problem, namely, the failure to adjust the state's ambitions to its reduced means.

The fiscal crisis illustrates the central thesis of this book: that the issue of transition in Russia is intertwined with the complex problem of redefining and rebuilding the state and its relationship to society. The very concept of "tax" in a market economy is poles apart from that of a state-owned command economy. It is a contract with society, which allows the removal of private property subject to rules agreed to through the legislative process, in exchange for the provision of public goods as specified by law. The orderly collection and allocation of tax monies requires settled relations among the various levels of government, a single national currency in which taxes must be paid, and a shared understanding of rights and responsibilities by the main parties concerned.

None of these conditions obtains in Russia today.

The epidemic of tax evasion

Russians are paying fewer and fewer taxes. Taxes unpaid or delayed, as a share of the total economy, have been climbing steadily since the beginning of the post-Soviet era, but beginning in 1996 tax evasion took off like an epidemic. The Russian state is unable to collect even two-thirds of the taxes called for in the official budget.[2] Almost half of taxes actually paid are not in real money, but in various forms of promissory notes, offsets of government debts, and even barter. According to the State Tax Service, only 16% of all registered businesses pay their taxes in full and on time; some 50% comply occasionally; while 34% ignore the tax collector altogether.[3]

The worst offenders are well known to the tax collectors, because they are the biggest companies in the country: 40% of all tax arrears, according to the State Tax Service, are owed by 100 largest companies (see table 9.2).[4] But even these numbers overstate the extent of compliance, since many tens of thousands of businesses avoid registering at all and thus largely escape the tax collectors' notice.[5]

Tax evasion in its present form is a post-Soviet phenomenon, but the psychology it represents is nothing new. In the Soviet era, enterprise managers survived by concealing from the planners their true resources and

[2] Determining precisely what share of budgeted revenues the government is able to raise at any one time is a slippery proposition, because the yardstick keeps changing. The official budget, voted into law by the parliament, contains spending and revenue targets that everyone realizes are unrealistic. The government then "sequesters" a portion of the approved expenses, and sets a new (and more realistic) revenue target to meet them. But the government is unable to raise even the "sequestered budget" revenues.

[3] *Russian Economic Trends*, No. 1 (1997), pp. 14–15.

[4] *Russian Economic Trends*, No. 3 (1997), p. 15.

[5] *Russian Economic Trends*, vol. 1 (1997), pp. 14–15; see also EBRD, *Transition Report 1997*, p. 121.

Table 9.2 *The spread of company tax arrears (in percent of GDP, end of period)*

	1994	1995	1996	1997	1998 (Q2)
Tax arrears	2.3	3.1	4.6	6.0	8.4
Arrears to off-budget funds	n.a.	0.9	4.2	5.7	7.8
Total		4.0	8.8	11.7	16.2

Source: Russian Economic Trends, No. 3 (1998), p. 75.

operations. Dissimulation and misreporting were the very core of the system.[6] As a result, the Soviet economy was not so much planned as negotiated. Today's massive tax evasion and "tax collection by plea bargain" are a continuation of some of the most deeply ingrained traits of Soviet behavior.

Indeed, tax evasion emerged almost as soon as Gorbachev began his attempts to reform the command economy in 1987 by increasing the latitude of enterprise managers. To lower their reportable profits, enterprises charged one another artificially low prices, which they offset under the table with bartered goods.[7] They spun off subsidiaries in remote locations with weaker regional tax offices. They lessened their employees' tax bills by finding ingenious ways of adding to their unreported income. One popular mechanism was to buy a group insurance policy for the enterprise's workers, which could be charged as a deductible cost of business; the paid-up proceeds of the policy would subsequently be credited, tax-free, to the employees' bank accounts.[8] In short, from the beginning enterprise managers set the pattern for the massive tax evasion that has since become the norm.

Tax evasion, to be sure, is not restricted to Russia. In the United States, the Internal Revenue Service estimates that evasion of individual and corporate taxes costs the Treasury more than 20% of taxes due, on the order of $100 billion every year. Data from the IRS's Tax Compliance Measurement Program suggest that two-thirds of US corporations are

[6] The classic work on the subject is Joseph A. Berliner, *Factory and Manager in the Soviet Union* (Cambridge, Mass.: Harvard University Press,1957). For a systematic description, see Ed A. Hewett, *Reforming the Soviet Economy: Equality vs. Efficiency* (Washington, D.C.: Brookings Institution, 1988), chapter 4, "The Soviet Economic System as it Actually Operates."

[7] In 1991 to combat the widespread practice of selling below cost the law was changed to provide that for tax purposes a good or service cannot be sold below its *sebestoimost'*; this rule remains in effect today.

[8] Sergei Sinel'nikov, *Biudzhetnyi krizis v Rossii: 1985–1995 gody* (Moscow: "Evraziia," 1995) pp. 44, 59–62.

"non-compliant," with unreported profits averaging 12% of their reported profits. The larger the corporation, US studies show, the larger the gap between unreported and reported profits.[9] In every Western economy there is a substantial underground economy, whose revenues are largely unreported and untaxed; and there is substantial underpayment by the official economy.

But if tax leakage is a universal fact, the measure of a good tax system is the extent to which it keeps the problem in bounds. In Russia the problem is out of control. The government has experimented with amnesties and deferrals and forced bankruptcies, none of which has brought much response. It has tried focusing on broad categories of delinquent taxpayers, using a combination of appeals and threats. Banks, rock groups and pop singers, travel agencies and tour operators, lotteries, direct-sale houses, casinos, and even fortune-tellers – all large earners of undeclared income – have come under scrutiny by government tax inspectors, but to little avail. To go after large taxpayers, the government in 1997 created a special high-level enforcement body and even gave it a name calculated to strike fear into the hearts of tax evaders – the Temporary Extraordinary Commission, or VChK, the initial name of the KGB at the beginning of the Soviet era. None of these ploys has worked.

Yet the government's uncertainty is understandable: it reflects deep underlying dilemmas in the design of tax policy.

Dilemmas of Russian tax policy

If there is one thing that all Russians can agree on, it is that the Russian tax system is terrible. It is so complex and inconsistent that, as the Russians say, "even the devil would break his leg." The system is jerry-built with bits and pieces left over from the Soviet era, overlaid with a veneer of post-Soviet reforms. The administration of it is unfair, capricious, unpredictable, and conflictual. The system is impossible to obey and all too easy to beat. Above all, it fails to meet the two essential criteria of any tax system: to bring in adequate state revenues while not stifling or distorting the economy.

Compared to modern fiscal systems in the west, the Russian system has a number of built-in "Soviet-era" defects:[10]

---

[9] Joel Slemrod, ed., *Why People Pay Taxes: Tax Compliance and Enforcement* (Ann Arbor, Michigan: The University of Michigan Press, 1992), p. 1–4. See particularly the chapter by Eric Rice, "The Corporate Tax Gap: Evidence on Tax Compliance by Small Corporations," pp. 125–166.

[10] Joel McDonald and Michael Alexeev, "Note on the Current Russian Tax System and Proposed Reforms" (Unpublished note prepared for the OECD Committee on Fiscal Affairs, Paris, France, May 1997)

1. *It taxes the wrong things and the wrong taxpayers*: The Russian tax
   system tends to tax gross revenues rather than profits, and corporations rather than individuals.
2. *It overstates the taxable base*: Most businesses still use Soviet-era
   accounting rules, which were designed to monitor physical production and account for the proper expenditure of state funds. The
   Russian system severely limits the deductibility of items that are considered normal business expenses in the west, such as insurance,
   travel, advertising, and business entertainment.
3. *It requires too many records and reports*: Russian tax collectors require
   very detailed accounting records and frequent reports. Much of this
   information is useless to the tax authorities, but assembling it and processing it imposes high costs on both the taxpayers and the tax collectors.
4. *It focuses on the "visible" businesses inherited from the Soviet era:* As the
   Russian economy has shifted from production to consumption, services, and small business, the tax system has failed to follow. It is
   administratively simpler to concentrate on the "visible" officially registered large enterprises. Meanwhile, most new businesses try to stay
   underground.

Russians complain their taxes are too high, especially for such a deeply
depressed economy. They may have a point: despite the post-Soviet
decline, the share of official GDP collected in Russia is comparable with
the United States and Japan, and much higher than most other countries
with similar income levels.[11] But the real trouble is in the way the burden
is apportioned.[12] Much of the pressure of the tax collector falls on large
enterprises; indeed, according to Aleksandr Pochinok, head of the
Russian Ministry for Tax Collection, nineteen large companies account
for over two-thirds of federal tax revenues.[13] The industrial and construction sectors, which produce 40% of official GDP, bear most of the tax
burden. At one extreme, the oil and pipeline sector, which generates some
12% of GDP, pays over 25% of total taxes;[14] at the other extreme, the
banking sector, at the height of its prosperity, generated only 4% of tax
revenues.[15] Finally, Russia collects only a small share of its revenues from
individual income taxes.

The tax collectors' natural temptation is to go after the big visible
targets first, mainly the large commodity exporters. The largest delin-

---

[11] *Russian Economic Trends*, "Special Report: Taxes in Russia" (Monthly Update, December
1997, by Internet).   [12] EBRD, *Transition Report 1997*, p. 121.
[13] "Chetyre udara Pochinka," *Ekspert*, December 1 1997, by Internet.
[14] "Special Report: Taxes in Russia," op. cit.
[15] *Russian Economic Trends*, No. 1 (1997), p. 16.

quent enterprises can be intimidated through pressure and threats of restructuring and foreclosure, measures that can be implemented relatively quickly, or so the government hopes. At the other extreme, dealing with the myriad unofficial businesses is more difficult, requiring a delicate combination of tax reform and tougher police power. The trade-off is between immediate results – at the cost of worsening the fundamental sources of the disease – and the much more uncertain and long-term results of reforming the system.

So far the Russian government, caught up in the daily battle to stay solvent, has stressed the near-term approach, while postponing reform. In the first instance, this has meant building up the enforcement system.

Building an enforcement system

Designing the tax system and setting collection priorities are difficult enough. In addition, the Russian government since 1991 has had to build a tax-collection system practically from scratch.

On a balmy August afternoon a few years ago Muscovites watched open-mouthed as Tax Police officers in ski masks and battle dress slid down ropes from the roof of a Moscow apartment building to the balcony of Sergei Mavrodi, the creator of a notorious pyramid scheme called MMM.[16] They arrested him for tax evasion and fraud and took him off to jail, but were later unable to convict him, and Mavrodi is still a free man today.

The Mavrodi episode differed only in its drama from hundreds of similar scenes enacted every day throughout Russia. There is a tax war going on. But the authorities, though they may have all the weapons of the state at their disposal, are losing.

In the Soviet era the main tax-collecting agent was the financial departments of the provincial governments (in Russian, the *finansovye otdely* of the *oblispolkomy*). These were regional bodies (although technically they also reported to the USSR Ministry of Finance) and like most offices at the provincial level they were, as a rule, weak and underpaid. But this hardly mattered, since tax collection and enforcement were not critical functions in the Soviet fiscal system.[17]

In 1990 the government merged the regional tax collectors into a new State Tax Service, responsible for all tax collection.[18] The Tax Service was

---

[16] Associated Press photograph, published in the *Los Angeles Times*, August 23 1994.
[17] Christine I. Wallich, ed., *Russia and the Challenge of Fiscal Federalism* (Washington, D.C.: The World Bank, 1994), pp. 26–27.
[18] Dmitri Georgievich Chernik, *Nalogi v rynochnoi ekonomike* (Moscow: IUNITI Publishers, 1997), p. 354. In March 1991 the Russian government passed its own republic-level laws creating a Russian tax service, reinforced by a key presidential decree in December.

initially a weak and understaffed force of about 100,000.[19] To cover all of Moscow, there were barely more than 1,000 tax inspectors.[20]

By now the Tax Service has doubled in size, and the inspectors' skills are being upgraded. The Service has regional training centers in Moscow, St. Petersburg and Nizhnii Novgorod, and its more promising specialists are being trained in the prestigious Finance Academy of the Ministry of Finance.[21] In addition, in cooperation with the OECD, the European Community, and the Danish Tax Service, an International Tax Training Center is operating in Moscow, which trains personnel from all over Russia. The Tax Service itself has risen in status: it is now classified as a ministry, which puts its chief, in theory, on a par with other senior financial officials such as the finance minister.

Even so, the tax inspectors are stretched very thin. In Moscow alone, the inspectors are responsible for patrolling over 400,000 registered businesses.[22] Each inspector must cover several dozen of them single-handed – checking the enterprise's books, its debts and receivables, its previous tax payments, its bank accounts. The pressure on tax inspectors has grown steadily, as the number of Russian businesses has increased. In 1992, there were only 270,000 taxpaying entities, most of them large state enterprises. By 1996, there were over six million. But the real challenge still lies ahead. If in coming years the Russian tax system gradually shifts from its present focus on corporate taxes to taxes on individuals, as is the practice in other advanced countries, the Russian tax Service will somehow have to patrol tens of millions of returns, a task that would be utterly beyond it today.[23]

At first, tax inspectors had few weapons at their disposal. They could levy fines, but the amounts involved represented hardly more than a slap on the wrist – only about $64,000 in fines, for example, were levied for the entire city of Moscow in the first half of 1993.[24] But the tax inspectors were still a threat to private businessmen, because they could freeze a business's bank accounts, stopping it in its tracks. As time went on, the tax inspectors learned to use the power of penalties and fines.

But then tax evaders began to fight back.

[19] *Rossiiskaia gazeta*, February 16 1993
[20] Maksim Rubchenko et al., "Nalogovaia sistema: den′gi dyrochku naidut," *Kommersant*, July–August 1993 (No. 35), pp. 15–17.
[21] For more complete information on efforts to upgrade the skills of the tax inspectors, see Chernik, op. cit., p. 360ff. Chernik is the head of the Moscow tax inspectorate and an expert on tax law.   [22] *Kommersant-Daily*, January 27 1996, p. 2.
[23] Actually, as Moscow tax expert Joel McDonald observes, the extent of the strain will depend on the direction of reform. If the personal income tax is kept simple and there is final withholding on most types of income such as wages, dividends and interest, as well as no itemized deductions, then there may not be many returns filed, and the task will be manageable for the inspectors.
[24] Rubchenko, "Nalogovaia sistema," *Kommersant*, op. cit.

Fighting the "red rooster"

Collecting taxes has become a high-risk profession. Tax inspectors face threats of violence and attacks on their offices. Arson – traditionally known in Russia as "turning loose the red rooster" – has become a favorite weapon of recalcitrant taxpayers. Tax inspection offices have been set ablaze, and in some places the tax inspectors' homes as well. Tax inspectors have been shot at, beaten up, and blackmailed. In some cases, their children have been kidnapped. The effect in many places is to deter tax inspectors from entering the premises of businesses or to pursue inquiries into dangerous cases.

It is not always necessary to intimidate tax inspectors; bribery and corruption are widespread. The State Tax Service has an internal review department (*kontrol'no-revizionnoe upravlenie*) to handle complaints against tax inspectors, but internal inspections are spotty and abuses are widespread, especially in the poorer and more distant regions.[25]

To protect the Tax Service – but also to police it – in March 1992 President Yeltsin signed a decree creating a Tax Police, modeled on Italy's "Guardia dei Finanzi."[26] Headed by a former KGB officer, Sergei Almazov, and staffed by former military, police, and KGB officers, the Tax Police grew quickly to over 20,000.[27] Each branch of the Tax Service throughout the country, and especially Moscow's 36 tax inspection districts, has its own complement of tax police for protection and enforcement. (Most of the tax inspectors are unarmed women; most of the tax police are armed men.)

Searching for unreported profits or illegal income, the Tax Police have the right to use force to enter any place of business, including a private residence suspected of being an office. They need no search warrant. The only restriction is that they must inform the Procuracy within 24 hours of entry. They have the same powers as the Tax Service to sequester records and to freeze bank accounts for periods of up to one month.[28] Little wonder that a leading Western accounting firm, in a monthly newsletter to its clients in Moscow, offered a rubrique called, "What to Do When the Tax Police Arrives." The first advice, "Stay calm."

The Tax Police soon began to pay their way. A favorite *modus operandi*

---

[25] Interview with the head of the State Tax Service's *kontrol'no-revizionnoe upravlenie*, Anatolii Mel'nichenko, in *Russkii telegraf*, December 11 1997, by Internet; also *Kommersant-Daily*, December 11 1997, by Internet.

[26] The presidential decree was followed up by a law on the tax police, dated 24 June 1993. See Chernik, op. cit., p. 354.

[27] *Kommersant*, No. 6 (21 February 1995), p. 60. In March 1999 Sergei Almazov was replaced by Viacheslav Sotaganov, who had previously headed internal security in the Ministry for Tax Collection.   [28] *Kommersant-Daily*, October 7 1994, p. 8.

of the Tax Police is to arrive right after the tax inspector has just left –
partly to check up on her. Thus the harassed Russian businessman frequently faces a double-barreled tax audit.[29] Senior Tax Police officers
trumpet that the Tax Police has become the most cost-effective operation
in the Russian government, returning 50 rubles of clear "profit" for every
ruble spent on it.[30]

Yet such claims are unconvincing. Behind the Tax Police's upbeat
claims is a story of weakness and frustration. Until 1996 the Tax Police
lacked the authority to conduct their own investigations. Once they had
identified a potentially criminal case, it was the job of the regular police
(MVD) to investigate it and bring it to court. But the MVD, which lacked
trained tax investigators, was notoriously unenthusiastic. With their
hands full chasing violent criminals, the police put off prosecuting "soft"
crimes like tax evasion. Fewer than 8% of the cases brought to the MVD
by the Tax Police ever reached the courts.[31]

Since 1996 the powers of the Tax Police have been strengthened; it can
conduct its own investigations and bring cases before the courts.[32] But
the courts are still reluctant to convict. Only two brief articles of the
Criminal Code deal with tax evasion, and they require the prosecution to
prove intent. So far, it has been easy for defense lawyers to get their clients
off with only light fines, arguing that their clients were absent-minded or
sloppy.[33]

The Tax Police face one problem in common with the tax inspectors-
lack of funds. The central government pays the tax policemen's salary, but
for the rest (buildings, telephone, etc.) they depend on the good will of the
local governor, whose support frequently comes with strings attached.
Over time the tax police, like the tax service, may answer more to the
regions than to the federal center.[34]

By far the greatest power in the hands of the tax inspectors and the tax
policemen is the power to harass. Both services can freeze bank accounts,
confiscate assets, and levy fines. For a small businessman it hardly matters
whether the case goes to court or whether he can ultimately recover funds
confiscated in a raid – he is likely to be out of business in any case. Thus,
as the tax collectors grow stronger and tougher, a more and more pressing
issue is taxpayers' rights.

---

[29] *Kommersant-Daily*, October 7 1994, p. 8.
[30] See for example *Segodnia*, November 26 1994.
[31] *Ekonomika i zhizn'*, No. 2 (January 1996), p. 3.
[32] *Kommersant-Daily*, December 20 1995, p. 14.
[33] *Kommersant-Daily*, February 24 1995, p. 2.
[34] Interview with Sergei Almazov, director of the Tax Police, "My – spetssluzhba," *Ekspert*,
No. 5 (February 8 1999), pp. 12–14.

The problem of taxpayers' rights

Imagine that the Russian tax collector knocks at your door, and informs you that you are being fined for having violated a tax ordinance. First, it is frequently the case that you have no idea what that ordinance may be. The modest number of published laws and regulations on tax matters is dwarfed by the vast quantity of unpublished "letters," "orders," and "telegrams" issued by government agencies, chiefly the Tax Service and the Ministry of Finance – in clear violation of Article 15 of the Constitution, which provides that no unpublished statute shall have force of law.

When new regulations are issued, they frequently apply retroactively and before the relevant statutes are even published, despite the fact that Article 57 of the Constitution forbids retroactive taxation, as does the Basic Law on the Tax System.

Some small progress is being made, at least, in informing Russian taxpayers of their liabilities. In 1994 the Tax Service began publishing a journal, "Tax Service Herald" (*Vestnik nalogovoi sluzhby*). Regional tax inspectorates publish their own newsletters. Moscow's tax inspectorate publishes its own newspaper, *Nalogi* ("Taxes"), and its own journal.[35] The government daily, *Rossiiskaia gazeta*, publishes most government decrees. Several business newspapers carry articles and columns on developments in the tax system. And many law firms and accounting firms have sprung up, specializing in advising businesses on the tax system.

Recent laws have bolstered taxpayers' rights. Under the newly adopted Part I Tax Code the Tax Service is no longer allowed to demand immediate payments of fines; instead the taxpayer may appeal the case to higher levels of the tax service as well as the arbitration courts. The new code also takes away the Tax Service's authority to make changes in tax laws through agency regulations (*normativnye akty*). The Tax Police's power to conduct investigations is subject to some new restrictions.[36]

But such laws are unlikely to change the basic situation, because the government needs money, and the powers of the courts are weak. Moreover, the tradition under which government agencies legislate through regulations is too strong to break. Yet so long as taxpayers' rights are as weakly enforced as they are today, the greater is the temptation for taxpayers to defend themselves by any means available – through backdoor political influence, through ever more elaborate dissimulation, or through violence.

---

[35] Chernik, op. cit., p. 371.

[36] *Kommersant*, No. 6 (21 February 1995), p. 65. This is a controversial point, however. The Yabloko Party opposes the Tax Code in its present form, arguing that it will increase the repressive powers of the state. See *Izvestiia*, November 4 1997, by Internet.

Yet in the end, the core failing of the enforcement system is that it is equipped to deal with only one of the three faces of tax evasion – namely, the average-sized, officially registered business. The tax service and the tax police are virtually powerless in dealing with the other two faces – the largest enterprises, which are too powerful for them to go after, and the myriad unregistered businesses that disappear into the unofficial economy. We look now at the unofficial economy, then at the problem of dealing with the large, well-connected businesses.

How to beat the tax collector

The unofficial economy is not a faraway place somewhere over the next hill; it is right in the midst of the official economy. Even in the Soviet era many Russians lived with one foot "on the left." Nearly all do today.

The underground economy is present everywhere. Inside every officially registered enterprise there are unregistered private businesses, funneling profits out the back door. Practically every Russian business-man chooses at the margin how much of his activity to conduct "above ground" and how much not, and what share in cash versus barter. Most operate in both economies, and the main factor in their decision is taxes. Increased state pressure on known delinquents, for example, increases their incentive to spin off unregistered "daughter companies." Thus a bad tax regime drives the legitimate economy underground or into the "virtual economy" of barter and wechsels.[37]

The best way to evade taxes is to leave no paper trail, and the best way to do that is to deal in cash. In the Soviet period cash represented only a small part of the money supply. Most transactions took the form of trans-fers from one state bank account to another, and were thus easily tracked. (In Russian practice bank accounts are referred to as "non-cash" – *beznal* – as opposed to cash in banknotes, called *nal*.)[38]

But with the rise of the private sector Russians have found more and more ingenious ways of turning "non-cash" into "cash." By 1996 some 30% of all money transactions were in cash,[39] and the spread of illegal cash had become an epidemic. In Moscow alone the leakage of recorded bank accounts into unrecorded cash was running at $40 million a day, and the government's top financial officials admitted they had run out of ways of fighting back.[40]

Illegal cash is called "black cash" (*chernyi nal*). "Black cash" has

---

[37] Daniel Kaufman and Aleksandr Kaliberda, op. cit.
[38] These terms are actually short for *beznalichnye den'gi* (non-cash monies) and *nalichnye den'gi* (cash monies).   [39] *Finansovye izvestiia*, March 15 1996, p. 2.
[40] *Kommersant-Daily*, March 7 1996, p. 1.

become a way of life in Russia, and it fuels the vigorous informal economy. The tax service estimates that as much as 40% of all taxable revenues escape taxation by being transacted in cash instead of interbank transfers.[41] The cash problem is aggravated by the fact that credit cards and checking accounts, unknown in the Soviet period, are still in their infancy in Russia.

Practically every organization in Russia, whether private or public, keeps two sets of books. The first is the official books, which are reported to the authorities and on which taxes are paid. The second is the unofficial kind, the "accounting out of the safe" ("*seifovaia bukhgalteriia*"), which is strictly cash and strictly unreported. Every deal has a cash component on the side, frequently paid in dollars. As a result, reported transactions either take place at cost or at a low margin, which keeps profits taxes at a minimum – while the actual profits are paid under the table in cash.

Similarly, most private companies have a "dual salary" system. Employees receive one part in rubles, duly recorded with income taxes properly withheld. The other part comes in an envelope, in dollars, and is usually the larger of the two. This portion is called the "*konvertirovannaia zarplata*" – a play on words that means simultaneously, "converted salary" and "envelope salary."[42]

To fight back, the government has passed laws requiring the use of cash registers to record cash transactions. The first such law, passed in 1993, had little effect. There were simply not enough cash registers available in Russia to enable every small business to have one. Now cash registers have become more common, but businessmen have found many ingenious ways of beating them. The simplest dodge is to record only part of the price of a transaction; the money that ends up in the till is only a fraction of the sale. To fight this, a new law was passed in 1996, giving the tax inspectors the right to make spot purchases, and then to demand to see the contents of the register.[43]

As tax law and enforcement become tougher and more sophisticated, tax evaders become ever more ingenious. As the Russian private economy evolves and becomes more open to the outside world, the sources of tax leakage multiply. Banks which are supposed to transfer their clients' taxes to the state frequently delay doing so for periods up to a year, using the "float" to make extra profits. Insurance companies are a favorite avenue for tax evasion: tax authorities estimate that nine out of ten insurance

---

[41] Rubchenko, "Nalogovaia sistema," *Kommersant*, op. cit.
[42] The "converted salary" avoids the 40% payroll taxes that apply to reported wages, and until its repeal in 1996, the 38% "excess wages tax" that applied to wages paid above a small minimum threshhold.   [43] *Kommersant-Daily*, April 12 1996, p. 8.

companies systematically evade tax laws, by such means as fictitious policies and inflated settlements.

Many Russians shelter their money from the tax collector outside the country. Estimates of Russian capital flight vary wildly, with estimates running from 20 to 300 billion dollars in net capital flow out of the country[44] The classic way to export capital is to understate the quoted price of exported goods or to inflate the price of imported items and services. The difference between the quoted price and the real one is paid by the Western partner – frequently an offshore office of a Russian company – into a bank account in the West. A variant on the technique is to import fictitious services from a foreign company (again, typically a Russian offshore partner); this is known as "importing air."[45]

The use of offshore subsidiaries has become a highly-developed art form among Russian businessmen. There are over 60,000 Russian offshore companies operating throughout the world.[46] So much of the Russian private sector has moved offshore that most large deals automatically carry a large offshore component; for example, when a building changes hands in Russia only a fraction of its value will be paid and declared inside the country; the rest will be settled from one Cyprus or Cayman Islands offshore account to another.

Contraband and shuttle trade are additional sources of tax leakage. The break-up of the USSR added nearly 12,000 kilometers of new external border for Russia's border troops to patrol, nearly all easy overland routes. Across these borders Russian traders – most of them ordinary women who have gone into trade to make ends meet – pass virtually without hindrance, making some 30 million trips each year. What they declare at entry points amounts to one-quarter of total Russian imports, and is taxed at a special low rate, causing a loss of up to $400 million a year in tax receipts.[47] What they do not declare is anyone's guess.

Lastly, the best defense against the tax collectors is not to use money at

[44] *Izvestiia,* March 6 1996, p. 7; *Kommersant-Daily,* March 2 1996, p. 2. The higher figure, which is more than ten times greater than the estimates of the State Customs Committee ($20 billion 1992–95) and the Russian Central Bank ($28.7 billion over the same period), comes from a report by Mikhail Khaldin, "Kapital Rossii: poteriat' ili preumnozhit'?" prepared under the aegis of the Russian Business Roundtable. While the estimates of the government agencies probably fall short of the true figure, Khaldin's numbers appear out of line, especially since they do not include 1995. Capital flight of $300 billion would be comparable to the capital transfers caused by the first oil shock, and would have a much more noticeable impact worldwide. A figure of $50 billion may be closer to the mark.

[45] These examples come from *Kommersant,* No. 6 (21 February 1995), pp. 60–63.

[46] *Izvestiia,* March 6 1996, p. 7.

[47] *Kommersant-Daily,* March 7 1996, p. 1, citing then-deputy economics minister Sergei Ignat'ev.

all. By one estimate, over 50% of the payments between industrial companies take place in barter and other non-money instruments, while among the largest industrial companies the share reaches three-quarters.[48]

Thus the Russian tax authorities face three forms of evasion: that of the "virtual economy" (the large industrial companies that operate on barter and quasi-monies), that of the "shadow economy" (small unregistered businesses that operate on cash only), and that of the "offshore economy." In reality, all three overlap, and any given Russian businessman or manager may be involved in all three at once.

Many countries live with a large unofficial economy. Once such an economy comes into existence, it is difficult to undo, because at bottom it reflects society's mistrust of the state and its promises. In a striking experiment, province authorities in Nizhnii Novgorod a few years ago declared an amnesty and instituted a new progressive tax system for small business. The reformers' expectation was that small entrepreneurs would come forward to take advantage of the favorable conditions offered. But to their astonishment, the response was virtually nil. If the experience of Nizhnii Novgorod is any guide, the reformers' hope of rolling back the unofficial economy through tax reform may be overoptimistic.

The Nizhnii Novgorod experiment also points to something else: the federal authorities are not the only players in the Russian tax crisis. Russia's provinces and republics have emerged as powerful competitors for tax revenues.

Center vs. regions: the issue of revenue-sharing[49]

In Russia power has traditionally been concentrated at the center. Only when the center was weak or divided has power leaked to the localities. The 1990s have been one of those times. The central government's control over many of the key levers of power has eroded: the power to coerce, to hire and fire key officials, to allocate key resources, and to grant or withhold monies. The big winners have been the local political leaders in the provinces and the major cities.

But will this new balance of power last? Gradually, it is being codified in laws, including the 1993 Russian constitution and also a series of bilateral

---

[48] Clifford G. Gaddy and Barry W. Ickes, "Beyond a Bailout: Time to Face Reality about Russia's Virtual Economy" (Washington, D.C.: Brookings Institution, July 1998). Available by Internet from the Brookings Institution website, http://www.brook.edu.

[49] This section owes much to the insights of Chris Speckhard, who as a graduate student at Georgetown in the spring of 1994 wrote an excellent analysis of center-regional tax issues, "The Politics of Fiscal Federalism in Russia."

treaties. Russians are gradually becoming accustomed to a new order, in which the central government in Moscow shares wealth and power. If enough time passes and the present arrangements are not reversed, the Russian political system may evolve into something it has never been in its past – a federal system of government.

The answer will depend in part on who controls the purse. In the years since 1991 both revenues and expenditures have been transferred downward to the regional governments. The regional governments' share of tax revenues currently fluctuates around 50%,[50] and if subsidies and transfers are included, the regional share goes up to more than 60%.[51] A new division of duties is evolving, in which the regional governments are responsible for health, welfare, basic education, housing, transportation, and public utilities.[52] The regional governments receive – at least in principle – a corresponding share of tax revenues.

At least, that is the theory. Reality is a good deal more complex. As a World Bank study concludes, "The system is not a system, but a collection of ad hoc, negotiated, nontransparent agreements whose effects are not well understood."[53]

From the beginning, the Russian reformers put the cart before the horse. The regions were so anxious to gain control over a share of revenues that they negotiated a new system of revenue assignments before it was clear what their spending responsibilities would be. This has led to constant bargaining between the center and the regions. The center tries to recapture revenues, while "pushing the deficit downward" by reassigning expenditures to the regional governments. The division of major taxes is renegotiated periodically, while responsibility for expenditures shifts with each year's budget.[54]

The result is a noisy and disorderly game in which neither side admits what it is really up to. The Ministry of Finance, in the name of fiscal rectitude, tries to limit the leeway of the regional governments to develop an independent tax base. The regional governments respond by developing ad hoc coping mechanisms which pass the buck back to the federal level. For example, regional governments pressure local enterprises to keep providing social services or infrastructure investments, then they press locally-owned banks to lend to the enterprises to cover the resulting

---

[50] *Russian Economic Trends*, various quarterly issues.
[51] Richard M. Bird, Robert D. Ebel, Christine I. Wallich, eds., *Decentralization of the Socialist State: Intergovernmental Finance in Transition Economies*, World Bank Regional and Sectoral Studies (Washington, D.C.: The World Bank, 1995), p. 354.
[52] An extensive listing of expenditure assignments will be found in Bell, Ebel, Wallich, eds., op. cit., pp. 329–331.   [53] Bell, Ebel, and Wallich, eds., op. cit., p. 337.
[54] Bell, Ebel, and Wallich, eds., op. cit., p. 372.

deficits.[55] The enterprises, strapped to repay the local loans, then delay paying taxes to the center.

But the most potent threat is that the regional governments will negotiate special tax regimes directly with the center, or withold tax payments altogether. What enables them to do so is political weakness at the center.

In the battle with the regions, the central government has two major trumps remaining – control over exports of certain key commodities, chiefly crude oil and gas, and redistribution of income from rich provinces to poor. Through ownership of pipelines, inspection by the customs service, the granting and withholding of export licenses, and the like, the federal government is still able to coerce the regional governments. But if the economy continues to liberalize and the government removes the last controls from foreign trade, even that lever will lose strength.

The federal government's final lever is redistribution of tax revenues. There are only a handful of "tax donors," i.e., regions that are prosperous enough that their tax payments exceed the amounts transferred back to them from the center. The rest are net recipients – and thus dependent on the central government's largesse, as it redistributes the surplus from the richer regions to the poorer. Moscow was, at least until August 1998, the most extreme case of a "donor." The city and its surrounding province provided over one-third of the taxes paid to the federal government. The other "donor" regions are a shifting list, but as a rule there are a fewer than a dozen, typically including St. Petersburg, the provinces of Nizhnii Novgorod, Perm', Samara, Sverdlovsk, and the two resource-rich *okrugi* of West Siberia, Khanty-Mansiisk and Yamalo-Nenetsk.[56] All the other regions of the Russian Federation are dependent to varying degrees on transfers. The extreme case is the depressed North Caucasus, where half of the ten regions with the lowest tax take are located.[57]

Initially the transfers were made largely on the basis of political influence and back-room bargaining, which gave the federal government maximum leverage. Gradually the system is becoming more transparent and predictable, as ad-hoc transfers give way to formula-based grants.[58] But the federal government, increasingly pressed by falling revenues, often fails to make good on the promised transfers, even as the regional governments face growing spending obligations. This threatens to undo the recent progress toward a more transparent system, and opens up the system once again to political negotiation.[59]

Thus the decentralization of political power that has occurred since

[55] Bell, Ebel, and Wallich, p. 348.   [56] *Rossiiskaia gazeta*, November 1 1997, by Internet.
[57] *Russian Economic Trends*, No. 2 (1997), p. 134.
[58] *Russian Economic Trends*, No. 3 (1997), p. 24.   [59] *Ibid.*, pp. 23–24.

1991 complicates immensely the state's fiscal problems. To be sure, as state bodies the regional authorities share the center's interest in bringing in revenues to support public spending. But regional politicians are also interested in protecting local industries; indeed, they are frequently stakeholders in them. More and more, regional politicians compete with one another and with the center to grant their largest employers tax breaks and concessions. Thus they add to the political leverage enjoyed by the largest businesses.

The battle against loopholes, exemptions, and other temptations

Tax evasion begins at the top. While small and medium-sized businesses defend themselves against the tax collector by fading into the unofficial economy, the largest businesses and the best-connected interests stand their ground and negotiate exemptions and concessions. According to the European Bank for Recovery and Development, exemptions, tax deferrals, and other tax concessions amount to over 7 percent of Russian GDP.[60] If that gigantic loophole could be closed, it would wipe out most of the Russian budget deficit.

But the preferential treatment given to large interests will never be closed off entirely, for two reasons. First, they are well connected. Second, they frequently invoke good causes, such as the need to maintain investment or employment, that are guaranteed to get a sympathetic hearing from politicians. Initially well-intentioned measures turn into end-runs around the fiscal system, as politicians struggle to satisfy all constituencies together with insufficient funds. One famous example, now shut down, was the so-called "30–70 reserve rule," which allowed enterprises to retain 30% of their profits as "wage reserves," which could not be touched by the tax collector, so as to pay off back wages to workers. In 1995 this one loophole accounted for two-thirds of the back taxes of Russian enterprises. There is no lack of similar good causes.

To target the largest enterprises, the government has attempted to create new tools. In October 1996 former prime minister Chernomyrdin established a "Temporary Extraordinary Commission" (VChK) to go after the largest tax debtors. On paper the VChK's powers were formidable. If a delinquent enterprise could not produce an acceptable schedule for paying off its back taxes and fines – or did not stick to the schedule agreed upon – then the government could force the enterprise into bankruptcy.

[60] European Bank for Reconstruction and Development, *Transition Report 1997* (London: EBRD, 1997), p. 121.

The VChK soon found it had stirred up a hornet's nest. Provincial officials leapt to the defense of "their" enterprises. Courts either failed to act on the cases brought by the federal bankruptcy authorities, or dragged their heels.[61] After its first several months of operation, the VChK found that the tax arrears of the 29 initial enterprises it had targeted had actually grown, and of the hundreds of bankruptcy actions taken by the Federal Bankruptcy Agency, fewer than a fifth were actually being implemented.[62]

Accordingly, the government changed tack. Bankruptcy was too blunt an instrument, as VChK officials conceded, because the government could not simultaneously institute bankruptcy proceedings against 90% of the enterprises in the country.[63] Instead, the VChK devised a complicated arrangement under which the tax debts of the delinquent enterprises would be restructured as bonds. If an enterprise defaulted on these, a controlling stake in its shares would be taken over the by the government, to be auctioned off to the highest bidder. But one year after the plan was announced, only three large enterprises were restructuring their tax debts, and the government's attempts to seize the assets of two oil refineries only ignited controversy and opposition.[64]

Even when large enterprises pay, they do so mostly in various forms of "quasi-money." According to federal officials, of 100 rubles paid to the treasury by large enterprises, only 6.5 per cent is in real money. Most of the rest is paid in so-called "offsets" (*zachety*) – an arrangement under which the enterprise can deduct from its taxes amounts owed to it by government bodies such as the military.[65] The federal treasury is then left holding the bag when the enterprises claim the resulting receivables as tax credits.[66]

The use of such offsets has itself become a major loophole in the budgetary process, enabling state bodies of all sorts (particularly local public agencies, known as *biudzhetniki*) to evade budgetary restrictions by pur-

---

[61] The commercial courts (*arbitrazhnye sudy*) have not been entirely inactive on the bankruptcy front. The journal of the Supreme Arbitration Court, *Vestnik Vysshego Arbitrazhnogo Suda Rossiiskoi Federatsii*, publishes a list of of all bankruptcy decisions issued by the local commercial courts. In 1997 these totaled over 1,200. But from inspection of the list it is apparent that the overwhelming majority of the cases involve very small local firms.

[62] For the beginnings of the VChK campaign, see *Russian Economic Trends*, vol. 5, no. 3 (1996), pp. 108–110; the subsequent phase of disillusionment is analyzed in *same*, No. 2 (1997), pp. 105–111.   [63] Ibid.

[64] *Segodnia* and *Russkii telegraf*, both December 9 1997, by Internet.

[65] Interview with Petr Karpov on the Russian television news program *Vesti*, December 29 1997, by Internet.

[66] Interview with former finance minister Aleksandr Livshits, "Ia khochu, chtoby reformy v Rossii skoree zakonchilis'," *Izvestiia*, August 28 1997, by Internet.

chasing goods and services on credit. In effect, the combination of tax deferrals and offsets has become a new form of "soft budget constraint," which allows nominally privatized enterprise managers to continue postponing the restructuring of their businesses.[67] In the fall of 1997, hoping against hope to increase the share of "live money" in tax collections, President Yeltsin banned all *zachety*, effective January 1998.[68] But the ban was soon countermanded by the Duma and *zachety* are still thriving.[69]

A similar problem arises when the government attempts to seize the assets of tax delinquents. The Tax Police, trying to sell off seized assets to convert at least some of their value into cash, has landed in the auction business. To help them in this unfamiliar territory, the Tax Police have enlisted "commercial organizations" to sell off seized assets, an obvious potential source of corruption.[70]

Yet the government did score one major victory in its battle against large tax delinquents. In the spring of 1997 the Russian gas giant, Gazprom – far and away the country's richest company and the source of over one-quarter of all federal revenues – agreed under pressure to pay $2.5 billion in back taxes. Gazprom had argued that it should not be required to pay taxes on gas sales that it had not yet been paid for itself, but when the government threatened to break up the company, it paid up by borrowing money from abroad. Yet after the August 1998 crash, when Gazprom could no longer raise the cash to pay its taxes in "live money," the government was forced to accept zachety from Gazprom as it does from everyone else.

On balance, then, the government's efforts to target the large enterprises have had little success. If the government cannot net even the biggest fish, then what chance does it have against the smaller fry who slip through the net unnoticed?

None at all, says a growing chorus of critics – until the tax system is reformed. Hence the momentum behind the effort to scrap the old system and replace it with a comprehensive Tax Code.

Reforming the system: the Tax Code

After more than five years of work, Russian tax experts have written a comprehensive Tax Code that addresses the tax system's worst problems.

[67] See the analysis of offsets and their effects in Special Report, Liam Halligan, Pavel Teplukhin, and Dirk Willer, "Subsidization of the Russian Economy," *Russian Economic Trends*, vol. 5, no. 1 (1996), pp. 109–128; and *Ibid*, No. 3 (1997), pp. 110–111.
[68] *Izvestiia*, November 15 1997, by Internet.
[69] Andrei Galiev, Tat'iana Lysova, "Ego velichestvo Zachet," *Ekspert*, No. 3 (January 25 1999), p. 34.
[70] *Izvestiia*, September 26 1997; *Ekho Moskvy*, November 20 1997, both by Internet.

Part I, which revises the broad rules of the tax system, is now in effect. But Parts II and III, which supply much of the essential detail, have been postponed.

Any tax reform plan must address three dilemmas:

1. *How to reform when the wolf is at the door?* Any radical overhaul of the tax system is likely to be time-consuming and disruptive. While it is being implemented tax revenues are likely to fall. Yet this is the one thing the Russian government cannot afford, because the entire policy of macreconomic stabilization depends on keeping deficits under control.

2. *How to balance between taxpayers' rights and coercion?* A "civilized" tax administration depends on voluntary compliance in judicious combination with punishment and force. In the long run, enforcement through police power alone is self-defeating, since society responds by going underground. Yet in Russia in the short run there is no alternative to force, since the means to elicit normal compliance do not yet exist.

3. *How to share tax power with the regions without losing control?* Over the last decade power has leaked massively from the center to the regions, and tax power along with it. If the federal government fights to regain control of revenues, it risks tax revolt by the regions. But if it acquiesces in overly generous revenue-sharing, it has no money left for national programs.

Critics charge that the government and the parliament, by failing to enact the entire Tax Code and adopting a series of stop-gap tax measures instead, have opted for short-term expediency. Moreover, they believe, the version of Part One that is now law is excessively favorable to taxpayers and will hamper tax collection. Finally, the key issues in center-region allocation have been left unresolved. In short, at this writing (spring 1999) tax reform is still at an early stage.

The Duma's actions sum up the central problem of the Russian tax system: the citizens – and their representatives – resist lowering the government's obligations, yet refuse to give it the tools it needs to pay for them. This, it may be argued, is the way politicians behave everywhere; but the Duma's deputies enjoy the special luxury of not having to account for their behavior to their voters. The Duma may have the power of the purse in theory; but in practice the deputies bet that if the government cuts spending or accumulates mountains of debt – or if the president violates the constitution and raises taxes by decree – the voters will blame the executive branch and not the legislature. Given this atmosphere, the future of tax reform is uncertain.

Conclusion: taxes and state power

"What kind of state and society is our 'free economy' leading us to?" mused Boris Yeltsin early in 1996. "The market by itself is no panacea.... We must increase the role of the state."[71] Well before the crash of August 1998, both reformers and their opponents agreed that the state was the central problem. For the market reformers, that meant strengthening the state's role as referee over a private economy. For conservatives, who returned to power in the central government after the August crash, strengthening the state meant at least a partial return to state ownership and direct investment.[72] But regardless of how the words were interpreted, "rebuilding the state" became the central slogan of the Russian government in the second half of the 90s.

But the goal of both market reformers and conservatives sounds strangely hollow when confronted with reality. To the casual eye the Russian state still seems ever-present. The massive official buildings left over from the Soviet era, the policemen on every street corner and roadside, the long lines to get official papers – it all seems very familiar from the Soviet past. When faced with a problem, businessmen and *babushki*, out of old habit, still look to the government for a solution, or blame it for not providing one. Government officials bustle about with dossiers filled with vast programs, and they still talk as though the state were as powerful as in Soviet times. But in reality the Russian government resembles a ruined aristocrat trying to hang on to the family estate and keep up appearances. Much of the outward appearance is a shell.

The shrinking of the state is not in itself a bad thing. Indeed, it is a necessary thing. A market economy needs a smaller state than the all-encompassing Soviet giant that owned every factory and planned every commodity of consequence. Theorists of market transition praise the "depoliticization" of the economy that goes with privatization, price liberalization, and decontrol of trade,[73] and some of the shrinkage has indeed been due to the reformers' deliberate policies. But since about 1993 most of the shriveling of the state has been involuntary, driven by the decline in

---

[71] Boris Yeltsin, "Priglashenie k budnichnoi rabote v gosudarstve," *Rossiiskie vesti*, September 25 1997.

[72] The most systematic exposition of these views is the memorandum addressed by members of the Economics Section of the Russian Academy of Sciences to the newly-confirmed Primakov government in September 1998, published in the press under the title, "Doklad Abalkina," *Kommersant-Daily*, September 15 1998.

[73] Andrei Shleifer, "Government in Transition," (Cambridge, Mass.: Harvard Institute of Economic Research Discussion Paper Series, Discussion Paper Number 1783, October 1996)

revenues. It is, in effect, shrinkage by leakage. The retreat is forced and unplanned. There has been no systematic effort to rethink and reshape state structures and functions – or ambitions.

The current shrinkage by attrition, as the state withdraws – trench by trench, so to say – is a highly damaging process.

1. *It breeds constant conflict:* Tax collectors and citizens are forced into a perpetual war to conceal and discover revenues. The conflictual relationship between state and society generates mistrust and hostility instead of the compliance and cooperation upon which most fiscal systems in mature market economies ultimately rest.

2. *It generates deception and pretense:* The government consents to excessive spending targets to gain passage of the budget through the parliament, and then resorts to massive "sequestering"of legally appropriated funds to keep deficits within bounds. Legislators vote for politically popular spending measures, without having to bear the responsibility for funding them, while the executive branch is forced to violate the law to limit the damage. The result is an elaborate dance of deception that fools no one, least of all the citizens.

3. *It forces all players into short-range firefighting:* The daily battle to raise revenues, cover essential spending programs, and finance the deficit absorbs the energies of Russian officials and prevents them from focusing on the longer-range tasks of legal and regulatory reform, military reform, institition-building, and the like.

It is no wonder that the government's victory over inflation was short-lived. Macroeconomic stabilization in 1995–97 was achieved mainly through brute-force sequestering by the Ministry of Finance of legally appropriated government expenditures, including wages and pensions. This was not a sustainable policy, because it depended on the willingness of a handful of individuals to keep enforcing a politically unpopular policy. They preferred to borrow instead, and the result was disaster.

A longer-term consequence of Russia's fiscal failure is economic and social distortion. Much of Russian state spending these days consists of what amounts to social welfare transfers – to the unreformed military and the farm sector, to the state bureaucracy, to a handful of depressed industries, but above all to the middle class, in the form of underpriced heat and light, housing subsidies, and municipal services. The loser is investment – both the foregone investment of corporations that must pay excessive taxes and cover local welfare programs, and the social investment that the state fails to make in education, scientific research, justice, and health.

The Russian tax crisis is in first instance a revolt against a bad tax system. Comprehensive tax reform – starting with the adoption of a Tax

Code – is the beginning of the right answer. But once an improved tax system is in place, then starts the much harder part – persuading the Russian people to pay their taxes. That is clearly not going to happen tomorrow, yet without a more reasonable tax system the process will not even begin.

"Russian capitalism will be to capitalism as Russian socialism was to socialism. Russia will do to markets and democracy what it did to Marxism, Christianity, and the Enlightenment.   Edward L. Keenan, Harvard historian

10   Conclusion: halfway to the market – Russia on the eve of the twenty-first century

Houston, Winter 1999:
Mikhail Khodorkovskii had shaved off his trademark black moustache. Still only thirty-six, he suddenly looked more like the elder statesman of business than the young entrepreneur who founded "Menatep" only a decade ago.

"Where will the next wave of entrepreneurs come from?" I asked him. "Most of my generation of entrepreneurs have now left Russia, "he replied," some after their first ten million, some after their first hundred million. Their entrepreneurial skills were lost to the country, and they have not been replaced. Then we had a 'dark decade' in which young people did not complete their education, but went into private business instead, to make money fast. Consequently, they never got the right training, and when everything collapsed last August, they were unprepared and helpless."

"But now there's a new crop of kids," Khodorkovsky went on, "who have been educated in the West and are coming back to Russia. They have business training, but they're still lacking the toughening experience (*zakalka*) of actually working in Russia, plus the connections and networks. It will be another five years before they really get going. When they do they will be better than we were."[1]

Yuzhno-Sakhalinsk, July 1998:
At the far eastern end of Russia, on the former penal colony of Sakhalin Island, Western oil companies are working with the local government to turn this remote province into a showcase for foreign investment. Galina Pavlova, an energetic former biologist, directs a special department for offshore oil and gas development that reports straight to a supportive governor who is the island's most enthusiastic salesman. Sakhalin is racing ahead while other provinces stand still, looking at Sakhalin, as the Russian phrase goes, "with square eyes." "They're all fighting among themselves," says Pavlova. "Here we're all on the same team."

---

[1] Author's interview, February, 1999.

The island is desperately poor and losing population. Outside Pavlova's office, on the main square where Karl Marx Street meets Communist Avenue, Lenin still points the way, just as he does in most other provincial capitals. But there are signs of change everywhere. As people here say, "there is diamond dust in the air."

In July 1998, as the Russian government struggled day by day to head off financial collapse, international financial institutions assembled an emergency $22.6 billion external-assistance package, including $11.2 billion in new loans from the International Monetary Fund, to help the Russian reformers support the ruble and stay solvent. All to no avail. In the worldwide post-mortem that followed the August crash, thoughtful people debated whether the West should have done more – or less. Stanley Fischer, a genial and able man who as deputy general manager of the IMF managed Russian policy during those crucial months, summed up the West's rationale: "Russia is special. It was a good bet. It might have worked."[2]

Yet in broader perspective it is clear that some sort of reckoning was inevitable. If the crash of August 1998 had not occurred when it did or in precisely the same form, something like it was bound to come. The government's bankruptcy was ultimately a reflection of deep flaws in the entire architecture of post-Soviet Russia. As the chapters of this book have argued, the flaws boil down to three:

- The new institutions of the private sector were geared above all to extracting a quick return from export revenues and short-term foreign lending, and they proved vulnerable when the world economy turned down in mid-1997.
- The spread of market institutions was uneven and incomplete, and in the space of a decade the market penetrated only part-way into the Russian economy and the fabric of society, while crime and corruption penetrated far more deeply.
- Russians at all levels were ambivalent about the changes surrounding them; and the resulting lack of strong popular support for market reforms bred constant political conflict that paralyzed the adaptation of the state to the requirements of a market economy.

It could hardly have been otherwise. The main lesson of the Russian Nineties is that building a market society in a country from which the market, and money, and private property-and indeed the very foundations of civil society-had been systematically eradicated over the course of seven decades, has proved to be a far larger undertaking than optimistic theories of transition allowed for. Moreover, market transition was never

---

[2] Address to the U.S.–Russia Business Council, Washington, D.C., December 11, 1998.

the single-minded goal of more than a handful of Russians. For the over-whelming majority, the aim was to get rich, to gain power, or simply to survive.

What has changed as a result of the crash of 1998? On the one hand, very little. World commodities prices have already largely recovered, and Russian export revenues are heading back to the high levels of the mid-1990s. Money from exports will flow into the service economy, as it did before, reviving the fortunes of the rich and of the middle class. By that time a new president will be in place. A new political leadership will return, one way or another, to the unfinished business of the Nineties, including a renegotiation of Russia's tattered relations with international lenders. Russia's prospects – and Russia's problems – will return to where they were in 1997–98.

Yet in a deeper sense, the crash of 1998 changed everything. It was the end of an illusion, the bursting of a bubble. It exposed how little had actu-ally been built, and how fragile the new economy really was. It showed the fragility of the emerging middle class and it underscored the powerful inertia of the virtual economy. It revealed that the macroeconomic stabil-ization of 1995–98 had no basis, apart from the massive "sequestering" of wages and pensions. Indeed, the government's massive expropriation of its creditors in 1998 was no different in essence from the government's repeated expropriations of its weaker citizens throughout the 1990s. The crash of 1998 made everything clear.

The erasing of the illusory gains of the Nineties signified a loss of pre-cious time and capital. Russia started the decade with significant assets: the developed oil and gas fields and mineral deposits inherited from the Soviet Union, the goodwill of its own population and the international community, and the hopeful entrepreneurial energy of its youngest and most talented citizens. All of these have now been depleted, and they will not be renewed.

August 1998 also produced a major political realignment. With the col-lapse of the major banks the role of the oligarchs as political kingmakers was abruptly weakened. The political power of all but the largest com-modity exporters has shrunk, and the city of Moscow has likewise lost much of its tax base and its clout. In their place reigns an uneasy coalition of provincial governors and city mayors, parliamentary opposition, the "power elites" of the police and the intelligence services, and the rem-nants of the Soviet planning and military-industrial bureaucracy. These are likely to be the dominant groups after the coming leadership succes-sion as well.

More significantly, along with the balance of political power, the balance of political rhetoric has shifted against market reform and the

West. Words like "market" and "privatization" have become negatives; "state control" is the new slogan of the day. The last radical reformers have either left the government or have begun to speak the new language. In the upcoming political succession, all of the candidates speak of nothing but strengthening the state. With the August crash it was as though the marquee above the political theater abruptly changed. "Transition" – last year's flop-is gone. When it may be revived is anyone's guess.

Yet the forces of change that were loosed in the mid-1980s are still at work, and they have already transformed the face of Russia. The wealth of the country has passed largely into private hands. Money, however distorted its forms, has returned to a central role in the economy. Many of the key institutions of a market economy now exist. A new body of laws is being written and the courts are beginning to apply them. Hundreds of thousands of new private businesses, big and small, operate in an environment governed by market forces. The borders are largely open to the flow of people and goods. The younger half of the Russian population has crossed the emotional divide marking the end of socialism.

On this reading, the new political leadership of the country – whatever form it finally takes after the coming succession – will have no choice but to come to terms with the evolving reality of Russia. In this last chapter we explore what this means. What strengths and weaknesses does Russia bring to the opening of the new century? What forces for change and what constraints will shape it?

Russia's "barbell" economy

After the Soviet collapse the Russian economy traded one imbalance for another. Material production and services changed places. In 1990, the Russian economy produced roughly one-third services and two-thirds material products (that is, manufactured goods, food, and raw materials); by the late 1990s these proportions were nearly reversed.[3] With much of its manufacturing capacity idled and its GDP reduced by more than 40%,[4] Russia became a "barbell" economy, producing raw materials at one end, and trade and services at the other.

Russia has been saved by its exports. Commodities producers with

---

[3] In 1996 the official GDP consisted of 48.3% services and 42.8% goods, the remainder being made up largely of taxes. Since that time, the share of services has undoubtedly grown further, especially in the shadow economy, which is understated in Goskomstat statistics.

[4] According to Goskomstat, Russian GDP declined by 43% between 1989 and 1996. As discussed elsewhere, Goskomstat's revised methodology includes some of the shadow economy but not all. (*Russian Economic Trends*, January 1998, by Internet)

something to export have been hurt the least and have been the first to turn around, both in the early 1990s and after 1998. The decline of internal oil consumption enabled Russia to maintain its oil exports to the west, despite a drop of nearly 50% in oil production. The gas industry became the other main prop of the economy, providing more than half of Russia's energy and export revenues nearly equal to those of oil.[5] Russia also exported "embodied energy," in the form of chemicals, fertilizers, and ferrous and non-ferrous metals. If it had not been for its energy abundance and its exportable resources, the Russian economy today might look more like that of Ukraine or Belarus. Even now, despite lower world prices, the commodity export sector remains Russia's mainstay

But Russia's manufacturing, light industry, food processing, and agriculture have been devastated by a combination of vanishing state orders, depressed per-capita incomes, foreign competition, and the break-up of the Soviet economic space. Significantly, the decline of this sector began in the mid-1980s (see table 10.1). Part of this collapse was to be expected, especially that of defense procurement, which has been on the order of 80%, but the size and breadth of the drop are a source of economic and political vulnerability for the future. These sectors are the core of the "virtual economy," which though much reduced remains politically and emotionally powerful.

The barbell economy is also unbalanced in the way profits from export revenues flow through it. A substantial part leaves Russia as capital flight (or to be more precise, it is export revenue that never re-enters the country). Much of the rest, prior to 1998, supported the Moscow-based financial-industrial empires. Banking profits fueled the boom in construction and services (mainly in Moscow) but above all paid for a vast influx of imported consumer goods.

The export-producing regions themselves received relatively little of the export revenue, although even that modest share touched off local booms in the most favored regional cities, such as those of the oil-rich Khanty-Mansiisk region and the Volga and Urals, particularly Nizhnii Novgorod, Samara, Cheliabinsk, Tol'iatti, and Perm'.[6] Their new wealth was unevenly spread, even within a single region or city. In the Urals city of Cheliabinsk, for example, export-led fertilizer plants boomed while the tractor plants stood idle. In the statistics, the region looked as though it was turning around. But on the ground, a few were doing well from the export boom while the rest were passed by.

---

[5] The gas industry was Leonid Brezhnev's posthumous gift to Russian capitalism. Beginning in the mid-1970s the gas industry became one of the top investment priorities of the Soviet government, and one of its last success stories. It is difficult to imagine how Russia would have survived the Nineties without a vigorous gas industry.

[6] "A Statistical Look at Russia's Regions," *Russian Economic Trends*, No. 2 (1997), p.128.

Table 10.1 *The collapse of Russian manufacturing, 1985–1996*

	1985	1990	1996
Employment in manufacturing (millions)	8.3	7.5	4.2
Machine tools (thousands)	97.9	74.2	12.1
Tractors (thousands)	261	214	14.0
Combines (thousands)	112	65.7	2.5
Trucks (thousands)	688	665	134
Trolleys (units)	2416	2305	127
Metal-stamping machines (thousands)	37.1	27.3	1.2

Source: Goskomstat RF, *Rossiiskii statisticheskii ezhegodnik 1997*, by Internet

Commodities exports are still the mainstay of the Russian economy today. The ruble lost three-quarters of its real value in a matter of months after August 1998, imports plummeted, and Russia's balance of payments, which had deteriorated badly in 1997–98, returned to a healthy surplus. Thus, such limited solvency as the Russian economy retains at the end of the 1990s is once again due mainly to the export sector.

Yet the cushion that Russia still enjoys today will not last. Its steel mills, oil and gas wells, aluminum smelters, nickel mines, and gold and diamond fields are running down. The export inheritance – a free gift, as it were, from the Soviet Union – will wind down steadily if the new owners continue to squander it. To renew it, they must invest. But so far, investment is not happening.

The Russian investment crisis

As fast as the Russian economy has declined, investment has dropped even faster. Overall, gross fixed investment declined from 45% of GDP in 1989 to 21% in 1996.[7] Since GDP itself declined by over 40% during the same period, capital spending in absolute terms dropped by over three-quarters.[8]

---

[7] These numbers are based on a reconstruction of GDP and investment numbers in 1995 prices. The basis for this analysis is discussed in Andrei V. Poletaev, "Investment in National Product Accounts," *Russian Economic Trends*, no. 3 (1997), pp. 122–130.

[8] Calculations of GDP decline vary widely, depending on conventions used. The estimate used here is GDP by expenditure in 1995 prices, given in Poletaev, op. cit. The general picture of a 75%-plus decline in gross investment is matched by Goskomstat numbers for "expenditures for new construction and equipment," which declined from an index of 326 in 1990 to 79 in 1997. (Source: *Russian Economic Trends*, No. 1 1997, pp. 108–109, updated from the *Russian Economic Trends* web site.)

That is extraordinary enough, but the real story is *net* fixed investment, i.e., what is left after allowance for the depreciation of the existing capital base. Net fixed investment has been negative since 1995; in other words, Russia's entire capital base has been shrinking. By 1997 net fixed investment was *minus* 10% of GDP,[9] and has continued to decline since then.

The drop in investment has been particularly severe in industry. In the hardest-hit sectors, such as agriculture, light industry, and manufacturing, gross investment has declined by over 80%. Military investment, particularly in procurement of conventional weapons, has practically vanished. But even sectors with large export revenues, such as the energy sector, have suffered investment declines of between one-half and two-thirds.[10]

The implications of these numbers are dramatic. Gross fixed investment has fallen well below the average for OECD countries, and far behind the rate of East Asia and other emerging markets[11] (at least, until the onset of the Asian economic crisis). At this rate, Russia could fall far behind the world's newly industrializing economies.

The source of the investment crisis is a combination of low domestic savings, limited foreign investment, and government deficits. What investment remains comes mainly from the retained earnings and depreciation deductions of private companies.

Low domestic savings There is considerable debate among economists over how much Russians are saving, but all agree that the share of Russian savings going into investment is very low. Most domestic savings are held in dollars, which are used by households as a liquid reserve (especially necessary in view of the general absence of checking or other convenient banking services). Most of this never ends up in banks, and is therefore unavailable for investment.[12]

High government deficits and borrowing Unable to balance their budgets, the central and regional governments have cut back practically all investment in industry and agriculture. As a result, investment from government sources has declined to only one-third of the total. Much of

---

[9] Poletaev, op. cit..

[10] See Philippe H. LeHouerou, *Investment Policy in Russia*, Studies of Economies in Transformation, No. 17 (Washington, D.C.: The World Bank, 1995)

[11] For tables on comparative investment levels, see LeHouerou, op. cit., p. 58. At the time of that report, Russian investment levels were still on a par with major OECD countries, but have slipped further since then.

[12] For reviews and discussions of the savings issue, see *Russian Economic Trends*, No. 1 (1997), pp. 84–89 and No. 3 (1997), pp. 67–70.

that goes into housing construction. Meanwhile, until 1998 the government borrowed from the Russian private capital market on a vast scale, at interest rates that crowded out practically all long-term private investment. Not only is the government hardly investing itself, but its punitive taxation and heavy borrowing prevented the private sector from doing so either.

Weak foreign investment During the same period, direct foreign investment has been insignificant, totalling under $20 billion (cumulative) through 1998.[13] On a per-capita basis, foreign investment in Russia lags far behind Eastern Europe, especially Hungary and Czechoslovakia. Russia is in direct competition for capital with emerging markets throughout the world (a point that Russians initially resisted but now increasingly acknowledge), but in that race Russia has so far been a loser.

Fortunately, there may be more investment taking place than the statistics suggest. Net fixed investment is biased downward because of very large depreciation allowances, which apply to all fixed capital on the Russian companies' books. Much of that capital consists of worn-out plant that will never be brought back into production and should be written off. For a variety of reasons (including significant tax advantages) Russian managers are reluctant to remove it from their books. Thus net investment appears smaller than it actually is. In addition, below a certain money amount investment need not be reported.

Clearly, many Russian companies are investing more than they say they are. One popular dodge is to contract "offshore": let's say a Russian company contracts for a building worth a million dollars. It pays the contractor half the value in Russia, and the other half offshore. The resulting building is recorded at half its true value, and thus investment is also understated by half. A good deal of the pre-1998 building boom in Moscow, in particular, was based on such offshore arrangements.

Still, these qualifications do not change the basic picture of an economy that is living largely on its inheritance. The oil industry is a key example. After seven years of continuous decline, Russian oil production stabilized in 1995–97. But the stabilization was entirely the result of better management of existing fields – essentially "old oil" – not of investment in new ones. Within a few more years Russian oil production will begin to decline again, unless new fields are developed on a large scale. This will require capital spending on the order of $10–11 billion a year, as opposed to the $3–4 billion the oil industry is spending today. The lower figure is

---

[13] PlanEcon, Inc., *Review and Outlook for the Former Soviet Republics* (Washington, D.C.: October 1998), p. 24.

being covered by the Russian companies' own retained earnings and depreciation allowances, but any significant increase in investment will require foreign resources.

Even more important than investment in physical capital is investment in people. But Russian spending on education, scientific research, and the like has also collapsed. Reported funding for research and development in 1996, for example, was 1.75% of GDP, less than one-third the levels typical of Soviet times.[14]

Since the August crash there has been much talk in Russia of the need for an "industrial policy," which would channel investment preferentially to the so-called "real economy," mainly to resurrect the Soviet-era manufacturing sector. But there is only one way such capital could be obtained – by taxing away the surplus of the commodities exporters, or even by renationalizing them outright. A high tax burden is tolerable so long as the government is merely capturing the rent from "Soviet commodities", the capital costs of which are long sunk. But the next generation of "post-Soviet" raw materials will not support such high taxes. The Soviet era skimmed the cream of the best and cheapest deposits, and the next generation will be higher in cost, as the law of diminishing returns sets in. In the future the commodities industries – oil, gas, metals, etc. – will yield fewer taxes than today, not more.

In short, "industrial policy," as imagined by today's Russian conservatives, is a dream. The reality is that Russia's economy will remain lopsidedly unbalanced toward exportable raw materials for the foreseeable future. But that prospect is not politically acceptable among the groups now dominant in Moscow. It is therefore likely that some sort of state-led industrial policy will be attempted in coming years. The result will be to take resources away from Russia's strongest sectors and reallocate them to the weaker ones, at the very time when investment in the next generation of commodities is urgently needed.

Potential for growth and wealth: toward a Russian economic miracle?

What do extreme sectoral imbalance and lack of investment imply for growth? In the near term, Russia can draw on reserves of underemployed labor and raw materials and underused plant and equipment. There is also room for productivity gains, as the emerging private sector learns to combine resources more efficiently and to adapt to the market. The basket of goods produced by the post-Soviet economy, as it moves away

[14] Goskomstat RF, *Rossiiskii statisticheskii ezhegodnik 1997*, by Internet.

from capital and defense goods for which there are no longer buyers, toward consumer goods and services for which there is large pent-up demand, automatically gains in value from the shift. There is enough capital, from domestic retained earnings and savings, to support a modest level of "maintenance" investment. So long as the country remains at peace, and there is reasonably orderly leadership, all the necessary elements are present for at least a modest near-term recovery.

It is over the longer term, past the next five to ten years, that serious questions arise. In an earlier book, *Russia 2010*, my co-author Daniel Yergin and I examined the possibility of an "economic miracle" in Russia, a scenario that we called *chudo* (from the Russian word for "miracle"). Our key argument was that two things are necessary for an economic miracle – secure property rights and stable money, meaning above all low inflation.[15]

Russia will have difficulty ensuring these. Property rights are weakened and distorted by the lack of a strong legal system (and the resulting weak enforcement of contracts); by organized crime and corruption; by the predatory and unpredictable tax system; and by the continuing battle for control of the most valuable properties. But the greatest source of inefficient property rights is the persistence of "soft budget constraints" in a variety of forms, especially tax and wage arrears, and the prevalence of barter and quasi-monies.

As for stable money, it is under threat from government spending, budget deficits, and state debt. The state faces an expensive welfare burden, yet for the foreseeable future it will have difficulty raising revenue to cover its expenditures, so long as Russians evade paying taxes. In the last few years the government has reined in spending by the brute-force mechanism of "sequestering," i.e., not disbursing legally appropriated funds. But in the long run, this is not politically sustainable. In a weak political system deficit spending is a constant temptation. The consequence is a chronic tendency toward large government debt and a heavy burden of debt service.

Russia, the Asian model, and the Asian crisis

Russian politicians frequently invoke the "Asian model" as an example for Russia. But on examination the experience of the Asian Rim economies is practically irrelevant for Russia.

Throughout the Asian Pacific Rim private savings rates are high, labor costs low, and governments small and fiscally austere. Despite the prevalence of corruption and cronyism, many of the Asian states have

[15] Daniel Yergin and Thane Gustafson, *Russia 2010 And What it Means for the World* (New York: Vintage Books, 1994), Chapter 12.

competent bureaucracies and well-trained planners. The broad formula
for Asian success has been export-led growth, backed by state cooperation with large private-sector manufacturing conglomerates to promote
investment and protect domestic markets. But Asian exports have not
been limited to raw materials; indeed, the story of the Asian economic
miracle has been one of steady movement toward higher-value products,
embodying more and more advanced technology. Much of this movement has been coordinated by the state and the private sector working in
effective partnership. Though the "Asian model" has been tarnished
recently by the Asian economic crisis, there is no reason why the basic
formula will not continue to work in the future.

Russia has the negative elements of this Asian formula, but not the positive ones. The large Russian conglomerates have so far been more interested in empire-building or exporting their capital offshore than in
investing to renew their assets, restructuring their operations, or developing new products. Russia's economy is led by exports, but does not have an
"export-led strategy" in the sense of an active forward-looking cooperation between state and industry. Russian efforts to use state power to build
world-class high technology were a failure even in Soviet times, with the
partial exception of military industry. The bureaucracy, apart from a
handful of skilled technocrats at the top, lacks modern skills and is poorly
acquainted with world trends and practices. The relationship between the
state and the private sector is on the whole unpredictable and antagonistic.

With an economy so unbalanced in favor of commodities production,
and with so little new investment taking place, and with a state so weak
and unskilled, how will Russia fare in the coming century?

Can Russia compete in the twenty-first century?

The opening decades of the next century will see low commodities prices
and intense competition among commodities producers. New technologies, particularly information technology, are revolutionizing every phase
of natural-resource production, causing costs to drop steadily around the
world. In the resulting buyers' market, consuming countries will be in a
strong position to impose taxes (such as environmental "carbon taxes")
that will take away much of the commodities' value to producers. A high-
cost resource producer such as Russia, located far from markets and
saddled with an obsolete industrial base, will be positioned far down the
competitive ladder.

In contrast, the main new sources of wealth in the twenty-first century
are likely to be based on services and consumer products, also powerfully
driven by technology. The list of likely leading sectors – information and

computers, global finance, media and entertainment, tourism and transportation, biomedicine and health delivery, luxury and leisure goods, environment and food – is a sobering one for Russia, because in none of them is Russia a leader or even a significant player. Russia's shrinking population of under 150 million is not large enough to be an adequate domestic market for world-class service industries. Its skills, biased toward heavy engineering and the industrial shopfloor, are those of the early twentieth century, not those of the twenty-first. Despite some notable exceptions, such as cellular telephony, Russia has few opportunities to leapfrog over its Soviet legacy into a leading position in the coming world.

Even in military technology, the pride of the Soviet central planners and the centerpiece of the Soviet industrial and technological system, Russia is likely to trail. The next century's weapons will be based on new technologies that Russia is not now developing. A decade of depression and turmoil has dispersed much of the Russian scientific base, and it is not being renewed. In the 1920s and 30s, when Russia faced a similar crisis, Stalin's answer was to concentrate the country's resources and talent on military technology and industry. Would Russia be willing to pay the same price again – and even if it did, could it succeed?

Beyond these obstacles, the most powerful long-term brake on Russia's progress is the half-way state of its economy, caught as it is in a no man's land between socialism and the free market. There are three main problems:

Incomplete market institutions: In today's market economies, more than half of the value of goods and services comes from specialists who manage time, risk, and distance, such as insurance companies, pension funds, commodities markets, credit-rating agencies, law firms, telecommunications and software services, financial information companies, and knowledge-based industries of all kinds. Such "transaction services" made up only a small part of the Soviet economy, which was dominated by production,[16] but they are the essential support for a developed market economy. The Russian response to the sudden need for such services was impressive, yet distorted by the corrupt environment of the Nineties. Much remains to be done, and much to be redone.

Barriers to the free movement of resources: in a market economy the major

---

[16] Douglass C. North, Institutions, Institutional Change, and Economic Performance (Cambridge: Cambridge University Press, 1981). It is an interesting exercise to analyze the Soviet economy from the perspective of production costs vs. transaction costs. Because of its focus on production, the command economy kept transaction costs low, yet by the 1970s and 80s this underdevelopment had become a brake on the evolution of the command economy.

"factors of production" – commodities, land and real estate, labor, capital, and knowledge – must be able to change hands and move freely to their most productive uses within the national market. That is far from the case in Russia today. Labor is one example. Lack of developed housing and real estate markets, residence restrictions, lack of skills and information-all these prevent Russian workers from finding and filling new jobs wherever they arise. Certain commodities, such as land, can hardly be traded at all. Goods cannot be shipped cheaply or reliably, because of the universal presence of criminals. Money cannot show its face, for the same reason, plus the fear of the taxman. Until factors of production can flow normally, the Russian economy can never be efficient.

Restricted market entry and exit: In Russia founders of new businesses face a host of obstacles, ranging from complex licensing requirements to lack of small-business credit. At the province level, the rules favor well-connected locals and outsiders are frequently prevented from operating. Many businesses simply never get off the ground-not because of the verdict of the market but because of crime and political corruption. But "market exit" is equally sticky: a large and well-connected company is practically impossible to shut down. Bankruptcy laws are still weak, and companies that have been declared insolvent continue to operate.

A national marketplace simply does not yet exist yet in Russia. As a telling illustration, could a business such as Amazon.com, the Internet bookstore, even get off the ground in Russia? There is no lack of enthusiastic young businessmen who might try it, and no shortage of readers. But there are too few computers and servers and usable phone lines; the mails would not deliver the books reliably; and there are only weakly developed, and largely local, credit-card networks to pay for them. The entire Internet phenomenon, which is revolutionizing the basis for business and trade in the West, is at best conceivable in Moscow, impossible in the rest of the country.

The stark conclusion is this: on its present course Russia will not produce an "economic miracle," whether of the German–Japanese 1950s vintage or that of the East Asian 1980s. The Russian economy will very likely grow over the next five to ten years; it may even grow at initially impressive rates, depending on the health of the world economy. But unless the fundamental constraints are relieved, Russia's growth will level off after that.

That is why continued economic liberalization and institutional reform are so crucial for the future of Russia. But will there be a "second generation" of market reforms? Not immediately, that is clear. The political appeal of market reform is exhausted for now. Russia's next leader may attempt to reinforce the power of the state and its control over the economy, through the application of "industrial policy" and possibly even partial renationalization. At the same time, the private sector is presently on the defensive, too poor and too demoralized to forge ahead on its own. In the next few years the conservatives may have their turn.

Continuing forces for change

But this book's central argument is that the forces of change loosed since the mid-1980s have not yet run their course. Many of these forces are positive and reinforce the constituency for further market reform in the longer run.

Demographic, cultural, and social forces: As Russia enters the new century, a new post-Soviet generation is rising to leading positions, not just in Moscow but throughout the country. Many of its members, those in their early thirties today, have lived their entire professional lives in the world of Gorbachev's perestroika and the post-Soviet market economy. For this generation, the end of the Soviet era was not a shock but a liberation. They are aware of the outside world, of international practices and trends, and they understand opportunity and competition. Increasingly, they are not engineers but lawyers, accountants, and economists, and they have the marketing and financial skills needed for business. They have no illusions about Russia's present weaknesses and they do not hesitate to look to the outside world for models.

A growing share of the Russian population, compared to the early days of the market reforms, has a concrete understanding of what it means, for better and for worse, to live in a market economy. Unlike the early days, the Russian people increasingly judge market reforms on the basis of their real economic interests, not vague and abstract impressions. At the moment, their judgment is largely negative, and there is nostalgia for the past. But as it becomes increasingly apparent that the state and the remnants of the Soviet economy are too weak to provide jobs and welfare at more than poverty levels, Russians will continue their migration to the private sector.

As voters, the post-Soviet generation have broadly supported the government's reforms. The main problem is that many younger Russians do not vote at all. Paradoxically, this is not because they reject the changes that have taken place in their lifetimes, but because they take them for granted. However, if Russia repeats the experience of other countries, younger Russians will vote in larger numbers as they grow older and found families. Meanwhile, at the other end of the spectrum, the generation of pensioners who are the main constituency of the neo-communist parties is gradually moving off the stage. In short, demographic change is gradually consolidating the potential support for the changes that have taken place, by bringing forward a generation of people who have never experienced anything else.

Economic forces: The long-term economic forces for change are even more important. Opportunities for making money through asset-stripping and speculation have already declined, drying up the concentrated flow of rents generated by the immediate post-Soviet transition, and forcing managers to begin looking for efficiency gains instead. If the value of the ruble stays low, imports will be contained and domestic consumers will become the market of choice for a growing range of Russian producers, enabling the economy to diversify. As the economy turns around, it will generate demand for better services in banking, insurance, accounting, legal services, and advertising, causing these sectors, which handle the "transaction costs" of a market economy, to grow and mature.

So far most privatized enterprises have not restructured or invested on any large scale, but as the domestic market grows the competitive pressures to do so will increase.[17] Enterprises are already being forced to think about cutting costs, marketing their products and developing new ones. There will be growing pressure to extend privatization to areas of the economy where it has been held back until now, especially land ownership and the so-called natural monopolies.

The private sector is already a source of demand for better public services. An increasing number of Russian businessmen want better protection of property rights, sound money, tax reform, and the removal of obstacles to new enterprise. When they do not get them, they turn to private providers, for education, health care, retirement and pensions – and also for private protection, recovery of loans, and enforcement of contracts. In the near term, this weakens the public sector, but in the long run it will create pressure on the state to improve its services.

These are powerful forces, yet they will act only if the political system remains open and the private sector is not suppressed by massive coercion. Will Russians continue to support liberal reform? Or will they lose patience with an experiment that is proving so difficult, and yield to the easy temptation to "restore order"? Is there support for wholesale reaction?

---

[17] See the series of articles on restructuring published under the title, "Improvizatsiia s petlei na shee," *Ekspert*, No. 4 (1998). pp. 26–39.

Economic performance and political acceptance

Public opinion polls consistently report that most Russians feel worse off than in 1991 and that they have little faith that the economy will improve. As the 1990s draw to a close, there is little sign of any change in this pattern. In answer to the question, "How would you evaluate the economic situation of Russia?" negative answers overwhelm positive answers, as they consistently have since the survey first began in 1993. Except that instead of margins of 5 to 1, since the August crash the margin for the negatives has swelled to 8 to 1.[18]

With reviews like that, why have Russians not swept away both the market and the reformers? Strangely, Russians' sour answers to pollsters do not match their behavior in the voting booth. Russian voters have gone to the polls four times since 1993, and each time the opposition has failed to gained a majority of the votes. Why?

A careful analysis of the 1995 parliamentary election and the 1996 presidential poll suggests some answers.[19] Russians do not only vote with their pocketbooks. Despite the recent upheavals in Russian society, Russians' attitudes and votes have been shaped more by social characteristics such as age, education, place of residence, or prior membership in the Communist Party. Despite their deep concern about the economy and their own fortunes within it, voters have tended to put politics ahead of economics.

This finding implies that if the Russian economy does not perform brilliantly in coming years, it is not a foregone conclusion that the voters will reject it for pure "pocketbook" reasons. Russian politicians have instinctively perceived this. Boris Yeltsin's strategy in the 1996 presidential election virtually ignored economic issues, and aimed at turning the election into a referendum on the threat of a return to communism. Yeltsin "waved the bloody shirt" – and it worked.[20]

But waving the bloody shirt will not work again. By the next round of elections – parliamentary elections in 1999 and presidential elections in 2000 – the government and the reformers will finally have to run on their record. Russians will be asked to vote, not on how much they themselves are making, but on how much the "oligarchs" made, and how. If the dominant

---

[18] Nationwide survey by the All-Russian Center for the Study of Public Opinion (VTsIOM), 12–28 January 1999, by Internet. In July 1998 negative answers outweighed positives by 79% to 15%. In September 1998 the margin was 91% to 5%. By January 1999 it had settled back somewhat to 85% to 10%.

[19] Timothy J. Colton, "Economics and Voting in Russia," *Post-Soviet Affairs*, vol. 12 (No. 4), pp. 289–317.

[20] Timothy J. Colton, *Transitional Citizenship: Voting in Post-Soviet Russia* (Cambridge, Mass.: Harvard University Press, forthcoming)

issues are not only economic decline and poverty, but also inequality, crime, and corruption, then the opposition stands a good chance of winning.

What then? Let us try to visualize the scenario that might follow. A right-wing or a left-wing president would almost certainly try to raise the level of state spending for a variety of causes, such as industrial investment, social spending, and defense. He would attempt to overturn the privatization of key properties. He would increase the level of coercion to combat tax evasion, and launch an aggressive anti-corruption campaign.

The initial economic impact of such measures would be severe. Private businessmen would retreat further into the shadows and shelter even more capital abroad. Tax receipts, instead of increasing, would drop. The few remaining foreign investors would withdraw and interest rates would rise sharply. State deficits would increase and inflation would return.

At this point, the government would face the choice between escalation and retreat – much as the communists did at the end of the 1920s. Yet this is not the Russia of the 1920s. Seventy years ago, Russia was still in the throes of a radical, anti-Western, anti-bourgeois revolution. The country was ruled by a hard and determined group of men who had seized power by force of arms and by the end of the 1920s had built the basis for a dictatorship. The militant workers who backed them saw the world in class terms, and were only too willing to listen to tales about rich peasants or profiteering merchants.[21]

There is little parallel to the 1920s today. The political system is too deeply fractured for any politician, even the president, to be able to respond to obstacles with escalation to more radical measures. There are no powerful mass parties that can call armies of supporters into the streets. Even the coercive forces – the army, the police, and the many special forces that bear arms – are deeply divided, making a coup a virtual impossibility.

Indeed, Russia appears fearful above all of political radicalism. In the winter of 1999, in answer to the question, "How would you evaluate the political situation in Russia," 62% of respondents said that they feared a breakdown of order and the rise of anarchy.[22] Such answers suggest that victory in the coming elections is more likely to go to the party and the candidate that can calm the voters' anxiety rather than attempt to rouse their righteous rage.

Despite the upheavals of the last decade and the widening gap between haves and have-nots, Russian society does not appear particularly polarized politically. Surprisingly, Russian sociologists find there has been little

---

[21] For valuable insights into popular attitudes toward the private businessmen in the 1920s, see Alan M. Ball, *Russia's Last Capitalists: the NEPmen, 1921–1929* (Berkeley: University of California Press, 1987)

[22] Nationwide survey by VTsIOM, February 19–22, 1999, by Internet.

change in Russians' basic perceptions and values since the late 1980s. The great changes in Russian society, they say, occurred in the previous two generations, with the move to the cities and the rise of educational levels and standards of living. By the late 1980s a new Russian urban culture had formed, founded on a large professional class, largely free of ideology and potentially supportive of liberal political values.[23] As a group of Russian scholars concludes, "There is no crisis in Russian values."[24]

But one far-reaching change has occurred in the last decade: Russians have increasingly disengaged from the state. As recently as the 1980s, writes sociologist Iurii Levada, a typical Russian still defined himself as a "state person" (*chelovek gosudarstvennyi*), meaning someone who served the state, identified with its symbols, and relied on the state's benevolent support in return.[25] But that is no longer the case. Young people, especially, now expect little from the state, and care less about its goings-on.[26] Russian society may have entered a "post-mobilizational" phase, in which Russians identify more with personal values such as family, language, birthplace, ethnic group, and home region, than with the state.

This divorce from the state, if it is real, has a positive side. It means Russians are likely to make fewer demands on it. There is little sign of the explosion of popular political participation that has typically accompanied the great political revolutions of the past. As political scientist Stephen Holmes writes, "Postcommunist man has not been, so far, mobilized in extremist movements because he has not been, so far, mobilized for anything at all. He remains politically inert."[27]

For these reasons, even an opposition victory in the upcoming elections is unlikely to lead to a massive reversal of the changes of the last decade. Just as the political system is presently too weak to be an effective partner to Russia's new capitalism, so also its very weakness prevents it from being a mortal threat. But Russians' disengagement from the state may also mean that there is little popular support for the kind of systematic state-building required to build a civil market society. The present social revolution in Russia is unusual in modern experience, in that so far it is leading to a weaker state, not a stronger one.[28]

[23] Moshe Lewin, *The Gorbachev Phenomenon: a Historical Interpretation* (Berkeley: University of California Press, 1991)

[24] See the articles by Iurii A. Levada, N. Tikhonova, B. Dubin, and A. Vishnevskii, in Tat'iana I. Zaslavskaia, ed., *Kuda idet Rossiia? Al'ternativy obshchestvennogo razvitiia.* Proceedings of an international symposium held under the auspices of the Interdisciplinary Academic Center for the Social Sciences, December 15–18 1994 (Moscow: "Aspekt Press," 1995), pp. 208–247.   [25] Levada, loc. cit., p. 222.

[26] B. Dubin, loc. cit., p. 239.

[27] Stephen Holmes, "Cultural Legacies or State Collapse? Probing the Postcommunist Dilemma," in Michael Mandelbaum, ed., Post-Communism: Four Perspectives (New York: Council on Foreign Relations, 1996), p. 35.

[28] The idea that social revolutions lead to stronger states is associated particularly with

This can be read two ways. The negative reading is that the relationship between society and state will remain poised where it is today, somewhere between corrupt coziness and antagonism. The state will not be strong enough either to impose an industrial policy or to build systematically a regulated market environment. Russia will continue to muddle along.

But there is a more positive reading. It is, perhaps, not entirely a bad thing that the Russian state is weak at the present stage. The void left by receding state power was what enabled Russian society to evolve toward a market economy in the first place. An early strengthening of state power would be harmful, because the present generation of Russian bureaucrats, at least below a handful of top officials, does not have the skills or the attitudes needed to build a productive partnership with the private sector – any more than does the present generation of Russian businessmen. The present state-society relationship, flawed as it is, may be better than any presently feasible alternative.

Against this backdrop, Russian society is continuing to evolve. If voters do not reverse the changes at the polls, then Russia may be granted precious time for the positive trends described in this book to continue working. Muddling along rather than economic miracle, may turn out to be Russia's formula for progress. A new generation is coming to maturity, with different skills, experiences, and attitudes from their parents and grandparents. They may, in time, bring fresh answers to the unresolved relationship of state and society.

The answers to the questions raised in this book, then, could be these: Capitalist Russia may not be rich in the coming decades, but it may produce enough growth and wealth to survive and keep on evolving. The transition to capitalism Russian-style may not win the hearts of Russians, but it may – just possibly – be tacitly accepted as the system best suited to the urban and middle-class people that the Russians have become. For a country that has had its fill of historical tragedy and radical ideological experiment, an emerging market society – with all its flaws – could provide the setting in which Russians can use their talents and their energies as they see fit. And that would be more than good enough.

footnote 28 (*cont.*)
Theda Skocpol's influential work, *States and Social Revolutions: a Comparative Analysis of France, Russia, and China* (Cambridge: Cambridge University Press: 1979) An essential part of Skocpol's reasoning is that old regimes collapse when they are unable to stand up to international competition, whether military or economic. To a considerable extent, the collapse of the Soviet regime fits the Skocpol pattern, and the recent example of the East Asian states suggests that strong states continue to play an essential role in economic adaptation. See Peter Evans, "The State as Problem and Solution: Predation, Embedded Autonomy, and Structural Change," in Stephan Haggard and Robert R. Kaufman, eds., *The Politics of Economic Adjustment: International Conflicts, Distributive Conflicts, and the State* (Princeton, NJ: Princeton University Press, 1992), pp. 139–181.

Bibliography

GENERAL

Alfred D. Chandler, *The Visible Hand: the Managerial Revolution in American Business* (Cambridge, MA: Harvard University Press, 1977)

J.C.D. Clark, *English Society 1688–1832* (Cambridge: Cambridge University Press, 1985)

Oliver C. Cox, *The Foundations of Capitalism* (New York: Philosophical Library, 1959)

Orlando Figes, *A People's Tragedy: The Russian Revolution, 1891–1924* (New York: Viking Penguin, 1997)

Thomas L. Friedman, *The Lexus and the Olive Tree* (New York: Farrar, Straus and Giroux, 1999)

Alexander Gerschenkron, *Economic Backwardness in Historical Perspective* (Cambridge, MA.: Harvard University Press, 1962)

John Gray, *False Dawn: The Delusions of Global Capitalism* (New York: The New Press, 1999)

Gregory Guroff and Fred V. Carstensen, eds., *Entrepreneurship in Imperial Russia and the Soviet Union* (Princeton NJ: Princeton University Press, 1983)

Albert O. Hirschman, *Journeys Toward Progress: Studies of Economic Policy-Making in Latin America* (New York: 20-Century Fund, 1963)

Samuel P. Huntington, *Political Order in Changing Societies* (New Haven, CN.: Yale University Press, 1968)

Ronald Inglehart, "The Renaissance of Political Culture," *American Political Science Review*, vol. 82, no. 4, December 1988, pp. 1204–1230.

John Maynard Keynes, *The Collected Writings of John Maynard Keynes* (London: Macmillan, 1971)

David S. Landes, *The Unbound Prometheus: Technological Change and Industrial Development in Western Europe from 1750 to the Present* (Cambridge: Cambridge University Press, 1969)

Douglass C. North, *Structure and Change in Economic History* (New York: Norton, 1981)

Douglass C. North, *Institutions, Institutional Change, and Economic Performance* (Cambridge: Cambridge University Press, 1981)

Alain Peyrefitte, *La Société de Confiance* (Paris: Editions Odile Jacob, 1995)

Henri Pirenne, *Histoire économique et sociale du Moyen Age* (Paris: Presses Universitaires de France, 1969)

Karl Polanyi, *The Great Transformation: the Political and Economic Origins of our Times* (New York: Rinehart, 1944)

Pavel A. Primachenko, *Russkii torgovo-promyshlennyi mir* (Moscow: "Planeta" 1993)

Adam Przeworski, *Democracy and the Market* (Cambridge: Cambridge University Press, 1991)

Hans Rogger, *Russia in the Age of Modernization and Revolution, 1881–1917* (London: Longman, 1983)

Joseph A. Schumpeter, *Capitalism, Socialism, and Democracy* (London: George Allen and Unwin, 1944)

Adam Smith, *An Inquiry into the Nature and Causes of the Wealth of Nations* (Chicago: Encyclopaedia Britannica, 1952)

Daniel Yergin and Joseph A. Stanislaw, *The Commanding Heights: the Battle between Government and the Marketplace that is Remaking the Modern World* (New York: Simon and Schuster, 1998)

THE SOVIET AND GORBACHEVIAN BACKGROUND, POST-SOVIET POLITICS:

Alan M. Ball, *Russia's Last Capitalists: the NEPmen, 1921–1929* (Berkeley: University of California Press, 1987)

Joseph A. Berliner, *Factory and Manager in the Soviet Union* (Cambridge, MA.: Harvard University Press, 1957)

Jean Farneth Boone, "Trading in Power: The Politics of Soviet Foreign Economic Reform, 1986–1991" (Doctoral dissertation, Georgetown University, 1998)

Rose Brady, *Kapitalizm: Russia's Struggle to Free its Economy* (New Haven, CN.: Yale University Press, 1999)

Archie Brown, *The Gorbachev Factor* (Oxford: Oxford University Press, 1996).

Timothy J. Colton, *Transitional Citizenship: Voting in Post-Soviet Russia* (Cambridge MA: Harvard University Press, forthcoming).

M. Steven Fish, *Democracy from Scratch: Opposition and Regime in the New Russian Revolution* (Princeton NJ: Princeton University Press, 1995)

Timothy Frye, *The State and the Market: Governing the New Russian Economy* (Ann Arbor, MI: University of Michigan Press, 1999)

Marshall Goldman, *Lost Opportunity: Why Economic Reforms in Russia Have not Worked* (New York: W.W. Norton, 1994)

Mikhail Gorbachev, *Memoirs* (New York: Doubleday, 1996)

Gregory Grossman, "Gold and the Sword: Money in the Soviet Command Economy," in Henry Rosovsky, ed, *Industrialization in Two Systems* (New York: Wiley, 1966), pp. 204–236.

Gregory Grossman, "Introduction," in Grossman, ed., *Money and Plan* (Berkeley, University of California Press, 1968), pp. 1–16.

Ed A. Hewett, *Reforming the Soviet Economy: Equality vs. Efficiency* (Washington, D.C.: Brookings Institution, 1988)

Jerry F. Hough, *Democratization and Revolution in the USSR, 1985–1991* (Washington D.C.: The Brookings Institution, 1997)

Janos Kornai, *The Socialist System: the Political Economy of Communism* (Princeton NJ: Princeton University Press, 1992)

Moshe Levin, *The Gorbachev Phenomenon: an Historical Interpretation* (Berkeley: University of California Press, 1991)

John Lloyd, *Rebirth of a Nation: an Anatomy of Russia* (London: Michael Joseph, 1998)

Michael Mandelbaum, ed., *Post-Communism: Four Perspectives* (New York: Council on Foreign Relations, 1996)

Leonid M. Mlechin, *Evgenii Primakov: istoriia odnoi kar'ery* (Moscow: "Trentrpoligraf," 1999)

L. Nikiforov and T. Kuznetsova, "Sud'ba kooperatsii v sovremennoi Rossii," *Voprosy ekonomiki*, No. 1 (1995), pp. 86–96.

David Remnick, *Lenin's Tomb: the Last Days of the Soviet Empire* (New York: Random House, 1993)

David Remnick, *Resurrection: the Struggle for a New Russia* (New York: Random House, 1997)

Lilia Shevtsova, ed., *Rossiia politicheskiaia* (Moscow: Carnegie Endowment for International Peace, Moscow Center, 1998)

Lilia Shevtsova, *Yeltsin's Russia* (Washington, D.C.: Carnegie Endowment for International Peace, 1999)

Robert Skildelsky, *The Road from Serfdom: The Economic and Political Consequences of the End of Communism* (New York: Viking Penguin, 1996)

Steven L. Solnick, *Stealing the State: Control and Collapse in Soviet Institutions* (Cambridge, MA: Harvard University Press, 1998)

Stephen White, *After Gorbachev*, fourth edition (Cambridge: Cambridge University Press, 1993)

Stephen White, Richard Rose, Ian McAllister, *How Russia Votes* (Chatham, New Jersey: Chatham House Publishers, 1997)

Daniel Yergin and Thane Gustafson, *Russia 2010 and What It Means for the World* (New York: Random House, 1994)

BUILDING A MARKET SYSTEM

MANAGING THE TRANSITION

Leonid Abalkin, *V tiskakh krizisa* (Moscow: Institut ekonomiki Rossiiskoi Akademii Nauk, 1994)

Leonid Abalkin et al., "Doklad Abalkina" (press version of the joint memorandum issued by members of the Economics Section of the Russian Academy of Sciences), *Kommersant Daily*, September 15 1998.

Michael V. Alexeev and James A. Leitzel, "Tax Arrears and Barter in Russia," *Eurasia Economic Outlook*, Wharton Econometric Forecasting Associates, June 1998, pp. 1.3–1.6.

Alice H. Amsden, Jacek Kochanowicz, Lance Taylor, eds., *The Market Meets its Match: Restructuring the Economies of Eastern Europe* (Cambridge, MA.: Harvard University Press, 1994)

Anders Aslund, *How Russia Became a Market Economy* (Washington, D.C.: Brookings Institution, 1995)

Anders Aslund, ed., *Economic Transformation in Russia* (New York: St. Martin's Press, 1994)

Anders Aslund, ed., *Russian Reform at Risk* (New York: St. Martins Press, 1995)

Olivier Jean Blanchard, Kenneth A. Froot, and Jeffrey D. Sachs, eds., *The Transition in Eastern Europe*, 2 volumes, National Bureau of Economic Research (Chicago: University of Chicago Press, 1994)

Aleksandr Buzgalin, *Perekhodnaia ekonomika: kurs lektsii po politicheskoi ekonomike* (Moscow: "Taurus Prosperus," 1994)

Christopher Clague and Gordon C. Rausser, eds., *The Emergence of Market Economies in Eastern Europe* (Cambridge MA: Blackwell, 1992)

Simon Clarke, ed., *Management and Industry in Post-Communist Russia: Social Divisions in the Transition to a Market Economy* (Cheltenham: Edward Elgar, 1994).

Simon Commander and Christian Mumssen, "Understanding Barter in Russia," Working Paper No. 37, European Bank for Reconstruction and Development (London: December 1998)

European Bank for Reconstruction and Development, *Transition Report 1994* (London: EBRD, 1994)

European Bank for Reconstruction and Development, *Transition Report 1997* (London: EBRD, 1997)

European Bank for Reconstruction and Development, *Transition Report 1998* (London: EBRD, 1998)

Boris Fedorov, *Zametki ob ochevidnom* (Moscow: ONIKS, 1995)

A.A. Frenkel', *Ekonomika Rossii, 1992–1995: Tendentsii, analiz, prognoz* (Moscow: "Finstatinform," 1995)

Roman Frydman, Kenneth Murphy, and Andrzej Rapaczynski, *Capitalism with a Comrade's Face: Studies in the Postcommunist Transition* (Budapest: Central European University Press, 1998)

Clifford G. Gaddy and Barry W. Ickes, "Beyond a Bailout: Time to Face Reality about Russia's Virtual Economy" (Washington, D.C.: Brookings Institution, July 1998). Available by Internet from the Brookings Institution website, http://www.brook.edu.

Clifford G. Gaddy and Barry W. Ickes, "Russia's Virtual Economy," *Foreign Affairs*, September–October 1998, pp. 53–67.

Egor Gaidar, "Novye zadachi: vybor za nami," *Voprosy ekonomiki*, No. 9 (1994), pp. 4–10.

Egor Gaidar, *Sdelai razumnyi vybor: besedy s izbirateliami* (Moscow: "Demokraticheskii vybor Rossii," 1995).

Egor Gaidar, ed., *Ekonomika perekhodnogo perioda: ocherki ekonomicheskoi politiki postkommunistecheskoi Rossii, 1991–97* (Moscow: Institut ekonomicheskikh problem perekhodnogo perioda, 1998).

Sergei Glaz'ev, *Poltora goda v Dume* (Moscow: "Gals Plius," 1995)

Institut ekonomicheskikh problem perekhodnogo perioda, "Krizis finansovoi sistemy Rossii: osnovnye faktory i ekonomicheskaia politika," *Voprosy ekonomiki*, No. 11 (1998), pp. 36–64.

Vladimir Ispravednikov, *Ekonomicheskaia reforma: prioritety i mekhanizmy*, published under the aegis of the Institut novykh khoziaistvennykh struktur i privatizatsii, Russian Academy of Sciences (Moscow: "Luch," 1993)

Simon Johnson, Daniel Kaufman, and Andrei Shleifer, "The Unofficial Economy in Transition," *Brookings Papers on Economic Activity*, No. 2 (1997).

Daniel Kaufman and Aleksandr Kaliberda, "Integrating the Unofficial Economy into the Dynamics of Post-socialist Economies: A Framework of Analysis and Evidence," World Bank Policy Research Paper 1691, Washington D.C., December 1996.

Boris Khorev, *Anti-rynok: avantiurizm razrushaet Rossiiu* (Moskva: "Paleia," 1994)

David Lane, ed., *Russia in Transition: Politics, Privatization, and Inequality* (London: Longman, 1995)

Philippe H. LeHouerou, *Investment Policy in Russia*, Studies of Economies in Transformation, No. 17 (Washington, D.C.: The World Bank, 1995)

Jim Leitzel, *Russian Economic Reform* (London: Routledge, 1995)

Aleksandr Livshits, *Ekonomicheskaia reforma v Rossii i ego tsena* (Moscow: "Kul'tura," 1994)

Vladimir Mau, "Politicheskaia priroda i uroki finansovogo krizisa," *Voprosy ekonomiki*, No. 11 (1998), pp. 4–19.

Ronald I. McKinnon, *The Order of Economic Liberalization: Financial Control in the Transition to a Market Economy* (Baltimore: Johns Hopkins University Press, 1993)

Peter Murrell, "What is Shock Therapy? What Did it Do in Poland and Russia?" *Post-Soviet Affairs*, vol. 9, no. 2 (April-June 1993), pp. 111–140.

Joan M. Nelson, "The Politics of Economic Transformation: Is Third World Experience Relevant in Eastern Europe?" *World Politics*, vol. 45 (April 1993), pp. 433–63.

Iu. M. Osipov and I.N. Shurgalina, eds., *Perekhody i katastrofy: opyt sotsial'no-eko-nomicheskogo razvitiia* (Moscow: Izdatel'stvo Moskovskogo Universiteta, 1994).

Nikolai Ia. Petrakov, *Russkaia ruletka: ekonomicheskii eksperiment tsenoiu 150 mil-lionov zhiznei* (Moscow: "Ekonomika" 1998)

Vladimir Popov, *Ekonomicheskie reformy v Rossii: tri goda spustia* (Moscow: Rossiiskii nauchnyi fond, 1994)

V.V. Radaev and A.V. Buzgalin, eds., *Ekonomika perekhodnogo perioda* (Moscow: Izdatel'stvo Moskovskogo Universiteta, 1995)

V.V. Riabov and A.Z. Seleznev, eds., *Ekonomicheskii i politicheskii kurs Rossii*, Rossiiskaia akademiia upravleniia, otdel kompleksnykh issledovanii, vypusk III (Moscow, 1993)

Richard Rose, "Toward a Civil Economy," *Journal of Democracy*, vol. 3, no. 2 (April 1992), pp. 13–26.

Russian Federation, Ministry of Economics, "O perspektivakh razvitiia eko-nomicheskoi situatsii v 1997 i zadachakh sotsial'no-ekonomicheskogo reformirovaniia (Unpublished report to the Russian government, January 1997)

Jeffrey Sachs. *Poland's Jump to the Market Economy* (Cambridge, MA.: MIT Press, 1993)

Jeffrey D. Sachs, "Prospects for Monetary Stabilization in Russia," unpublished paper, prepared for the Conference on Economic Transformation in Russia, Stockholm School of Economics, June 1993.

Jeffrey D. Sachs, "Russia's Struggle with Stabilization: Conceptual Issues and Evidence" (Washington D.C.: World Bank Annual Conference on Development Economics, April 28–29 1994)

Joseph Stiglitz, "Whither Reform? Ten Years of the Transition" (Keynote Address at the World Bank Annual Conference on Development Economics, April 28–30 1999, Washington, D.C.)

Daniel S. Treisman, "Fighting Inflation in a Transitional Regime: Russia's Anomalous Stabilization," *World Politics*, vol. 50 (January 1998), pp. 235–65.

Vladimir Vlaskin and Vladimir Pashkov, *Ekonomicheskaia krakha: chto zhe dal'she?* (Saratov: "Slovo," 1994)

David Woodruff, "It's Value that's Virtual: Bartles, Rubles, and the Place of Gazprom in the Russian Economy," Working Paper Series No. 11, Program on New Approaches to Russian Security, Davis Center for Russian Studies, Harvard University, January 1999.

David Woodruff, *Money Unmade* (Ithaca, New York: Cornell University Press, 1999)

Grigorii Yavlinsky, *Laissez-Faire vs. Policy-Led Transformation: Lessons of the Economic Reforms in Russia* (Moscow: Center for Economic and Social Research, 1994)

Tat'iana I. Zaslavskaia, ed., *Kuda idet Rossiia? Al'ternativy obshchestvennogo razvitiia.* Proceedings of the second annual international symposium held under the auspices of the Interdisciplinary Academic Center for the Social Sciences, December 15–18 1994 (Moscow: "Aspekt Press," 1995)

Tat'iana I. Zaslavskaia, ed., *Kuda idet Rossiia? Sotsial'naia transformatsiia postsovetskogo prostranstva.* (Proceedings of the third annual international symposium held under the auspices of the Interdisciplinary Academic Center for the Social Sciences, January 12–14 1996 (Moscow, "Aspekt Press," 1996)

PRIVATIZATION, CORPORATE GOVERNANCE, AND PROPERTY RIGHTS

S. Aukutsionek and E. Belianova, "Uzhestochaiutsia biudezhetnye ogranicheniia rossiiskikh predpriiatii?" *Mirovaia ekonomika i mezhdunarodnye otnosheniia*, No. 7 (1994), pp. 40–48.

Nicholas Barberis, Maxim Boycko, Andrei Shleifer, Natalia Tsukoanova, "How Does Privatization Work? Evidence from the Russian Shops," *Journal of Political Economy*, vol. 104, no. 4 (1996), pp. 764–790.

Joseph Blasi et al., *Kremlin Capitalism: Privatizing the Russian Economy* (Ithaca, NY: Cornell University Press, 1997)

Maxim Boycko, Andrei Shleifer, Robert W. Vishny, "Privatizing Russia" (Washington, D.C.: Brookings Panel on Economic Activity, September 9–10, 1993)

Maxim Boycko, Andrei Shleifer, Robert Vishny, *Privatizing Russia* (Cambridge, MA.: MIT Press, 1995)

Anatolii Chubais, "Peremena uchasti," *Otkrytaia politika*, No. 2, 1994, pp. 13–20.

"Corporate Governance," Survey Section of *The Economist*, January 29 1994, pp. 3–18.

Simon Clarke et al., "The Privatization of Industrial Enterprises in Russia: Four Case Studies," *Europe-Asia Studies*, vol 46, no. 2 (1994), pp. 179–214.

Padma Desai, "Russian Privatization: a Comparative Perspective," *The Harriman Review*, vol. 8, no. 3 (August 1995).

Peter Dittus and Stephen Prowse, "Corporate Control in Central Europe and Russia: Should Banks Own Shares?" Policy Research Working Paper 1481 (Washington D.C.: The World Bank, June 1995)

Roman Frydman, Katharina Pistor, Andrzej Rapaczynski, "Exit and Voice after Mass Privatization: The Case of Russia," *European Economic Review*, vol. 40 (1996), pp. 581–588.

William T. Gormley, ed., *Privatization and its Alternatives* (Madison, Wisconsin: University of Wisconsin Press, 1991)

William T. Gormley, ed., "Privatization Revisited" (Unpublished paper prepared for the Twentieth Century Fund, Conference on Privatization, New York, N.Y., May 4 1993)

Paul Holden and Sarath Rajapatirana, *Unshackling the Private Sector: a Latin American Story*, Directions in Development Series (Washington, D.C.: The World Bank, 1995)

Barry W. Ickes and Randi Ryterman, "Roadblock to Economic Reform: Inter-Enterprise Debt and the Transition to Markets," *Post-Soviet Affairs*, vol. 9, no. 3 (1993), pp. 231–252.

Janos Kornai, "The Soft Budget Constraint," *Kyklos*, vol. 39, no. 1 (1986), pp. 3–30.

Gary D. Libecap, *Contracting for Property Rights* (Cambridge: Cambridge University Press, 1989)

Ira W. Lieberman and John Nellis, eds., *Russia: Creating Enterprises and Efficient Markets*, World Bank Studies of Economies in Transformation, No. 15 (Washington, D.C.: The World Bank, 1995)

Michael McFaul and Tova Perlmutter, eds., *Privatization, Conversion, and Enterprise Reform in Russia* (Boulder, Colorado: Westview Press, 1995)

Nizhegorodskii prolog: ekonomika i politika v Rossii (Moscow: EPITsentr, 1992)

John Nellis, "Time to Rethink Privatization?" Paper prepared for the IMF Conference on "A Decade of Transition," Washington, D.C, February 1–3, 1999.

V. Oborotova and Aleksandr Y. Tsapin, "The Privatization Process in Russia: an Optimistic Color in the Picture of Reform" (Columbus, Ohio: Mershon Center, Ohio State University, 1993)

PlanEcon, Inc., "Voucher Auctions in the First Phase of Russian Privatization and the Emergence of Voucher Investment Funds," *PlanEcon Report*, vol. 10, No. 33–34 (October 4 1994).

Vladimir Polevanov, *Tekhnologiia velikogo obmana* (Moscow: 1995). [Printed pamphlet, containing no indication of publisher]

William H. Riker and Itai Sened, "A Political Theory of the Origin of Property Rights: Airport Slots," *American Journal of Political Science*, vol. 35, no. 4 (November 1991), pp. 951–69.

Blair Ruble, *Money Sings: The Changing Politics of Urban Space in post-Soviet Yaroslavl* (Cambridge: Cambridge University Press, 1995)

Ratna Sahay and Carlos A. Vegh, "Dollarization in Transition Economies: Evidence and Policy Implications," IMF Working Paper WP/95/96 (Washington, D.C.: International Monetary Fund, September 1995)

Andrei Shleifer, "Establishing Property Rights" (Washington D.C.: World Bank Annual Conference on Development Economics, April 28–29 1994)

Darrell Slider, "Privatization in Russia's Regions," *Post-Soviet Affairs*, vol. 10, no. 4 (October-December 1994), pp. 367–396.

David Stark, "Recombinant Property in East European Capitalism," *American Journal of Sociology*, vol. 101, no. 4 (January 1996), pp. 993–1027.

Pekka Sutela, "Insider Privatization in Russia". *Review of Economies in Transition*, 1994.

Aleksey Tkachenko, "Malaia privatizatsiia v Rossii," Helsinki, Bank of Finland Working Paper, April 1993.

BUILDING NEW FINANCIAL INSTITUTIONS

Brunswick Brokerage, *Russian Equity Guide 1995* (Moscow: Trinity Press, 1995).

Mikhail Dmitriev and Dmitrii Travin, *Rossiiskie banki: na iskhode zolotogo veka* (St. Petersburg: "Norma," 1996)

Mikhail E. Dmitriev, M.Yu. Matovnikov; L.V.Mikhailov, L.I Sycheva, "Russian Banks in 1995–96: Focus on the Balance Sheets of Moscow Banks (manuscript, 1997).

Timothy Frye, "Governing the Russian Equities Market," *Post-Soviet Affairs*, vol. 13, no. 4 (1997), pp. 366–395.

Dmitrii Grishankov, Svetlana Lokotkova, Andrei Shmarov, "U vlasti – krupnooptovaia partiia," *Ekspert*, No. 12 (October 31 1995), pp. 16–22.

Joel S. Hellman, "Breaking the Bank: Bureaucrats and the Creation of Markets in a Transitional Economy" (Ph.D. Thesis, Columbia University, 1993)

Frank Knowles, "The Russian Banking System: At the Crossroads" (London: Merrill Lynch, European Fixed Income Research, October 1997)

Frank Knowles and Dan McGovern, "Russia and Russian Banks: Adjusting to Global Financial Instability" (London: Merrill Lynch, Emerging Markets Research, November 1997)

Investing in Russia's Securities Market: an Independent Assessment of the State of Play (Middlebury, Vermont: Geonomics Institute, December 1996)

Juliet Ellen Johnson, "Banking in Russia: Shadows of the Past," *Problems of Post-Communism*, May-June 1996, pp. 49–59.

Juliet Ellen Johnson, "The Russian Banking System: Institutional Responses to the Market Transition," *Europe-Asia Studies*, vol. 46, no. 6 (1994), pp. 971–995.

G. Kasatkin, "Investitsionnyi klimat v Rossii: luchshe ne stalo," *Rynok tsennykh bumag*, No. 12 (1995), pp. 28–31.

Roland Nash and Dirk Willer, "Share Prices in Russia: the Reasons for Undervaluation," *Russian Economic Trends*, vol. 4, no, 2 (1995), pp. 111–127.

Russian Central Bank, "Sovremennoe sostoianie bankovskoi sistemy Rossii" (December 1998), by Internet (http://www.cbr.ru/system/overview.html)

Russian Federation, Russian Securities Commission, "Problemy razvitiia kollektivnykh investorov v Rossii" (Unpublished report to the Russian government, March 1997)

Russian Federation, Russian Central Bank, *Programma restrukturizatsii bankovskoi sistemy Rossiiskoi Federatsii* (October 5 1998 draft), reprinted in *Kommersant-Daily*, October 14 1998, by Internet

Russian Federation, Russian Central Bank, *Programma neotlozhnykh mer po restrukturizatsii bankovskoi sistemy Rossiiskoi Federatsii* (October 19 1998 draft)

Jeffrey Williams, *The Economic Function of Futures Markets* (Cambridge: Cambridge University Press, 1986)

World Bank, "Rossiia: Bankovskaia sistema v perekhodnyi period" (Moscow: World Bank, 1997)

THE SOCIAL FABRIC FOR A MARKET SYSTEM

Harley Balzer, "A Shadow Middle Class for a Shadow Economy" (paper presented at the XXIX Annual Convention of the American Association for the Advancement of Slavic Studies, Seattle, Washington, November 20–23 1997)

M.K. Gorshkov, A.Iu. Chepurenko, F.E. Sheregi, eds., *Rossiia v zerkale reform: khrestomatiia po sotsiologii sovremennogo rossiiskogo obshchestva*, Russian Independent Institute for Social and National Problems (Moscow: "Akademiia," 1995)

Simon Johnson and Daniel Kaufman, "In the Underground" (Paper prepared for the IMF Conference on "A Decade of Transition: Achievements and Challenges," February 1999)

G.S. Khromov, *Nauka, kotoruiu my teriaem* (Moscow: 1994)

Marina Krasil'nikova, "Sklonnost' k sberezheniiam i potrebleniiu," *Ekonomicheskie i sotsial'nye peremeny: monitoring obshchestvennogo mneniia*, No. 3 (1997), pp. 25–30.

Zoia Kupriianova, "Real'naia i professional'naia professional'naia mobil'nost' v Rossiiskoi Federatsii," VTsIOM (Russian Center for Public Opinion Research) *Monitoring obshchestvennogo mneniia: Informatsionnyi biulleten'*, No. 4 (July-August 1997), pp. 26–30.

Natalia Mikhailovna Rimashevskaia, "Sotsial'nye posledstviia ekonomicheskikh transformatsii v Rossii," *Sotsiologicheskie issledovaniia*, No. 6 (1997), pp. 55–65.

Mikhail N. Rutkevich, "Transformatsiia sotsial'noi struktury rossiiskogo obshchestva," *Sotsiologicheskie issledovaniia*, No. 7 (1997), pp. 3–19.

Evgenii Starikov, "Marginaly, ili razmyshleniia na staruiu temu: 'Chto s nami proiskhodit?'" *Znamiia*, No. 10 (October), 1989, pp. 133–162.

I.N. Veselkova et al., "Nekotorye demograficheskie tendentsii v Rossiiskoi Federatsii," *Zdravookhranenie Rossiiskoi Federatsii*, No. 3 (1994), p. 32.

POVERTY AND INEQUALITY

Timothy Heleniak, "Dramatic Population Trends in Countries of the FSU," *Transition*, vol. 6, nos. 9–10 (September-October 1995), pp. 1–5.

Jeni Klugman, "Poverty in Russia: an Assessment," World Bank Report No. 14110–RU (Washington, D.C.: The World Bank, June 1995)

Richard Rose, "New Russian Barometer VI: After the Presidential Election," Studies in Public Policy No. 272 (University of Strathclyde, Center for the Study of Public Policy, 1996)

Richard Rose and Evgenii Tikhomirov, *Trends in the New Russia Barometer,*

1992–1995, University of Strathclyde Center for the Study of Public Policy, Studies in Public Policy No. 256 (Glasgow, Scotland: University of Strathclyde, 1995)[Publications of the CSPP are accessible by Internet, http://www.strath.ac.uk:80/departments.CSPP.]

UNEMPLOYMENT AND SECONDARY EMPLOYMENT

Vladimir Gimpel'son, "Politika rossiiskogo menedzhmenta v sfere zaniatosti," *Mirovaia ekonomika i mezhdunarodnye otnosheniia*, No. 6 (1994), pp. 5–20.

Simon Johnson, John McMillan, and Christopher Woodruff, "Job Creation in the Private Sector: Poland, Romania, Russia, Slovakia, and Ukraine Compared" (Paper presented at the IMF Conference on "A Decade of Transition: Achievements and Challenges," February 1999)

A. Kashepov, "Problemy predotvrashcheniia massovoi bezrabotitsy v Rossii," *Voprosy ekonomiki*, No. 5 (1995), pp. 53–62.

E. Khibovskaia, "Vtorichnaia zaniatost' kak sposob adaptatsii k ekonomicheskim reformam," *Voprosy ekonomiki*, No. 5 (1995), pp. 71–79.

Eduard Viktorovich Klopov, "Vtorichnaia zaniatost' kak forma sotsial'no-trudovoi mobil'nosti," *Sotsiologicheskie issledovaniia*, No. 4 (1997), pp. 29–45.

M. Toksanbaeva, "Legko li byt' ekonomicheski aktivnym?" *Voprosy ekonomiki*, No. 5 (1995), pp. 80–89.

THE NEW RUSSIAN ENTREPRENEURS, FINANCIAL–INDUSTRIAL GROUPS, AND SMALL BUSINESS

A. Arkhipov, G. Batkilina, and V. Kalinin, "Gosudarstvo i malyi biznes: finansirovanie, kreditovanie i nalogooblozhenie," *Voprosy ekonomiki*, No. 4 (1997), pp. 141–151.

A. Blinov, "Maloe predprinimatel'stvo i bol'shaya politika," *Voprosy ekonomiki*, No. 7 (1996), pp. 39–45.

Konstantin Borovoi, *Tsena svobody* (Moscow: "Novosti" 1993)

I.M. Bunin, ed., *Biznesmeny Rossii: 40 istorii uspekha* (Moscow: Izdatel'stvo AO "OKO," 1994)

I.M. Bunin, ed., *Finansovo-promyshlennye gruppy i konglomeraty v ekonomike i politike sovremennoi Rossii* (Moscow: "Tsentr politicheskikh tekhnologii" 1997)

A. Chepurenko, "Problema finansirovaniia v rossiiskom malom biznese," *Voprosy ekonomiki*, No. 7 (1996), pp. 59–66.

Finansovo-promyshlennye gruppy i konglomeraty v ekonomike i politike sovremennoi Rossii (Mosckva: Tsentr politicheskikh tekhnologii, 1997)

Timothy Frye and Andrei Shleifer, "The Invisible Hand and the Grabbing Hand," *American Economic Review Papers and Proceedings*, vol. 87, no. 2 (May 1997), pp. 354–358.

Vladimir Gimpel'son, "Novoe rossiiskoe predprinimatel'stvo: istochniki formirovaniia i strategii sotsial'nogo deistviia," *Mirovaia ekonomika i mezhdunarodnye otnosheniia*, No. 7 (1993).

Simon Johnson and Gary W. Loveman, *Starting Over in Eastern Europe: Entrepreneurship and Economic Renewal* (Boston, MA.: Harvard Business School Press, 1995)

V.A. Lepekhin, *Obshchestvenno-politicheskie protsessy v srede predprinimatelei.* Issue No. 5 of the "Seriia obozrenii k pervomu kongressu rossiiskikh predprinimatelei," general editor A.S. Orlov (Moscow: Kruglyi stol biznesa Rossii, Akademicheskii tsentr 'Rossiiskie issledovaniia,' 1994)

Michael Maccoby, *The Gamesman: the New Corporate Leaders* (New York: Simon and Schuster, 1976)

A.S. Orlov, ed., *Rossiiskoe predprinimatel'stvo: sotsial'nyi portret,* Issue No. 7 of the Seriia obozrenii k pervomu kongressu rossiiskikh predprinimatelei (Moscow: Kruglyi stol biznesa Rossii, Akademicheskii tsentr 'Rossiiskie issledovaniia,' 1994)

A.S. Orlov, "Maloe p'redprinimatel'stvo: starye i novye problemy," *Voprosy ekonomiki,* No. 4 (1997), pp. 130–140.

A. Panarin, "Paradoksy predprinimatel'stvo, paradoksy istorii," *Voprosy ekonomiki,* No. 7 (1995), pp. 62–73.

Vadim Radaev, ed., *Stanovlenie novogo russkogo predprinimatel'stva (sotsiologicheskii aspekt)* (Moscow: Russian Academy of Sciences, Institut ekonomiki, Mezhdistsiplinarnyi akademicheskii tsentr sotsial'nykh nauk, 1993)

Vadim Radaev, "O nekotorykh chertakh normativnogo povedeniia novykh rossiiskikh predprinimatelei," *Mirovaia ekonomika i mezhdunarodnye otnosheniia,* No. 4 (1994), pp. 31–38.

Peter Rutland, "Business Lobbies in Contemporary Russia," *The International Spectator,* vol. 32, No. 1 (1997), pp. 23–37.

Karen E. Simeone, "Locomotive of Prosperity: Small Entrepreneurship in Russia" (unpublished seminar paper, Georgetown University, December 1997)

Rair Simonian, "Predprinimatel'stvo i vlast'," *Dialog,* Nos. 5–6, 1993.

V. Stepin, "Kul'tura i stanovlenie tsivilizovannogo rynka v Rossii," *Voprosy ekonomiki,* No. 7 (1995), pp. 74–81.

A. Tsyganov, "Predprinimatel' i vlast': problemy vzaimodeistviia," *Voprosy ekonomiki,* No. 6 (1997), pp. 97–103.

Nicolo de Vecchi, *Entrepreneurs, Institutions, and Economic Change: the Economic Thought of J.A. Schumpeter* (London: Edward Elgar, 1995)

A. Vilenskii, "Etapy razvitiia malogo predprinimatel'stva v Rossii," *Voprosy ekonomiki,* No. 7 (July 1996), pp. 30–38.

N. Zarubina, "Rossiiskoe predprinimatel'stvo: idei i liudi," *Voprosy ekonomiki,* No. 7 (1995), pp. 82–90.

Viktor A. Zevelev, *Malyi biznes – bol'shaia problema Rossii* (Moscow: "Menedzher" 1994)

HEALTH AND POPULATION

Igor' Alekseevich Gundarov, *Pochemu umiraiut v Rosssii, kak nam vyzhit'? (Fakty i argumenty)* (Moscow: "Media sfera," 1995)

E.M. Andreev, ed., *Demograficheskie perspektivy Rossii* (Publication of the Otdelenie demografii of the Institut statistiki i ekonomicheskikh issledovanii, Goskomstat Rossii) (Moscow: Respublikanskii informatsionno-izdatel'skii tsentr, 1993)

Murray Feshbach, ed., *Environmental and Health Atlas of Russia* (Moscow: "Paims," 1995)

Ol'ga Dmitrievna Zakharova, "Demograficheskie protsessy v Rossiiskoi Federatsii i stranakh novogo zarubezh'ia," *Sotsiologicheskie issledovaniia*, No. 7 (1997), pp. 60–69.

CRIME AND CORRUPTION

Scott Anderson, "Looking for Mr. Yaponchik: the Rise and Fall of a Russian Mobster in America," *Harper's*, December 1995, pp. 40–51.

Clifford Gaddy, Jim Leitzel, and Michael Alexeev, "Mafiosi and matrioshki: organized crime and Russian reform," *Brookings Review*, vol. 13, no. 1 (Winter 1995), pp. 26–30.

Diego Gambetta, *The Sicilian Mafia* (Cambridge, MA.: Harvard University Press, 1995)

Stanislav Govorukhin, *Velikaia kriminal'naia revoliutsiia* (Moscow: "Andreevskii Flag" 1993)

Harry I. Greenfield, *Invisible, Outlawed, and Untaxed: America's Underground Economy* (Westport, Connecticut: Praeger, 1993)

Marie-Laurence Guy, "La criminalité organisée "tous azimuts": l'exemple de la Russie," *Relations Internationales et Strategiques*, vol. 20 (Hiver 1995), pp. 116–128.

Stephen Handelman, *Comrade Criminal: the Theft of the Second Russian Revolution* (London: Michael Joseph, 1994)

Stefan Hedlund and Nicolas Sundstrom, "Does Palermo Represent the Future for Moscow?" (Unpublished paper prepared for the NAS/NRC Workshop on "Economic Transformation: Institutional Change, Property Rights, and Corruption," Washington, March 708, 1996.

Robert Klitgaard, *Tropical Gangsters* (New York: Basic Books, 1990).

Vadim Kolesnikov, *Ekonomicheskaia prestupnost' i rynochnye reformy* (Sankt-Petersburg: "Izdatel'stvo Sankt-Petersburgskogo Universiteta ekonomiki i finansov," 1994)

Ol'ga Kryshtanovskaia, "Mafioznyi peizazh Rossii." *Izvestiia*, September 21 1995, p. 5.

Morton Paglin, " The Underground Economy: New Estimates from Household Income and Expenditure Surveys," *Yale Law Journal*, vol. 103 (1994), pp. 2239–57.

Georgii Podlesskikh and Andrei Tereshonok, *Vory v zakone: brosok k vlasti* (Moscow: "Khudozhestvennaia literatura, 1994)

William L. Riordan, *Plunkitt of Tammany Hall* (New York: E.P. Dutton, 1963)

V.M. Rybkin, ed., *Prestupnost' v Rossii v devianostykh godakh i nekotorye aspekty zakonnosti bor'by s nei* (Moscow: "Kriminologicheskaia Assotsiatsiia," 1995)

Laurent Ruseckas, "Corruption and Economic Efficiency in the Soviet and Post-Soviet Systems: From Good to Bad to Worse" (Unpublished paper, Columbia University, December 1995)

Georgii Satarov, M.I. Levin, M.L. Tsirik, "Rossiia i Korruptsiia" (Report sponsored jointly by the Council on Foreign and Defense Policy and the "Information for Democracy" Fund), published in *Rossiiskaia gazeta*, February 19 1998.

Louise I. Shelley, "Organized Crime in the Former Soviet Union," *Problems of Post-Communism*, January/February 1995, pp. 56–60.

Louise I. Shelley, "Privatization and Crime: The Post-Soviet Experience," *Journal of Contemporary Criminal Justice*, vol. 11, no. 4 (December 1995).

Louise I. Shelley, *Policing Soviet Society: The Evolution of State Control* (London: Routledge, 1996)

Andrei Shleifer and Robert Vishny, "Corruption". *The Quarterly Journal of Economics*, August 1993.

Konstantin M. Simis, *The Corrupt Society: the Secret World of Soviet Capitalism* (New York: Simon and Schuster, 1982)

Hernando de Soto, *The Other Path* (New York: Harper and Row, 1989)

Vladimir G. Treml and Michael V. Alexeev, "The Second Economy and the Destabilizing Effect of its Growth on the State Economy in the Soviet Union: 1965–1989" Berkeley-Duke Occasional Papers on the Second Economy in the USSR, Paper No. 36 (Bala Cynwyd, Pa.: The WEFA Group, December 1993)

Vladimir G. Treml and Michael V. Alexeev, "The Growth of the Second Economy in the Soviet Union and its Impact on the System," in Robert W. Campbell, ed., *The Postcommunist Economic Transformation* (Boulder, Colorado: Westview Press, 1994), pp. 221–248.

Federico Varese, "Is Sicily the Future of Russia? Private Protection and the Rise of the Russian Mafia," *Archives Européennes de Sociologie*, vol. 35 (1994), pp. 224–258.

Federico Varese, "Some Misconceptions Regarding the Russian Mafia," testimony to the United States Senate Committee on Foreign Relations, Washington, D.C. May 15 1995. (Published in A. Van Boren, ed., *Russian Organized Crime: A White Paper Report*. Washington, D.C.: United States Senate, The Committee on Foreign Relations).

CIVIL SOCIETY

M. Steven Fish, "The Emergence of Independent Associations and the Transformation of Russian Political Society", *The Journal of Communist Studies*, Vol. 7, September 1991.

M. Steven Fish, "Who Shall Speak for Whom? Democracy and Interest Representation in Post-Soviet Russia", in Alexander Dallin (ed.), *Political Parties in Russia*. (Berkeley: Berkeley University Press, 1993)

Andranik Migranian, "Vzaimootnosheniia individa, obshchestva i gosudarstva v politicheskoi teorii marksizma i problemy demokratizatsii sotsialisticheskogo obshchestva," *Voprosy filosofii*, No. 8 (1987), pp. 75–91.

Andranik Migranian, "Na puti k grazhdanskomu obshchestvu," *Sovetskaia kul'tura*, October 7 1989.

Andranik Migranian, "Dolgii put' k evropeiskomy domu," *Novyi Mir*, No. 7, 1990, pp., 166–184.

Andranik Migranian, "Grazhdanskoe obshchestvo," in Iurii Afanasev and Mark Ferro, eds., *Opyt slovaria novogo myshleniia* (Moscow, "Progress," 1989), pp. 446–453.

Putnam, Robert, *Making Democracy Work: Civic Traditions in Modern Italy.* (Princeton NJ.: Princeton University Press, 1993)

INFRASTRUCTURE, SECTORS, AND REGIONS

T. Alimova et al., "Strategii povedeniia semeinykh fermerskikh khoziaistv," *Voprosy ekonomiki*, No. 1 (1995), pp. 47–56.

Albert Bressand and Catherine Distler, *La Planète Relationnnelle* (Paris: Flammarion, 1995)

Murray Feshbach, *Ecological Disaster: Cleaning up the Hidden Legacy of the Soviet Regime* (New York: The Twentieth Century Fund Press, 1995)

Clifford G. Gaddy, *The Price of the Past: Russia's Struggle with the Legacy of a Militarized Economy* (Washington, D.C.: The Brookings Institution, 1997)

Peter Kirkow, "Regional Warlordism in Russia: the Case of Primorskii Krai," *Europe-Asia Studies*, vol. 47, no. 6 (1995), pp. 923–947.

Peter Kirkow and Philip Hanson, "The Potential for Autonomous Regional Development in Russia: the Case of Primorskiy Kray," *Post-Soviet Geography*, vol. 35, no. 2 (February 1994), pp. 63–88.

Arbakhan Magomedov, "Politicheskie elity rossiiskoi provintsii," *Mirovaia ekonomika i mezhdunarodnye otnosheniia*, No. 4, 1994, pp. 72–82.

O. Meliukhina and E. Serova, "K probleme monopolizma v sfere pererabotki sel'skokhoziaistvennoi produktsii," *Voprosy ekonomiki*, No. 1 (1995), pp. 66–75.

Boris Nemtsov, *Provintsial* (Moscow: "Vagrius," 1997)

Kevin O'Prey, *A Farewell to Arms? Russia's Struggle with Defense Conversion* (New York: Twentieth Century Fund, 1995).

S. Pavlenko, "Regiony i regional'naia politika," *Voprosy ekonomiki*, No. 9 (1994), pp. 11–16.

V. E. Seliverstov, ed., *Federalizm i regional'naia politika: problemy Rossii i zarubezhnyi opyt* (Publication sponsored by the Siberian International Center for Regional Studies, Institute for the Economics and Organization of Industrial Production, Siberian Division of the Russian Academy of Sciences) (Novosibirsk: "IEiOPP SO RAN," 1995)

E. Serova, "Predposylki i sushchnost' sovremennoi agrarnoi reformy v Rossii," *Voprosy ekonomiki*, No. 1 (1995), pp. 32–46.

V. Uzun, "Nizhegorodskaia model' reformirovaniia sel'skokhoziaistvennykh predpriiatii," *Voprosy ekonomiki*, No. 1 (1995), pp. 57–65.

THE ROLES OF THE STATE

Peter Evans, "The State as Problem and Solution: Predation, Embedded Autonomy, and Structural Change," in Stephan Haggard and Robert R. Kaufman, *The Politics of Economic Adjustment* (Princeton NJ: Princeton University Press, 1992), pp. 139–181.

Peter Evans et al., eds., *Bringing the State Back In* (Cambridge: Cambridge University Press, 1985).

Paul Langford, *A Polite and Commercial People: England, 1727–1783* (Oxford: Oxford University Press, 1989)

S.V. Pirogov, ed., *Gosudarstvennoe regulirovnie sotsial'no-ekonomicheskikh protsessov v usloviiakh rossiiskikh reform* (Moscow, Institute of Economics of the Russia Academy of Sciences, 1993)

J.H. Plumb, *The Growth of Political Stability in England, 1675–1725* (London: Pelican, 1950).

J.G.A. Pocock, "Authority and Property: the Question of Liberal Origins," *Virtue, Commerce, and History: Essays on Political Thought and History, Chiefly in the Eighteenth Century* (Cambridge: Cambridge University Press, 1985)

Pierre Rosanvallon, *L'Etat en France de 1789 à Nos Jours* (Paris: Seuil, 1990)

Andrei Shleifer, "Government in Transition," (Cambridge, MA.: Harvard Institute of Economic Research Discussion Paper Series, Discussion Paper Number 1783, October 1996)

Andrew Shonfield, *Modern Capitalism: The Changing Balance of Public and Private Power* (Oxford, 1965)

Boris Yeltsin, "Priglashenie k budnichnoi rabote v gosudarstve," *Rossiiskie vesti*, September 25 1997.

MONETARY AND FINANCIAL POLICY

William E. Alexander, et al., *Systemic Bank Restructuring and Macreonomic Policy* (Washington, D.C.: International Monetary Fund, 1997)

Brigitte Granville, *The Success of Russian Economic Reforms* (London: Royal Institute of International Affairs, 1995)

World Bank, *Russian Economic Reform: Crossing the Threshold of Structural Change* (A World Bank Country Study) (Washington, D.C.: The World Bank, 1992).

INDUSTRIAL AND INVESTMENT POLICY

Lev Freinkman, "Financial-Industrial Groups in Russia: Emergence of Large Diversified Private Companies," *Communist Economies and Economic Transformation*, vol. 7, No. 1 (1995), pp. 51–65.

Jane E. Prokop, "Industrial Conglomerates, Risk Spreading, and the Transition in Russia," *Communist Economies and Economic Transformation*, vol. 7, No. 1 (1995), pp. 35–49.

Irina Starodubrovskaia, "Financial-Industrial Groups: Illusions and Reality," *Communist Economies and Economic Transformation*, vol. 7, No. 1 (1995), pp. 5–19.

SOCIAL AND WELFARE POLICIES

Anders Aslund and Mikhail Dmitriev, eds., *Sotsial'naia politika v period perekhoda k rynku: problemy i resheniia* (Moscow: Carnegie Endowment for International Peace, Moscow Center, 1996)

Lev Freinkman and Michael Haney, "What Affects the Regional Governments' Propensity to Subsidize?" Policy Research Working Paper 1818 (Washington, D.C.: The World Bank, August 1997)

Michael Mandelbaum and E. Kapstein, eds., *Social Policy and Social Safety Nets in the Post-Communist Economies* (Armonk, N.Y.: M.E. Sharpe, 1997)

Organization for Economic Cooperation and Development, Center for

Cooperation with the Economies in Transition, *The Changing Social Benefits in Russian Enterprises* (Paris: OECD, 1996)

Michal Rutkowski, ed., *Russia's Social Protection Malaise: Key Reform Priorities as a Response to the Present Crisis* (Washington, D.C.: World Bank, April 1999)

THE LEGAL FRAMEWORK

Harold J. Berman, *Justice in the USSR: An Interpretation of Soviet Law* (Cambridge, MA.: Harvard University Press, 1963)

Harold J. Berman, "The Rule of Law and the Law-Based State with Special Reference to the Soviet Union," in Donald J. Barry, ed., *Toward the "Rule of Law" in Russia? Political and Legal Reform in the Transition Period.* (Armonk, NY, and London: M.E. Sharpe, 1992).

A.D. Boikov, "Sudebnaia reforma: obreteniia i proschety," *Gosudarstvo i pravo*, No. 6 (1994), pp. 13–22.

Natalie Brand, "The Development of Intellectual Property Law in Russia: Its History, Successes, and Problems" (Unpublished seminar paper, Georgetown University Russian Area Studies Program, Spring 1995)

Lane Blumenfeld, "Russia's New Civil Code: The Legal Foundation for Russia's Emerging Market Economy," *The International Lawyer*, vol. 30, no. 3 (Fall 1996), pp. 477–515.

William E. Butler, *Soviet Law*, 2nd edition (London: Butterworths, 1988)

Thomas Carothers, "The Rule of Law Revival," *Foreign Affairs*, vol. 77, no. 2 (March/April 1998), pp. 95–106.

Laurent Cohen-Tanugi, *Le Droit sans l'Etat: sur la Démocratie en France et en Amérique* (Paris: Presses Universitaires de France, 1985)

V.A. Dozortsev, "Problemy sovershenstvovaniia grazhdanskogo prava Rossiiskoi Federatsii pri perekhode k rynochnoi sisteme," *Gosudarstvo i pravo*, No. 1 (1994), pp. 26–35.

Laura Engelstein, "Combined Underdevelopment: Discipline and Law in Imperial and Soviet Russia," *American Historical Review*, vol. 98, no. 2 (April 1993), pp. 338–353.

Iurii Vasil'evich Feofanov, *Bremia vlasti* (Moscow: "Politizdat," 1990)

Iurii Feofanov, *O vlasti i prave: publitsisticheskie etiudy* (Moscow: "Iuridicheskaia literatura," 1989)

Lawrence M. Friedman, *Total Justice* (New York: Russell Sage Foundation, 1994)

Todd S. Foglesong, "The Soviet Judiciary and Perestroika" (unpublished paper prepared for the 4th SSRC Workshop on Soviet Politics, University of Toronto, Summer 1991)

Grazhdanskii kodeks Rossiiskoi Federatsii, Parts I and II (with an introductory essay by V.F. Yakovlev, chairman of the Higher Arbitration Court of the Russian Federaltion) (Moscow: "Kontrakt," 1996)

Kathryn Hendley, "Legal Development in Post-Soviet Russia," *Post-Soviet Affairs*, vol. 13, no. 3 (1997), pp. 228–251.

Kathryn Hendley, Barry W. Ickes, Peter Murrell, and Randi Ryterman, "Observations on the Use of Law by Russian Enterprises," *Post-Soviet Affairs*, vol. 13, no. 1 (1997), pp. 19–41.

James Willard Hurst, *Law and the Conditions of Freedom in the Nineteenth Century United States* (Madison, Wisconsin: University of Wisconsin Press, 1956)

Eugene Huskey, "Government Rulemaking as a Brake on Perestroika," *Law and Social Inquiry*, vol. 15, no. 3 (1990), pp. 419–432.

Eugene Huskey, "The State-Legal Administration and the Politics of Redundancy," *Post-Soviet Affairs*, vol. 11, No. 2 (1995), pp. 115–143.

John Henry Merryman, *The Civil Law Tradition*, 2nd. edition (Stanford, CA: Stanford University Press, 1985)

"O rabote arbitrazhnykh sudov Rossiiskoi Federatsii v 1995–96 godakh," *Vestnik vysshego arbitrazhnogo suda Rossiiskoi Federatsii*, No. 4 (1997), pp. 131–135.

Katharina Pistor, "Supply and Demand for Contract Enforcement in Russia: Courts, Arbitration, and Private Enforcement," *Review of Central and East European Law*, vol. 22, no. 1 (1996), pp. 55–87.

Richard Rose, "Toward a Civil Economy," *Journal of Democracy*, vol. 3, no. 2 (April 1992), pp. 13–26.

Robert Sharlet, "Russian Constitutional Crisis: Law and Politics under Yeltsin," *Post-Soviet Affairs*, vol. 9, no. 4 (October-December 1993), pp. 314–336.

Robert Sharlet, "Transitional Constitutionalism: Politics and Law in the Second Russian Republic," *Wisconsin International Law Journal*, vol. 14, no. 3 (1996), pp. 495–521.

Gordon B. Smith, *Reforming the Russian Legal System* (Cambridge: Cambridge University Press, 1996)

Peter H. Solomon, Jr., Legality in Soviet Political Culture: A Perspective on Gorbachev's Reforms," in Nick Lampert and Gabor T. Ritterspoon, eds., *Stalinism: its Nature and Aftermath: Essays in Honor of Moshe Lewin* (London: Macmillan, 1992)

Peter H. Solomon, "The Limits of Legal Order in Post-Soviet Russia," *Post-Soviet Affairs*, vol. 11, no. 2 (1995), pp. 89–114.

Peter H. Solomon, Jr., ed., *Reforming Justice in Russia, 1864–1994: Power, Culture, and the Limits of Legal Order* (Armonk, NY, and London: M.E. Sharpe, 1996).

Peter H. Solomon, Jr., *Soviet Criminal Justice under Stalin* (Cambridge: Cambridge University Press, 1996)

V.F. Yakovlev, "O novom grazhdanskom kodekse Rossii i ego primenenii," introductory essay to the text of the Civil Code, *Grazhdanskii kodeks Rossiiskoi Federatsii*, Parts I and II (Moscow: "Kontrakt," 1996)

V.F. Yakovlev, speech to the annual plenum of the Higher Arbitration Court, 19 February 1997, excerpted in "S plenuma Vysshego Arbitrazhnogo Suda Rossiiskoi Federatsii, *Vestnik Vysshego Arbitrazhnogo Suda Rossiiskoi Federatsii*, No. 4 (1997), pp. 5–14.

V.F. Yakovlev, speech at a meeting on the results of the year 1998, 15 February 1999, "Tendentsiia k povysheniiu roli arbitrazhnykh sudov sokhraniaetsia," *Vestnik Vysshego Arbitrazhnogo Suda Rossiiskoi Federatsii*, No. 4 (1999), pp. 5–16.

THE TAX SYSTEM

Richard M. Bird, Robert D. Ebel, Christine I. Wallich, eds., *Decentralization of the Socialist State: Intergovernmental Finance in Transition Economies*, World Bank Regional and Sectoral Studies (Washington, D.C.: The World Bank, 1995)

Dmitri Georgievich Chernik, *Nalogi v rynochnoi ekonomike* (Moscow: IUNITI Publishers, 1997)

Jon Craig, John Norregaard, and George Tsibouris, "Russian Federation," in Teresa Ter-Minassian, *Fiscal Federalism in Theory and Practice* (Washington, D.C.: International Monetary Fund, 1997), pp. 680–701.

Joel McDonald and Michael Alexeev, "Reforming the Russian Value-Added Tax," *Russia Business Watch* (monthly magazine of the US-Russia Business Council), March, 1997, pp. 41–45.

Joel McDonald and Michael Alexeev, "Note on the Current Russian Tax System and Proposed Reforms" (Unpublished memorandum prepared for the OECD Committe on Fiscal Affairs, Paris, France, 30 May 1997)

G. Semenov, "Ratsionalizatsiia vzaimootnoshenii mezhdu federal'nym i regional'nymi biudzhetami: puti obnovleniia nalogovo-biudzhetnovo mekhanizma," *Voprosy ekonomiki*, No. 9 (1994), pp. 38–51.

Sergei Shatalov, "Nalogovyi kodeks – ne panatseia, a sredstvo pod"ema ekonomiki," *Rynok neftegazovogo oborudovaniia*, No. 10 (1997), pp. 6–8.

Sergei Sinel'nikov, *Biudzhetnyi krisis v Rossii: 1985–1995 gody* (Moscow: "Evraziia," 1995)

Joel Slemrod, ed., *Why People Pay Taxes: Tax Compliance and Enforcement* (Ann Arbor, MI: The University of Michigan Press, 1992)

Pekka Sutela, "Fiscal Federalism in Russia," *Review of Economies in Transition*, No. 7 (1994), pp. 5–27.

Christine I. Wallich, ed., *Russia and the Challenge of Fiscal Federalism* (Washington, D.C.: The World Bank, 1994)

MISCELLANEOUS

Gosudarstvennyi komitet Rossiiskoi Federatsii po statistike (Roskomstat), *Sotsial'no-ekonomicheskoe polozhenie Rossii: operativnaia informatsiia)*, monthly report (Moscow).

Government of the Russian Federation, Center for Economic Reform, *Russian Economic Trends*, quarterly.

International Monetary Fund, *Russian Federation* (IMF Economic Reviews, No. 8 1993) (Washington, D.C.: June, 1993)

"Kto est' kto v Rossiiskom pravitel'stve" (Moscow, "Panorama," September 1992).

S.B. Lavrov, ed., *Geopoliticheskie i geoekonomicheskie problemy Rossii*. Proceedings of a symposium held on the occasion of the 150th anniversary of the Russian Geographic Society in St. Petersburg, October 1994. (St. Petersburg: "Progress-Pogoda," 1995)

Sergei Rogov, "Military Reform and the Defense Budget of the Russian Federation" CIM 527 (Alexandria, VA: Center for Naval Analyses, August 1997)

JOURNALS AND NEWSPAPERS

IN RUSSIAN

Delovoi mir
Ekspert (weekly)
Finansovye izvestiia
Izvestiia
Kapital (Russian-language edition of *The Moscow Times)*
Kommersant-Daily
Kommersant (weekly)
Mezhdunarodnaia ekonomika i mezhdunarodnye otnosheniia (monthly)
Monitoring obshchestvennogo mneniia: Ekonomicheskie i sotsial'nye peremeny (The
    website of the VTs IOM is http://www.wciom.ru
Moskovskie novosti (weekly)
Neft' i kapital
Nezavisimaia gazeta
Politiia
Rossiiskaia gazeta
Russkii telegraf
Rynok tsennykh bumag (monthly)
Segodnia
Sotsiologicheskie issledovaniia (bimonthly)
Statisticheskoe obozrenie (bimonthly)
Vestnik Vysshego Arbitrazhnogo Suda (monthly)
Voprosy ekonomiki (monthly)
Zakon (monthly)

IN ENGLISH

The Christian Science Monitor
The Economist
The Financial Times
The Los Angeles Times
The Moscow Times
The New York Times
The Wall Street Journal
The Washington Post

CIS Law Notes (monthly newsletter of the law firm of Patterson, Belknap, Webb,
    and Tyler)
Europe-Asia Studies (formerly *Soviet Studies*)
Morbidity and Mortality Weekly Report (Newsletter of the Massachusetts Medical
    Society)
Post-Soviet Affairs (formerly *Soviet Economy*)
Post-Soviet Geography (formerly *Soviet Geography*)
Russian Economic Trends (quarterly publication of the Russian European Centre
    for Economic Policy)

Russia Business Watch (newsletter of the US-Russia Business Council)

Russian Commerce News (publication of the Russian-American Chamber of Commerce)

Rule of Law Consortium Newsletter (publication of the ARD/CHECCHI Joint Venture)

Transition (monthly newsletter of the World Bank, Macroeconomics and Growth Division, Policy Research Department)

Russia Portfolio (monthly newsletter on securities published by Global Investor Publishing)

INTERNET RESOURCES

Internet Securities

National News Service (*Natsional'naia sluzhba novostei*)

Russian Economic Trends, monthly updates and special reports

Russia Online

Website of the Russian Securities Commission (http://www.fe.msk.ru/win/info-market/fedcom/rnews

Goskomstat RF, *Rossiiskii Statisticheskii ezhegodnik* (annual, available by Internet through Internet Securities)

Index